TRANSLATION TECHNIQUE
IN THE PESHITTA TO JOB

SOCIETY OF BIBLICAL LITERATURE

DISSERTATION SERIES

David L. Petersen, Old Testament Editor
Pheme Perkins, New Testament Editor

Number 137

TRANSLATION TECHNIQUE
IN THE PESHITTA TO JOB
A Model for Evaluating a Text with
Documentation from the Peshitta to Job

by
Heidi M. Szpek

Heidi M. Szpek

TRANSLATION TECHNIQUE IN THE PESHITTA TO JOB
A Model for Evaluating a Text with Documentation from the Peshitta to Job

Scholars Press
Atlanta, Georgia

TRANSLATION TECHNIQUE IN THE PESHITTA TO JOB
A Model for Evaluating a Text with Documentation from the Peshitta to Job

Heidi M. Szpek

Ph.D., 1991
University of Wisconsin-
Madison

Advisor:
Michael V. Fox

© 1992
The Society of Biblical Literature

Library of Congress Cataloging in Publication Data
Szpek, Heidi M.
    Translation technique in the Peshitta to Job: a model for evaluating a text with documentation from the Peshitta to Job / Heidi M. Szpek.
        p. cm. — (Dissertation series; no. 137)
    Originally presented as the author's thesis (Ph.D.)—University of Wisconsin, 1991.
    Includes bibliographical references.
    ISBN 1-55540-761-7 (alk. paper). — ISBN 1-55540-762-5 (pbk.: alk. paper)
    1. Bible. O.T. Job. Syriac—Versions—Peshitta. 2. Bible. O.T. Job—Translating. 3. goriac language—Grammar.   I. Title. II. Series: Dissertation series (Society of Biblical Literature); no. 137.
BS1415.5.S95   1992
223'.1043—dc20   92-34963
                                                              CIP

Printed in the United States of America
on acid-free paper

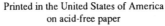

ראשית חכמה קנה חכמה
ובכל־קנינך קנה בינה

"The beginning of wisdom is this: Acquire wisdom;
but with everything you acquire, acquire understanding."
(Prov. 4:7)

To my mentors
Dr. Michael V. Fox and Dr. Bernard Grossfeld

who have given me wisdom and understanding,
as well as knowledge

Table of Contents

Abbreviations

adj.	adjective
Adv	Adverb
AJSL	*American Journal of Semitic Languages and Literature*
Amos	Amos
BDB	Brown, Francis, S.R. Driver and Charles A. Briggs. *A Hebrew and English Lexicon of the Old Testament.* Oxford: Clarendon Press, 1975.
Bib	*Biblica*
BZAW	*Beihefte zur Zeitschrift für die alttestamentliche Wissenschaft*
c.	common
CBQ	*Catholic Biblical Quarterly*
1 Chron.	1 Chronicles
2 Chron.	2 Chronicles
Conj	Conjunction
DO	Direct Object
Dt.	Deuteronomy
Eccl.	Ecclesiastes
Est.	Esther
Ex.	Exodus
Ezek.	Ezekiel
Ezra	Ezra
f.	feminine
Gen.	Genesis
Hab.	Habbakkuk
Heb.	Hebrew
Hos.	Hosea
HUCA	*Hebrew Union College Annual*
Is.	Isaiah
ICC	International Critical Commentary
Interj	Interjectory Particle
IO	Indirect Object
JA	*Journal of the Royal Asiatic Society*
JBL	*Journal of Biblical Literature*
JBLMS	*Journal of Biblical Literature Monograph Series*
Jer.	Jeremiah
Joel	Joel
Josh.	Joshua
JSS	*Journal of Semitic Studies*
JThS	*Journal of Theological Studies*
Judg.	Judges
K	Ketib
1 K	1 Kings

2 K	2 Kings
KJV	King James Version
Lev.	Leviticus
LXX	Septuagint
m.	masculine
Mal.	Malachi
Micah	Micah
MT	Masoretic Text
n.	noun
Nah.	Nahum
Neg	Negation
Neh.	Nehemiah
NT	*Novum Testamentum*
Num.	Numbers
OT	Old Testament
p.	person
P	Peshitta
PPh	Prepositional Phrase
pl.	plural
Prov.	Proverbs
Ps.	Psalm
Q	Qere
QTg	Qumran Targum
RSV	Revised Standard Version
Ruth	Ruth
S	Subject
s./sg.	singular
1 Sam.	1 Samuel
2 Sam.	2 Samuel
Sem	*Semitica*
S	Symmachus
SL	Source Language
STh	*Studia Theologica*
SubCl	Subordinate Clause
Syr.	Syriac
T	Temporal Element
Tg.	Targum
TL	Target Language
TO	Targum Onkelos
Q	Theodotian
V	Verb
V	Vulgate
VT	*Vetus Testamentum*
VT Suppl	*Vetus Testamentum Supplement*
Zach.	Zachariah
ZAW	*Zeitscrift für die alttestamentliche Wissenschaft*
Zeph.	Zephaniah

List of Diagrams

I

Introduction

Throughout the ages travellers such as the ancient Egyptian Wen-Amon, the Greek Herodotus, the medieval Marco Polo, and the more modern Amelia P. Edwards, Gertrude Bell and Sir Richard Francis Burton were compelled to record not only their daily experiences and observations, but also their innermost reflections on their travels in order to preserve for posterity (or for their financiers) a journal that would hopefully be of use to future travellers, arm-chair or otherwise.

Would that we had this same zest for recording, as well as a plethora of diaries from the hand of another group of literary adventurers, the translators: those men (and women) whose world revolved around the written word, as they journeyed through their translational adventures. Imagine a diary in which were recorded the literary verve, the daily dilemmas and the inspirational sparks which guided their hands and minds in solving each translational puzzle.

One might ask: What purpose would such a record serve? Who would profit from such a diary? To anyone involved in translating or evaluating a translation, i.e. comparing a target text to a source text, a reference tool such as this would be invaluable. There would be no question as to whether a translator had a different *Vorlage* before him, sought help from other Versions, simply errored, or felt compelled to depart from his source text because of ideological beliefs. His diary would provide the answers.

True we have, for example, the biblical quotations of Ephraem Syrus (4th C.E.) and Aphraates (5th C.E.) or the early commentaries of Jacob of Edessa (c. 8th C.E.) and Bar Hebraeus (13th C.E.) on the Peshitta, the target text we will be working with, but these are second hand and once again not the comments of the original translator. Thus,

1

lacking this resource, an evaluator has but one recourse: to play the role
of literary archaeologist.

The archaeologist excavates the earth seeking to uncover artifacts
which will provide clues to the cultural characteristics of an earlier
civilization. As for the literary archaeologist the text is his excavation
site. The words, components of words, or combinations of words contain
the artifacts which, if systematically excavated, collected and analyzed,
can reveal the data to reconstruct the intellectual forces that filled the
mind and moved the hand of the translator.

The archaeologist has a wide variety of tools and scientific texts to
aid in his endeavor. But what of the literary archaeologist? Herein lies
the objective of this dissertation:
(1) to present the first systematic study of translation features in the
Peshitta to the book of Job (P-Job); and in doing so (2) to develop a
systematic model that can be used to excavate, i.e. evaluate, P-Job and
other target texts in order to extract and explain not only unique
translation techniques and significant departures from the source text, but
also account for the expected equivalences necessitated only by language
difference.

The Peshitta: Name, Origin and Language

The name Peshitta (ܦܫܝܛܬܐ) is the term given to the translation of
the Old Testament into Syriac, an east Aramaic dialect. Geographically,
Syriac was used both as a spoken and literary language from Edessa in
Upper Mesopotamia as far south as Northern Syria. Temporally, it
spanned the early pre-Christian centuries until the 8th C.E., at which time
it lost prominence to Arabic and was relegated to use in a few remote
districts and in religious services.[1]

While the word Peshitta means "simple, plain" the exact
connotation of this term is not altogether certain. It may indicate a
version prepared for the common populace, a version relatively free of
paraphrase or "simple" in contrast to the more complex Syro-Hexaplar
text.[2] The *Vorlage* from which the Peshitta was translated is generally

---

[1] Theodor Nöldeke, *Compendious Syriac Grammar* (London, 1904), p. xxx.
[2] See L. Haefeli, *Die Peschitta Des Alten Testamentes* (Münster, 1927), p. 5;
E. Würthwein, *The Text of the Old Testament* (Grand Rapids, Michigan: William B.

assumed to be the Hebrew text; however, as we will see, influence from the Aramaic Targumim and from the Greek versions, in particular the Septuagint, cannot be discounted.

The provenance of the Peshitta is obscure. Current scholarship is divided into three schools of thought:

(1) in the first century C.E. the Kingdom of Adiabene was converted to Judaism, hence the need for a translation in their own language, Syriac;[3]

(2) the Peshitta originated in Edessa, the major Aramaic capital of Christianity in the second century C.E.;[4]

(3) the translation of the Peshitta was gradual, beginning with a period of oral transmission, then initially written down by Jewish savants and finally reworked by Christian hands. Evidence exists of both Jewish influence in the form of Targumic and Midrashic parallels, especially in the Pentateuch,[5] and of Greek influence from the Septuagint, especially in Isaiah, the Psalms and Minor Prophets,[6] thus giving credence to this gradual process of textual development.[7]

Text of P-Job Used

The manuscript used for our study of the target text, P-Job, is the critical edition of Codex Ambrosianus prepared by L.G. Rignell under the direction of the Peshitta Institute of the University of Leiden.[8] It is written in Estrangela, the oldest of three Syriac scripts; the other two being Nestorian, used mainly in the east, and Jacobite, used in the west. It

---

Eerdmans Publishing Co., 1979), p. 80; F.E. Deist, *Towards the Text of the Old Testament* (Pretoria: N. G. Kerkboekhandel Transvaal, 1978), p. 143.

[3] See Deist, p. 143; Würthwein, p. 80; Paul Kahle, *Cairo Geniza* (1959), p. 270f.

[4] See Deist, p. 143; Würthwein, p. 81.

[5] See A. Vööbus, "Der Einfluss des altpalästinischen Targums in der Textgeschichte der Peschitta des Alten Testament." *Le Museon* LXVIII (1955): 215-218; *Peschitta und Targumim des Pentateuches: Neues Licht zur Frage der Herkunft der Peschitta aus dem altpalästinischen Targum* (Stockholm, 1958); Y. Maori, *The Peshitta Version of the Pentateuch in its Relation to the Sources of Jewish Exegesis.* Doctoral Dissertation. (Hebrew University, 1975).

[6] See W.E. Barnes, "On the Influence of the Septuagint on the Peshitta." *JThS* II (1901): 186-187.

[7] See J.H. Hospers, "Some Remarks with Regard to Text and Language of the Old Testament Peshitta," in Festschrift für Prof. J. van der Ploeg, *Von Kanaan bis Kerala* (1982): pp. 443; P. Kahle, *Cairo Geniza*, p. 265f; J. Pinkerton,"The Origin and Early History of the Syriac Pentateuch," *JThS* 15 (1914): 41.

[8] *The Old Testament in Syriac According to the Peshitta Version* (Leiden: E.J. Brill), 1982.

dates from the 6th C.E. and is one of the oldest extant complete Syriac texts of the Old Testament.[9] The critical apparatus accompanying the Leiden edition contains variants from 43 other manuscripts up to and including those belonging to the 12th C.E., as well as numerous lectionary readings. The nature of these variants is mainly orthographic, e.g. plene/ defective forms (ܟܢܐ/ܟܐ), uncontracted/contracted forms (ܩܕܡܝܐ /ܩܕܝܬ ܠܐ), the presence of Seyame (two dots indicating plurality) and obvious errors, e.g. omission of consonants. As the text of P-Job was compared to the MT the critical apparatus was consulted, but given the orthographic nature of the variants they had little effect on the morphology of the text.

Previous Studies of the Peshitta of Job

The end of the 19th century witnessed the publication of three major studies on the P-Job. The first two were doctoral dissertations by E. Stenij (1887) and A. Mandl (1892); the third a series of articles by E. Baumann (1898-1900) elaborating on their dissertations. The emphasis of each of these studies was the text-critical value of the P-Job for the study of the Hebrew text.

E. Stenij's dissertation, entitled *De Syriaca Libri Iobi Interpretatione quae Peschita Vocatur*,[10] was prefaced with an introductory section on the general nature of the Peshitta.[11] His analysis consisted of two parts: a chapter by chapter, verse by verse notation of the variants in the editions, texts and manuscripts of the P-Job; and a list of corrections which he accepted in the text of the Peshitta.

A. Mandl's dissertation, entitled *Peschitta zu Hiob nebst einem Anhang über ihr Verhältniss zu LXX und Targum*,[12] similarly contained background information on the Peshitta. His interest, however, was not in collecting intra-versional variants, but rather with first investigating

---

[9] The date 1006/7 appears on the manuscript but this date is believed to be the date at which the text was presented to a monastery and not the date when its was copied. See Deist, pp. 147-148.
[10] Helsingforsiae, 1887.
[11] Stenij discussed such topics as the current editions of the Peshitta (#1), the name Peshitta (#2), its age (#3), the religious persuasion reflected in the Peshitta (#4). He likewise included a current index of relevant literature (#5).
[12] Budapest: Universität Leipzig, 1892.

the general character of the translation of P-Job. This characterization
was divided into twelve headings:

  1. dissolution of metaphors
  2. peculiar treatment of verbs and nouns
  3. insertion of words for the purpose of greater clarity
  4. irregular sentence construction
  5. avoidance of anthropomorphisms and anthropopathisms
  6. rendering Hebrew roots by similar sounding Syriac roots
  7. incorrect derivation of verbal and nominal forms
  8. misunderstanding or too free of translation
  9. peculiarity of exegesis
  10. phonetic mistakes
  11. following a reminiscence from a parallel verse
  12. addition of words or double translations

For each item he provided a few pertinent examples.

Next Mandl noted the divergencies from the Hebrew text. These
variants he explained under the following headings for which he likewise
provided a select number of examples:

  1. assumption or non-assumption of a *mater lectionis*
  2. mistakes
  3. transposition
  4. loss or omission of letters
  5. loss or omission of words
  6. incorrect sentence division
  7. incorrect verse division
  8. dittography
  9. *Vorlage* of a different text

He then devoted a section to divergent vocalizations of the Heb. text
as inferred from the Peshitta's readings. And finally, he concluded with
a discussion of the relationship of the Peshitta to the LXX and the
Targum, providing congruencies with each version.

While Mandl was content with citing a few examples to illustrate
each of his points, not so E. Baumann. His series of articles, entitled "Die

Verwendbarkeit der Pesita zum Buche Ijob für die Textkritik,"[13]
contained an exhaustive list of variants and examples. Like Stenij he
provided the intra-version variants for P-Job (1898). His study (1899),
also, contained a collection of doublets and additions with parallels in the
other versions; a list of errors; a characterization of the Peshitta;[14] and
the Peshitta's relationship to the Versions with a chapter by chapter list of
congruencies. The remainder of his research (1899-1900) was a
comparison of the Peshitta and Hebrew text with verse by verse notes on
the differences. He closed with a list of emendations to the Hebrew text
based on readings in the Peshitta.

Following Baumann's study, research on the P-Job was relegated to
textual notes in commentaries on Job,[15] with one exception: E. Dhorme's
A Commentary on the Book of Job, 1926.[16]   In his Introduction he
briefly analyzed the text of P-Job.[17]   He simply cited the passages where
Peshitta agreed with the LXX and Tg; where it diverged from the
Hebrew; incorrect readings and defective vocalizations; double
translations, transpositions, omissions, compressions; confusion of
Hebrew and Aramaic roots; and errors in the Syriac.

It must be emphasized that in each of these studies the main
objective was to evaluate the Peshitta in its role as a textual witness to the
Hebrew text. Even in Mandl's and Baumann's analyses of the character
of the Peshitta, this purpose was evident. Interest in translation
techniques never extended beyond the most simplistic types: addition,
omission, or the doublet. As for motivations for changes, appeal most
often was made to language difference or misunderstanding. Thus, the
Peshitta, as an independent entity reflective of a unique ideology and
worthy to be studied in its own right, was not an immediate concern.

---

[13] *ZAW* 1889: 305-338; 1899: 15-95, 287-309; 1900: 177-307.

[14] Baumann analyzed the Peshitta's translation of the particles הן, הנה, and נא; the
conjunctions, prepositions, the copula, suffixes, number, tense, voice, personal names,
questions, poetic form and anthropomorphism.

[15] See, for example, the following commentaries: S.R. Driver and G.B. Gray, *A
Critical and Exegetical Commentary on the Book of Job* , The International Critical
Commentary (Edinburgh, 1977); Norman C. Habel, *The Book of Job*, The Old
Testament Library (Philadelphia: Westminster Press,1985); Marvin H. Pope, *Job: A
New Translation with Introduction and Commentary,* The Anchor Bible (New York:
Doubleday & Company, Inc., 1983); H.H. Rowley, *The Book of Job* , The New
Century Bible Commentary (Grand Rapids: Wm. B. Eerdman's Publishing Co., 1983).

[16] New York: Thomas Nelson Publishers, rpt. 1984.

[17] See specifically Chapter Twelve: Text and Versions: #6 The Peshitta, pp. ccxvi-
ccxviii.

Background of the Translation Technique Model

The model of translation technique (TT Model) presented in the following chapter was developed from and owes its impetus to studies in two disciplines: Biblical Studies and Linguistics. These two disciplines influenced the formation of one or more of the four parts in this model. For the sake of reference the four parts of the model are:

I.   Element of translation
II. Technique of adjustment
III. Motivation for change
IV. Effect on meaning

In the field of biblical studies foremost is the work of M. Goshen-Gottstein. In his "Theory and Practice of Textual Criticism: The Text Critical Use of the Septuagint," Goshen-Gottstein provides a valuable list of interpretive "assumptions", tucked away in a footnote, which he uses to explain a variant between the LXX and MT.[18] These are:

1. purely linguistic reasons
2. influence from parallel verse
3. complication by inner-Greek variants
4. implicit to explicit exegesis
5. Midrashic interpretation

These five assumptions, with slight modifications, are included in Part Three: motivation for change in the text.

Once again from the field of biblical studies, P. Kyle McCarter's *Textual Criticism: Recovering the Text of the Hebrew Bible* provided the basic subcategories for the adjustments in Part Two.[19] In Chapter II "The Causes of Textual Criticism" he cites four main changes that can occur in a text:

---

[18] M. Goshen-Gottstein, "Theory and Practice of Textual Criticism: The Text Critical Use of the Septuagint" in *Text and Language in Bible and Qumran* (Jerusalem: Orient, 1960): 138, n. 20.

[19] P. Kyle McCarter, Jr., *Textual Criticism: Recovering the Text of the Hebrew Bible* (Philadelphia: Fortress Press, 1986).

1. changes that expand the text
2. changes that shorten the text
3. changes that do not effect length
4. deliberate changes

The first three became the three major adjustments in Part Two: addition, omission, and substitution. Deliberate changes was classified under motivations for a change (Part Three), rather than as an adjustment.

E. Tov's and B.G. Wright's article "Computer-Assisted Study of the Criteria for Assessing the Literalness of Translation Units in the LXX" demonstrated how useful statistics, charts and diagrams can be for more clearly presenting my data.[20]

In the field of linguistics, most influential is the classic work on translation by Eugene A. Nida, *Towards a Science of Translating.*[21] His emphasis on all areas of linguistics in the translation process is evident in the TT Model, especially in the fourfold classification of each element of translation in Part One under the headings: grammar, syntax, semantics, style. Most influential, however, was his chapter on techniques of adjustment. There he lists three major changes - addition, subtraction and alteration - with subcategories for each containing an amalgam of types: some grammatical, some stylistic, some semantic and some phonological in nature.[22] It must be noted, however, that Nida was presenting guidelines for adjustments that might be necessary and permitted in preparing a translation. Thus, his concern was with the

---

[20] E. Tov and B.G. Wright, "Computer-Assisted Study of the Criteria for Assessing the Literalness of Translation Units in the LXX," *Textus* XII (1985):149-187. These same sentiments were likewise echoed by G. Marquis, "Word Order as a Criterion for the Evaluation of Translation Technique in the LXX and the Evaluation of Word-Order Variants: As Exemplified in LXX-Ezekiel," *Textus* XIII (1986):59-83; and A. Aejmelaeus, "What Can We Know about the Hebrew *Vorlage* of the Septuagint?," *ZAW* 99 (1987/2): 58-89. Marquis, like Tov and Wright, also employs charts and even a bargraph to display his results.

[21] Eugene A. Nida, *Towards a Science of Translating* (Leiden: E.J. Brill, 1964).

[22] Nida, *Towards a Science of Translating*, p. 226ff. Nida's subcategories for addition are: filling out elliptical expressions, obligatory specification, additions required because of grammatical restructuring, amplification from implicit to explicit status, answers to rhetorical questions, classifiers, connectives, categories of receptor language which do not exist in the source language, doublets; for subtraction are: repetition, specifications of reference, conjunctions, transitionals, categories, vocatives, formulae; and for alteration are: sounds, categories, word classes, order, clause and sentence structure, semantic problems involving single words, semantic problems involving exocentric expressions.

source and receptor languages. By contrast, the TT Model is concerned with evaluating an already existing translation (target or receptor language) in comparison with the MT (the source language) from the perspective of a third language, and determining the techniques of adjustment already employed, rather than which ones should be employed.

The examination of an existing translation by the TT Model is partially similar to Nida's methodology for analyzing different types of translations.[23] He developed the following three step plan:

1. number lexical units of the source-language text
2. use asterisk, italics and small capitals to indicate omissions, additions and structural modifications
3. possibly expand this system by indicating significant semantic elements, e.g. objects = O, abstract = A.

Through this analysis he attempted to determine the general stage of translation exhibited.[24] The three stages are:

1. literal transfer - "word for word" translation
2. minimal transfer - only alterations necessary to conform to receptor language, i.e. obligatory alterations
3. literary transfer - optional modifications

By contrast, the system I have developed:

1. examines lexical and grammatical elements of the target-language text in comparison with the source-language text;
2. uses the four part system of the TT Model to indicate the element of translation, type of adjustment, motivation, and effect on meaning for each adjustment to the text;
3. analyzes the results in such a fashion as to determine more than just the general stage of a translation.

---

[23] Nida, *Towards a Science of Translating*, p. 185ff.
[24] Nida, *Towards a Science of Translating*, p. 184.

The manner of analyzing the results was influenced by the final major impetus for this study from the field of linguistics, the work of Th. Bynon. In her textbook, *Historical Linguistics*, she discusses what she terms "cultural reconstruction via the lexicon".[25] She states:

> Invaluable information concerning the history of languages can be derived from not only an examination of a language's internal structure, but also through its lexicon. The lexicon can provide information about the social, cultural, geographical and political nature of a language group.[26]

It is Bynon's concept that a language's culture can be reflected in its lexicon that is significant, and is here taken one step further. Just as a language's lexicon might yield information on any or all aspects of its culture, so too might the translation techniques and changes in meaning reflect the ideology or, more poetically speaking, "the voice of the translator."[27] Thus, by systematically analyzing the translation techniques and changes in meaning, a more specific characterization of the translator and translation can be uncovered. Specific is the key word here. Too often characterizations of translations are general, vague and more intuitive (on the part of the investigator), with but a few examples of each characteristic provided which could be interpreted in one way by one scholar and yet another way by yet another scholar.[28]

Other entries in this model, such as voice and suffix in the area of grammar or the motivations ambiguity and implicit to explicit exegesis, are included in many studies. In fact, many seem to be universal topics encountered in studies of translation technique, so much so that credit cannot be given to any one individual.[29]

---

[25] Th. Bynon, *Historical Linguistics* (Cambridge: Cambridge University Press, 1985), pp. 272-280.

[26] Bynon, *Historical Linguistics*, p. 272.

[27] See Jackson Mathews, "Third Thoughts on Translating Poetry," in *On Translation*, ed. Reuben A. Brower (Cambridge, Massachusetts: Harvard University Press, 1959), p. 67.

[28] See, for example, the remarks by E. Tov and B.G. Wright ("Computer-Assisted Study," p. 151) concerning this generalizing tendency. For examples of this generalization see the outlines of A. Mandl's and E. Baumann's studies of the Peshitta to Job in the previous chapter. Mandl in particular provided but a few examples for each characteristic.

[29] See, for example, E. Baumann, "Verwendbarkeit der Peshita zum Buche Ijob für die Textkritik." *ZAW* (1898):305-338; (1899):15-95, 287-309; (1900): 177-307; Donald H. Gard, "The Exegetical Method of the Greek Translator of the Book of Job." *JBLMS* 8 (Pennsylvania: Society of Biblical Literature, 1952); A. Mandl, *Die Peschitta zum Hiob*. Dissertation. (Leipzig, 1892); Eugene A. Nida, *Towards a Science of Translating*

Thus, no one study has provided the background from which the TT Model has emerged, but rather a mixture of concepts, classifications and methods drawn from both biblical studies and linguistics have contributed to and resulted in the nascence of this model. Throughout the explanation of the Model, those scholars whose terminology has been borrowed or modified will be indicated in the footnotes.

(Leiden: E.J. Brill, 1964); Harry M. Orlinsky, "The Character of the Septuagint Translation of the Book of Job." *HUCA* 28 (1957): 53-74; 29 (1958): 229-271; 30 (1959): 153-167; A. Sperber, ed., *The Bible in Aramaic, Vol. IVB: The Targum and the Hebrew Bible.* (Leiden: E.J. Brill, 1973); Heidi M. Szpek, *Similes and Metaphors in the Targumim: A Comparative Study of the Translational Techniques used by the Aramaic Targumim to the Pentateuch for Similes and Metaphors of the Hebrew Bible.* Unpublished M.A. Thesis (University of Wisconsin-Milwaukee, 1983); and E. Tov, *The Text-critical Use of the Septuagint in Biblical Research.* Jerusalem Biblical Studies (Jerusalem: Simor LTD., 1981).

II

Model of Translation Technique

The model of translation technique proposed here is based on the premise that the act of translation can be conceptualized as a systematic process involving four interconnected components. These basic components are:

> ELEMENT OF > ADJUSTMENT > MOTIVATION > EFFECT ON
> TRANSLATION   MEANING

Just as phonology uses the term phoneme to describe the smallest unit of sound, morphology uses morpheme for the smallest unit of meaning and lexicography uses lexeme so too should we have a term to describe a unit of translation. At present, lacking a formal term to describe this unit, we will have to be content with the more wordy designation "element of translation" or "translational element" to describe each individual element or item that is encountered by a translator.[1] These elements will be classified in conjunction with the major branches of linguistics, i.e. whether they are elements of grammar, semantics, syntax or style. While phonology is also a major branch of linguistics, changes in this area are directly associated with semantics, and as such will be discussed under that category.

Adjustment refers to the type of change that occurs to a element of translation in its transference from source to target language. The main

---

[1] The term element of translation rather than unit of translation is used, because in biblical studies "unit of translation" usually refers to a larger section of text or pericope.

of translations in all areas of linguistics, syntactically based adjustments and semantically oriented alterations.

Motivation refers to the reason or cause that prompted an adjustment to an element of translation. The nature of these motivations can be linguistically based (e.g. language difference, linguistic interference, aural error), contextually based (e.g. intra-/inter-verse influence, parallel verse influence, implicit to explicit exegesis, ambiguity, redundancy), or culturally based (e.g. ideological alterations).

The last component is concerned with the effect an adjustment has on the meaning of the text. Two factors will be considered in this section: meaning relation and perspective. Meaning relation refers to the semantic relationship that occurs between the source text and the target text for each item translated. Relations are classified under five headings: clarity, confusion, synonymy, antithesis and innovation. Perspective refers to the point of view from which an effect on meaning is classified: reader/aural recipient, translator and evaluator.

Whether the translator was consciously or unconsciously aware of his actions each and every time transference occurred between source and target language, his work still involves these key points of contact.[2] By approaching the concept of translation in such a fashion, we can then go back and use this same four-step process to analyze and evaluate a target text in order to uncover the translation techniques of any given translator for any given text. In essence, then, the model proposed here is both a model for describing the process of translation and a model for evaluating an already existing translation. It includes the components necessary for describing and evaluating those translational elements that diverge from the source text, as well as those that indicate a minimal or even Ø degree adjustment in the transfer from source to target text.

---

[2] In "The Translation Process and the Character of the Septuagint" (*Textus* VI [1968]: 8), C. Rabin stated that many translators practiced verbal linkage, that is an "automatic response to certain recurring stimuli, so the translator soon uses words or phrases as a response to verbal stimuli rather than acts of conscious choice."

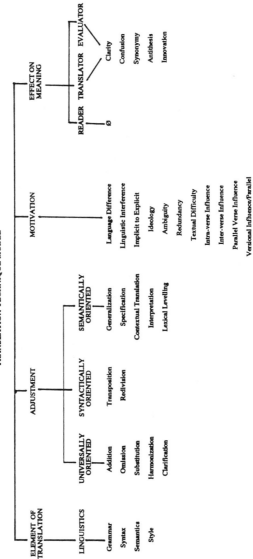

TRANSLATION TECHNIQUE MODEL

It must be noted that the subcategories listed in this diagram of the translation model are those that occur in P-Job, hence they are not finite. Studies of other books, be they in the Peshitta, Targum, LXX, etc., would no doubt uncover additional subcategories. For example, Homer Heater's study of anaphoric translation in the LXX to Job would be listed under Addition.[3] However, the overall scheme with its four major categories and their primary subcategories would remain the same.

In the following detailed description of this model the intent is to simply define each item and provide a relevant example, not to explain all the problems or divergences that occur elsewhere in a given example. This type of analysis will be done in Chapters III through VII, where the TT Model is applied to P-Job in detail.

I. Element of Translation

As stated above each element of translation is classified according to its placement in the field of linguistics according to four headings: grammar, syntax, semantics and style.

1. Grammar.

Under grammar the topics of gender, number, person, pronoun, tense, voice, word class, and suffix come into consideration. Other items, such as mood, might also be included here; however, in the text of P-Job variants of this nature do not happen to occur.

a. Gender. The concern of the subject of gender is the replacement of a masculine form with a feminine one and vice-versa. This gender replacement may occur in any part of speech. So, for example, in Job 1:4 P replaces the Heb. m. numeral שלשת in construct with the feminine form ܬܠܬ for agreement with the feminine אחיתיהם "their sisters":

MT   והלכו בניו ועשו משתה בית איש יומו ושלחו
      וקראו ל ש ל ש ת אחיתיהם לאכל ולשתות עמהם:

P   ܘܐܙܠܝܢ ܗܘܘ ܒܢܘ̈ܗܝ ܘܥܒܕܝܢ ܡܫܬܝܐ ܒܒܝܬ ܓܒܪ ܒܝܘܡܗ ܀

---

3 *A Septuagint Translation Technique in the Book of Job*, The Catholic Biblical Quarterly Monograph Series 11 (Washington, DC: The Catholic Biblical Association of America, 1982).

ܡܫܕܪܝܢ ܗܘܘ ܘܩܪܝܢ ܠܬܠܬ ܐܚܘܬܗܘܢ. ܠܡܐܟܠ
ܘܠܡܫܬܐ ܥܡܗܘܢ.

b. Number. Number refers to the replacement of a Heb. singular form by a plural Syr. form, a Heb. plural by a Syr. singular, or a Heb. collective plural by a simple Syr. plural form. This variation in number may effect all parts of speech. Thus in 1:22 the Heb. m.s. demonstrative זאת is replaced by the m.pl. form ܗܠܝܢ.

MT בכל־זאת לא־חטא איוב "In all this Job did not sin"

P ܘܒܗܠܝܢ ܟܠܗܝܢ ܠܐ ܚܛܐ ܐܝܘܒ. "In all these (things) Job did not sin"

In 2:6 the Heb. singular noun בידך "into your hand" is replaced by the plural ܒܐܝܕܝܟ "into your hands". And in 8:19 it is a verb that undergoes a change in number:

MT . . . ומעפר אחר יצמחו. "and from the dust other(s) will sprout"(pl.)

P . . . ܘܡܢ ܥܦܪܐ ܐܚܪܢܐ ܢܥܒܐ "and from the dust another will sprout"(sg.)

c. Person. The parts of speech effected by a change in person are verbs, pronouns, and suffixes. So, for example, in 7:13b P renders the Heb. 3pms. ישא by the 1cs ܐܬܠܒܒ:

MT ישא בשיחי משכבי: "my bed will ease (lit. lift up) my complaint."

P ܘܐܬܠܒܒ ܡܢ ܛܘܪܦܐ ܕܡܫܟܒܝ. "and I will take heart from the agitation of my bed."

In 14:14b P records the 3pms pronominal suffix where MT has the 1pcs:

MT   כל־ימי צבאי איחל   "all the days of my service I
                                                                would wait"

P ܟܘܡܗ ܕܚܝܘܬܗ̈ ܘܡܣܟܐ ܠܟܠܗܘܢ "and all the days of his
                                                              youth he waits"

d. Pronoun. Pronoun refers to a change not only in an independent
pronoun, but also to a variation in the relative pronoun.   In 9:6a a
personal pronoun is explicit P:

MT   המרגיז ארץ ממקומה   "(He) who shakes the earth
                                                              from its place"

P ܡܢ ܕܐܙܝܥ ܐܪܥܐ ܡܢ ܫܪܫܗ "he who shakes the earth from
                                                              its root"

And in 3:16 it is a relative pronoun that is explicitly stated:

MT   כעללים לא־ראו אור: "like children (who) have
                                                              never seen light"

P ܘܐܝܟ ܥܘ̈ܠܐ ܕܠܐ ܚܙܘ ܢܘܗܪܐ "and like newborn babes who
                                                              have never seen light"

e. Tense. Tense refers to a difference in tense between the Hebrew and
its Syriac correspondence. So, for example, the Heb. yiqtol in 1:7 - with
its multiplicity of temporal possibilities[3] - is defined more precisely by
the Syriac's use of the participle:

MT   ויאמר יהוה אל־השטן מאין תבא
P   ܘܐܡܪ ܡܪܝܐ ܠܣܛܢܐ. ܡܢ ܐܝܡܟܐ ܐܬܐ ܐܢܬ.
"And the Lord said to the adversary, 'From whence do you come?'"

---

[3] See GKC #107; Bruce K. Waltke and M. O'Connor, *An Introduction to Biblical
Hebrew Syntax* (Eisenbrauns, 1990), p. 497ff.   The topic of tense in Hebrew and
Syriac is dealt with in depth in Chapter III Grammar: Tense.

f. Voice. The term voice indicates that a change from active to passive or passive to active state has occurred. So, for example, in 3:3 the active Heb. והלילה אמר "and the night (which) said . . ." is translated by the passive statement ܗܡ ܕܐܬܐܡܪ ܒܗ "and the night in which it was said . . .".[4]

g. Word Class.[5] The term word class is used to designate a change in parts of speech, e.g. a Syriac noun is used to translate a Hebrew adjective or a Hebrew noun is rendered verbally. An example of this kind can be found in 3:17 where the Heb. noun רגז "raging" is translated by the infinitive construct ܠܡܪܓܙܘ "to provoke anger":

MT   שם רשעים חדלו רגז   "there the wicked cease raging"

P .ܠܡܪܓܙܘ ܡܢ ܚܠܘ ܗܠܝܢ ܗܬܡܢ "for there the ungodly
                                                      cease from provoking anger"

Likewise in 10:17c the Heb. noun חליפות "changes" is rendered verbally by P's ܡܫܚܠܦ ܐܢܬ "you change":

MT חליפות וצבא עמי   "(lit.) changes and a host are with me"

P .ܥܠ ܚܝܠܐ ܐܢܬ ܡܫܚܠܦ ܘ̈ܡܢ "and you change hosts against me"

h. Suffix. The term suffix indicates that a variation exists in a pronominal suffix on a verb, noun, or preposition. This variation may be the addition or omission of the suffix. So is the case in 2:6 where the pronominal suffix of Heb. הנו "Behold, he" is deleted by P. Variation may also take the form of an alternate orthographic representation of a suffix, e.g. a verbal suffix is translated by a Lamedh object marker with a pronominal suffix. Such is the case in 7:8:

---

[4] P's change in voice in this specific case may also be in response to the uniqueness of this Heb. figure of speech - personification - with P's translation in effect dissolving it.
[5] See E. Nida, *Toward A Science of Translating* (Leiden: E.J. Brill, 1964), p. 234, who lists word class as a subcategory of Techniques of Adjustment: Alteration.

MT לֹא־תְשׁוּרֵנִי עִין רֹאִי   "the eye of the one who sees me will
                                       not behold me"

P ‏ܠܐ ܬܚܕܐ ܠܝ ܥܝܢܐ ܕܚܙܝ ܠܝ   "the eye of the one who sees
                                       me will not rejoice for me"

2. Syntax

Translation techniques involving changes in syntax can be referred
to under four headings: word, phrase, clause, or sentence. The larger
units of syntax - discourse, narrative sequence - will not be given separate
headings, for when these larger units are examined the changes which
occur can be traced back to an alteration at a smaller level such as word,
phrase, or sentence.[6]

a. Word. The designation word indicates that an adjustment has
occurred for a single word, thereby affecting the syntax. So, for
example, in 1:13 it is the omission of an equivalent for Heb. יין "wine",
functioning as the direct object, which alters the word order from T S S
V V DO PPh to T S S V V PPh.   Compare the Heb. and Syr. texts:

PPh	DO	V	V	S	S	T
בבית אחיהם	יין	ושתים	אכלים	ובנתיו	ובניו	היום ויהי

הבכור :

"And so it was one day his sons and his daughters (were) eating and
drinking wine in the house of their eldest brother."

V	V	S	S	T
‏ושתין	אכלין	ובנתה דאיוב	בנוהי	‏הוא וביומא

‏בביתה דאחוהון רבא
              PPh

"And so it was one day the sons and daughters of Job were eating
and drinking (in) the house of their eldest brother."

b. Phrase. The next level of syntax which can undergo alteration is the
phrase. Phrase refers to "a group of words used as an equivalent of a

---

6 Technically these larger units could be included for the sake of completeness, for the
possibility might exist of, for example, the transposition of two paragraphs.

single word class".[7] They are often classified according to the kind of word around which they are constructed, e.g. a noun, verb or prepositional phrase.[8] An alteration involving syntax at the phrase level is found in 1:14a. Here the dative לה "to him" has been added:

```
        V/S        PPh    V     S
MT    ויאמר  אל־איוב  בא   ומלאך
```

"And a messenger came to Job and said,"

```
        PPh    V/S        PPh      V        S
P    .ܠܗ  ܘܐܡܪ ܠܗ  ܠܘܬ ܐܝܘܒ  ܐܬܐ  ܡܠܐܟܐ
```

"And a messenger came to Job and said to him,"

c. Clause. There are two main categories of clauses: independent and dependent. An independent clause is a complete statement, i.e. a sentence, that is capable of standing alone. The dependent clause, by contrast, is as its name states, dependent on another statement, the sentence, for completion. Like the phrase, the dependent clause is composed of a group of word that function like a single word, e.g. like an adjective, that in some way modifies the independent clause. The dependent clause is distinct from the phrase in that predication is realized whereas in a phrase it is not.[9] One such example of syntactic change at the clausal level occurs in 6:4a/b:

```
MT    רוחי  שתה  חמתם  אשר        עמדי  שדי  חצי  כי
```

"For the arrows of Shaddai are with me,
    whose wrath my spirit drinks;"

```
P  ܟܠ ܓܝܪ ܓܐܪܘܗܝ. ܕܥܫܝܢܐ ܒܒܣܪܝ. ܘܚܡܬܗܘܢ ܫܬܝܐ ܠܪܘܚܝ.
```

"For the arrows of the Mighty One are in my flesh
    and their fury drinks up my spirit; "

---

[7] Waltke and O'Connor, *Hebrew Syntax*, p. 68.

[8] Waltke and O'Connor, *Hebrew Syntax*, p. 68.

[9] Waltke and O'Connor, *Hebrew Syntax*, pp.68-69; 77-80.

In the MT the second stich contains a relative clause "whose wrath
my spirit drinks", further modifying חצי שׁדי "the arrows of Shaddai"
in stich one. P, by contrast, replaced the Heb. relative pronoun with a
waw conjunctive, thus reading two independent clauses for the Hebrew
independent plus dependent relative clause.[10]

d. Sentence. The final level of syntax included here is the sentence. As
stated above the sentence is an independent clause in which predication is
realized.[11]   Here, too, alterations can be found that affect word order.
In 1:7b the direct object of the first clause (את יהוה) is transferred to
the second clause. Note the change in word order:

                    V   DO   S   V
       MT   ויען השׂטן את יהוה ויאמר   "And the adversary answered
                                              the Lord and said,"

       P   ‡ ܠܡܪܝܐ ܘܐܡܪ ܣܛܢܐ ܘܥܢܐ   "The adversary answered and
                                              said to the Lord,"
            DO/PPh   V   S   V

In the detailed examination of syntax in P-Job (Chapter IV) we will
look at adjustments in these levels as they pertain to word order and
clausal relationships involving the waw conjunctive.

3. Semantics

Adjustments in semantics are noted by one of the following terms:
root, word, or phrase. Larger units, such as clause or sentence, will not
be used, because the alterations that occur in these larger units can be
traced to one of the lower levels.

a. Root. The term root is used to designate an adjustment that has been
made in one or more of the radicals of a root. It is in this category that
problems of a phonological nature are included.[12] So, for example, in
6:10 P renders Heb. חילה "anguish" > הול/חיל I by ܚܝܠܐ "strength" >

---

[10] Many commentators (Dhorme, Habel, Pope, ICC), like the P, treat the Heb. relative
clause as if it were a simple independent statement.

[11] *The Sentence in Biblical Hebrew* (The Hague: Mouton Publishers, 1980), p. 23.

[12] The possibility of course exists that some phonological problems may be due to a
different *Vorlage*, rather than confusion of letters or homographs.

ܫܟܼ/ܐܟܼ II, thus clearly confusing homographs. Another example, involving the erroneous identification of a root letter (ר/ד confusion), is found in 6:7. Here Heb. דוי "illness" is confused by P with the root רוה, hence its translation ܪܘܐ "drunkard".

b. Word. When an adjustment has been made that in some way simplifies, specifies, or clarifies the meaning of an individual word the term word will be used to represent this semantic level. Consider, for example, the term נערים "lads" in 1:16:

אש אלהים נפלה מן־השמים ותבער בצאן ובנערים ותאכלם
"... and the fire of God came down from the heavens and burnt
the sheep and young men and consumed them ... "

P replaces the general Heb. נערים "lads" with a more specific term ܪܥܘܬܐ "shepherds", thereby defining the particular role of the נער in this context. A similar specification of the term נער occurs in 1:19 where P translates with the term ܥܠܝܡܐ "unmarried youths", likewise more contextually appropriate.

c. Phrase. Designating an adjustment by the phrase level of semantics indicates that an alteration has occurred involving more than a root letter, more than an individual term, but rather an entire phrase. Consider the following two examples of P's treatment of semantics at the phrase level:

(1:12)

ויאמר יהוה אל־השטן הנה כל־אשר־לו בידך MT
"And the Lord said to the adversary,
Behold all which is his (is) in your hand."

P ܡܐܡܪ ܡܪܝܐ ܠܣܛܢܐ.
ܗܐ ܟܠ ܡܕܡ ܕܐܝܬ ܠܗ ܡܫܠܡ ܒܐܝܕܝܟ.
"And the Lord said to the adversary,
Behold everything which is his is delivered into your hands."

P adds the participle ܡܫܠܡ "is delivered", implicit in the Heb. phrase הנה כל אשר־לו־בידך "Behold all which is his (is) in your

hand". Thus, in this example it is through addition that P adjusts the
semantics of the Heb. phrase to conform to the translator's explicit style
of expression. In the next example, it is by omission that P treats an
unacceptable Heb. phrase:

(1:15)
MT   :ואמלטה רק־אני לבדי להגיד לך
        "And only I alone escaped to tell you."

P   .ܐܢܐ ܕܐܚܘܝܟ ܒܠܚܘܕܝ ܐܢܐ ܘܐܬܦܠܛܬ
        "And I alone escaped that I might tell you."

The MT preserves a reading that is highly emphatic. This stich
begins with a cohortative, followed by an emphatic particle רק followed
by the independent pronoun (אני) already contained in the initial verbal
form (אמלטה), and finally concluded with another emphatic particle
with suffix (לבדי). P handles this redundancy by omitting a translation
for Heb. רק . This omission is likewise attested to in 1:16,17,19 where
this same phrase occurs.

4. Style
The final category of linguistics, that of style, refers to those
elements of choice which an author can impart to a text for aesthetic
reasons. These are elements such as figurative language or sentence type,
or devices such as parallelism, assonance or alliteration. In the detailed
analysis of style (Chapter VI) three subtopics are examined: Figurative
language, Idiom, and Sentence Type.
a. Figurative Language. The term figurative language is a broad
designation for any alteration that occurs in a figure of speech. The
alteration effected is also quite varied. It might be one in which one
figure of speech is transformed into another, a figure of speech is
completely dissolved, or a new figure of speech is added.[13]   So, for
example, in 6:12a a metaphor is converted into a simile by the addition of
the comparative particle ܐܝܟ "like, as":

---

[13] See E. Nida, *The Theory and Practice of Translation,* p. 107.

MT   אם־כח אבנים כחי

"or is my strength the strength of stones?"

P   ܐܠܐ ܐܝܟ ܚܝܠܐ ܗܘ ܕܟܐܦܐ ܚܝܠܝ.

"is my strength like the strength of stones?"

In 12:20a a figure of speech is removed. There Heb. שׂפה "lip", a metonymy for "speech", is rendered ܡܡܠܠܐ "speech" in P.

b. Idiom. The designation idiom might be included in the above figurative language, because an idiom is a figure of speech. However, due to the frequency in which an alteration involving idiom does occur it deserves mention as a separate item. Alteration of idiom most frequently involves either the removal or replacement of a Hebraic idiom or the addition of a Syriac one. In 1:10a P replaces the Hebrew idiom with a Syriac one:

MT   הלא־את שׂכת בעדו ובעד־ביתו

"Have you not placed a hedge about him and about his house?"

P   ܐܢܬ ܐܢܬ ܐܝܟ ܣܡܬ ܐܝܕܟ ܥܠܘܗܝ ܘܥܠ ܒܝܬܗ

"Have you rested your hand upon him and upon his house."

P removes the Hebrew idiom שׂךְ בעד "to place a hedge about" meaning "to protect"[14] and replaces it with a less picturesque Syriac one ܐܝܕ ܣܡ "to rest the hand", also meaning "to protect".[15]

In 1:14 P replaces a simple Hebrew verb חרשׁ "to cut in, engrave, plough, devise" in the phrase הבקר היו חרשׁות "the oxen were ploughing" with a Syriac idiom ܢܓܕ ܦܕܢܐ "to lead the yoke", i.e. ܘܬܘܪܐ ܗܘܘ ܢܓܕܝܢ ܦܕܢܐ "the oxen were leading the yoke", that is "the

---

[14] See Francis Brown, S.R. Driver, C.A. Briggs, *Hebrew and English Lexicon of the Old Testament* (Oxford: Clarendon Press, 1975), p. 962a, s.v. שׂוךְ.

[15] See J. Payne-Smith, *Syriac English Dictionary* (Oxford: Clarendon Press, 1979), p. 73a, s.v. ܣܡ ; R. Payne-Smith, *Thesaurus Syriacus*, p. 742, s.v. ܣܡ

oxen were ploughing".[16] The Syriac language does contain the cognate root √ܚܪܬ "to dig out, hollow out, furrow";[17] however, the translator choose to incorporate an idiom, possibly for stylistic variety or possibly √ܚܪܬ may be used with less frequency.

c. Sentence Type. Sentences are frequently classified by purpose: declarative, interrogative, imperative, and exclamatory.[18] It is an alteration according to this classification to which sentence type refers. Additional sentence subtypes, such as the rhetorical question or the conditional sentence, can also be included here. An example of sentence type occurs in 1:8b. There P records an exclamatory sentence for the Heb. interrogative question. This is achieved by reading the interjectory particle ܗܐ "behold" for the Heb. interrogative Heh:

MT   השמת לבך על־עבדי איוב
             "Have you considered my servant Job?"

P   ܗܐ ܣܡܬܗ ܠܒܟ ܥܠ ܥܒܕܝ ܐܝܘܒ.
             "Behold you have considered my servant Job!"[19]

II. Adjustment.

The second major portion of the translation model is adjustment. Adjustment refers to a variety of processes that can be performed upon a element of translation in its transference from source to target text. These processes are addition, omission, substitution, harmonization, clarification, transposition, redivision and a variety of semantically oriented alterations.

---

[16] See J. Payne Smith, p. 82b, s.v. ܕܒܪ ; p. 434b, s.v. ܦܠܚ. ; R. Payne-Smith, p. 811, s.v. ܕܒܪ .

[17] See J. Payne Smith, p. 160a, s.v. ܚܪܬ ; R. Payne-Smith, p. 1388, s.v. ܚܪܬ .

[18] John C. Hodges, Mary E. Whitten & Suzanne S. Webb, *Harbrace College Handbook,* 10th ed. (San Diego: Harcourt Brac Jovanich Publishers, 1986), p. 24.

[19] For this well attested phonological correspondence Heb. ה > Syr. ܗܐ , suggestive of an aural error, see Chapter VI: Style: Sentence Type: Interrogatives.

1. Addition.

An adjustment termed addition refers to the presence of an extra element in the translated text. Thus, with addition the translated text length is increased. This "plus"[20] may be at the level of the morpheme, word, phrase, clause, or sentence.

a. Morpheme. The term morpheme is used to indicate a bound morpheme, that is the smallest unit of meaning that can not function independently, such as a pronominal suffix or a plural ending.[21] An example of this kind is found in 9:26b where P adds a pronominal suffix that may very well be implicit in the Heb. text:

MT   :עלי־אכל   יטוש   כנשר

"like an eagle (that) rushes upon (its) food."

P   ܐܝܟ ܢܫܪܐ ܕܦܪܚ ܥܠ ܡܐܟܘܠܬܗ.

"like an eagle which circles over its food."

b. Word. The designation word refers to the addition of a free morpheme, that is a single self-sustaining term in which predication is not realized[22]. An example of this type is found in 7:6a in which P adds the noun (ܓܓܘ) for precision:

MT   ימי קלו מני־ארג   "My days are swifter than a loom,"

P   ܝܘܡܬ̈ܝ ܩܠܝܠܝ̈ܢ ܡܢ ܓܓܘ .

"My days are swifter than the thrum of looms,"

---

[20] See E. Tov, *The Text-critical Use of the Septuagint in Biblical Research* (Jerusalem Biblical Studies 3, Jerusalem: Simor Ltd., 1981), p. 186f.

[21] This notion of dependence versus self-sustaining is a necessary criteria for distinguishing a morpheme from a word. Consider, for example, the word בֵּיתוֹ "his house". In English we have two free morphemes: his and house. In Hebrew there are also two morphemes, however, one is bound (וֹ-), the other is free (בית). Thus, when a change occurs in a bound morpheme it will be classified under morpheme, when it occurs in a free morpheme it will be classified under word.

[22] In the Semitic languages it is necessary to define a word as a free morpheme without predication realized, for predication can occur within a single word, as for example the verbal form אמר "he said". An addition of this sort would then be listed under sentence.

c. Phrase. The term phrase is used to indicate an addition of a phrase, that is a group of words functioning as a single word in which predication is not realized. [23] So, for example, in 42:3a P adds a prepositional phrase ܒܡܠܐ "with words":

> MT   מי זה מעלים עצה בלי דעת
>
> "Who is this (who) darkens counsel without knowledge?"

> P   ܡܢܘ ܗܢܐ ܕܡܟܣܐ ܬܪܥܝܬܐ ܒܡܠܐ ܕܠܐ ܐܝܕܥܬܐ.
>
> "Who is this who takes counsel with words without knowledge?"

d. Clause. Addition at the clausal level refers to the insertion of a dependent clause.[24] Job 3:1b contains one such example. Here it is the addition of a relative clause:

> MT   ויקלל את־יומו: "And he cursed his day."

> P   ܘܠܛ ܠܝܘܡܐ ܕܐܬܝܠܕ ܒܗ.
>
> "And he cursed the day in which he was born."

e. Sentence. As previously explained the term sentence is used to refer to an independent, self-sustaining statement, in which predication is realized.[25] Addition at the sentence level in the P-Job occurs infrequently. However, one such example of the incorporation of an entirely new sentence occurs in 31:34:

> MT   כי אערוץ חמון רבה ובוז־משפחות יחתני
>
>   ואדם לא־אצא פתח:
>
> "For I would tremble a great tumult,
>   and the contempt of families would terrify me.
> Then I would be silent, I could not go forth (from my) door."

> P   ܐܢ ܕܚܠܬ ܡܢ ܣܘܓܐܐ ܕܥܡܐ. ܐܠܐ ܣܡܟܐ ܗܘ ܕܒܝܬܐ ܐܬܟܢܫ

---

[23] See above pp. 20-21.

[24] See above pp. 21-22.

[25] See above p.22.

ܘܓܒܪ̈ܐ ܠܐ ܐܗܦܟܬ ܒܬܪܥܐ. <u>ܘܒܡܡܠܠܐ ܕܣܦ̈ܘܬܐ ܠܐ ܪܫܬ.</u>
<u>ܒܘܙ̈ܚܘܗܝ ܕܐܠܗܐ ܡܟܟܢܝ.</u>

"And if I had trampled the strength of many
- even though the multitude of families has destroyed me;
and I did not turn men away at the gate;
<u>and I did not pay heed to the discourse of the lips</u>
<u>then the provocations of God would have humbled me."</u>

One rather specific type of addition that occurs in P-Job is paraphrase. Paraphrase by definition is the restatement of a word(s) in other words that results in the same general semantic information. It differs from a simple addition to the text in that it replaces a given word with another equivalent expression that does not use the original term. Thus, in a sense it is also a type of substitution that results in a longer but synonymously parallel expression. An example of paraphrase has already been discussed for 1:14 under Style: idiom. There P paraphrased the Hebrew verb חרשׁ in the phrase הבקר היו חרשׁות "the oxen were ploughing". Rather than using the root ܚܪܬ "to dig out, hollow out, to furrow"[26] the translator used the Syriac idiom ܕܒܪ ܦܕܢܐ "to lead the yoke", i.e. ܬܘܪ̈ܐ ܗܘܘ ܕܒܪܝܢ ܦܕܢܐ "the oxen were leading the yoke" that is "the oxen were ploughing".[27]

Another specific type of addition that occurs in the P-Job is the doublet, i.e. a second translation of an existing word, phrase, clause or entire verse in the Hebrew text.[28] Doublets are found in the P-Job from word to sentence level. In 12:14a an example of a doublet at the word level occurs. There P translates the Heb. particle הן by both possible translations ܗܐ ܐܢ "behold, if":

MT <u>הן</u> יהרוס ולא יבנה
"<u>Behold/If</u> he tears down, then it will not be rebuilt,"

26 See J. Payne-Smith, p. 160a, s.v. ܚܪܬ.

27 See J. Payne-Smith, p. 82b, s.v. ܕܒܪ; p. 434b, s.v. ܦܕܢ.

28 See the discussion of doublets, for example, in E. Baumann, "Verwendbarkeit", (1899): 15ff; A. Mandl, *Peschittha zu Hiob*, p. 20; A. Sperber, *The Bible in Aramaic*, Vol IVB, pp. 245-46, 414-15.

P   ‎ܡܐ ܐܟ ܣܬܪ ܘܬܡ ܟܕ.

"Behold, if he demolishes, who can rebuild?"

In 9:17a an example of a doublet at phrase level can be found:

MT   אשר־בשׂערה ישׁופני   "who bruises me by the storm,"

P   ‎ܘܒܟܠ ܪܬܝܐ ܕܪܫܝ ܒܬܬܡܦܐ ܬܠܣܣ.

"for He smote me in every part of my head with force,"

P here translated Heb. בשׂערה by both orthographic possibilities:
(1) erroneously understanding Heb. שְׂעָרָה "storm, tempest" as שַׂעֲרָה
"hair", hence the paraphrastic ‎ܟܠ ܕܪܬܝ ܕܪܫܝ "in every part of my
head";
(2) making the correct association of Heb. שׂערה with שְׂעָרָה (= סְעָרָה)
"storm, tempest", but then translating interpretively by ‎ܒܬܬܡܦܐ "with
strength".

In 29:3a P preserves a second rendering of a clause. Compare the
Heb. and Syr.:

MT   בהלו נרו עלי ראשׁי
"When He shined His lamp upon my head,"

P   ‎ܘܣܠܐܬܗ ܕܒܕ ܠܠܠ ܕܝ ܪܬܝ ܟܬܦܘܣܡ ‎ܪܬܘܟ‎ܡ ܠܠܗ.
"He placed his awe upon my head,
when He spread His lamp upon me."

P translates this Heb. stich twice, although each does not contain the
identical grammatical elements. The first Syr. stich incorporates the Heb.
עלי ראשׁי (underscored words) in its translation; alters the tense from a
Heb. infinitive construct > Syr. perfect; and interprets Heb. נרו "His
lamp" as ‎ܪܬܘܠܬܗ "his awe".The second translation incorporates Heb.
נרו (bold face words), i.e. ‎ܡܠܬܝܟ; retains the infinitive; and translates
Heb. עלי ראשׁי simply as ‎ܠܠܗ "upon me".

2. Omission.

The adjustment of omission involves the exclusion of a morpheme, word, phrase, clause, or sentence with no replacement.[29] Thus, the text length is shortened. The meaning of each term designating a level is identical to that given in the preceding section, hence what follows are the examples of each of the four subcategories of omission.

a. Morpheme. In 5:5a the omission of a morpheme is found in the lack of the pronominal suffix of Heb. קצירו "his harvest":

MT   אשר קצירו רעב יאכל

"whose harvest the hungry consumes,"

P   ܘܢܣܒ ܚܨܕܐ ܟܦܢܐ.

"for the hungry consumes the harvest,"

b. Word. In 1:13 an omission of a word occurs. There P preserves no translation for Heb. יין "wine":

MT   ויהי היום ובניו ובנתיו אכלים ושתים יין
                 בבית אחיהם הבכור:

"And so it was one day his sons and his daughters (were) eating and drinking wine in the house of their eldest brother."

P   ܘܗܘܐ ܝܘܡܐ ܘܒܢܘܗܝ ܘܒܢܬܗ ܕܐܝܘܒ ܐܟܠܝܢ ܗܘܘ ܘܫܬܝܢ
                 ܒܝܬ ܐܚܘܗܘܢ ܒܟܘܪܐ

"And so it was one day the sons and daughters of Job were eating and drinking (in) the house of their eldest brother."

c. Phrase. Job 11:15a contains an example of omission of a phrase. There P lacks a translation for Heb. ממום "without (lit. from) blemish":

MT   כי־אז תשא פניך ממום והיית מצק ולא תירא:

"for then you will lift up your face without blemish,
and you will be firmly established and not afraid."

---

[29] If another item or element is added for the omission this would more properly be called substitution, for which see below p.32f.

P ܘܡܟܝܢ ܐܝܕܝܟ ܬܪܝܡ. ܘܡܢ ܟܐܒܐ ܠܐ ܬܕܚܠ.

"And then you will raise your hands,
and you will not be afraid from adversity."

d. Clause. In 27:5a P omits translating the Hebrew protasis:

    MT   חלילה לי אם־אצדיק אתכם

    "Far be it for me if I declare you right!"

    P   ܚܣ ܠܝ.

    "Far be it for me, (until I die . . .)"

e. Sentence. In 30:7 it is an independent clause ינהקו "they bray" that is omitted in P:

    MT   בין־שׂיחים ינהקו   "Between the shrubs they bray,"

    P   ܘܬܚܘܬ ܫܩܝܦܐ "and beneath steep rocks,"

3. Substitution.

All translation involves the act of substitution, that is replacing an element from the source text with the nearest equivalent in the target text. The choice of substitute is clearly governed by the rules of the target language with the ultimate result being a synonymous proposition. Examples of this kind are found in all areas of linguistics. One such example can be found in 9:5b:

    MT   אשׁר הפכם באפו: "who overturns them in His anger."

    P ܘܗܦܟ ܠܗܘܢ ܒܪܘܓܙܗ "and [He] overturns them in His anger."

Lacking a 3ppl objective suffix, Syriac is forced to find an alternate means of representation.[30] Syriac possesses two possibilities: the enclitic ܐܢܘܢ / ܐܢܘܢ or the preposition Lamedh with the 3p. pronominal suffix

---

[30] See Nöldeke, p. 45f, #63-65; p. 226f, #287-288; and Th. Robinson, p. 77f.

ܩܛܠ- / ܝܩܛܠ-. In the present verse the translator chose the latter option, replacing the Heb. verbal suffix (ם‎֖) with the pronominal suffix on the Lamedh object marker (ܠܗܘܢ).

Consider another example of substitution. The Hebrew tenses possess a far greater range in meaning than those in Syriac.[31] In order to adjust for this fluidity in meaning, the translator of P often had to translate a verb according to the meaning implied in the MT, rather than following the given structural form of the verb. Such is the case, for example, in 3:11. Following the implicit past time frame, P replaces the Heb. yiqtol forms אמות and אגוע with the qatal forms ܡܝܬܬ and ܣܦܬ:

MT :וְאֶגְוָע יָצָאתִי מִבֶּטֶן אָמוּת מֵרֶחֶם לֹא לָמָה
"Why did I not die at birth,
  come forth from the womb and perish?"

P ܠܡܢܐ ܠܐ ܡܢ ܡܪܒܥܐ ܡܝܬܬ.
ܡܢ ܟܪܣܐ ܢܦܩܬ. ܣܦܬ ܘܝ
"Why did I not die from the womb,
  and from conception why did I go forth
  that I have perished?"

All substitutions, however, do not necessarily result in an "exact" or "near-exact equivalent," thereby preserving the synonymy of the text,[32] nor are all governed by a motivation of language difference. In other words text length may go unchanged, but through substitution caused, for example, by ideological concerns the effect on meaning can be quite innovative. Many substitutions of this kind will be seen in the application of this model to P-Job in the following chapters.

---

[31] For the meaning of the Syriac tenses see Nöldeke, p. 202ff, #255f - esp. #264-268 on the imperfect; and Robinson, p. 53. For the Hebrew tenses see GKC #106ff - esp. 107b for this example from Job (3:11); Bruce K. Waltke and M. O'Connor, *An Introduction to Biblical Hebrew Syntax* (Eisenbrauns, 1990), Chapters 29-37; and Seow, pp. 92,141,158; and Thomas O. Lambdin, *Introduction to Biblical Hebrew* (New York: Charles Scribner's Sons, 1971), #44 and 91.

[32] See p. 35 for a discussion of equivalency between source and target texts.

4. Harmonization.

Harmonization is a process whereby in the transference from source to target language an element is altered - be it in terms of number, gender, person, etc. - in order to better accord with an element in the surrounding environment. It is a secondary adjustment, for harmony between elements is achieved through addition, omission or substitution. An example of harmonization achieved by substitution occurs in P at 7:14:

MT   ותחתני   בחלמות ומחזינות   תבעתני:
            "And you scare me with dreams,
            and you startle me from/more than visions."

P   ܘܗܐ ܐܙܝܥܬܢܝ ܒܚܠܡܐ. ܘܒܚܙܘܢܐ ܐܠܨܬܢܝ.
            "And behold you terrified me with dreams,
            and you startled me with visions."

P substitutes ב "in, with" for Heb. מִן "from", thus harmonizing this preposition with the ב in stich one.

5. Clarification.

Clarification, like harmonization, is a secondary adjustment, for it involves the addition, omission, substitution, redivision or transposition of a translational element due to an ambiguity in the source text with the intent, at least from the translator's perspective, of bringing clarity to the text. So, for example, in 3:20 P translates the Heb. active יתן in the clause למה יתן לעמל אור "Why does he/one give light to the oppressed" by the passive ܢܬܝܗܒ "Why is light given to the labourers?", thereby removing the uncertainty of the unnamed subject "he".[33]

6. Syntactically Oriented.

a. Transposition. Transposition is a type of alteration that belongs to the area of syntax. It involves the movement of a word or phrase to a new

---

[33] See p. 90 where this verse is further discussed.

position within a clause. In 3:7b we see an example of transposition of the subject and prepositional phrase:

     PPh S   V

MT   :אל־תבא רננה בו   "May a ringing cry not enter into it!"

P ܘܠܐ ܬܥܘܠ ܒܗ ܬܫܒܘܚܬܐ "And may praise not enter into it!"
    S   PPh   V

b. Redivision. Redivision is the term used to describe the creation of new stich or verse boundaries in the target text. So, for example, in 9:21 P erroneously recognized the semantic boundary between stichs, construing נפשי as the subject of the following verb, rather than the direct object of the preceding verb:

MT   :תם־אני לא־אדע נפשי אמאס חיי

    "I am innocent?! I do not know myself! I loathe my life!"

P   ܬܡܝܬ ܐܢܐ ܘܠܐ ܝܕܥ ܐܢܐ. ܢܦܫܝ ܐܡܣܬ ܚ̈ܝܝ

    "I am innocent, but I do not know! My soul abhors my life!"

7. Semantically Oriented.

In comparative semantic analyses between source and target languages the term lexical correspondence is used to designate the target language's lexical choice for a source language's lexeme.[34] The term equivalence has also been used to describe this relationship; however, equivalence tends to be confused with the term "equal". And, as will shortly be seen, complete "equality" or "synonymity" does not exist in language.[35] So, for example, in 3:18 P selected the root ܫܠܐ "to be still, cease, rest" for translating Heb. שאנן "to be at ease". This same Syr. root is also used for Heb. שקט "to be silent" in 3:13; for חדל "to cease" in 3:17; and for שלה/שללה "to be quiet, at ease" in 3:26, thus resulting in

---

[34] See E. Nida, *Towards a Science*, p. 213, where however he subdivides lexical correspondences into: literal, manufactured and borrowing. Here it is used just to indicate a basic correspondence.

[35] See E. Tov, pp. 101ff for the subject of Greek-Hebrew equivalents. The issue of synonymity in meaning is discussed below, pp.51f.

a secondary adjustment termed lexical levelling. This term and four other semantically oriented adjustments that occur in the P-Job are discussed below.

a./b. Generalization and Specification.[36] For an explanation of the terms generalization and specification appeal can be made to what in Linguistics is called componential analysis. This approach attempts "to break down meaning into its minimal components".[37] These minimal components are indicated by plus and minus values. The first marker is usually a syntactic one indicating to what part of speech the word belongs, the others are semantic indicators. Thus, Heb. אִישׁ "man" and מֶלֶךְ "king" are analyzed as having the following components:

א י שׁ	מ ל ך
+noun	+noun
+animate	+animate
+human	+human
+male	+male
+adult	+adult
-first-in-power	+first-in-power

Both terms share the general components of [noun-animate-human-male-adult]. The more specific feature [first-in-power] is what distinguishes them. When a translator provides a correspondence that contains less semantic markings than the source language, this is generalization. Specification is just the opposite, translating with a term that is componentially more sophisticated than the source language. Consider the following two examples.

Generalization. In 6:30 P contains the more general term פהבי "my mouth" for the more specific Heb. חכי "my palate":

MT :‏היש־בלשוני   עולה   אם־חכי   לא־יבין   הוות‎

"Is there iniquity in my tongue,
or does my palate discern calamity?"

---

[36] See E. Nida and C. Taber, *Theory and Practice*, p. 108, where they use the terms generic and specific in contrast to generalization and specification in the TT Model.
[37] Ullmann, *Meaning and Style: Collected Papers*, Language and Style Series (Oxford: Basil Blackwell, 1973), p. 35.

ܘܠܐ ܐܝܟ ܕܠܟ ܢܚܘܐ ܠܘܬܟ ܐܘ ܦܘܡܝ ܠܐ ܢܡܠܠ ܩܘܫܬܐ. P

"(cont. from v. 24) lest there be iniquity in my tongue,
or my mouth does not speak truth."

Hebrew חֵךְ and Syriac ܦܘܡ can be analyzed as having the following
components:[38]

חֵךְ	ܦܘܡ
+noun	+noun
+part of body	+part of body
+part of head	+part of head
+facial orifice	+facial orifice
+used in breathing	+used in breathing
+takes in water/	+takes in water/
nourishment	nourishment
+roof of mouth	

Thus, both חֵךְ and ܦܘܡ share six components. חֵךְ, as a particular
part of the mouth, possesses one additional one which sets it apart from
the term ܦܘܡ and makes it more specific. P removes this specification
by descending the ladder of components by one rung.
Specification. An example of specification has already been seen in the
explanation of Word under Semantics above. The MT at 1:16 read:

אֵשׁ אֱלֹהִים נָפְלָה מִן־הַשָּׁמַיִם וַתִּבְעַר בַּצֹּאן וּבַנְּעָרִים וַתֹּאכְלֵם
"and the fire of God came down from the heavens and burnt the
sheep and young men and consumed them "

P replaced the general Heb. נערים "lads" with the more specific
term ܪܥܘܬܐ "shepherds". The components of these two words are:

---

[38] A bit of arbitrariness does exist in selecting components. This is one of the
weaknesses of this approach. See S. Ullmann, *Language and Meaning*, p. 35f.
Although scholars may differ in this selection process, the concept of going from a more
complex to a less complex lexeme is still obvious.

נ ע ר	ܪܥܝܐ
+noun	+noun
+animate	+animate
+human	+human
+male	+male
+young	+young(?)
	+pastoralist
	+tends sheep

Thus, P has defined the role of the Heb. נער "lad" by translating with a componentially more complex term ܪܥܝܐ "shepherd".

c. **Contextual Translation.** A semantic alteration is termed a contextual translation when P has replaced a rare, difficult, or unclear term, including the *hapax legomena*, with a term that is appropriate to the given context. Consider, for example, Heb. √בלג "to smile" in 9:27b:

MT   אעזבה פני ואבליגה:

"I will relax my countenance and <u>smile</u>."

P   ܐܢ ܐܫܒܘܩ ܗܘ ܚܘܫܒܝ. ܐܘ ܡܠܬܗܝ. ܟܪܝܐ ܠܝ.

"If I leave off my thoughts or my words, <u>I am grieved</u>."

Heb. בלג "to smile" occurs four times in the Old Testament: Amos 5:9; Ps. 39:14 and twice in Job, here (9:27) and 10:20. In each case P translates contextually, here with ܟܪܝܐ ܠܝ "I am grieved", in Job 10:20 and in Ps. 39:14 by ܐܬܬܢܝܚ "I will be at rest"; and in Amos 5:9 with ܢܫܬܒܩ "be permitted".

d. **Interpretation.** A semantic alteration is termed interpretation when the translation can be shown to explain the meaning of a Heb. word, phrase, or clause. An example of interpretation at the word level is found in 8:14. There Heb. מבטחו "his trust" is rendered ܒܝܬܗ "his house":

MT אֲשֶׁר־יָקוֹט כִּסְלוֹ וּבֵית עַכָּבִישׁ מִבְטַחוֹ:

"Whose confidence snaps and <u>whose trust</u> is the spider's house."

P ܡܬܦܣܩ ܘܡܬܬܒܪܐ ܣܒܪܗ ܘܐܝܟ ܒܝܬܐ ܕܓܘܓܝ <u>ܒܝܬܗ</u>.

"And his trust is broken and <u>his house</u> is the spider's house."

e. Lexical leveling. Lexical leveling is the term used to indicate a type of semantic alteration in which one word is used to translate a variety of terms that are in the same semantic range:

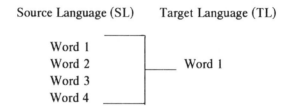

Source Language (SL)   Target Language (TL)

An excellent example of this process can be found in 4:10-11. Here the Hebrew text contains five terms for a lion:

MT שַׁאֲגַת <u>אַרְיֵה</u> וְקוֹל <u>שָׁחַל</u> וְשִׁנֵּי <u>כְפִירִים</u> נִתָּעוּ:
<u>לַיִשׁ</u> אֹבֵד מִבְּלִי־טֶרֶף וּבְנֵי <u>לָבִיא</u> יִתְפָּרָדוּ:

"The roar of the lion and the cry of the lion,
and the teeth of the young lions are broken.
The lion perished for lack of prey,
and the sons of the lioness are dispersed."

P ܢܗܡܬܐ <u>ܕܐܪܝܐ</u> ܘܩܠܐ ܕܓܘܪܝܐ <u>ܕܐܪܝܐ</u>. ܘܫܢܐ <u>ܕܐܪܝܘܬܐ</u> ܐܬܬܒܪ.
<u>ܐܪܝܐ</u> ܐܒܕ ܡܢ ܕܠܝܬ ܠܗ ܬܒܪܐ. ܘܒܢܝ <u>ܐܪܝܘܬܐ</u> ܐܬܒܕܪܘ.

"The roar of the lion and the cry of the lion's whelp,
and the teeth of the lionnesses are broken.
The lion perished for lack of his possessing prey,
and the sons of lionesses have been scattered abroad."

P translates all terms referring to a "lion" by the simplest equivalent ܐܪܝܐ here and similarly throughout Job.[39] Note, however, for Heb. שׁחל P does add ܓܘܪܝܐ "whelp" for specification, so too in 10:16 and 28:8.

Hebrew (SL)   Syriac (TL)

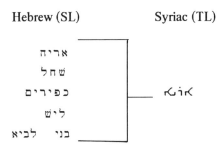

Furthermore, lexical levelling, as we will see, is a secondary process, for it results from the generalization, specification, contextualization or interpretation of lexemes, as well as from the loss of variety dictated by language difference, i.e. a target language that lacks the lexical variety of the source language.[40]

III. Motivation.

The third major portion of the translation model is motivation. Motivation refers to the reason or cause that prompted the translator to initiate an adjustment in the transference from source to target text, in so far as this can be deduced from the end product.

a. Language Difference.   When translation occurs between any two languages, no matter how closely related the languages are they still contain differences that make them distinct.   The term language difference is used to refer to these differences that, on the surface, appear to be departures from the source text, but in fact are only language specific, i.e. the only way a given language has of expressing itself. Consider P's translation of the Heb. in 4:17:

---

[39] See also 10:16; 28:8; 38:39. See also A. Gelston, *The Peshitta of the Twelve Prophets* (Oxford: Clarendon Press, 1987), p. 141, where he notes a similar treatment of words for "lion" in P to the Dodekapropheton.

[40] The secondary nature of this process is amply demonstrated in Chapter V: Semantics: Lexical Levelling.

Heb. :האנוש מאלוה יצדק אם מעשהו יטהר־גבר
"Can a man be more righteous than God?,
or can a man be purer than his Maker?"

P. ܐܢܫ ܡܢ ܐܠܗܐ ܢܙܕܩ ܐܘ ܡܢ ܡܥ̈ܒܕܘܗܝ ܢܬܕܟܐ ܓܒܪܐ.
"(Shall) man be declared more righteous than God?
or man be purer than his Maker?"

Language difference required the translator of P to represent a
simple interrogative in a manner indicative of its own language.
Although Syriac has no exact lexical correspondence for this Heb.
interrogative particle, it does have options: non-representation of the
interrogative Heh with context determining the question; the particle
ܕܠܡܐ to introduce an indirect interrogative; or the replacement of a
question by its answer in the form of an exclamatory affirmative
statement.[41] Here, P used the first and most common option: non-
representation and context.

b. Linguistic Interference.[42]   Linguistic Interference is the term used
to indicate the interference that can occur in all areas of linguistics when
languages come into contact, in particular when translation occurs
between languages belonging to the same language family for cognate
elements can easily be confused. Consider Job 7:15:

MT   ותבחר מחנק נפשי   "My soul chose strangulation,
      מות מעצמותי: death rather than my bones."

P   ܘܒܚܪܬ ܢܦܫܝ ܡܢ ܚܘܒܠܐ ܘܓܪ̈ܡܝ ܡܢ ܡܘܬܐ.
"And you have examined/observed (sic.) my soul
from destruction and my bones from death."

---

[41] See Chapter VI Style: Sentence Type: Interrogatives for P's treatment of Hebrew
interrogative sentences.
[42] See M. Silva, *Biblical Words & Their Meaning: An Introduction to Lexical Semantics*
(Grand Rapids, Michigan: Zondervan Publishing House, 1983), p. 86.

P directly adopted the Heb. בחר√ "to choose", assuming it to be a cognate of the Syriac ܒܚܢ√ which, however, means "to examine, observe; test, try (silver)" in Syriac. Hence, this is either a case of linguistic interference in the area of phonology/ semantics, whereby the similarity in languages resulted in an erroneous equivalent, which in turn resulted in a confusion in meaning;[43] or a West Aramaic element in P-Job, for in West Aramaic בחר√ means "to choose".[44]

c. Implicit to Explicit Exegesis.[45] Implicit to explicit exegesis indicates that an implied element in the source text is explicitly expressed in target text. In 5:14, for example, four times an implicit Heb. preposition is explicitly expressed in the P:

> MT: יומם יפגשו־חשך   וכלילה ימששו בצהרים
> "(In) the daytime they meet (as in) darkness,
> and at noon-time they grope as (in) the night."

> P   ܐܝܟ ܒܨܦܪܐ ܡܓܫܝܢ ܘܒܐܝܡܡܐ.
>   ܘܐܝܟ ܒܠܠܝܐ ܡܓܫܝܢ ܒܛܗܪܐ.
> "They grope around <u>in</u> the daytime <u>as in</u> the dark,
> and they grope at noon as <u>in</u> the night."

d. Ideology. The term ideology refers to "the body of ideas reflecting the social needs and aspirations of an individual, group, class, or culture".[46] The translator, as a representative of his culture group, may at times have felt compelled to adjust an element in the source text that was in some way contrary to his set of beliefs. This is termed an ideologically motivated adjustment.

Past cultures that have left a rich legacy of artifactual remains, including literary works, make it easier to recreate and formulate their

---

[43] See below in Part Four of the TT Model where this verse is further discussed as an example of Effect on Meaning: Confusion.

[44] See Jan Joosten, "West Aramaic Elements in the Old Syriac and Peshitta Gospels." *JBL* 110/2 (1991): 274, where she similarly cites P's use of ܒܚܢ√ in John 3:18 ܒܪܐ ܒܚܝܪܐ which can only mean "chosen son".

[45] See the discussions of implicit to explicit exegesis in M. Goshen-Gottstein, "Theory and Practice," p. 138, n. 20; P. Kyle McCarter, *Textual Criticism*, p. 34; and E. Nida, *Toward a Science of Translating*, p. 228f.

[46] *The American Heritage Dictionary*, (2nd College Edition, 1982).

ideology. Likewise, a contemporary culture is a living example of its ideological system, hence an ethnographical study can easily be undertaken and used to understand their set of beliefs. However, in the case of the Peshitta (and Syriac literature), all that is preserved of the Syriac people and culture is the written word; thus the Syriac ideological system must be recreated by what is termed "cultural reconstruction via the lexicon".[47] "The lexicon can provide information about the social, cultural, geographical and political nature of a language group."[48] Just as a language's lexicon can yield information on any or all aspects of its culture, so too might the translation techniques and changes in meaning reflect it's ideology. Consider the following passage:

(6:30) MT   :ה_וות_ לא־יבין אם־חכי   עולה היש־בלשוני
  "Is there injustice on my tongue?,
  or cannot my palate discern <u>calamity</u>?"

P. ܩܘܫܬܐ ܠܠܡܠ ܡܡܠܐ ܠܐ ܦܘܡܝ ܐܢ . ܥܘܠܐ ܒܠܫܢܝ ܐܝܬ ܕܠܡܐ
  "Lest there is iniquity in my tongue,
  or my mouth does not speak <u>truth</u>."

Heb. הוות "calamities" is rendered ܩܘܫܬܐ "truth" in P, רגושתא "tumult" in the Tg, συνεσιν "judgment,understanding" in the LXX, and *stultitia* "folly, foolishness, simplicity" in the Vulgate, thus all attest to the uncertainty of the meaning of this Heb. term. However, it is evident that P and LXX present positive concepts whereas Tg. and Vulgate present negative ones. This Heb. term occurs twice elsewhere in Job, where the translator of Job seems to have understood its meaning (6:2 ܕܗܡܝ רכדני "what has befallen me"; (30:13 ܕܗܡܝ ܕܗܒ ܠܠ "over what has befallen me"). Thus in the present verse, P's translation may be ideologically motivated, more specifically a theological dilemma. Here the translator attempts to harmonize the patient, optimistic Job of the prologue and epilogue with the vocative, loquacious, complaining Job of the dialogue by avoiding any negative attributes to issue forth from the mouth of Job.   Hence, it is not that the palate of Job has

---

[47] Th. Bynon, *Historical Linguistics* (Cambridge: Cambridge University Press, 1985), pp. 272-280.
[48] Th. Bynon, *Historical Linguistics*, p. 272.

understood/discerned/experienced calamities, i.e. that he has spoken
wrongly/harshly, but rather that his mouth has only brought forth
truth.[49]

e. Ambiguity. In his *Seven Types of Ambiguity*, William Empson
commenced with his definition of ambiguity: "any verbal nuance,
however slight, which gives room for alternative reactions to the same
piece of language."[50] In its simplest form, he maintained, "a word or a
grammatical structure is effective in several ways at once."[51] Thus,
ambiguity can occur in the meaning of a word itself or as the result of a
common word in a peculiar context. It can occur because of an
uncertainty in a word's syntactic role. Then too, ambiguity need not be
limited to the word level, semantics or syntax, but can extend into the
realm of style and the figurative use of words and to larger units of
discourse, i.e the phrase, clause and sentence. One example of ambiguity
involving semantics at the word level is found in 21:20:

MT : יִשְׁתֶּה   שַׁדַּי   וּמֵחֲמַת   כִּידוֹ   עֵינָו   יִרְאוּ
"May his eyes see his misfortune,
and may he drink from the wrath of Shaddai!"

P   ‏ܘܢܚܙܝܢ ܥܝܢܘܗܝ ܐܒܕܢܗ. ܘܡܢ ܚܡܬܗ ܕܐܠܗܐ ܢܫܬܐ.
"And may his eyes see his destruction,
and may he drink from the wrath of God!"

Heb. כִּיד "misfortune" is a *hapax legomenon* whose meaning is
determined by conjecture. Because of the ambiguity in the meaning of

---

[49] Further examples of the Peshitta's tendency to harmonize the character of Job occur in
6:30;7:7;9:35;10:1,7,12, to name but a few. This topic is dealt with more fully in
Chapter VII.

[50] 2nd ed., London, 1949, p. 1. Empson's seven types of ambiguity are: detail is
effective in several ways at once; two or more alternative meanings are fully resolved into
one; two apparently unconnected meanings are given simultaneously; alternative
meanings combine to make clear a complicated state of mind in the author; fortunate
confusion, as when the author is discovering his idea in the act or writing; what is said is
contradictory or irrelevant and the reader is forced to invent interpretation; full
contradiction, marking a division in the author's mind.

[51] Empson, p. 1.

this *hapax* form, P was prompted to translate contextually with ܐܒܕܢܐ "destruction".[52]

f. Redundancy. An alteration that is prompted by redundancy means that the target text, P, has omitted some element of the source text, MT, that is superfluous or unnecessary. Consider, for example, 38:29b:

MT   וכפר שמים מי ילדׁו:
       "And who bore (it) the hoarfrost of heaven?"

P   ܘܓܠܝܕܐ ܕܫܡܝܐ ܡܢܘ ܐܘܠܕܗ.
       "And who begat the hoarfrost of heaven?"

The 3pms suffix on ילד is resumptive, referring back to "the hoarfrost". Unless the Heb. text is translated in a poetically more literal fashion - "and the hoarfrost of heaven, Who bore it?" - this suffix is redundant. P appears to have considered this suffix redundant and, hence, omitted it in its translation.

g. Textual Difficulty. An alteration is said to be motivated by a textual difficulty when the Heb. text presents a form that consonantally or vocalically may be questionable. So, for example, in 24:6a it is a Qere/Ketib situation that requires P to make a choice:

MT   בשדה בלילו יקׁצׁירו
       "They will harvest/make harvest his fodder in the field."

---

[52] The possibility exists that the Hebrew text the translator of P used might have had פיד "destruction" rather than כיד, a suggestion forwarded by many commentators (see Dhorme, p. 317; ICC, p. 148; and BDB, p. 810a, s.v. פיד). The Versions also suggest a term for "destruction, ruin" not necessarily just פיד (cf. LXX την εαυτου σφαγην; Vg. *interfectionem suam*; Tg. תבירריה). פיד occurs four times in the OT. Thrice in Job (12:5;30:24;31:29) and once in Prov. (24:22). The first two Job passages are textually difficult and the exact correspondences used by P are not easily distinguished. In Job 31:29 ܬܒܪܐ is used by P, which, however, is the usual equivalent of Heb. איד throughout Job (18:12;21:17,30;31:3,23). In Prov. 24:22 both איד and פיד occur. איד is rendered ܬܒܪܐ (as in Job) and פיד = ܣܘܦܐ. Hence, uncertainty does exist as to whether P translated פיד not כיד or even איד in the present passage (21:20). Nonetheless, ambiguity does exist in whatever term existed for the translator of P.

P   ܘܒܚܩܠܐ ܢܚܨܕܘܢ ܕܠܐ ܕܝܠܗܘܢ ܣܥܪܗܘܢ.

"And in a field they will reap fodder which is not theirs."

Heb. יַקְצִירוּ: Qere יִקְצוֹרוּ (Qal imperfect in pause), Ketib יַקְצִירוּ (Hiphil imperfect) is rendered ܢܚܨܕܘܢ "they will harvest (Peal imperfect) following the Qere.

h. Intra-Verse Influence. A motivation that is classified as intra-verse influence indicates that within a verse itself some grammatical element has caused an alteration in another element. In 3:9 it is the plural number in the first stich which causes an alteration in the second:

MT   יחשכו כוכבי נשפו יקו־לאור ואין
              ואל־יראה בעפעפי־שחר:

"May the stars of its twilight grow dark,
may it hope for light but there be none,
may it not look into the eyelids of dawn."

P. ܢܚܫܟܘܢ ܟܘܟܒܐ ܕܨܦܪܐ. ܢܣܟܘܢ ܠܢܘܗܪܐ ܘܠܐ ܢܗܘܐ ܠܗ
              ܘܠܐ ܢܚܙܐ ܒܙܠܝܩܝ ܨܦܪܐ.

"May the stars of dawn grow dark,
may they hope for light but there will be none to it;
and it will not see into the rays of dawn."

P renders the singular Heb. יקו by the plural ܢܣܟܘܢ, thus preserving the plural subject "stars" of the first stich in place of the singular implicit subject "the day" of the Heb. text.

i. Inter-verse Influence. Inter-verse influence refers to an alteration in a verse prompted by a grammatical element found not in the same verse but in an adjacent one. Consider the topic of number in 27:16:

MT   אם־יצבר כעפר כסף   וכחמר יכין מלבוש:

"Though he heaps up silver like dust,
and he piles up clothing like clay;"

P ܐܢ ܢܟܢܫܘܢ ܣܐܡܐ ܐܝܟ ܥܦܪܐ.
ܘܐܝܟ ܛܝܢܐ ܢܬܩܢܘܢ ܠܒܘܫܐ.

"If they will gather silver like dust,
and they will be furnished (with) clothing like clay;"

P preserves 3pmpl verbal forms where the Heb. reads 3pms, thus continuing the 3ppl verbal forms begun in v. 13b (יקחו) and continued in vv. 14-15 (תבכינה, יקברו, ישבעו, ירבו). This same v e r b a l harmonization occurs in the following verse (27:17) for the first verbal form (Heb. יכין > Syr. ܢܬܩܢܘܢ).[53]

j. Parallel Verse Influence[54]   Similar to the previously described motivations (#h,i) is parallel verse influence. Whereas intra-/inter-verse influence describe alterations based on grammatical similarity, parallel verse influence involves semantic similarity. Thus, a semantic parallel within or between verses results in an alteration in a given verse. Consider for example the closing of Job 2:10:

MT   . . . בכל־זאת לא־חטא איוב בשפתיו:
"In all this, Job did not sin with his lips."

P   ܘܒܗܠܝܢ ܟܠܗܝܢ ܠܐ ܚܛܐ ܐܝܘܒ.
ܐܦ ܠܐ ܓܕܦ ܥܠ ܐܠܗܐ ܒܣܦܘܬܗ.
"And in all these things, Job did not sin,
indeed he did not blaspheme God with his lips."

P adds the underscored phrase from 1:22 where it served as an interpretive explanation of Heb. ולא נתן תפלה לאלהים "and he did not ascribe unseemliness to God". The catalyst for this addition was no doubt the phrase בכל זאת לא חטא איוב "in all this Job did not sin" which occurs in both verses.

k. Versional Influence/Parallel. Versional influence indicates that a departure in the target text directly owes its provenance to a reading in

---

[53] P also translates the 3pms verbal suffixes in vv. 14-15 by the 3pmpl suffix, taking עריצים in v. 13b as the referent rather than אדם רשע in v. 13a as in the MT.
[54] See M. Goshen-Gottstein, "Theory and Practice", p. 138, n. 20; P. Kyle McCarter, *Textual Criticism*, p. 28.

one of the versions. Versional parallel refers to a reading in the target text that is similar to one in a version; however, direct borrowing or dependence is not indicated, because of the nature of the translational element. Versional parallels are most obvious when implicit to explicit exegesis is indicated or when a very obvious error or ambiguity in the source text could easily lead any target language to yield the same results. The designation versional influence, thus, will be reserved for those cases in which the P and another Version contain a similar reading that departs from the MT, but in no way is implicit or could have been achieved through a very obvious error in reading the MT or an ambiguity in the MT. An example of versional parallel in P with LXX is found in 7:15a:

MT   ותבחר מחנק נפשׁי   "And my soul chose strangulation"

P   ܚܘܬܢܝ ܢܦܫܝ ܡܢ ܐܒܕܢܐ
      "And you have tried my soul from destruction"

LXX Απαλλαξεις απο πνευματος μου
     την ψυχην μου
     "You will remove my life from my spirit"

P, like the LXX, records a 2pms verb (ܒܚܢܬ) where the Heb. has a 3pfs form (תבחר), thus construing Heb. נפשׁי as the direct object rather than the subject. This error could easily be independently arrived at by both P and LXX, for Heb. תבחר is a homograph for the 2pms and 3pfs forms.

l. Error. A motivation is termed an error when a difference between the source text and translated text results from a mistaken assumption on the part of the translator as to what he believes he is hearing or seeing, at least from the perspective of an evaluator.

a. Aural. An aural error is an error in hearing. An example of this error occurs in Job 11:6. There Heb. כפלים "double" is rendered ܩܦܠܐ "inner chambers/ treasures". Note the interchange in the velars Kaph and Qoph. An aural error is clearly indicated. In Job 41:5 P likewise erroneously translated this term, reading ܢܦܠܐ "falls" in contrast to Is. 40:2 where P translates with ܐܥܦܐ "double; twice as much".

b. Visual. A visual error is one which resulted from an orthographic difficulty similar to what was defined as a textual difficulty above; however in this case the error is unintentional. This can be illustrated by the P's translation of the Heb. in 6:7b:

MT :המה כדוי לחמי "They are like illness (in) my bread,"

P .ܬܘܒ ܐܝܟ ܗܘܝ ܐܬܟܬܫܬ ܐܦ
"Indeed my battle laments like a drunkard,"

P confused דוי (√דוה) with the √רוה - ד/ר confusion - hence, it translated ܗܘܝ.

The terms intentional and unintentional are also relevant to the issue of motivation. Intentional is used to describe an adjustment that is consciously and deliberately made by the translator, unintentional implies that the translator was unaware of the change made in the text. However, classifying the above motivations as intentional or unintentional is not always clearcut. There are those that can easily be assigned to either category. So, for example, a visual error (ד/ר confusion as in 6:7 above) is most likely unintentional, whereas language difference adjustments (e.g. Heb. interrogative Heh > Syr. Ø) are clearly intentional. Most motivations have the potential of being intentional or unintentional depending on a given situation. Thus, in terms of the translator's intent, each motivation must be evaluated in each circumstance. The final decision will no doubt also contain an element of subjectivity on the part of the evaluator of the translation.

IV. Effect on Meaning

The final portion of the translation model is effect on meaning. The adjustments (section II) to a given element of the text (section I) prompted by one or more motivations (section III) are then evaluated in terms of their effect on the meaning of the text. Two important factors must be considered: meaning relation and perspective. Meaning relation refers to the semantic relationship that occurs between the source text and the translated text for each item translated. Relations are classified under

five headings: clarity, confusion, synonymy, antithesis, innovation.[55]
Perspective refers to the point of view from which an effect on meaning
is classified. Three perspectives are considered: reader/aural recipient of
the translated text, translator of the text and evaluator of the translated
text.

I. Meaning Relations

1. Clarity.

Clarity in the text can result from any adjustment, can affect any
linguistic area and be initiated by any one or more of the motivations
discussed above. An example to illustrate this point is found in 3:1:

> MT   :אחרי־כן פתח איוב את־פיהו ויקלל את־יומו
> "After this Job opened his mouth and cursed <u>his day</u>."

> P. ܗܢܐ ܟܕ ܗܟܢܐ ܦܬܚ ܐܝܘܒ ܦܘܡܗ ܘܠܛ. ܠܝܘܡܐ ܕܐܬܝܠܕ ܒܗ
> "And afterwards Job opened his mouth
> and cursed <u>the day in which he was born</u>."

In the Heb. text the reference to יומו "his day" is somewhat
ambiguous. Precisely which of Job's days is being cursed? P clarifies
this obscurity by replacing the 3pms pronominal suffix with the
dependent clause ܕܐܬܝܠܕ ܒܗ "in which he was born". Thus, reference
is clearly to Job's day of birth.

2. Confusion.

The same adjustments and motivations that bring a clarity to the
text in other instances produce the opposite purpose, that is confusion.
Consider the following example from 7:15:

---

[55] The terms synonymy and antithesis are borrowed from Lowth's classic classification
of Hebrew parallelism. See David Noel Freedman, Prolegomenon to George B. Gray's,
The Forms of Hebrew Poetry (KTAV Publishing House, 1972), p. ix. See also S.
Ullmann's, *Language and Style,* p. 50, who uses the terms thesis, antithesis, and
synthesis from Hegelian dialectics to describe these meaning relations.

MT   ותבחר מחנק נפשי   "My soul chose strangulation,
         מות מעצמותי: death rather than my bones."

P   .ܪܬܘܡ ܢܡ ܝܬܡܪ̈ܓ ܗ̇ܝܐ ܐܕܒܘܐ ܢܡ ܝܫܦܢ ܬܘܚܒ

"And you have examined/observed (sic.) my soul
from destruction and my bones from death."

The Hebrew text here is a bit problematic. If we accept the
following syntactical analysis the above translation results: V DO S //
DO PPh. P, however, appears to have:
(1) analyzed the Heb. word order as V PPh DO // DO PPh;
(2) directly adopted the Heb. √בחר "to choose" which, however, means
"to examine, observe; test, try (silver)" in Syriac;[56]
(3) and understood the Heb. *hapax legomenon* מחנק as a noun with
prefixed preposition מן, hence, its translation ܐܕܒܘܐ ܢܡ.

Even were we to translate the preposition מן in the Syriac by the
comparative ("And you have examined my soul more than destruction
and my bones more than death") or make נפשי "my soul" the subject,
which is orthographically possible, ("And my soul has examined more
than destruction and my bones more than death"), the resulting
translations would still be illogical from any perspective. P's translation
in this case clearly results in a confusion of meaning unless we accept
√ܒܚܪ as a West Aramaic element which, like Hebrew, would mean "to
choose".[57] Our resulting proposition would be "and you chose my soul
more than destruction and my bones more than death", a still somewhat
perplexing statement.[58]

3. Synonymy.

Just as Lowth distinguished varieties of synonymous parallelism, so
too can levels of synonymy be found with regard to meaning relations.
As R. van den Broeck states "complete equivalence does not exist".[59]

---

[56] The motivation is clearly linguistic interference or West Aramaic influence, see p.41f.
[57] See above p. 41f.
[58] See below, Chapter III Grammar, p.64 where this example is further discussed.
[59] "The Concept of Equivalence in Translation Theory: Some Critical Reflections." In
Literature and Translation: New Perspectives in Literary Studies with a Basic

However, levels of synonymous variation can and have been distinguished. John Lyons defined synonymy on the basis of two conditions: (i) interchangeability in all contexts, and (ii) identity in both cognitive and emotive import.[60] Complete synonymy occurs when the second condition is met, total or absolute synonymy when the first is met. Following these requirements, he suggests four kinds of synonymy:

1. complete and total synonymy
2. complete, but not total
3. incomplete, but total
4. incomplete, and not total.[61]

This scheme may work fine within one language, as, for example, when describing such synonyms as vixen: female fox as cognitive synonyms or father: daddy as emotive synonyms, but it is not as effective when describing meaning relations between languages.[62]

Furthermore, at times we will be considering the meaning relation between entire propositions rather than only the semantic relationship between individual items. So, for example, we will see the introductory formula "And N1 answered N2 and said" translated into Syriac as "And N1 answered and said to N2". Describing the relationship between the Hebrew proposition and the Syriac one as totally or completely synonymous seems inadequate. They do contain the same information. The lexemes are identical in both languages at variance only is so far as they structurally have to conform to the grammatical rules of their respective languages. They do, however, differ syntactically, requiring the addition of the preposition "to" in Syriac.[63] Slight variations in synonymy such as this need to be accounted for when classifying the

---

Bibliography of Books on Translation Studies, James S. Holmes, Josè Lambert & Raymond van den Broeck, eds. (Leuven/Belgium: Acco, 1978), p. 36.

[60] *Introduction to Theoretical Linguistics* (Cambridge: University Press, 1969), p. 448.

[61] *Introduction to Theoretical Linguistics*, p. 448ff. See also John Lyons, *Language and Linguistics: An Introduction* (Cambridge: University Press, 1981), p. 148ff, 290ff; *Language, Meaning and Context* (Chaucer Press, 1981), p. 50f.

[62] Lyons, too, acknowledges this point when he states "even descriptive synonymy across languages is far less common, except in the more or less specialized subparts of their vocabularies . . . It would be absurd to maintain that there is no such thing as inter-language (or indeed inter-dialect) synonymy. . . . we must recognize that word-for-word translation is generally impossible between any two natural languages. *Language and Linguistics: An Introduction*, p. 151.

[63] See Chapter IV: Syntax, p. 111f., where this example is discussed more fully.

meaning relation between source and target text. With this necessity in mind, S. Ullmann's study of synonyms is helpful in describing the levels of synonymy between languages. He delineated nine levels by which synonyms can be distinguished:[64]

1. one term is more general than another
2. one term is more intense than another
3. one term is more emotive than another
4. one term may imply moral approbation or censure where another is neutral
5. one term is more professional than another
6. one term is more literary than another
7. one term is more colloquial than another
8. one term is more local or dialectal than another
9. one of the synonyms belongs to child-talk.

Three of these levels have been most applicable and prevalent in the comparative analysis of P-Job: intensity (#2), literary style (#6), and moral approbation/ censure (#4). To these three I am adding an additional level: structure, that is one term or item differs only in its formal structure from the other without altering the meaning of the text, e.g. the Heb. interrogative Heh > Syr. Ø morpheme.[65]

a. Intensity. Synonymy with variation at the level of intensity is concerned with a change of emphasis from the MT, in particular a variation in the use of exclamatory or interjectory particles, the verbal nuances of command - the imperative, jussive, cohortative - and the infinitive absolute when used in its emphatic capacity. Consider one such example in 3:7:

MT   ‏הנה הלילה ההוא יהי גלמוד   אל־תבא רננה בו:‏
"Behold, may that night be barren,
Let not a ringing cry enter into it."

---

[64] *Semantics: An Introduction to the Science of Meaning,* Oxford: Basil Blackwell, 1970, pp. 142-143. Ullmann's classification is developed from an earlier study by W.E. Collinson, "Comparative Synonymics: Some Principles and Illustrations", *Transactions of the Philological Society,* 2nd ed., 1939, pp.54-77.

[65] See Chapter VI Style: Sentence Type-Interrogatives where P's treatment of Interrogatives is discussed in detail.

P   ܟܠܠܗ ܗܘ ܗܘܢܐ ܢܗܘܐ ܥܩܪܐ. ܘܠܐ ܬܐܬܐ ܒܗ ܬܫܒܘܚܬܐ.

> "Let that night be barren,
> and may praise not enter into it."

P omits translating the initial exclamatory Heb. הנה "behold". The
motivation may be inter-verse influence with v. 6 which similarly begins
with הלילה ההוא, that is without הנה. No meaning change is effected
due to this omission, hence the meaning relation is synonymous, but the
level of intensity has changed. The Heb. contained one exclamatory
particle and two jussives, whereas P contains only the jussives.
b. Structure. When an effect on meaning is labelled synonymous with
variation at the level of structure this indicates that only a structural
change has occurred. A structural change can occur in any area of
linguistics, for example, in Grammar: Tense P's use of the passive voice
for the Heb. impersonal active, the equivalent of a passive, yields the
same meaning albeit in a structurally different form; in the area of
syntax, P's tendency to standardize word order, i.e. V S IO DO PPh, is
just a structural change that need not even be considered a change in
intensity or emphasis - the usual explanation for variation in Heb. word
order. Under style one specific case in 4:17 can be cited concerning
Sentence type: Interrogative:

MT   האנוש מאלוה יצדק   אם   מעשׂהו יטהר־גבר:

> "Can man be more righteous than Eloah?
> or can man be more pure than his Maker?"

P. ܐܢܫܐ ܕܝܢ ܐܠܗܐ ܥܘܪܡ. ܐܘ ܡܢ ܕܝ ܕܒܗܘܢ ܕܬܘܪܬܐ ܗܘ ܢܬܕܟܐ.

> "Can man be declared more righteous than God?
> or man bc more pure than his maker?"

Syriac has no precise equivalent for the Heb. interrogative Heh.
Questions must often be inferred from emphasis, context, or as Nöldeke
states "the enfolding of clauses".[66] More specifically, the disjunctive

---

[66] *Compendious Syriac Grammar*, James A. Crichton, tr. (London: Williams &
Norgate, 1904), #372.

question, as we have in 4:17, is indicated by the interrogative Heh in stich one followed most frequently by the particle אם introducing the alternative. In Syr. the correspondence of Heb. ה . . . אם is simply א< . . . Ø, a change in formal structure necessitated by language difference. The meaning then is still synonymous with variation only at the level of structure.

c. Literary Style. Synonymy with variation at the level of literary style refers to an alternate way of turning a phrase while yet preserving the same basic meaning. Consider P's creation of an idiom in 9:32:

MT :כי־לא־איש כמוני אעננו נבוא יחדו במשפט
"For there is not a man like me (that) I might answer him,
(that) we might come together in judgment."

P. ܕܓܒܪܐ ܗܘ ܠܐ ܕܐܝܬ ܐܟܘܬܝ ܕܐܬܠ ܠܗ ܦܬܓܡܐ
ܘܢܐܬܐ ܐܟܚܕܐ ܠܕܝܢܐ.
"For there was not a man who is like me
that I might (lit.) give to him a word,
and we might come together for judgment."

Heb. אעננו "I might answer him" is rendered ܐܬܠ ܠܗ ܦܬܓܡܐ "I might give to him a word", hence the creation of an idiom as a correspondence to the Heb. verb ענה√ "to answer". The √ܬܠ is used in Syriac - as is amply illustrated by its appearance in the book of Job. Hence, P's usage is not based on language difference, but more likely stylistic preferences. This idiom is found a number of times in Job, all of which still preserve the basic connotation of "to answer, give a reply".[67] Thus, the effect on meaning is synonymous with variation only in stylistic presentation; with P we might state the style is now heightened or elevated in its use of a figure of speech, in contrast to the Heb. ordinary language.

d. Moral Approbation/Censure. Job 10:3 opens with the phrase הטוב לך "Is it good/ advantageous for you (that you oppress, that you despise the labour of your hands and you shine upon the counsel of the wicked?"), a

---

[67] See Chapter VI Style: Idiom for a complete discussion of this Syriac idiom.

statement ostensibly offensive in that it might be construed to bear the implications that God takes pleasure or receives gain by oppressing His (supposedly good) creations, while favouring the wicked. The Peshitta subtly alters this statement, not to the extent that it is totally removed or rewritten, but rather the implications still remain, but are now clothed in gentler garb. Consider P's translation:

.ܝܢܐܝܢ ܐܬܗܢܐܠ ܐܢܬ ܐܬܕܡܣܢ ܐܢܬ ܚܠܛܝܢ ܝܠ ܢܒ ܐܠ
.ܬܪܐܝܢ ܐܥܝܪܢ ܐܬܝܢܬ ܠܠܢ

> "Is it not enough for you that you oppress
> and you despise the labour of your hands,
> and you look upon the opinion of the wicked?"

P's translation "not enough" still carries the connotation that God is oppressing, but it lacks the blatant harshness of the Hebrew connotation of 'taking pleasure in this act'. Thus, the basic idea of oppressing still exists in P and is synonymous with the MT, but P's synonym differs in that it is morally less offensive than the Heb.

4. Antithesis.

The meaning relation termed antithesis is concerned with opposites in meaning. Within this category levels have been attempted,[68] but in studying P-Job the relation of antithesis is rare and any attempt to finely subdivide has proved fruitless. Of those passages where antithesis does occur, however, two sublevels are apparent: antonymy and contradiction. When an item is the direct opposite, i.e. "Job said" versus "Job did not say", this is antonymy. Contradiction, by contrast, is the near opposite, e.g. "Job said" versus "Job might have said". Consider the following two examples of antithesis from Job:

18:5 MT   אם אור רשעים ידעך ולא־יגה שביב אשו:
> "Indeed the light of the wicked will be extinguished,
> and the flame of his light will not shine."

---

[68] See John Lyons, *Semantics*, Vol. 1 (Cambridge: Cambridge University Press, 1977), p. 270ff, where he discusses Opposition and Contrast. Contrast is used as the most general term, opposition is restricted to binary contrasts (male: female), and antonymy to gradable opposites (big: small).

P .ܡܐܢܘ ܟܐܘܘܡܐܝ ܡܐܗ 9ܟܐ .ܝܟܝܘ ܟܘܝܝܪ ܟܝܝ 9ܟܐ

"And indeed the lamp of the wicked will be extinguished,
and indeed the flame of his light will shine."

37:15   MT   :עננו   אור   והופיע   עליהם   בשׂום־אלוה   התדע

"Do you know when Eloah placed [a command] upon them,
and caused the light of his clouds to shine?"

P   .ܝܢܡܠܝ ܟܡܠܟ ܡܡܪ ܘܡܡܪ ܢܒܝܢ ܐܘܟ ܝܘ ܟܡ
                         .ܝܡܢܝܠܝܝ ܟܝܡܢ ܟܠܢ

"Behold you know what God placed upon them,
and He revealed the light of his clouds."

In the first example (18:5) P's omission of the negative particle לא
in stich two - or its replacement with the emphatic אף - has led to the
direct antithesis of the Heb.: MT "the flame of his light will not shine" >
P "the flame of his light will shine". If sub-levels of antithetic meaning
were cited this would be antonymy, the direct polar opposite.

In the second example (37:15), the Heb. interrogative Heh has been
replaced by the exclamatory particle הא - an interesting phonological
correspondence well attested to in the P-Job. This substitution alters a
Heb. rhetorical question "do you know", begging the negative response
"you do not know", into an exclamatory "Behold you know", hardly the
equivalent of the Heb. implied negation. The level of antithesis
demonstrated here is what is termed converse or contradiction, that is a
statement that is the opposite of another, but not the exact polar opposite,
much like north and south are antonyms, i.e. polar opposites, but north
and south-west are also opposites, not polar, but contradictory.

5. Innovation.

The term innovation is used to describe a meaning relation which
results in a completely new meaning in the target text, as compared to
that preserved in the source text. In some cases this new meaning has a
linguistic basis, while in others it is a total neologism. In 16:15b one such
innovative relation occurs:

MT שׂק תפרתי עלי גלדי ועללתי בעפר קרני:
"I have sewn sackcloth upon my skin,
and I have thrust my horn into the dust."

P ܡܣ ܟܡܘܗܐ ܕܚܒܝܢ ܥܠ ܡܫܟܝ. ܘܦܠܦܠܬ ܒܥܦܪܐ ܪܫܝ.
"I have put sackcloth upon my skin,
and I have sprinkled my head with dust."

In the second stich Heb. ועללתי בעפר קרני "I have thrust my horn into the dust" is a phrase used to express humiliation. It is the antithesis of raising one's horn as a sign of pride and exaltation. The √עלל III "to insert, thrust" is a *hapax legomenon* with this meaning. This may have led to the alteration of this idiom in the P, where it is replaced with a more commonly used idiom, an idiom more parallel to and appropriate with "putting on sackcloth" in stich one: "to sprinkle dust on one's head" (ܘܦܠܦܠܬ ܒܥܦܪܐ ܪܫܝ). Sackcloth and ashes are commonly used to signify mourning in the OT. Hence, the P has rendered √עלל in light of this usage, with קרני being equated with the "the head" and בעפר representing a dative of instrument, rather than of place. Hence, P preserves a stich that is innovative in relation to its Heb. counterpart by reason of ambiguity (√עלל), intra-verse influence (stich one) and parallel influence (the biblical concept of sackcloth and ashes = mourning) and a new perspective on קרני and בעפר.

II. Perspective

In the preceding paragraphs as each meaning relation was explained and illustrated by examples, such verbal modalities as "might, may, could, it seems possible, etc." were used when assigning a meaning relation. This uncertainty in wording stems from the inherent ambiguity that exists in the second factor involved in effect on meaning, namely perspective. As stated perspective refers to the point of view from which an effect on meaning is classified. Three perspectives are at once apparent: reader/aural recipient of the translated text, translator of the text and evaluator of the translated text:

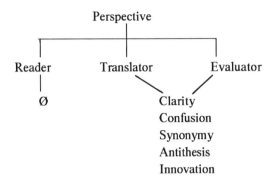

The common reader or more likely the aural recipient of the translated text would most likely be exposed to the text in a non-academic setting, i.e. religious service or private reading (?). We cannot assume that he (or she) had access to, familiarity with or even the language skills necessary to read and understand the Hebrew text, much less make a comparison of the two by which to judge the translation's faithfulness. If the individual possessed these skills the need for a translation would be superfluous. Thus it is not too presumptuous to state that classifications under effect on meaning do not reflect the common man's perspective. To him the meaning of the text is just that which is presented to him. The meaning relations - clarity, confusion, synonymy, antithesis, innovation - have no place in his world. The text is as its stands. Thus, if I read, write or in any way present a line of translated text to another (non-academic) person - be it from the P, the LXX, or a line from any translated text - the reader has no way of determining the faithfulness of the translated word. Thus, the effects on meaning described here are not from the perspective of the lay reader.

The translator and evaluator, by contrast, are naturally more actively involved. Both have the source text at their disposal - although not necessarily the same source text - and both are aware of an effect on meaning. However, the degrees of awareness may not be identical, for a given line of translated text may be seen differently, in terms of semantic relations, by the translator and the evaluator. Consider, for example, the presence of the polysemous idiom נשׂא פנים in the text of Job. As will later be shown, this idiom has four meanings, thus presenting an obvious

ambiguity.[69] When the translator provides his translation he may believe
he is clarifying the text.   If he erroneously selects the wrong choice for
this polysemous idiom, to the evaluator, he is in fact creating a new
meaning. The translator, however, may be unaware of this discrepancy.
Thus, while both share the same possibilities for semantic relations their
choice for an individual case need not be the same.

---

[69] See Chapter VI Style: Idiom.

III

Grammar

By virtue of their placement in the Northwest Semitic language family - Hebrew under the Canaanite branch, Syriac under the Aramaic branch - it is hardly surprising to find shared, as well as distinct grammatical characteristics. Therefore, language difference is a primary motivation for certain grammatical adjustments in P. However, in some cases, what appeared to be just a language difference adjustment at first glance, on closer examination proved otherwise. This occurs most prominently in the sub-topic of tense.

Language difference, however, is not the only motivation prevalent in the area of grammar. Intra-/inter-verse influence, explicit exegesis and error are likewise evident. Synonymy with variation in structure and style is the most common effect on meaning, but clarity, innovation and an occasional antithetic proposition also occur.

Gender

Gender adjustments in P-Job are represented by a very meagre data supply. This is due to chance; the necessary grammatical environments that might necessitate such changes do not exist. Those passages that do contain a gender adjustment were motivated by intra-verse influence, ambiguity and language difference. Consider the following verses:

1:4b M T: שלחו וקראו <u>לשלשת</u> אחיתיהם לאכל ולשתות עמהם
"And they sent and summoned their three sisters to eat
and drink with them."

61

P   ܢܫܬܓܘܪ̈ ܗܘܘ ܗܘܘ ܘܩܪܘ ܠܬܠܬ ܐܚܘܬܗܘܢ. ܠܡܐܟܠ
ܘܠܡܫܬܐ ܠܘܬܗܘܢ

"And they sent and summoned their three sisters to eat
and drink with them."

Intra-verse influence, in particular number-noun agreement, has
motivated the translator of P to record the feminine numeral ܬܠܬ
"three" where the Heb. reads with the masculine שלשת. The effect on
meaning is synonymy with variation only in structure. In the following
example, ambiguity in syntax has resulted in the translator interpreting
the 3pfs verb תבחר , with נפשי as its subject, as a 2pms verb with
נפשי as the object.

7:15 MT   ותבחר מחנק נפשי   מות מעצמותי:
        (1) "And my soul chose strangulation (and) death rather than
            my bones."
        (2) "So my throat prefers strangling, my bones desire death."

P   ܘܓܒܝܬ ܢܦܫܝ ܡܢ ܐܒܕܢܐ ܘܓܪ̈ܡܝ ܡܢ ܡܘܬܐ.
        "And you have tried/observed (sic.)/chosen my soul
        from destruction, and my bones from death."

The Hebrew of this verse is a bit problematic. Early commentators
presented the first translation above, understanding נפש "soul" in its
most common and literal capacity and retaining the preposition מן in
stich two.[1]   More recent commentators (Habel, Pope) treat the
preposition מן in stich two as an enclitic mem, thereby paralleling the
syntactic structure of the first stich and resulting in the second
translation.[2] Note also נפש is rendered by the less common, but attested,
translation "throat".

P's translation clearly confused the syntax of stich one, placing the
preposition מן of stich two before מות. The effect on meaning of these

---

[1] See Dhorme, pp. 106-107 who also reads עצמותי "my bones" as עצבותי "my
suffering"; and ICC, p. 72.
[2] See Habel, pp. 152-153 and Pope, p. 58, 62.

adjustments is innovative and also somewhat confusing. The new meaning is not solely due to the alteration in gender and number, but more so to linguistic interference with the verbal root בחר . This root was either directly transferred into Syriac, where, however, it carries the meaning "to try, observe" and not "to choose", or is a West Aramaic element in P-Job bearing the meaning "to choose".[3] This linguistic interference has resulted in a somewhat meaningless proposition. However, if we construe the preposition ܒ as a preposition of means (ܒ = "by"), then some sense can be made of this proposition: "and you have tried/chosen my soul by destruction and my bones by death".

In the next example, Heb. טוֹב - n.m.s "prosperity, happiness, welfare"[4] - is translated by Syr. ܛܒܬܐ - adj.f.pl "good" = n. "that which is good, prosperity",[5] thus not only a change in gender, but also a change in number. The motivation is purely one of language difference. Stylistically, the Syriac language prefers this grammatical form when the substantive "prosperity, goodness" is denoted. This adjustment occurs similarly throughout Job and in the Old Testament.[6]

21:13 MT   יכלו בַטוֹב ימיהם וברגע שאול יחתו׃
   "They spend their days in prosperity
   and in a moment they go down to Sheol."

  ܕܡܒܠܝܢ ܒܛܒܬܐ ܝܘܡܬܗܘܢ. ܘܒܥܓܠ ܠܫܝܘܠ ܢܚܬܝܢ
   "spending their days in goodness (f.pl.)
   and quickly descending to Sheol."

The effect on meaning is synonymy with variation only in literary style. In the next example, gender change is not the only adjustment made by the translator of P, thereby resulting in an innovative meaning:

---

[3] See above Chapter II, pp. 38 and 47f.

[4] See BDB, pp. 373-374, s.v. טוב.

[5] See Payne Smith, pp. 165-166, s.v. ܛܒ.

[6] For examples in Job, see טוב in 2:10;7:7;30:26;36:11 and רע in 1:1,8;2:3,10; 28:28;30:26; 31:29. In only three places in the OT does P not translate with the adjectival form (Hos 10:1; Pss 23:6;25:13;103:5).

24:25   MT   :אם־לא אפו מי יכזיבני וישׂם לאל מלתי
          "If it is not so, who will prove me a liar
          and show that there is nothing (in) my word?"

P   .   ܗܐܠ ܗܘܐ ܗܝܟܢܐ ܗܕܐ ܒܘܪܒ
          ܗܘܬܘܨܒ ܡܕܡ ܐܠܗܐ ܒܠܬܗܕ‡
          "And if it was not so, his anger will prove me a liar,
          and my word will be reckoned before God."

An erroneous understanding of the Hebrew syntax of the second
stich has prompted P to translate the Heb. object מלתי as the subject -
hence the change in gender for subject-verb agreement - and to
incorrectly recognize the vocalization of Hebrew לְאַל "for nought" as
לְאֵל "to God".

Number

The topic number refers to the following substitutions:

Heb. singular	>	Syr. plural
Heb. plural	>	Syr. singular
Heb. dual	>	Syr. plural

In P-Job there are 150 cases of a Heb. singular rendered by a Syr.
plural; 51 cases of a Heb. plural translated by a Syr. singular; and one
case of a Heb. dual by a Syr. plural.

Substitution of number occurs in any part of speech where the
possibility of number exists. Thus it is a demonstrative in 1:22 (Heb.
זאת > Syr. ܗܠܝܢ); adjectives in 2:10 (Heb. הטוב > Syr. ܛܒ̈ܬܐ; Heb.
הרע > Syr. ܒܝ̈ܫܬܐ); a verb in 3:9 (Heb. יקו > Syr. ܢܣܟܘܢ) and a
noun in 4:11 (Heb. לביא > ܐܪ̈ܝܘܬܐ).

The motivations for these adjustments are primarily language
difference, error and intra-/inter- verse influence. Implicit to explicit
exegesis, ambiguity and ideology are secondarily responsible. Effect on
meaning, as will shortly be seen, is primarily synonymy with variation in
structure or literary style and quite infrequently a innovative meaning.

1. Language Difference. Language difference is by far the most
common motivation for the substitution of numbers. Over one hundred
examples of Heb. singular > Syr. plural are attested to in the P-Job[7] and
forty cases of Heb. plural > Syr. singular.[8] Likewise the one occurrence
of a Heb. dual replaced by a Syr. plural (38:8) is motivated by language
difference. Consider the following representative examples:

1:22a MT   איוב   לא־חטא   בכל־זאת   "In all this Job did not sin"

P   ܐܝܘܒ ܚܛܐ ܠܐ ܗܠܝܢ ܒܟܠܗܘܢ
         "And in all these (things) Job did not sin"

17:1c MT   קברים לי׃   "the grave(s) [is ready] for me."
P   ܡܛܝܒ ܠܝ ܩܒܪܐ   "the grave is ready for me."

In 1:22 P renders the f.s. Heb. demonstrative, used collectively to
refer to Job's recent misfortunes, by the c.pl. demonstrative. By contrast,
in 17:1, the Heb. plural קברים, used stylistically, is rendered simply by
the singular in the P.[9] Both are motivated by language difference: P
prefers explicitness over against the Heb. collective usage of a singular or
stylistic usage of a plural. The effect on meaning, however, is still
synonymy with variation only in structure or literary style.

21:9a MT   בתיהם שלום מפחד   "their houses are safe from fear"

P   ܕܚܠܬܐ ܡܢ ܫܠܝܢ ܒܬܝܗܘܢ
         "their houses are safe from terror"

---

[7] For Heb. sg. > Syr. pl. see 1:22;2:6,10(3);3:5;4:4,11;6:23;7:21;8:4,8,19;9:22,
27;10:1,6,7,14,20,21;11:6;12:9,10,22;13:17;14;3,7;15:3,30,32,33,35;16:4,9,18;18:10;
19:8,12,17,19,26;20:27,29;21:2,5,6,9,12,16;22:16,21;23:2,11,12;24:6,8,9,14,15(2),
17,20;28:3,4,6,9,16(2),23;29:19(2),22,25;30:21,23,30;31:7,10,33,35;33:9,17,19;
34:11,16,22,37;36:9,11,23,24,25,29,30,32:37:4,11,13,16;38:6,17,30,34(2);39:7,13;
41:13(2),15; 42:10,11.

[8] For Heb. pl. > Syr. sg. see 6:4,25;8:13,19;9:5,28;14:19;15:5,20,24,28,34;16:11,19;
17:1,5;18:19;19:11;21:17,27,32;22:9(2),12,24,29;23:4;24:2,3,16;26:14;28:24;31:16,
39;33:15;38:20,33;39:6,30;41:6.

[9] See also Job 21:32 where קברות is similarly a plural of intensity and is rendered by the
singular in P.

P's adjustment in the number of Heb. שלום is once again dictated by language difference, as well as by intra-verse influence. Whereas the Heb. is more flexible in its agreement between the plural noun בתיהם and the singular noun שלום, functioning predicatively, the P is more strict in its adherence to agreement, hence its use of the plural adjective ܫܠܝܢ. Once again the meaning relation is synonymy with variation only in structure.

2:6a MT   ויאמר יהוה אל־השׂטן הנו בידך
"And the Lord said to the adversary, 'Behold he is in your hand.'"

P   ܗܐܡܪ ܡܪܝܐ ܗܘܐ ܠܣܛܢܐ ܗܐ ܡܫܠܡ ܒܐܝܕܝܟ.
"And the Lord said to Satan, 'Behold he is delivered into your hands.'"

In this final example, P records a plural ܐܝܕܝܟ as against the Heb. singular ידך, here with the extended meaning of "in your power". Elsewhere in Job, when יד connotes "power", P also records a plural number.[10] The meaning "in your power" can still be construed in the P, thus synonymy is once again present. One other possible cause can be mentioned, however, and that is error, specifically a visual error in mistaking a singular for plural.

2. Error. The Hebrew *Vorlage* the translator of the Peshitta had at his disposal was most probably not vocalized. Although the exact origin of the P is uncertain, legend and comparative studies with the Targumim and Septuagint place it in the early centuries of the Common Era. Excluding the use of *matres lectionis*, which early on were used in the Hebrew text, various systems of vocalization were not developed till much later, thus giving credence to the fact that the translator of P worked from an unpointed text. When the translator was faced with a consonantal homograph problems clearly arose as to what was the correct or accepted pronunciation. This is especially evident in the sub-topic of number. The translator clearly selected the "wrong" vocalization when compared to the

---

[10] See for example 6:23 and 10:7.

vocalization preserved in the MT. Thus, from the perspective of an evaluator, error has occurred. Consider the following examples:

a. Heb. singular > Syr. plural

7:21	עוֹנִי	as if	עֲוֹנֵי	thus	ܢܘܿܗ̈ܝ
21:2	מִלָּתִי	as if	מִלָּתֵי	thus	ܕܼ̈ܠ
21:6	פַּלָּצוּת	as if	פְּלָצוֹת (?)	thus	ܩܘܼ̈ܪ̈ܐ
30:30	עַצְמִי	as if	עַצְמֵי	thus	ܓ̈ܪ̈ܡܝ
42:10	רֵעֵהוּ	as if	רֵעֵיהוּ	thus	ܗ̈ܒܢ̈ܘܗܝ

b. Heb. plural > Syr. singular

9:28	עַצְּבֹתָי	as if	עַצְּבֹתֵי	thus	ܟ̣ܐܒ̈ܝ
11:8	גְּבֹהֵי	as if	גֹּבַהּ	thus	ܪܘܿܡ̣ܐ
11:14	אֹהָלֶיךָ	as if	אָהֳלֶךָ	thus	ܡܫ̈ܟܢܝܟ
18:19	מְגוּרָיו	as if	מְגוּרוֹ	thus	ܟܼ̣ܫܘܿܗܝ

Although error in misunderstanding the Hebrew pointing may have resulted in a change in number it did not produce any significant semantic changes. The meaning relation is still synonymy with variation in but literary style.

3. Intra-/Inter-verse Influence. In 21:9a (discussed above under Language Difference), intra-verse influence was also cited as a motivation for the alteration in number. There P read a plural adjective (ܫ̈ܠܝ) in contrast to the singular Hebrew (שׁלוֹם) in order to achieve noun-adjective agreement. Grammatical reasons within and between verses are often responsible for adjustments in number.[11] Consider the following representative examples:

---

[11] For Heb. sg. > Syr. pl. due to Intra-verse influence, see 3:9,16;4:4,11;6:15,20,29; 8:20;10:17,20;15:3;19:13,19;20:11;21:25,32;22:14,20;24:15,17,20,24;31:12,33;32:1; 34:14; 36:25;37:4;38:34;41:13;for Inter-verse influence, see 18:6;24:20;27:14,15,16; 28:19; 30:11,15(2); 35:10;36:25,29,32;37:3.
For Heb. pl. > Syr. sg. due to Intra-verse influence, see 4:7;12:7;15:20,24,28;16:19; 22:29; 24:16;32:11;42:8.

4:4   MT   כּוֹשֵׁל יקימון מליך   וברכים כרעות תאמץ:
      "Your words have upheld the stumbling man,
      and you have strengthened the tottering knees."

P   ܒܡ̈ܠܝܟ ܠܐ ܢܩܝܡܘܢ ܬܠܝܢ. ܘܒܘܪ̈ܟܐ ܕܙ̈ܝܥܢ ܠܐ ܬܫܪܪ‡
      "Your words will not raise the weak (pl.),
      nor will you strengthen the shaking knees."

P reads with the plural ܬܠܝܢ for Heb. singular כושל due to
intra-verse influence with stich two where the object is likewise in the
plural (ברכים כרעות). The effect on meaning is clearly still synonymy
with variation only at the level of structure. Explicit exegesis might also
be cited as a motivational factor, for although the Heb. preserves a
singular form it might be considered collective in that not just one
"stumbling man" is referred to, but "stumbling men" in general.[12] By
contrast, the following example (15:3) contains a number change
resulting once again in synonymy of meaning, but with variation at the
literary level:

15:3 MT   הוכח בדבר לא יסכון   ומלים לא־יועיל בם:
      "Should he reprove with a word which is unprofitable,
      or (with) words that have no profit in them."

P   ܠܡܟܣܘ ܒ̈ܡܠܐ ܕܠܝܬ ܒܗܝܢ. ܘܒ̈ܡܠܐ ܕܠܝܬ ܒܗܝܢ ܝܘܬܪܢ.
      "In order to reprove words which are ineffectual
      and with words in which there is no profit."

P again records a plural for the Heb. singular object motivated by
intra-verse influence with the second stich, no doubt for stylistic
preferences, thereby preserving plural objects in both stichs. As stated
synonymy is maintained.[13] The following two passages preserve

---

[12] Further examples of intra-/inter-verse influence yielding a change in number but
maintaining synonymy with only structural variation are found in 3:9,16;4:7,11; 6:15,
20;8:20;10:20;19:13;31:12;38:34.

[13] Further examples of intra-/inter-verse influence yielding a change in number but
maintaining synonymy with only stylistic variation are found in 6:29;12:7;15:20,24;
16:19;19:19;20:11;21:32;22:20,29;24:15,24;34:14;36:25;37:4;41:13.

examples of number changes that, by contrast have an innovative effect on meaning.

31:12 MT כי אשׁ היא עד־אבדון תאכל ובכל־תבואתי תשׁרשׁ:

"for that is a fire which consumes unto Abaddon,
and it roots at all my yields."

P ܘܢܘܪܐ ܗܝ ܕܐܟܠܐ ܠܐܒܕܢܐ ܐܟܠܐ. ܘܟܠܗܝܢ ܥ̈ܠܠܬܝ ܢܬܥܩܪܢ

"And that is light which consumes unto Abaddon
(destruction) and all my yields will be rooted up."

P has treated Heb. תבואתי "my yields" as the subject of the second stich as against the Heb. "sin of enticement" (v. 9) being understood as the implicit subject, hence the change in number, as well as in voice. The meaning has also been altered, albeit insignificantly. By contrast, the following passage contains a number change producing a significant semantic change:

32:1 MT וישׁבתו שׁלשׁת האנשׁים האלה מענות את־איוב
כי הוא צדיק בעיניו:

"So these three men ceased answering Job for he was
righteous in his eyes."

P ܘܫܠܝܘ ܗܠܝܢ ܬܠܬܐ ܓܒܪ̈ܝܢ ܕܒܥܝܢ ܗܘܘ ܠܡܚܝܒܘܬܗ
ܠܐܝܘܒ. ܡܛܠ ܕܗܘ ܗܘܐ ܙܕܝܩ ܒܥܝ̈ܢܝܗܘܢ.

"So these three men who sought to condemn Job ceased
because he was righteous in their eyes."

P reads "in their eyes" for the Heb. "in his eyes" under influence of the plural subject earlier in this verse.[14] Quite plausible, too, is a theological motivation on the part of the translator who saw Job's three friends convinced of his righteousness, thus their cessation in speech, in contrast to the MT's declaration that the friends stopped in their barrage of words, because Job truly believed in his own righteousness and hence their banter was of no avail. Clearly the theological implications of this

[14] Note also LXX and Sym. contain a similar reading.

alteration are more significant than in the previous example. The MT's statement portrays Job in a more self-righteous, haughty light, whereas the P now depicts him as a man who is truly upright in character so much so that he has convinced his friends of his innocence.[15]

P's overall treatment of number, thus, tends to be greatly influenced by language difference, error, intra-/inter-verse influence, as well as the translator and his language's natural tendency to be more explicit in translation. These adjustments are tendencies inherent in the Syriac language.The effect on meaning in all but a few cases is synonymy.

Person

Over sixty examples of change in person are found in P-Job, of these over fifty produce innovative meanings and many significant innovations. The most prevalent motivations are language difference and intra-/inter-verse influence; however error and versional influence are also significant.[16]

1. Language Difference/Error. Language difference is a frequent motivation for alterations in person. In the first example, language difference resulting in a synonymous meaning with variation only on the literary level is demonstrated:

21:22   MT   הלאל יל מד־דעת   והוא רמים ישפוט:
          "Can anyone teach God knowledge,
          (seeing) that He judges the high ones."

P   ܐܠܗܐ ܡܠܦ ܐܢܬܘܢ ܝܕܥܬܐ. ܕܗܘ ܠܪܡܐ ܢܕܘܢ.
          "(Do) you teach knowledge to God
          that He will judge the high ones?"

---

[15] See Chapter VII Conclusions where further examples of P's virtuous characterization of Job as exhibited by translational techniques are brought together. Further examples of number changes prompted by intra-/inter-verse influence resulting in an innovative meaning are found in 15:28;22:14;24:16,20;32:11;42:8.

[16] Examples of person changes prompted by versional influence/parallels occur in 7:13,15;9:19;10:16; changes prompted by error occur in 16:3;17:4;22:9;23:8; 26:14;31:12,31;34:9.

The Heb. 3pms verb is translated by the 2pms verb in the Peshitta (more specifically a m.pl. participle + 2pmpl pronoun). Thus, where the Heb. refers to an impersonal subject "anyone, one", the P specifically directs Job's words towards his three friends.[17]

In the next two examples, language difference is once again the primary motivation. However, this time the alteration in person results in an antithetic and an innovative meaning, respectively. In the first, 6:13, a particularly significant meaning is produced:

6:13 MT   האם אין <u>עזרתי</u> בי   ותשיה נדחה ממני:
            "Is it that my help is not in me
            and abiding success is driven from me?"

P   ‏ܗܐ ܠܝܬ <u>ܥܘܕܪܢܝ</u> ܒܝ ܘܦܘܪܩܢܗ ܐܬܪܚܩ ܡܢܝ.‏
        "Behold, his help is not in me
        and his salvation is far from me."

In the MT, Job asks "Is it that my help is not in me?" implying a negative declarative reply "My help is not in me", thus indicating that "his help" comes from a higher source, i.e. God. P, by contrast, specifically declares by the emphatic statement that "His (i.e. God's) help is not in me",[18] clearly the opposite of the MT. One other motivation, however, must be considered: error, specifically orthographic confusion of the Yodh and Waw. The translator of P may not have had any underlying theological motivation that prompted this reading, but simply fell prey to visual error. The next example of an innovative meaning in P is solely motivated by language difference; however, here the new meaning is not as significant as in 6:13:

12:4a MT   שחק לרעהו <u>אהיה</u>
            "I am a laughingstock to my friends,"

---

[17] Further examples of person changes motivated by language difference resulting in a synonymous effect on meaning are found in 34:17 and 37:5.

[18] For P's treatment of the Heb. interrogative sentence by an emphatic, see Chapter VI: Emphatic sentences, where this verse is discussed.

P   ‎.ܝܗܘܪܒܚܠ ܐܟܘܚܓ ܐܘܗܘ

"And he was a laughingstock to his friends,"

In the MT, Job calls himself a laughingstock. By contrast, in P, an impersonal, non-specific man, possibly in the same situation as Job, is referred to. The meaning is different from the Hebrew, but the significance of this alteration is clearly not as important as in the previous example.[19]

2. Intra-/Inter-verse influence. Intra-/Inter-verse influence is also a major motivation for alterations in person. They likewise produce synonymous and innovative meanings. The following verse contains an example of intra-verse influence yielding a synonymous effect on meaning with variation at the literary level.

38:11   MT   וָאֹמַר עַד־פֹּה תָבוֹא וְלֹא תֹסִיף

‎ו פ א ־יָשִׁית בִּגְאוֹן גַּלֶּיךָ:

"And I said, this far you may go and no farther,
and (lit.) here shall he set the pride of your waves."

P   ‎.ܦܣܘܬ ܐܠܘ ܝܬܐܬ ܐܟܪܗܠ ܥܕ ܐܢܐ ܬܪܡܐܘ

‎.ܟܝܠܓܕ ܐܬܘܐܓܒ ܢܘܩܒܬ ܐܟܪܗܘ

"And I said, unto here you may reach and no farther,
and here you will remain in the pride of your waves."

Heb. 3pms יָשִׁית "he shall set", with 'he' = God or, more probably, an impersonal subject = the passive voice, is translated by 2pms ‎ܬܒܩܘܬ "you will remain". Intra-verse influence with the 2pms forms in stich one clearly motivated this alteration, thus the referent is now uniformly 'the sea'. The meaning is still synonymous.[20] By contrast, the following example,16:3, contains a person change producing an innovative meaning.

---

[19] Further examples of changes in person due to language difference and resulting in a innovative meaning are found in 9:29;10:19;11:14;32:14.

[20] Further examples of changes in person due to intra-/inter-verse influence resulting in a synonymous meaning are found in 14:3,14;16:7,8,22;17:4,5,10,16;18:6,14,15; 19:15; 21:34;22:9;23:9;30:18;31:5,7,12;37:20;38:11;39:6.

16:3 MT :הקץ לדברי־רוח   או מה־ימריצך כי תענה

"Do windy words have an end?,
Or what disturbs you that you answer?"

P   ܠܐ ܬܟܐܐ ܠܢ̈ܘܚܝ ܒܡ̈ܠܐ.
          ܘܐܢ ܬܐܡܪ̈ܝܢ ܠܝ ܠܐ ܥܢܐ ܐܢܐ

"Do not sadden my spirit with words,
Even if you speak to me, I do not answer."

Person changes are not the only adjustments that occur in the P's
translation of this verse.[21] However, three changes in person and a
substitution in word class (Heb. n.m. קץ > Syr. ܬܟܐܐ) result in rather
distinct sentiments. In the Hebrew, after chastising the friends as
"miserable comforters", Job simply asks them when their "windy words"
will come to an end (16:3a) and then demands to be told what provokes
them to speak to him in such a fashion (16:3b). Thus, in the MT the
referent of the 2pms form of the pronominal suffix and the verb תענה is
the friends. By contrast, the P records a conditional statement. Even if
the friends do speak to Job, he will not condescend to reply. The
motivation is primarily inter-/intra-verse influence,[22] for in 16:3b the
2pmpl is introduced by Job's epithet מנחמי עמל כלכם "miserable
comforters are you all". The translator of P then maintained the second
person referent in 16:3. In the MT and P, the second person continues
through verse five. The importance of such a change is clearly not a
major theological issue; however, it does depict a rather forceful,
unyielding Job, a Job who refuses to be on the defensive and maintains his
ground.[23]

---

[21] In stich one Heb. הקץ, interrogative Heh + n.m.s., was erroneously identified as a
Hiphil verbal form (√קצץ), resulting in a confusion in syntax. Thus, the Heb. construct
chain became a DO (ܢܘܚܝ) and, with the addition of the preposition ܒ , a dative of
means ܒܡ̈ܠܐ. Both stichs are negated in the Peshitta. In the second stich, in addition to
the change in person, Heb. או מה . . . כי "or what . . . that" is transformed into a
conditional statement.

[22] Error might also be suggested as a motivation for Heb. ימריצך > Syr. ܬܐܡܪ̈ܝܢ , that
is confusion of roots מרץ and אמר.

[23] Further examples of adjustments in Person due to intra-/inter-verse influence and
resulting in an innovative meaning occur in 7:13;10:16;20:9;22:18;23:8,12,14;
38:10,23,34;42:8.

Pronoun

As explained in the Model of Translation Technique, the designation pronoun refers to an adjustment in an independent pronoun and the relative pronoun, as well as an enclitic pronoun or one functioning as a copula. The adjustments that are found in P-Job include omission and addition.[24] Most frequent by far is addition, with over 150 instances appearing P-Job. Omission is represented by a meagre data supply, only four examples.

Once again language difference plays a primary role in promoting an adjustment, followed closely by implicit to explicit exegesis. Less frequent are intra/inter-verse influence, redundancy, ambiguity, and versional influence. Of the 154 examples culled and examined very few have any other than a synonymous effect on meaning.

1. Omission. As stated only four cases of omission of a pronoun are extant in P-Job. These omissions were motivated by language difference (15:20;37:17), intra-verse influence (24:13), ambiguity (37:17) and redundancy (9:29), all yielding a synonymous effect on meaning with variation only in literary style. So, for example, in 9:29:

MT   אנכי ארשע   למה־זה הבל איגע:
       "(If) I am guilty, Why then do I labour in vain?"

P   ܗܐ ܐܢ ܐܬܚܝܒܬ. ܠܡܢܐ ܐܝܟ ܡܕܡ ܡܚܒܠ ܐܢܬ ܠܝ.
       "Behold, if I am guilty,
       Why do you destroy me like nothing?"

P omits translating the Hebrew demonstrative pronoun functioning in an emphatic capacity. As stated the effect on meaning is minimal, projecting a slightly less emphatic statement.

2. Addition. The majority of cases where a pronoun has been added by the translator of P are prompted by either language difference or implicit to explicit exegesis. In those cases where addition is due to language

---

24 Examples of substitution, e.g. where P reads an object pronoun for a Heb. suffix (1:5,15,16,17) or where P substitutes a relative pronoun for a Heb. conjunction or preposition, e.g. Heb. עד־אין מספר and אין חקר > Syr. ܕܠܝܬ and ܕܠܐ (5:9) also occur. However, the former is included under Grammar: Suffix and the latter under Semantics.

difference the pronoun in question is specifically an enclitic one. This type of addition results in synonymy in meaning with variation only at the level of literary style. Consider the following representative example:

4:6 MT הלא יראתך כסלתך תקותך ותם דרכיך:
"Is not your fear your confidence,
and the integrity of your ways your hope?"

P. ܟܡ ܕܛܠܬܝ ܗܘ ܠܗ ܗܘ ܓܠܬܝ ܗܘܘܒܟܝ ܘܗܕܟܒܘܬܗ ܐܘܪܚܬܝ.
"Behold, it is your fear that is your blame,
and your hope and the integrity of your way!"

In P the personal pronoun and enclitic pronoun are added in the first stich, thereby more precisely indicating the nominal subject and nominal predicate. This tendency of precision is well documented in P-Job.[25] In most cases the addition of the pronoun produces no radical change in meaning as in the present example. Note also in P to 4:6 the enclitic is not added in the second stich, indicating that the translator understood the nouns of stich two to be dependent on stich one, rather than a parallel independent proposition as in the MT.

Where implicit to explicit exegesis is the primary motivation it is the relative pronoun that is of concern. Effect on meaning is once again synonymy. However, this time variation is in structure rather than literary style. Consider the following example:

3:3 MT יאבד יום אולד בו והלילה אמר הרה גבר:
"Let the day in (which) I was born perish,
and the night (which) said, 'a male child has been conceived!"

P ܐܒܝܕ ܝܘܡܐ ܕܐܬܝܠܕܬ ܒܗ
   ܘܠܠܝܐ ܕܐܬܐܡܪ ܒܗ ܕܐܬܒܛܢ ܓܒܪܐ

---

[25] Further examples of the addition of an enclitic pronoun occur in 5:7,9,13,24; 6:11,12;7:1,17;8:9,13,19;9:2,4,5,6,7,10;10:4,5,7,10,20;11:9,11;12:2,10,13,16;13:1, 4,12,15,18;14:1,5;15:14,23;16:2;17:13;18:10,21;19:21;20:5,29;21:15,21,28,31;22:5, 11;25:6;26:6;27:2,13;28:23,28;31:2,4,11;32:7,8,13;33:3;34:17,19,35;35:8;36:4,24; 37:13; 40:19;42:5.

"Let the day in which I was born perish,
and the night in which it was said, 'a man has been conceived'!"

In both stichs the relative pronoun, enclosed in parentheses in the
MT, is implicit. Following the explicit tendencies of the translator of P,
both relative pronouns are represented. Note the resumptive pronoun has
also been added to the second stich, thus paralleling the first.[26] Likewise
many explicit representations of the relative pronoun find parallels in the
versions.[27]

Addition of a pronoun prompted by intra-/inter-verse influence is
poorly represented in the P-Job due to chance rather than intentional
reasons. The most prominent example occurs in 9:4-10 where the MT
preserves a doxology. Note also ambiguity and explicit exegesis are also
significant factors.

חכם לבב ואמיץ כח מי־הקשה אליו וישלם	4
המעתיק הרים ולא ידעו אשר הפכם באפו:	5
המרגיז ארץ ממקומה ועמודיה יתפלצון:	6
האמר לחרס ולא יזרח ובעד כוכבים יחתם:	7
נטה שמים לבדו ודורך על־במתי ים:	8
עשה־עש כסיל וכימה וחדרי תמן:	9
עשה גדלות עד־אין חקר ונפלאות עד־אין מספר:	10

4   "(He is) wise in heart and mighty in strength
      - who has hardened himself against him, and succeeded? -
5   He who removes mountains, and they know it not,
      when he overturns them in his anger;
6   He who shakes the earth out of its place,
      and its pillars tremble;
7   He who commands the sun, and it does not rise;
      who seals up the stars;
8   (He who) alone stretched out the heavens,
      and trampled the waves of the sea;

---

[26] Further examples of the addition of an implicit relative pronoun are found in 3:16;4:7,
8,19;5:4;7:2,9;9:26,32,33;10:7;11:3,19;13:5,9,13,28;14:7,12;15:3,22;16:22; 17:9,10;
18:21;20:15,26;21:18,27;24:5;26:2,3;27:13;28:1,5;29:11,16;30:1,15;31:12; 34:2, 7;
35:5,10;36:22; 37:2;38:2;40:2,11,27;41:26;42:3,15.

[27] See, for example, the parallel addition of the relative pronoun in the Versions in
5:4,9;7:2;9:4,26,32;10:7;13:9;20:15;21:27;28:1;29:16;30:15;34:7.

9 (He who) made the Bear and Orion;
the Pleiades and the chambers of the south;
10 (He who) does great things beyond understanding,
and marvellous things without number."

4 ܚܟܝܡ ܠܒܐ ܗܘ ܘܥܫܝܢ ܚܝܠܐ. ܡܢܘ ܐܬܩܫܝ ܠܘܬܗ ܘܗܘܐ ܫܠܝܢ
5 ܗܘ ܕܡܫܢܐ ܠܛܘܪ̈ܝܢ ܠܐ ܝܕܥ. ܘܗܦܟ ܠܗܘܢ ܒܪܘܓܙܗ.
6 ܗܘ ܕܐܙܝܥ ܐܪܥܐ ܡܢ ܥܩܪ̈ܝܗ ܘܥܡܘܪ̈ܝܗ ܪܥܠܝܢ.
7 ܗܘ ܕܐܡܪ ܠܫܡܫܐ ܘܠܐ ܕܢܚ. ܘܒܐ̈ܦܝ ܟܘ̈ܟܒܐ ܚܬܡ.
8 ܗܘ ܕܡܬܚ ܫܡܝܐ ܒܠܚܘܕܘܗܝ. ܘܕܪܟ ܥܠ ܬܘܩܦܗ ܕܝܡܐ.
9 ܗܘ ܕܥܒܕ ܟܝܡܐ ܘܥܝܘܬܐ. ܘܓܢܒܪܐ ܘܐܚܕ ܠܬܝܡܢܐ
10 ܗܘ ܕܥܒܕ ܪ̈ܘܪܒܬܐ ܕܠܐ ܣܟ. ܘܬܩ̈ܝܦܬܐ ܕܠܐ ܡܢܝܢ.

4 "He is wise of heart and powerful of strength,
- Who can be harsh toward Him and be successful? -
5 He who removes mountains does not know,
and who changes them by his anger.
6 He who shakes the earth from its roots
and its inhabitants reel.
7 He who commands the sun and it does not rise,
and He sealed over the face of the stars.
8 He who stretches out the heavens by himself
and treads upon the bottom of the sea.
9 He who made Pleides and Aldebaran
and the Orion and He enclosed the south.
10 He who made great (things) without limit,
and strong (things) without number."

In verse four, the translator of P has added the 3pms pronoun, thereby avoiding any ambiguity in subject. In the following verses the translator has not only added a relative pronoun (vv. 8-9), thus paralleling the earlier verses in the MT (vv. 5-9), but has also continued to add the 3pms pronoun (vv. 5-9). Thus, the Peshitta presents a uniform pattern of personal pronoun + relative pronoun (vv. 5-9) after the initial introductory pronoun in the beginning of this doxology (v. 4).[28] Thus, ambiguity, implicit to explicit exegesis and inter-verse influence were all influential in the translator's treatment of this Hebrew passage. These

[28] For Syriac's use of the relative pronoun with a "Correlative" word, i.e. the personal pronoun in 9:4, when the substantive antecedent is lacking, see Nöldeke, p. 183f, #236.

additions, however, did not affect the meaning of the text, but only presented a different literary style.

Tense

Although Hebrew and Syriac are both Semitic languages, thereby containing many common points, their verbal systems are not identical. The Hebrew tenses do not simply indicate the past, present, and future time frames. The time frame spanned by each form is much more complex.[29] In Syriac, whereas the Perfect and Imperfect may have originally indicated completeness and incompleteness, they have now, possibly under Greek influence, developed into the past and future tenses, with the participle filling the present tense position and a series of compound tenses providing finer verbal nuances.[30] The following chart presents a comparison of the Hebrew and Syriac verbal systems:[31]

Hebrew	Tense	Syriac
Stative; Completed Action; Experience; Instantaneous Action; Certitude; Conditional	< Perfect >	Past, esp. Completed Result; Future-Perfect in Conditions Either/Or Clauses and Hypothetical
Narrative Future	< Perfect Consecutive >	Ø
Incomplete Action; Frequentative/Habitual; Potential; Permissive; Desiderative; Obligative; Injunctive; Conditional	< Imperfect >	Future

---

[29] See Ronald J. Williams, *Hebrew Syntax: An Outline* (University of Toronto Press, 1984), pp. 29-40; GKC #106-116; or more recently Bruce K Waltke and M. O'Connor, *An Introduction to Biblical Hebrew Syntax* (Eisenbrauns, 1990), Chapters 29-37.

[30] See Nöldeke, #255-286; Robinson, pp. 53, 60.

[31] This chart is based on the studies of tense by Williams, Waltke and O'Connor for Hebrew, and Nöldeke and Robinson for Syriac.

Preterite (true past)	<	Imperfect Consecutive	>	Ø
Command	<	Imperative	>	Command
As Subject/Object; Genitive; Gerund; Purpose; Consequence; Degree; w/ prep. has temporal, clausal or concessive meaning	<	Infinitive Construct	>	Direction/Purpose w/ ܠ; Obligation, Necessity, Ability w/ ܐܝܬ or ܗܘܐ
As Subject/Object; Adverbial Accusative; Indicates Emphasis or Continuity to Verb; As genitive (rare); Substitute for finite verb;	<	Infinitive Absolute	>	Emphasis to Verb
Continuous Action; Immediate Imminent Action; Admissive Sense; Substantival	<	Participle	>	Active: Present, Future, Imminent Past Action Passive: Completion of Action Instead of Perfect

In addition, Syriac contains a systems of compound tenses using ܗܘܐ :

> Present: Participle + Personal Pronoun
> Continuous Past: Participle + Perfect of ܗܘܐ
> Pluperfect: Perfect + Perfect of ܗܘܐ
> Frequentative Past: Imperfect + Perfect of ܗܘܐ

With this comparison in mind it is hardly surprising to find such equivalences as:

Heb. Perfect > Syr. Continuous Past[32] or Participle[33]
Heb. Perfect Consecutive > Syr. Participle[34], Imperfect[35]
Heb. Imperfect > Syr. Participle[36]
Heb. Imperfect Consecutive > Syr. Participle,[37] Perfect[38] or
                                                      Continuous Past[39]
Heb. Participle > Syr. Continuous Past,[40] Imperfect,[41] Perfect[42]

The motivation which prompted such equivalences is simply language difference. Hebrew and Syriac do not use the verbal tenses in the same manner. In most cases context clarifies the intended time frame, as, for example, in 1:7a:

MT   ויאמר יהוה אל־השטן מאין תבא

"And the Lord said to the adversary,
'From whence do you come?'"

---

[32] See, for example, 3:13,25;10:13;29:16.

[33] See, for example, 3:18;6:3,17;7:4,9;9:5,28,30;10:14;11:11;12:9,21;13:2,18;14:2,11, 12; 15:9,23;17:11;18:21;19:25;20:11;21:7,18,24;22:13,28;23:10;24: 15,16;26:2,12; 27:19; 28:13,21,23;29:16;30:2,15,23;32:22;33:2,12,32;34:19; 35:5,6,15;38:4,12,18, 20,21,23; 39:1,2;42:2.

[34] See, for example, 7:4.

[35] See, for example, 11:19.

[36] See, for example,1:7;2:2;3:13,17,22;4:18;5:2;6:5,6,14,17,27,30;7:2,9,10,12, 19;8:3, 5,9;9:2,3,6,7,11,12,13,16,21,23,24,26,27,28;10:2,3,4,6,7,9,11,12,20;11:2,7,8,10, 11;12:11,14,15,17,19,20;13:3,7,8,9,10,13,14,15,16,19,24,25, 26,28;14:7,10,11,12, 14,18,21;15:3,4,5,12,13,15,22,26,35;16:3,6,13,22; 17:3,12;18:2;19:2,3,7;20:24;21:4, 7,11,12,13,15,22,26,27,31,32;22:3,14,17,29;23:6,8;24:7,14;25:3,4,5;26:11;27:8,9; 28:1,2,5,13,15,16,19,20,24;31:4,12,14;32:7,8,9,13,14,16,19;33:5,10,12,14,16,17, 29;34:3,9,11,12,14,15,17,20,21,28,29,31,37;35:3,6,7,9,12,13,16;36:5,6,7,8,22,26, 28;37:2,5,11,12,15,16;38:5,22,24,30,31,34,35,41;39:2,3,4,9-12,14,15,19-22,24-30; 40:2,5,8,9, 15,17,21,22,23,26,27,28,29,31;41:5,8-16,18,19,20,21,26;42:2.

[37] See, for example, 2:3,9,10;5:3;7:9;9:16,20;11:3,4,11;12:18,22,23,24,25;36:7.

[38] See, for example, 8:4;32:2,3;36:9.

[39] See, for example, 9:4.

[40] See, for example,1:13,18;2:8;23:7;32:4.

[41] See, for example, 3:9*;13:16*;15:16,34*;18:19*;20:18,28;30:13*;34:34 (* indicates MT contains a present existential statement not a participle that is rendered by the imperfect in P).

[42] See,for example, 4:11;9:32*;10:13*;11:14*;12:4;15:9;16:4*;23:6*;24:1,25*; 25:2; 26:7,8,9,10;28:4,14*;29:16*;31:27;32:1*,9*;39:5;40:19;41:26*;42:10*, 11* (* indicates MT contains a present existential statement not a participle that is rendered by the perfect in P).

P   .ܐܢܬ ܐܬܝܬ ܐܝܡܟܐ ܡܢ .ܠܣܛܢܐ ܡܪܝܐ ܐܡܪܗ

"And the Lord said to the adversary,
'From whence do you come?'"

The Hebrew text here contains the imperfect תבא referring to an
action in the present time.   In keeping with the temporal frame indicated,
the translator P used the participle with independent pronoun ܐܢܬ ܐܬܐ.
Adjustments under these conditions have no significant effect on the
meaning.   Thus the meaning relation would best be described as
synonymous with structural variation. However the Syriac text does tend
to provide more precision in temporal elements by its more defined
verbal system; thus clarity would also describe the meaning relation from
the perspective of the translator.
        Another example of verbal tense adjustment motivated by language
difference, but involving one particular root, is P's treatment of the Heb.
√ידע "to know".   Heb. ידע is a verb denoting experience or
perception.[43] Although it often, but not exclusively, occurs in the
perfect tense its aspect refers to a continual state.   In Syriac, by contrast,
the participle is used.   Thus, in P-Job, wherever ידע occurs in this
capacity, the translator used a participle.[44] So, for example, in 12:9:

MT   :מי לא־ידע בכל־אלה   כי יד־יהוה עשׂתה זאת

"Who does not know all these things,
    that the hand of the Lord has done this."

P   .ܗܠܝܢ ܟܠܗܘܢ ܒܟܠ ܝܕܥ ܠܐ ܕ ܡܢ
"Who does not know all these things,
    that the hand of the Lord has done these."

Thus, the translator of P has provided merely a structural
adjustment in his rendition, thereby preserving the meaning of the MT.
One other motivation, however, must be considered in this particular

---

[43] Williams, p. 30, #163.
[44] See 8:9;9:5,21;11:11;13:2,18;14:21;15:9,23;18:21;19:25;20:4;22:13;23:10; 24:15,16;
28:13,23;30:23;32:22;34:33;35:15;36:26;37:15,16;38:4,12,18,20,21,33;39:1,2;42:2.
See similar treatment of √אמן in 4:18;15:15,22;39:12.

case, as well as other cases of a Heb. 3pms perfect or Heb. m.s. participle being translated by a Syr. perfect: error. More specifically the translator may have incorrectly recognized the Hebrew vocalization. Such may be the case in 12:9; however, the uniformity of P's treatment of the √ידע throughout the text, argues against this. Error in recognizing proper vocalization is more probable, for example, in 4:11:

MT   ליׁש א ב ד מבלי־טרף   ובני לביא יתפרדו:
        "The lion perishes for lack of prey,
        and the lion cubs are scattered."

P   ܐܪܝܐ ܐܒܕ ܡܢ ܕܠܝܬ ܠܗ ܬܘܪܒܐ.
        ܚܒܠ ܐܪܝܘܬܐ ܐܬܒܕܪܘ.
        "The lion perished for his not having prey,
        and the lion cubs have been scattered abroad."

Having before him (most likely) an unvocalized text, the translator of P could have easily misconstrued the homograph אבד , now in vocalized text pointed as a m.s. participle אֹבֵד , as the 3pms perfect אָבַד, hence the Syriac ܐܒܕ. However, care must also be taken in distinguishing the Syr. participle and perfect forms, in particular the 3pms perfect and ms participle which are consonantly homographs. The participle is distinguished by a dot above the word, whereas the perfect receives a dot below the word. This system of dots is by no means completely accurate, nor necessarily uniform in a given manuscript.[45] Thus, in the present example, the translator may have retained the Heb. participle in his translation, but failed - he or a future copyist - to use a distinguishing dot.

Far more interesting and significant are the other than expected verbal equivalences or those equivalences for which language difference is not necessarily the primary motivation nor synonymous-structure the resulting effect on meaning. Consider the following:

---

[45] See Nöldeke, p. 8; and J.B. Segal, *The Diacritical Point and the Accents in Syriac* (Oxford University Press, 1953), esp. p. 15ff.

Heb. Perfect > Syr. Imperfect,[46] Infinitive Construct,[47]
        Imperative[48]
Heb. Imperfect > Syr. Imperative,[49] Infinitive Construct,[50]
        Perfect[51]
Heb. Imperfect Consecutive > Syr. Infinitive Construct,[52]
        Imperative,[53] Imperfect[54]
Heb. Imperative > Syr. Perfect,[55] Continuous Past[56] or
        Participle[57]
Heb. Participle > Syr. Infinitive Construct[58]
Heb. Infinitive Construct > Syr. Perfect,[59] Imperfect,[60]
        Participle,[61] Continuous Past[62]
Heb. Infinitive Absolute > Syr. Participle,[63] Perfect[64]

In most of these equivalences intra-/inter-verse influence resulted
in a variation in style while still preserving synonymy in meaning. This
is the case, for example, in 11:20:

MT   וְעֵינֵי רְשָׁעִים תִּכְלֶינָה וּמָנוֹס אָבַד מִנְהֶם

           וְתִקְוָתָם מַפַּח־נָפֶשׁ:

---

[46] See, for example, 5:20;8:7;9:31;11:20;15:20;18:6,17;24:8,11,16;27:6;30:8;31:35;
32:14;33:21, 24; 36:13,32;37:20,24.
[47] See 20:19.
[48] See 33:28.
[49] See 18:2;21:3;40:10.
[50] See 23:3.
[51] See 2:4,10;9:18;10:1;11:14;12:4;13:24;16:4,5,8,11;17:10;21:28;22:6,7,11; 23:9,14;
29:3,12;30:16-18,21,22;32:11;33:4,8,10,11,13;34:33,36;35:14,16.
[52] See 10:8.
[53] See 14:7.
[54] See 14:20;20:25;24:20;33:24,26,27;34:24;36:9,10;37:8.
[55] See 5:27;11:14.
[56] See 11:6.
[57] See 33:33.
[58] See 12:5.
[59] See 1:7;2:2;14:13;20:4;28:25,26;29:7;30:1;31:30,33;32:2;33:24;34:18; 37:15;38:8,
9,38.
[60] See 1:15,19;2:3;7:19;33:23;34:30;37:7,17;39:9;42:8.
[61] See 2:10;13:9;14:14;15:22;24:15;33:15,30;39:1;42:10.
[62] See 11:5;31:13.
[63] See 6:2.
[64] See 26:9;15:35.

"But the eyes of the wicked will fail
and escape has perished from them,
and their hope is the breathing out of life (i.e. to expire)."

P   ܩܢܝ̈ܗܘܢ ܕܪ̈ܫܝܥܐ ܢܚܫܟܢ. ܘܚܝܠܗܘܢ ܢܐܒܕ ܡܢܗܘܢ
             ܘܣܒܪܐ ܕܢܦܫܬܗܘܢ.

"But the eyes of the wicked shall grow dark,
and their strength <u>will perish</u> from them
and the hope of their souls."

The narrative at 11:20 provides the reader with a statement
contrasting the plight of the wicked with the earlier described fate of the
repentant man. The previous verses are set in the future time, as is stich
one of 11:20. In 11:20b, however, the time element has changed to the
past without noticeably disrupting the message. However, given the
preponderance of future references the translator of P was no doubt
motivated to harmonize the Heb. perfect אבד, thus his resulting
translation ܢܐܒܕ. Synonymy of meaning is still retained, although the
translator differs in his stylistic tendency for uniformity in tenses.

Another interesting tense treatment that betrays the translator's
style of narration is found in the equivalence Heb. imperfect > Syr.
perfect. The choice of equivalence is hardly unusual in itself, given the
possibility of a Heb. imperfect = old preterite. However, in more than
thirty passages the translator is presenting events or statements with clear
reference to the future or present time in the MT as already completed.
In some passages it is Job himself who speaks with future or present
reference,[65] but the translator has perceived Job not as intending to do
something, but as already having completed an act. Such, for example, is
the case in 16:4:

MT   גם אנכי ככם אדברה לו־יש נפשכם תחת נפשי
            אחבירה עליכם במלים ואניעה עליכם במו ראשי:
            "I also could speak as you do, if you were in my place;
            <u>I could join</u> words together against you,
            and <u>shake</u> my head at you."

---

[65] See 9:27;12:4;13:24;16:4,5,8;21:28;23:9,14;29:3,12;30:15-18,21,22.

P ܐܦ ܐܢܐ ܐܝܟ ܐܢܬܘܢ ܐܡܠܠ. ܐܝܬܘܦ
ܕܝܢ ܠܒܢ̈ܝ ܗܘܝ ܢܦܫ̈ܬܟܘܢ ܚܠܦ ܢܦܫܝ.
ܘܒܚܬܟܘܢ ܕܝܢ ܒܡ̈ܠܐ. ܘܐܢܝܕܬ ܥܠܝܟܘܢ ܒܪܝܫܝ.

"I also could speak as you, for if only you were in my place;
for I have examined[66] you with words
and I have shaken my head against you."

The tense adjustment here suggests that the translator "corrected" the text because Job has in fact already joined words and chastised his friends, rather than considering these actions - for Job has been doing just that. What we are dealing with then is rather a slight difference in narrating events. To the translator Job has been using words against his friends from the onset of his discourses and, hence, he has chastised or "shaken his head" against them; thus the perfect more properly depicts the temporal setting. The MT, by contrast, suggests that if Job desired he *could* be like his friends by battling with words. However, he will not stoop to this level, thus the imperfect tense is used to indicate a possible though not yet complete action. Thus, the P provides us with a translation that is somewhat contradictory to the MT, for the MT's "could join" and "could shake" suggests Job would not do these things, whereas the P clearly states that Job has.

This same change in temporal setting in P is found in statements uttered by the other characters in the book of Job.[67] So, for example, in a statement from the adversary in 2:4:

MT ויען השטן את־יהוה ויאמר עור בעד־עור
וכל אשר לאיש יתן בעד נפשו:

"And the adversary answered the Lord and said, 'Skin for skin
and all which a man has he will give for his soul."

P ܘܥܢܐ ܣܛܢܐ ܘܐܡܪ ܠܡܪܝܐ. ܡܫܟܐ ܚܠܦ ܡܫܟܐ
ܘܟܠܡܕܡ ܕܐܝܬ ܠܓܒܪܐ ܝܗܒ ܚܠܦ ܢܦܫܗ ܘܡܫܬܦܠܛ.

---

66 P's translation √ܒܚܐ suggests a confusion of the Heb. √חבר with √בחר. See Mandl, p. 22.
67 See 2:10;22:6,7,11;32:11;33:4,8,10,11,13;34:33,36;35:14,16.

"And the adversary answered and said to the Lord, 'Skin for skin
and all which a man has <u>he gives</u> for his soul that it might be saved.'"

The translator of P has rendered the Heb. יתן "he will give" by the
ms. participle ܝܗܒ "he gives", clearly seeing this statement as a reference
to Job, who has in fact just "been giving" everything but his life in the
previous chapter, rather than an unspecified "man". Hence, the translator
has harmonized the temporal setting in this passage to accord with the
events of the previous narrative.

Most adjustments in tense result in synonymy of meaning with
variation in style or more often in structure. However, there are a few
instances possibly prompted by ideological motivation that result in an
innovative meaning. Such is the case in the following two examples:

11:14 MT עולה: באהליך תשכן ואל־ הרחיקהו בידך אם־און
           "If iniquity is in your hand, put it far away,
            and let wickedness not dwell in your tents."

P   ܐܢ ܐܝܬ ܗܘܐ ܥܘܠܐ ܒܐܝܕܝܟ. ܪܚܩܗ ܗܘܐ ܠܗ.
           ܘܠܐ ܥܡܪ ܒܟܣܬܝܟ ܥܘܠܐ.
           "If there was iniquity in your hands, He put it far away,
            and iniquity did not dwell in your tent."

In the first stich, Heb. הרחיקהו - a Hiphil imperative with object
suffix - is translated by the Syr. ܪܚܩܗ ܗܘܐ ܠܗ , a compound tense:
Aphel participle + ܗܘܐ. The cause of this discrepancy is most likely an
error in recognizing the Hebrew vocalization, for Heb. הרחיקהו is
consonantly a homograph of not only the imperative but also the 3pms
perfect. The effect on meaning, at least from the perspective of an
evaluator, is clearly innovative. In the MT, Zophar extends a plea to Job
to "put iniquity far away"; by contrast in P it is an unnamed subject, most
likely God, who will perform the action.

In the next example, ideology rather than error may be responsible
for the change in tense and person in the final stich.

33:24   MT :כפר מֻצָאתִי שַׁחַת מֵרֶדֶת פְּדָעֵהוּ וַיֹּאמֶר וַיְחֻנֶּנּוּ

"And he was gracious to him and said,
'Deliver him from going down [into] the pit,
I have found a ransom.'"

P   ܐܠܗܐ ܚܝܘܗܝ ܠܐ ܕܢܚܘܬ ܦܘܩܝܗܝ. ܘܢܐܡܪ ܠܠܗܐ ܢܪܚܡ
ܘܗܘ ܢܫܟܚ ܦܘܪܩܢܐ.

"And he will have compassion on him and say,
'Deliver him that he will not go down to corruption,
and he will find salvation for himself.'"

The "he" of the MT refers to a mediator or angel "who could declare to man what is right" (33:23). It is this mediator who declares that he has found a ransom for Job. In P, the mediator is still the author of this declaration, but with a slight twist. It is not he, the mediator, who will procure the ransom, but Job himself who will find it. Thus the mediator brings hopeful tidings of help, but that is all. It is Job who must find the "ransom" himself.

Voice

Adjustments in voice involve the interchange of the active and passive voices. Thirty-five examples were found of a Syriac passive for a Hebrew active - eight of which are the Heb. impersonal active = a passive - and 22 examples of a Heb. passive > Syr. active. Ambiguity - more precisely ambiguity of subject or ambiguity over which voice is represented in the MT - is by far the most prevalent motivation. But language difference, error, versional influence/parallel and intra-/inter-verse influence are also documented. The effect on meaning is clarity (for those passages involving ambiguity), synonymy: structure,[68] synonymy: style[69] and innovation.[70] In the case of innovation, a

---

[68] See 1:15;4:19;7:3;14:12;20:8,19,22;22:9;30:15;31:31;32:18;34:11;36:21; 37:5;41:2.
[69] See 3:3,20;8:21;9:24;10:19;11:16;18:8,13;20:20,28;22:29;26:14;27:15;31:12;33:21; 36:8;37:4,10;38:38.
[70] See 9:15;14:20;21:33;22:16;24:4;30:5;31:31;33:19,26;34:20,37;36:17; 37:13;41:25. Some of these verses project a new meaning not only as a result of voice change, but also involve a semantic change. See, for example, 31:19,31;34:20;41:25. This will be dealt with in the chapter on Semantics.

number of verses project a new meaning not only as a result of voice
change, but also as a result of semantic change. These will be dealt with
in Chapter V.

1. Ambiguity. In 22 passages ambiguity in subject resulted in a Heb.
active > Syr. passive.[71] In 16 passages ambiguity in voice, i.e. where the
MT may contain an active or passive, resulted in a Heb. passive > Syr.
active.[72] Consider the two following examples:

3:20   MT   למה יָתֵּן לעמל אור   וחיים למרי נפש:
             "Why does He give light to the oppressed
             and life to those embittered of soul."

P   ܠܡܐ ܡܬܝܗܒ ܢܘܗܪܐ ܠܠܐܐ܂ ܘܚܝܐ ܠܡܪܝܪܝ ܢܦܫܐ.
             "Why is light given to the labourers,
             and life to those embittered of soul."

English translations and commentators differ as to the subject of
Heb. יתן in stich one.[73] Is God the implied subject or an impersonal
"one", i.e. "one gives light" = the passive "light is given". The translator
of P opted for the latter, hence מתיהב with נוהרא as the subject.
Note LXX (δέδοται) and Tg. (יהיב) also translate passively. The
translator's choice clarifies this ambiguity, hence the effect on meaning is
clarity. From an evaluator's perspective the effect on meaning is still
synonymy with variation in style, for the agent of this passive action,
although not explicitly stated, can still be understood as God.

In the following example ambiguity as to which voice occurs in the
MT, combined with intra-verse influence and an erroneous recognition of
the Hebrew pointing, resulted in the P's active for the MT's passive in
stich one.

---

[71] See 1:15,17;3:3,20;8:21;9:24;11:16;14:12;18:13;20:19,20,25;22:29;24:20; 26:14;
31:12;34:11,27;36:17,21;37:10,13.

[72] See 9:24;10:19;11:2;18:8;20:8;22:9,16;30:5;31:31;33:19,21,30;34:11,20; 37:4;41:25.

[73] See, for example, ICC, p. 38; Dhorme, p. 37; Habel, p. 99; and Pope, p.27 who see
'He' = God as the subject of Heb. יתן, whereas RSV and KJV translate יתן as the
impersonal active = a passive "light is given".

9:24 MT   אם־לא אפוא מי־הוא: פני־שפטיה יכסה   ארץ נתנה ביד־רשע

> "The earth is given into the hand of the wicked;
> He covers the faces of its judges - if not he, who then?"

P   אוֹ ארץ ממבה מאחא וגאיבי. מבאמאַם אַנַ מאַ הטשבי.
       אלא ואֹנְהַ מבה הבמאבבי.

> "The earth - He gives it into the hand of the wicked,
> and the faces of the judges are covered;
> but His anger, Who can endure?"

In stich one Heb. נתנה is a source of ambiguity in that it is a consonantal homograph for the Niphal 3pfs perfect and the Qal 3pms perfect + 3pfs suffix. The translator of P appears to have understood Heb. נִתְּנָה with ארץ as it subject, i.e. "the earth is given", as the Qal perfect + 3pfs suffix נְתָנָהּ , with ארץ functioning as a *casus pendens*, hence the translation אוֹ ارض ممבה "the earth - He gives it". Once again the effect on meaning for the translator is clarity, but for the evaluator synonymy with variation in style.

2. Language Difference. Fourteen examples occur in which a Heb. active > Syr. passive due to language difference.[74] In these passages the Heb. active is the impersonal use of the active, thus the equivalent of a passive. Since Syriac lacks this impersonal use the translator simply translated with a passive. Such is the case in 7:3b where Heb. מנו־לי "(impersonal) they appointed to me" = "nights of weariness were appointed to me" is translated by the passive אתמנביא which was, however, erroneously negated.

MT   כן הנחלתי לי ירחי־שוא   ולילות עמל מנו ־לי :

> "So I was allotted months of emptiness
> and nights of weariness were appointed (lit. they appointed) to me."

P   מבוא אַני אנאַ ל יַנחי סמֹאמי.
       מלליא ראֹלא וגבלא לא אתמבחמי ל.

---

[74] See 4:19;7:3;11:16(2);20:8,19,20,22,28;22:29;24:4;32:18;37:5;41:2.

> "Thus I inherited for myself worthless months,
> and nights of weariness were not reckoned to me."

3. Error. In 9:24 discussed above, we came across the verbal form
נחנה which could have presented an ambiguity to the translator in that it
is a homograph for the Niphal 3pfs perfect and the Qal 3pms perfect +
3pfs suffix. The translator chose the latter option. From the perspective
of an evaluator, as we now perceive the Heb. vocalization, this was an
error. In a number of other passages, error too may be the primary
cause for the discrepancy in voice between the MT and P. So, for
example, in 18:8:

MT   :כי־שֻׁלַּח ברשת ברגליו   ועל־שֹׁבכה יתהלך
      "For he is cast into the net by his own feet,
      and he walks upon the lattice."

P   .ܡܠܘ ܟܐܝܫܝ ܠܓ ܥܠ ܡܬܟܝ ܟܬܒܝ ܢܐܠܘ ܝܐܪܣܘ ܠܓܠ
      "Because he stretched out his foot into the net,
      and he walked upon the lattice."

The translator may have construed Heb. שלח (Pual) as a Qal
perfect or participle. The active Hithpael יתהלך in stich two may have
further influenced the translator in selecting the active voice in stich
one.[75]

4. Versional Influence/Parallel. The interchange of voice documented
in the P does find parallels in the Versions.[76] In a few examples,
versional influence rather than just a parallel seems quite plausible. So,
for example, in 12:14:

MT   :הן יהרוס ולא יבנה   יסגר על־איש ולא יפתח
      "If he tears down, it will not be rebuilt,
      (if) he imprisons a man, it cannot be opened."

---

[75] Further examples of intra-/inter-verse influence producing voice change occur in
14:2;18:8;22:9;24:4,20;27:15;30:15;36:8;37:10.
[76] See, for example, 3:20 (LXX,Tg); 4:19 (Vg); 7:3 (LXX,Tg); 8:21 (Vg); 18:13
(LXX); 20:8(2) (LXX,Vg); 22:29 (LXX,Tg, Vg); 31:31 (LXX, Vg); 34:11 (Θ); 34:37
(LXX); 36:17 (Vg); 37:4 (LXX,Tg.); 37:10 (Tg, Σ, Vg).

P ܗܦܘܣ ܢܒܢܐ ܐܝܟܐ ܟܕ̈ܗ ܐܝܟ ܘܗܢ . ܟܒܫ ܢܒܢܐ ܡܚܣ ܐܢ ܗܐ

"Behold, if (he) demolishes, who can rebuild?
and if (he) shuts (the door) in the face of a man, who can open?"

In this example the P does not merely contain voice changes motivated by error or stylistic preferences, but contains passive verbs couched in an interrogative statement. Both statements find direct parallels in the LXX: τις οικοδομησει "who will rebuild?" and τις ανοιξει "who can open?". Thus, in this particular case, direct influence with the LXX can be suggested.

5. Ideology. Two verses (9:15;21:33) illustrate voice adjustments motivated by ideology that result in an innovative meaning relation. Consider the first example, 9:15:

MT אֲשֶׁר אִם־צָדַקְתִּי לֹא אֶעֱנֶה לִמְשֹׁפְטִי אֶתְחַנָּן:

"Though I am innocent I cannot answer,
I must implore the favor of my opponent."

P ܐܠܐ ܐܝܪܝܬ ܗܘܝܬ ܠܐ ܐܬܬܢܐ . ܘܠܒܥܝ ܐܬܟܫܦ.

"Although I am justified, I will not be answered,
and I will make supplication to my judge."

In stich one, Job states: "Though I am innocent I cannot answer". What precisely does the apodosis mean? Who or what is it that Job cannot answer? Is it that he is unable to respond to the charges of guilt levelled at him, or is it that Job is unable to answer God? The immediate context (9:14,16ff) clarify that it is God that Job is unable to respond to, for he feels himself incapable of "matching words" (9:14) and even if God answered, Job does not believe He would "heed him" (9:16). The translator of P, however, perceived this statement from a different perspective. It is not a question of Job's inability, but simply that regardless of Job's justification he will not be answered. One wonders if the translator was influenced by Job's words in 9:16b "I do not believe he would heed me", thereby harmonizing the two stichs. Thus, in both it is not a matter of ability, but simply that Job will not be answered nor paid attention to. One further motivation cannot be discounted, namely error.

The translator may have misconstrued the Heb. Qal imperfect אענה as the Niphal imperfect, distinct only in vocalization.

In the next passage, 21:33, ideology is once again responsible for voice change and once again results in an innovative meaning:

MT   מתקו־לו רגבי נחל   ואחריו כל־אדם ימשוך
                         ולפניו   אין   מספר:

> "The clods of the valley are sweet to him,
> and after him all men will follow
> and before him an innumerable number."

P   ܚܠܝ ܠܗ ܦܢܟ̈ܐ ܣܠܟ̈ܐ. ܘܒܬܪܗ ܟܠ ܒܪ ܢܫܐ ܢܬܕܒܪ.
                   ܘܩܕܡܘܗܝ ܠܝܬ ܡܢܝܢܐ.

> "The deep hollows of the torrent swallow him,
> and after him every man will be led
> and before him an innumerable amount."

The immediate context of this passage relates the fate of the wicked, that is his rather effortless passing on to the grave. The MT (21:33b) states that every man follows the wicked to his grave, just as before countless others have gone. This statement is made in the active voice. By contrast, the P translates passively - every man will be led. The implications are hardly as significant as in the previous example, but it does leave open the questions Who leads? and Why are the dead being lead? Unfortunately the translator does not provide these answers.

Word Class

Although Hebrew and Syriac are both Semitic languages, this relationship does not necessarily dictate a similar use of word classes. Thus, where Hebrew uses an adjective predicatively Syriac use a participle (e.g. 17:12), where Hebrew uses a verbal noun Syriac uses a pure noun (e.g. 10:4), where Hebrew uses two nouns in construct Syriac uses a noun with a qualifying adjective (e.g. 7:3). Thus, it is hardly surprising to find language difference as the primary factor in explaining many word class choices by the translator of P. However, in this topic of Grammar, error is equally as significant in promoting word class

changes, with ambiguity[77] and intra-/inter-verse influence[78] also
occurring. Some of these word class changes find parallels in the
Versions.[79] In the case of changes due to language difference the effect
on meaning is only one of structural or stylistic differences. Ambiguity
and intra-/inter-verse influence find a variety of meaning relations. By
contrast, the majority of passages involving word class changes due to
error result in an innovative meaning relation.

1. Language Difference. Over thirty verses in P-Job contain word class
differences when compared to the MT due to language difference. The
majority have only a stylistic effect on meaning,[80] fewer are only
structurally different[81] and in one case an innovative meaning results
(29:5[82]). Consider the following verse:

6:10 MT   ותהי עוד נחמתי   ואסלדה בחילה <u>לא יחמול</u>
                                    כי־לא כחדתי אמרי קדוש:

> "This then would be my consolation;
> I would spring in anguish unsparingly
> for I have not concealed the words of the Holy One."

P. ܡܢܘ ܘܠܐܕ ܟܕܒ ܬܚܕܕ ܐܟܬܪܕܟܐ ܗܘܕ ܒܬܚ ܟܘܣܠܐ ܪܟܐ ܟܢܬܚ ܟܢܡܝܗ
.ܐܬܝܕܩ ܝܕܬܘܦܕ ܗܝܬܣܟܒ ܝܠܝܗ ܘܕ ܠܝܠܐܕ

> "And it again would be my comfort,
> and again I would be given over by strength unsparingly,
> for I did not swear falsely against the word of the Holy One."

The Heb. לא יחמול "lit. he/one will not have compassion/spare"
is an expression used adverbially with the meaning "unsparingly". In the
Hebrew it contains a negated Qal imperfect 3pms. By contrast, the P
preserves this expression as ܡܢܘܚ ܠܐ , that is a negated noun, carrying

---

[77] See 10:17;13:12;20:19;24:18;30:24.

[78] See 4:19;8:2;10:17;17:12;19:5,19;24:18.

[79] See 10:15 (LXX); 11:16 (LXX); 22:12 (Vg), 29 (LXX,Vg); 29:12 (LXX); 30:31
(LXX); 35:14 (LXX);

[80] See 7:3;11:16;12:21;15:10,34;22:2,10;26:10;29:7;30:13,28,31;31:30;33:3;34:3,8;
36:26;39:16;40:18.

[81] See 3:17;6:10;8:7;10:4,7,15;27:12;34:16,35;35:2;36:4;39:2.

[82] In the case of 29:5 many other adjustments occur, thus the innovative effect on
meaning is not solely due to the interchange of word class.

the same meaning "unsparingly". This same expression occurs four other times in the OT. In three cases the translator again used a noun ܣܡ (Job 16:13) or ܣܢܣ (Job 27:22; Isa 30:14) in place of the Heb. verb and in only one case is a verb used, more specifically the m.s. participle ܣܢܣ (Hab 1:17). Thus, language difference dictated the interchange of word classes. The meaning remains the same, albeit a slight structural difference.

2. Ambiguity/Intra-/Inter-verse Influence. In the next example, word class interchange prompted by intra-verse influence and ambiguity resulted in a stylistically different proposition by the translator of P.

10:15   MT   אִם־רָשַׁעְתִּי אַלְלַי לִי   וְצָדַקְתִּי לֹא־אֶשָּׂא רֹאשִׁי
                        שְׂבַע קָלוֹן וּרְאֵה עָנְיִי:

"If I am guilty, Woe to me!
and (if) I am righteous, I cannot lift my head,
full of disgrace and seeing affliction."

P   ܐܢ ܚܛܝܬ ܗܐ ܠܝ ܘܐܢ ܙܟܝܬ ܠܐ ܐܪܝܡ ܪܝܫܝ.
                        ܘܣܒܥܬ ܒܗܬܐ ܘܚܙܝܬ ܡܘܟܟܝ.

"If I have sinned, Woe to me!
and if I am innocent, I cannot lift up my head;
I am full of shame and I have seen my affliction."

    In the final stich, the MT contains the somewhat ambiguous phrase "full of shame and seeing affliction". Precisely how this stich accords with the previous two and in particular the part of speech to which רְאֵה belongs, has long been a matter for discussion.[83] Given this ambiguity and the first person verbal forms earlier in this verse the translator rendered the Hebrew noun and adjective by verbs. Note also the LXX verbalized the first clause, whereas the Targum verbalized the second. The effect these changes have on the meaning of the MT is still synonymy, albeit in a stylistically different form.

3. Error. In over thirty verses, error suggests itself as the most probable motivation for word class differences. The majority result in an

---

[83] See, for example, ICC, p. 64; Dhorme, pp. 151-152; Habel, p. 184; Pope, p. 81.

innovative meaning,[84] while the remainder produce only stylistic changes between the MT and P.[85] Compare the following two examples:

8:2   MT   ‏ עד־אן תמלל־אלה   ורוח כביר <u>אמרי</u>־פיך:

       "How long will you say these things,
       and the words of your mouth be a mighty wind?"

P. ‏ܦܘܡܟ <u>ܬܗܐ</u> ‏ܘܐܬܗܐ ‏ܬܩܘܡ . ‏ܡܠܠ ‏ܬܬܠܠ ‏ܐܡܬܝ ‏ܟܡܐ

       "How long will you say these things,
       and your mouth be full of a mighty wind?"

P's treatment of Heb. ‏ אמרי "words of" in the second stich suggests an error as indicated by its translation ‏ܬܗܐ "(your mouth) is full". Syr. ‏ܬܗܐ is a homograph for the f.s. noun "word"; however the syntax of this stich would require the construct state ‏ܬܠܬ "word of your mouth". Thus, ‏ܬܗܐ is more likely a verb √‏ܬܗܐ suggesting a confusion of the liquids Resh and Lamedh and a transposition of radicals. The change produces an innovative meaning, albeit an insignificant one, for it is not Job's words that are likened to a mighty wind, but his mouth. Given the context the implication could be that since the mouth is the organ of speech, Job's words are still in fact "windy ones".

In the following example, error results specifically in synonymy with variation in style.

14:12   M T   ‏ ואיש שכב ולא־יקום   עד־<u>בלתי</u> שמים לא יקיצו
                               ‏ ולא־יערו משנתם:

       "so man lies down and does not rise;
       until the heavens are no more they will not awake,
       nor be roused out of their sleep."

P. ‏ܢܬܬܥܝܪܘܢ ‏ܠܐ ‏ܟܕ ‏ܒܠܝ ‏ܥܕ . ‏ܩܐܡ ‏ܠܐ ‏ܘܬܘܒ ‏ܓܒܪܐ
                            ‏ ܫܢܬܗܘܢ ‏ܡܢ ‏ܢܥ ‏ܘܠܐ.

---

84 See 7:20;8:2;11:4;14:20;15:11;16:3,20;20:21;21:7;22:12,29;23:7,10,17; 24:17;28:4; 29:4,12;31:21;33:19,20,27;34:6;36:17,19,29;37:6.
85 See 14:12;19:5;21:3;24:15;30:13,31;35:14.

"And a man who lies down does not rise;
until the heavens are worn out they will not be awakened,
nor startled out of their sleep."

The translator of P erroneously identified Heb. בִּלְתִּי, a
substantive used as a particle of negation,[86] as a verb, possibly the
infinitive construct בְּלוֹת derived from the root בלה "to wear out",[87]
hence the participle ܒܠܐ. The effect on meaning is still synonymy with
variation in style, for both propositions, although couched in different
words, ultimately mean the same thing - until the heavens are gone they
will not awake, i.e. since the heavens will always be they will never
awaken.

Suffix

There are a little over a thousand verses in the book of Job. Most
verses contain at least one suffix. Where one is lacking another verse will
yield two or more; thus we have a data supply of at least a thousand
examples of a suffix. A comparative examination of Suffix between the
MT and P revealed twenty-seven verses in which a suffix was omitted,
thirty-nine verses in which a suffix was added, and forty-nine verses in
which the translator represented the suffix in a different manner. Thus,
P departed from the MT in a little more than ten percent of the
occurrences.

1. Substitution. The adjustment termed substitution, be it also called
replacement or alternate representation, is specifically concerned with
the element to which a suffix is affixed, that is, whether the suffix is
attached to a verb, a preposition, or an object marker. The following
equivalences were found:

---

[86] See BDB, p. 116b, s.v. בלה.
[87] See BDB, p. 115a, s.v. בלה.

Heb. verbal suffix > Syr. ܠ + suffix[88]
Heb. verbal suffix > Syr. ܟܝ + suffix[89]
Heb. verbal suffix > Syr. ܒ + suffix[90]
Heb. verbal suffix > Syr. ܥܠ + suffix[91]
Heb. verbal suffix > Syr. independent pronoun[92]
Heb. ל + suffix > Syr. verbal suffix[93]
Heb. את + suffix > Syr. verbal suffix[94]
Heb. על + suffix > Syr. verbal suffix[95]
Heb. אל + suffix > Syr. verbal suffix[96]
Heb. ב + suffix > Syr. verbal suffix[97]

The motivations for these changes are primarily language difference and implicit to explicit exegesis. Syriac, and Aramaic in general, often expresses a pronominal object by the Lamedh with suffix. So, for example, in 3:21:

MT   המחכים למות ואיננו   <u>ויחפ רהו</u>   ממטמונים:
"Who wait for death, but it comes (lit. is) not;
and <u>search for it</u> more than for hidden treasure."

P   ܘܕܡܣܟܝ ܠܡܘܬܐ ܘܠܝܬܘܗܝ. ܗܐ ܕܘܢܗ ܐܝܟ ܠܓܘܙܐ ܕܣܝܡܬܐ.
"Who wait for death, but there is none;
and <u>search for it</u> as if for hidden treasure."

In stich two the MT contains the verb יחפרהו containing a verbal suffix. P, by contrast, was required to indicate the object-suffix by means

---

[88] See 3:21;7:8;9:3,5,16;10:2,9,14;12:7,15,23(2),24;19:2;23:5;31:29;32:8;33:12,24; 37:12; 39:15;40:28.
[89] See 9:31,35.
[90] See 10:8;33:26.
[91] See 13:26.
[92] See 24:20;36:13;40:13.
[93] See 6:24;15:17;22:14;32:10;34:2.
[94] See 13:10,11.
[95] See 19:5.
[96] See 21:19.
[97] See 36:25.

of the object marker Lamedh with suffix, for in this particular case P
translated the Heb. imperfect consecutive with a participle, and participles
do not take object-suffixes in Syriac.

In other cases P inserts a preposition, which then carries the suffix,
because the meaning of that preposition is implicit or contextually more
appropriate than a simple verbal suffix. Likewise, there are cases where
the preposition bearing the suffix is omitted and represented by a verbal
suffix because the preposition is awkward or redundant in a given
context. So, for example, in 36:25 the translator omits the superfluous
prepositional complement ב in the phrase חזו־בו and renders with a
verbal suffix, hence ܫܘܚܕܗܝ .

36:25   MT   כל־אדם חזו־בו   אנוש יביט מרחוק.
             "All men have seen it, man regards (it) from afar."

P   ܘܒܢ̈ܝ ܐܢܫܐ ܫܘܚܕܗܝ ܘܚܪܘ ܒܗ ܡܢ ܪܘܚܩܐ.
         "And men have seen it, and they beheld (it) from afar."

What both examples have in common, and for that matter all cases
in this category of substitution, is their effect on meaning. Synonymy
still prevails, only the structure is different.
2. Omission.   Language difference, redundancy, error, intra-verse
influence and occasionally ambiguity[98] resulted in the omission of a
suffix in P-Job. Synonymy with variation in structure or style and
innovative meaning relations occur due to this omission.
a. Language Difference and Redundancy. In eight verses language
difference and redundancy go hand in hand as the motivations responsible
for omission of a suffix, for it is inherent in the Peshitta - at least in P-
Job - to omit redundant features of the MT. Four omissions result in a
synonymous meaning relation with variation at the structural level[99] and
four result in synonymy with variation in style.[100]

So, for example, in 3:21 (discussed above under substitution), the
translator of P omitted the suffix of ואיננו in the clause למות ואיננו

---

98 See 5:5;20:28.
99 See 3:21;33:14;37:13;40:2.
100 See 5:27;29:16;36:23;38:29.

המחכים "who wait for death but it is not". The suffix is somewhat redundant for the absolute form אין would still carry the same meaning "there is none", that is there is no death for those who wait. Thus, the translator used the unsuffixed ܠܝܬ , a slight stylistic difference. Note, however, error cannot totally be dismissed, for haplography (by the translator) with the Nun of אין and the following Waw conjunctive might account for the omitted ־נו suffix.

In 29:16, language difference and redundancy again resulted in the omission of a suffix.

MT   אב אנכי לאביונים   ורב לא־ידעתי אחקרהו:
"I was a father to the needy,
and the case (which) I did not know I searched it out."

P   ܐܒܐ ܗܘܝܬ ܠܬܒܪ̈ܐ. ܘܕܝܢܐ ܕܠܐ ܝܕܥܬ ܗܘܝܬ ܒܨܝܢܗ.
"I was a father to the unfortunate,
and a judgment which I did not know I searched out."

In the second stich the translator has omitted the redundant verbal suffix. The difference is only structural, thereby preserving synonymy with the MT.

b.   Error and Intra-verse influence.[101] In 3:21 above we saw an example of suffix omission that may have been caused by haplography (איננו > ܠܝܬ). The effect on meaning was merely a structural difference yielding synonymy.[102] Other cases do exist in which error produces a stylistic difference[103] and even an innovative meaning.[104] Consider the following two examples:

18:19   M T : לא נין לו ולא־נכד <u>בעמו</u>   ואין שריד במגוריו:
"He has no offspring or posterity among his people,
and there is no survivor in his places of sojourn."

---

[101] See 6:5;11:20;32:14;34:29 for other examples of intra-verse influence resulting in omission of a suffix which are not discussed below.

[102] See also 2:6;7:18;27:6;32:14 where error produces only structural changes.

[103] See 5:5;9:33;18:19;20:28;39:16.

[104] See 23:3,17;29:14;38:10.

P   ܠܐ ܥܕܪ ܠܗ ܡܐ ܘܠܐ ܕܘܟܪܢ ܒܥܡ̈ܐ.
         ܘܠܐ ܢܗܘܐ ܠܗ ܡܣܝܒܪ ܟܕ ܒܬܘܬܒܘܬܗ.

"He has no name and no memorial among the nation,
and there will be no remnant in his sojourning."

In stich one P omits translating the pronominal suffix (בעמו).
Haplography may once again be responsible for this omission, for note
the following Waw conjunctive. The effect on meaning is but a stylistic
change. By contrast, the following verse contains an omission that results
in an innovative meaning.

29:14   MT   צדק לבשתי וילבשני   כמעיל וצניף   מ ש פ ט י :
           "I put on righteousness and it clothed me;
           my justice (was) like a cloak and turban."

P   ܡܩܒܐ ܠܒܫܬ. ܘܠܒܫܢܝ ܐܝܟ ܦܪܝܣܐ ܘܐܟܠܝܠܐ ܕܕܝܢ̈ܐ.
           "I put on truth, and it clothed me
           like a mantle and a crown of judgment."

It is quite probable that the translator erroneously omitted
transcribing the Yodh suffix of Heb. משפטי. Note, however, that intra-
verse influence may also be responsible, for the translator clearing
interpreted the second Hebrew stich as the vehicle of comparison
dependent on וילבשני of stich one, i.e. as if the Hebrew read משפט
וילבשני כמעיל וצניף. Thus, the Hebrew pronominal suffix would
be semantically inappropriate. The meaning relation that is achieved is
clearly innovative. Furthermore, the LXX translates similarly, omitting
the pronominal suffix and joining stich two with one, thereby creating a
comparative statement; thus versional influence is suggested.[105]
3. Addition. Many of the same motivations that resulted in an omission
of a suffix likewise account for the addition of one. More specifically, in
P-Job, there are cases involving language difference, error, intra-verse

---

[105] The LXX reads Δικαιοσυνην δε ενδεδυκειν, ημφιασαμην δε κριμα ισα
διπλοιδι "Also I put on righteousness, and clothed myself with judgment like a
mantle". Versional parallels and in some cases influence also occur for omissions of
suffix in 2:6 (Tg.); 6:5 (LXX); 27:6 (LXX,Vg);38:10 (LXX); 38:29 (LXX,Vg); 39:16
(Tg.).

influence. Above all, the one that predominates is implicit to explicit exegesis. Meaning relations of synonymy, both in structure and style, and innovation result.

a. Language difference. Only three examples of addition of a suffix due to language difference occur in P-Job (3:17;17:9;22:9). All deal with a similar grammatical and syntactical structure, namely Heb. m. adj. in construct + dual noun > Syr. relative pronoun + m.pl. absolute adj. + plural noun + suffix:

3:17 Heb. יגיעי כח > Syr. ܐܝܠܝܢ ܕܠܐܝܢ ܒܚܝܠܗܘܢ
"weary ones of strength" "those who are weary in strength"
17:9 Heb. טהר־ידים > Syr. ܘܕܕܟܝܢ ܐܝܕܘܗܝ
"the pure of hands" "the one whose hands are pure"
22:29 Heb. שח עינים > Syr. ܘܕܡܟܝܟܢ ܥܝܢܘܗܝ
"the lowly of eyes" "the one whose eyes are lowly"

The difference is simply one of style, for the Syriac language does permit the use of an adjective in construct with a noun.[106] Thus, synonymy still prevails.

b. Error[107] and Intra-verse influence.[108] While haplography was cited as the cause for the omission of a suffix earlier, dittography may likewise be responsible for the addition of a suffix in 33:17.

MT להסיר אדם מעשה וגוה מגבר יכסה:
"to turn away man (from his) work,
and cut off pride from man."
P ܠܡܥܒܪܘ ܐܢܫܐ ܡܢ ܥܒܕ̈ܘܗܝ ܘܦܓܪܗ ܕܓܒܪܐ ܢܟܣܐ.
"to remove man from his affairs,
and cover the body of man."

---

106 See, for example, 3:20 (Heb. למרי נפש > Syr. ܠܡܪ̈ܝܪܝ ܢܦܫܐ); 9:4 (Heb. חכם לבב > Syr. ܚܟܝܡ ܠܒܐ ܗܘ; Heb. אמיץ כח > Syr. ܥܫܝܢ ܚܝܠܐ); 14:1 (Heb. קצר ימים > Syr. ܘܒܨܝܪ ܝܘܡ̈ܬܐ ܗܘ); 37:24 (Heb. כל־חכמי־לב > Syr. ܠܟܠܗܘܢ ܚܟܝ̈ܡܝ ܠܒܐ).

107 See 27:6 and 38:37 for examples of addition of a suffix not discussed in this section. Both result in only a structurally different text.

108 See 11:16;15:20*;16:22*;18:13*;28:23;34:11 (* indicates Innovation in P).

In stich one, the translator added the 3pms suffix, as if the Heb.
read מעשׂהו. The following Waw conjunctive suggests a possible
dittography on the part of the translator, but explicit exegesis cannot
totally be discounted. The effect on meaning is but a variation in
structure, thus still a synonymous meaning relation. By contrast in the
following example, 28:20, error once again may account for the addition
of a suffix in the final stich. Though a slightly innovative meaning may
prevail.

28:20   MT   :בִינה וה מקום זה ואי תבוא מאין והחכמה
             "From where does wisdom come?,
                and where is the place of understanding?"

P   .ܗܠܒܘܣܡܘܗ ܐܬܪܐ ܗܘ ܘܐܝܢܐ .ܐܬܝܐ ܐܝܡܟܐ ܚܟܡܬܐ
         "From where does wisdom come?,
            and what is the place of its/her understanding?"

P translated Heb. בִּינָה "understanding" as if it read בִּינָתָהּ "her
understanding" or more erroneously בִּינָהּ . The change in meaning at
first seems unsubstantial; however on closer look the MT suggests the
personification of two nouns: Wisdom and Understanding. The addition
of the suffix in P implies that there is only one entity, Wisdom, to whom
belongs the attribute of understanding. Thus, error and intra-verse
influence with stich one resulted in an innovative meaning. Note, also,
that the addition of the 3pfs suffix also occurs in the similar verse, 28:12.
c. Implicit to Explicit Exegesis. The majority of verses in which a suffix
is added can be attributed to explicit exegesis.[109] The effect on meaning
is still synonymy with variation at the structural level. Consider one
example, 13:18:

        MT   :אצדק כי־אני ידעתי משפט ערכתי הנה־נא
             "Behold, I have arranged (my) case;
                I know that I will be vindicated."

---

[109] See 9:26;11:16,20;13:3,18,22;14:15;17:6;18:9;20:12;21:5;23:9;24:12,15; 27:17;
28:23;29:9,18,25;30:24;32:10;33:8,17;34:29;38:37;41:4.

P   .ܝܒ ܗܡ ܐܢܗܪ ܐܢܐ ܚܝܠ ܘܝܕ. ܐܢܐ ܐܟܬܒ ܐܢܐ ܐܦ ܐܡ

"Behold, I also am bringing my judgment;
and I know that I am innocent."

The translator added the implicit pronominal suffix of Heb. מֹשְׁפַט
in stich one, thus ܕܝܢܝ. The LXX similarly preserves the possessive
pronoun. However the implicit nature of this pronoun suggests Versional
parallel rather than direct influence in this case.[110] In this particular
case, error, specifically a dittography with the following Yodh (ידעתי)
might be considered.

*   *   *

From the preceding analysis of eight areas of grammar we have
seen a plethora of grammatical elements that diverge from the MT. It is
no surprise to have found language difference as a significant factor
influencing many of these translational departures from the Hebrew text.
However, language difference was not the only influential motivation.
Intra-/inter-verse influence and error were equally as prevalent. Note
that these three motivations are universal in that they explain deviations in
almost every area of grammar examined. By contrast, motivations such
as implicit to explicit exegesis (see Pronoun and Suffix) and ambiguity
(see Voice) are more topic specific, that is they are motivations that more
properly pertain to only a few topics of grammar.

As for adjustments, substitution is by far the most common,
accounting for differences in all but two topics (see Pronoun and Suffix),
whereas addition and omission were found only in the areas of pronoun
and suffix.

An overall view of these adjustments in grammar on the effect on
meaning finds Synonymy-Structure the most prominent semantic relation
for Tense and Suffix; Synonymy-Style more prevalent for Gender and
Word Class; and equally distributed for the other topics. Innovative
propositions are most frequent in Person and fairly common for Voice
and Word Class. Clarity was most noteworthy for Tense and Voice
where it jointly served as an effect on meaning with Synonymy-Structure.

---

[110] For other versional parallels of an explicit suffix, see 14:15;17:6;32:10;33:8, all
LXX and Vg.

IV

Syntax

A comparative study of the syntax of the MT and P-Job would *seem* to be a relatively straightforward process owing to their language family relationship - as against, e.g., Greek and Hebrew. However, it becomes more difficult if we seek to isolate and evaluate departures that are *purely* syntactic in nature. In fact, of the more than one thousand verses in the text of Job, syntactical divergences occur in less than one hundred verses. The key word here is "purely" for in many cases, as we will see, an adjustment in grammar, semantics or style precipitated a subsequent syntactic change.

Our goal here is not to rewrite or restate the rules of Syriac grammar. This has been done by Theodore Nöldeke,[1] C. Brockelmann[2] and R. Duval.[3] And more recently the studies of G. Goldenberg,[4] I. Avinery,[5] T. Muraoka[6] and A. Guillaumont[7] have attempted to clarify those points of syntax not fully dealt with in the earlier studies.

---

[1] *A Compendious Syriac Grammar.* James A. Crichton, trans. (London: Clarendon Press, rpt. 1979).

[2] *Syrische Grammatik mit Paradigmen, Literatur, Chrestomathie und Glossar* (Leipzig: Veb Verlag Enzyklopädie, rpt. 1981).

[3] *Traitè de grammaire syriaque* (Paris, 1881).

[4] "On Syriac Sentence Structure" in *Arameans, Aramaic and the Aramaic Literary Tradition.* Michael Sokoloff, ed. (Bar-Ilan University Press, 1983): 97-140.

[5] "On the Nominal Clause in the Peshitta." *JSS* 22(1977): 48-49.

[6] "On the Syriac Particle ܐܘܟ." *Bibliotheca Orientalis* 34(1977): 21-22; "On the Nominal Clause in the Syriac Gospels." *JSS* 20(1975): 28-37.

[7] "La phrase dite "nominal" en syriaque." *Comptes rendus du Groupe Linguistique d'Etudes Chamito-Sèmitique* 5(1949): 31-33.

The earlier comprehensive works of Nöldeke, Brockelmann and Duval had in common their approach to syntax, namely dividing their studies into two parts: Parts-of-Speech (including word order) and Clausal Relationships. It is this division which will also be incorporated in the present study.

In the first part we will look at not so much the function of individual parts-of-speech - for adjustments here are covered under Grammar and Semantics - but more specifically word order, that is the position individual parts-of-speech hold in a sentence or proposition in the MT and how and why the P maintained or departed from this order. It is here that the language similarity between Hebrew and Syriac is quite apparent, for Syriac syntax allows for much the same word order as the Hebrew with but a few variations. It is these variations which will be examined for adjustment, motivation and effect on meaning.

The second part of this comparative study of syntax will examine clausal relationships. This in itself is an enormous undertaking, therefore, an examination of the waw conjunctive has been chosen as a test case. As defined by Bruce K. Waltke and M. O'Connor the role of the waw conjunctive is twofold: "it conjoins nouns on the phrasal level and it conjoins clauses."[8] It is P's treatment of the waw in this second role - clausal conjoining - that is examined here.

When specifically syntactic adjustments do occur they involve two adjustments that are unique to the area of syntax, namely transposition and redivision. Addition, omission and substitution occur as motivations in all areas of translation as demonstrated in the chapters on grammar, semantics and style, hence they are universal adjustments. However, in the area of Syntax they are infrequent as the major adjustment resulting in a syntactic change. This is no doubt due to the fact that in most cases a major semantic or grammatical change occasioned by these adjustments produced a secondary syntactic alteration. Consider, for example, 32:11b:

MT   עד־תבונתיכם   אזין   הן הוחלתי לדבריכם
עד־תחקרון מלין:

---

[8] *Biblical Hebrew Syntax*, p. 648, #39.2. Waltke and O'Connor do of course further define the type of clauses that are conjoined and how the waw functions under these circumstances.

"Behold, I waited for your words,
I gave ear to your reasons
While you searched for words."

P. ܢܘܬܠܠܝܗ ܪ ܟܘܬܐ ܘܬܘܬܗ ܘ ܢܘܢܠܢܘܗ ܠܢܝ ܕܘܬܫ ܟܗ
ܗܒ ܒܘܬܠ . ܢ ܘ ܢܘܬܘܝ

"Behold, I held my peace for you and for your words
and I gave ear until you finished
then I searched you out with words."

Each stich in P is syntactically distinct from the MT. In 32:11a the addition of a second direct object altered the MT's Interj + V/S + DO to the P's Interj + V/S + DO + DO. In 32:11b the translator of P construed the Heb. עד־תבונתיכם "to your reasons" as a subordinate verbal clause ܢܘܬܠܠܝܗ ܪ ܟܘܬܐ "until you finished",[9] hence altering the Heb. syntax of V/S + PPh to Conj + V/S + SubCl(Adv + V/S). In 32:11c, the P has not only transformed a clause dependent on 32:11b into an independent proposition, but in an attempt to harmonize this clause with 32:11a/b has altered the 2pmpl to the 1ps verbal form and then added a 2pmpl pronominal object. With these changes the syntax the P presents is naturally different from that of the MT. Thus, in this verse adjustments in semantics and grammar quite naturally also resulted in a secondary syntactic departure from the MT.

At times too it must be noted that the position a word holds in a proposition may go unchanged but its syntactic function is altered by virtue of a grammatical, semantic or stylistic change. Consider, for example, 7:10:

MT: לא־ישוב עוד לביתו ולא־יכירנו עוד מקמו:

"He will not again return to his house,
nor will his place any longer recognize him."

P ܡܢܝܬܠ ܒܘܬ ܢܒܘܬܫܗܒܬܪܟܐ ܡܘܬܠ ܒܘܬ ܠܦܗܡ ܟܗ .

"He no longer returns to his house,
and he no longer recognizes his place."

---

9 Dhorme (p. 478) suggests the P read עד תכליתכם "until your completion".

The translator of P understood Heb. מקמו as the direct object of
the verb rather than the subject, no doubt through analogy with stich one.
Thus, the Heb. word order of stich two Conj + Neg + V +DO + Adv + S
became Conj + Neg + V/S + Adv + DO. No rearrangement of the text
occurred - for מקמו = ܡܢ ܕܘܟܬܗ still holds the final position - but rather
a change in the syntactic function of a single word occurred.

I. Word Order

Of those instances involving departures from word order as
presented in the MT, language difference, ambiguity and error are the
predominant motivations. However, intra-/inter-verse influence, parallel
verse influence, ideology and versional parallels are also attested, albeit
infrequently. As stated above two adjustments predominate in departures
in word order: transposition and redivision. As for effect on meaning
synonymy with variation in style and innovation frequently result,
synonymy especially in cases of transposition due to language difference
and innovation especially where redivision within or between verses
occurs.   Clarity for the translator likewise occurs in those cases
involving ambiguity.
1. Transposition. Transposition is a specifically syntactic adjustment that
describes a rearrangement in word order. Language difference may be a
significant factor in promoting transposition, but ambiguity/error and
intra-verse influence are also present.
a. Language difference or Stylistic preferences?   Syriac word order,
much like Hebrew, permits a somewhat free arrangement of its principal
parts with variation dictated by emphasis or stylistic preferences.
Nöldeke points out that under certain circumstances, as in "purely verbal
sentences", the predicate takes precedence "but this is by no means a fast
rule."[10] However, in P-Job, there are numerous instances in which the
translator has chosen to "standardize" or present a more prosaic word
order as against the MT.[11]   Consider for example P's translation of the
Heb. אף־אני אחוה דעי found in 32:10b and 32:17b.

---

[10] *A Compendious Syriac Grammar*, pp. 258-259.
[11] For additional examples of transposition due to language difference resulting in a
synonymous meaning with variation only in structure or style see 3:7b,11;9:2b,3b,23;

32:10b   ܝܘܠܠ ܝ ܢܐܢܐܠܐܪ ܐܐܪ ܗܐܢ =

                Conj + Interj + S + V/S/IO + DO

32:17b   ܝܘܠܠ ܐܐܪ ܗܐ ܐܢܐܐܢ   =

                Conj + V/S + Interj + S + DO

In the first appearance of this clause P has regularized the word order, neatly arranging the parts of speech in standard form and even supplying an assumed indirect object. The effect on meaning is clearly synonymy. In the second occurrence the P provides an alternate word order, this time paralleling the MT in its precedence of the verbal form, but then transposing the interjectory particle and independent pronoun with the direct object. The effect on meaning is once again synonymy with variation only in style.

Precisely why the translator chose to vary the word order in each case, however, is unclear, especially when we consider the close proximity of these two semantically parallel phrases. Could it be for literary effect? or just an unconscious slip? Most of the transpositions in word order leave questionable the reason/cause for their adjustment. The translator may have merely chosen a more simplistic, standard word order, as against the MT's poetic license, with the intent of seeking greater clarity in the delivery of his message. There are cases, however, where the translator felt no regrets at reproducing the freedom in word order presented in the MT.[12] Therefore, language difference cannot be cited as the motivational factor; likewise intra-/inter-verse influence has been discounted in each case as well as versional influence.

Thus, in most cases of transposition the cause cannot clearly be delineated. However, in P's treatment of one particular type of phrase language difference may be indicated, namely in the formula "And N1 answered N2 and said". It is distinct from the standard speech

---

10:11b,19;12:11;13:6b,13b,16b,24,27a;15:3b,9b,16b;16:2a,8a,10c,22a;17:7,13b;18:6, 8,9,17;19:5,6,8,9,13,16,23;20:12;21:17a/c,19,24,32;22:4b,7,17;24:7;27:16a,20a;28:14 ,24,25,26;29:10,12,17,23;30:12,13,22,31;31:5,7a/b,15,16a/b,17,24,30a,35c,36,38,39; 32:3,10,15;33:2,5,6,10,28;34:4a/b,8,11,13;35:16;36:15;37:2a/b,8;38:1,6,10,13,19,28, 30, 34,36;39:5,7,9,29,30;40:4,9,10,13,26,30,31;41:11,13,19,24;42:3,11,17.

[12] In Chapter III, for example, see vv. 4a,6a,7a,11b,16a and 24. Note especially that in vv. 7 and 11 transposition occurred in one stich which contained a variation in word order due to emphasis, but not in the other stich which likewise contained a free arrangement of the parts of speech.

introductory formula "And N answered and said"[13] in that the object of
the speaker's words is specifically expressed. This type of clause occurs
nine times in P-Job. In four cases the adversary is the speaker and the
Lord the recipient of his words (1:7,9; 2:2,4) and in five cases the Lord is
the speaker and Job the recipient (38:1;40:1,3,6; 42:1). Note also in two
of these cases the Heb. also contains the prepositional phrase "from the
whirlwind" after the direct object, i.e. "And the Lord answered Job from
the whirlwind and said" (38:1;40:6). Compare the word order of the P
and MT in these clauses:

MT ויען השטן את־יהוה ויאמר > P ܪܟܬܐ ܠܡܬܒ ܐܪܟܬܐ ܗ ܡܬܐ ܟܠܝܘ ܪܟܐ

MT ויען יהוה את־איוב ויאמר > P ܟܪܢܟ ܐܟܬܐ ܐܟܪܝ ܗܟܬܐ ܗܪܝ ܐܟܬܐ

M T ויען־יהוה את־איוב מן סערה ויאמר > P ܠܠܒܠܟ ܡܪ ܐܟܢܟ ܐܟܬܐ ܗ ܐܪܝܟ ܐܟܬܐ

The MT presents the word order Conj + V + S + DO (+ PPh) +
Conj + V/S. Note that the DO (and PPh) is placed after the initial verb
and the final verb ויאמֶר is pointed with the Pathah indicating direct
discourse follows. By contrast, P presents the word order (Conj) + V + S
+ Conj + V/S + PPh1(= DO) (+ PPh2); hence the formula is now "And
N1 answered and said to N2 (from X)". The translator has transferred
the DO (and PPh) after the final verb, thus necessitating the object to be
stated in the form of a prepositional phrase as dictated by the semantics of
the verb √אמֹר "to say (to)". It is almost as if the translator of P was
translating another Hebrew formula "And N1 answered and said to
N2".[14] It is significant, too, that of the fourteen appearances of this
formula elsewhere in the Hebrew Bible, P makes a similar syntactic
adjustment in all but five cases.[15] In three of these cases the lack of
adjustment is understandable: in two the N2 is an expansive phrase better
suited in its original position (2 Sam 4:9 and 1 Kgs 12:13) and in one

---

[13] In the book of Job see 3:2;4:1;6:1;8:1;9:1;11:1;12:1;15:1;16:1;18:1;19:1;20:1; 21:1;
22:1;23:1;25:1; 26:1;32:6;34:1;35:1.

[14] See Gen 27:37,39;31:14,31,36,43; 1 Sam 1:17;29:9; 2 Sam 14:18; 1Kgs
1:43;2:22;13:6; Joel 2:19; Amos 7:14; Zech 3:4;4:6;6:5; Ruth 2:11; Ezra 10:2; 1 Chr
12:17; 2 Chr 34:15.

[15] See Josh 7:20;1 Sam 9:19;20:28,32;21:6;25:10; 2 Sam 15:21,43(42 in P);1 Kgs 1:36.

verse the N2 has been omitted (2 Kgs 7:2). Thus, in only two cases has P
not rearranged the formula (1 Sam 21:5[16] and 22:14).

Versional influence is not responsible for transposition in this
formula. The Targum parallels the MT and only once does the LXX
parallel P in its rearrangement (1:9). Thus, we may have here a
formulaic pattern that is preferable in the Syriac of the Peshitta (or at
least to the translator of P), indicating language difference as the cause.
Regardless of the precise motivation, in this case P's translation has the
same semantic effect, albeit in a stylistically different proposition, hence
synonymy still prevails.

b. Ambiguity/Error. The second most common reason for transposition
jointly involves ambiguity and error, ambiguity in that uncertainty may
exist as to the exact syntactic function of elements within a sentence, and
error in that the translator made the wrong selection where options
existed from the evaluator's perspective, given the current state of the
MT. This selection resulted in innovative propositions.[17]   Before
examining one such example a further comment must be made: wherever
ambiguity is cited as a motivation it must be remembered that from the
translator's perspective, clarity is the effect on meaning, for he no doubt
felt that his translation had clarified any uncertainty in the text. Now
consider the following example:

15:5 MT   כי יאלף עונך פיך   ותבחר לשון ערומים:
              "For your iniquity teaches your mouth,
                  and you choose the tongue of the crafty."

P   ܕܝܠܦ ܠܟ ܓܠܐ ܕܝ ܦܘܡܟ ܢܬܝ ܚܛܗܐ.
              ܘܬܪܥܐ ܐܝܬ ܕܒܠܫܢ ܢܟܠܐ ‡
              "For your mouth teaches sins,
                  and you take pleasure in the tongue of deceit."

The first stich clearly permits an ambiguity in subject and object;
however the Heb. is generally taken as presenting the word order Conj +
V + S + DO, hence "your iniquity" is the subject and "your mouth" the

---

[16] The lack of transposition is peculiar here for in the following verse, 21:6, P returns to
his usual tendency to place N2 at the end of the formula.
[17] See, for example, 15:29;17:11;18:13,14;22:30;36:7,18;39:12.

object. "Your mouth" as the object in the MT may seem peculiar, but analogy with the second stich - where "the tongue of the crafty", hence, also an organ of speech is the object - may have clarified this ambiguity. The P, by contrast, transposed the S and DO of the MT and erroneously choose "your mouth" as the subject. It clearly indicated "your sins" as the DO by pluralizing it, thus making certain it would not be construed as the subject of the singular verb. The meaning relation between the MT and P is clearly innovative, for it is no longer the iniquity man does that teaches his mouth to speak, but just the opposite. Man's mouth emits sins. To the translator, however, clarity was the effect on meaning, for to him his translation clearly preserved the meaning he believed the MT contained, albeit in a clearer proposition.

c. Intra-verse influence. Verses in which intra-verse influence is a significant factor in producing a transposition in word order are hardly as prolific as those in which language difference or ambiguity/error are the primary motivations.[18] One such example, however, occurs in 10:5a:

MT   הכימי אנוש ימיך   אם־שנותיך כימי גבר:
      "Are your days like the days of man,
      or are your years like the days of man?"

P   אם ܝܘܡܬܟ איך ܝܘܡܘܗܝ ܕܐܢܫܐ אܢܬ.
      אם ܫܢܝܟ איך ܝܘܡܘܗܝ אܢܬ ܕܓܒܪܐ.
      "Or are your days like the days of man?
      Or are your years like the days of man?"

In stich one the P has transposed the elements of the simile, placing the tenor (your days) before the preposition and vehicle (like the days of man). The motivation for this adjustment may be the syntax of the second stich in the MT where the more prosaic pattern of tenor + like + vehicle occurs. Then, too, one cannot discount the fact that it may be language difference that dictated the P present the more standard word

---

18 See also 3:20a;12:11;13:6b,13b;31:5 where language difference and intra-verse influence produced a transposition in syntax.

order in stich one.[19] P's transposition of the Hebrew syntax clearly does
not affect the meaning, providing but a stylistic difference.
2. Redivision. Redivision within a verse, that is between stichs, and
between verses occurs in a little over thirty places in P-Job. Three
motivations - ambiguity, error and intra-/inter-verse influence are the
chief motivations causing this adjustment, often all three working
together on a single verse(s). In all but a very rare case the effect on
meaning that results is innovative.[20]
a. Ambiguity/Error. Ambiguity and error, sometimes but not always,
go hand in hand as motivations prompting the redivision within and
between verses: ambiguity, in that the translator was simply uncertain
where the division should be, and error, in that he subsequently chose the
wrong place to divide. In the next example, it is precisely these causes
that prompted the translator to make a redivision within the MT verse:

20:15   MT חיל בלע ויקאנו   מבטנו יורשנו אל:
            "He swallows riches and vomits them up,
             God casts them out of his belly."

        P .מטמה בי מה אلבטהנ והلل ملאكלהמהته
               הטנה יהנהבכטה אלנكא
        "And the food which he swallowed he will bring it forth
         from his belly, and God will destroy it."

    In contrast to the MT, P divided this verse after מבטנו, hence
understanding מבטנו as dependent on ויקאנו. Intra-verse influence
might also be cited as influential in determining the placement of מבטנו,
for clearly the semantics of stich one does not preclude such a division.
The overall verse still contains the same information, albeit each
individual stich now presents it in a slightly different form.[21]

---

[19] For P's treatment of the interrogative in this verse, see Chapter VI: Style: Sentence
Type: Interrogatives. For P's treatment of similes see also Chapter VI: Style: Figurative
Language.
[20] See, for example, 15:16 כמים עולה איש־שתה ונאלח כי־נתעב אף. In P the
equivalent of Heb. איש is joined to stich one which, owing to the general nature of the
term איש in this verse, still yields the same meaning.
[21] Mandl (pp. 13,15) suggested that the P altered this metaphor because it was offensive.

In the next example, 38:28-29, error alone is responsible for redivision between verses, for the semantics of these two verses in no way projects a possible ambiguity.

MT   היש־למטר אב   או מי־הוליד אגלי־טל:

מבטן מי יצא הקרח   וכפר שמים מי ילדו:

"Does the rain have a father?
or who begat the drops of dew?
From whose womb does the ice come forth
and the hoarfrost of heaven, Who begat it?"

P

"Does the rain have a father?
or who begat the drops?
From whose womb have the dew and ice come forth?
and who begat the hoarfrost of heaven?"

P joined Heb. טל, the *nomen rectum* at the end of 28, to verse 29 as an additional accusative of יצא = נפק. Note it also added the waw conjunctive before the equivalent of טל and before the equivalent of קרח which now both hold the primary position. He then pluralized the verb יצא = נפק, thus unmistakingly indicating that both are the subjects of verse 29 and in no way belong to verse 28. This redivision resulted in an innovative proposition, albeit rather insignificant.[22]

b. Intra-/Inter-verse influence. In some cases the semantics within a verse or between verses may have led a translator to question the division of a verse, hence intra-/inter-verse influence prompted redivision. Note, however, error and ambiguity cannot totally be dismissed even in these circumstances, for the semantics may have led the translator to his

---

[22] Other examples of redivision prompted by ambiguity and/or error resulting in an innovative proposition occur in 9:21;15:23,24(Vg/Tg);16:10;19:24,26; 20:15,18, 25;21:34; 22:3-4,15-16;23:10-12(LXX w/ further redivisions);24:23-24;27:21; 28:4-5;30:17-18;31:26-27; 32:15-16;34:25-26,32-33;36:17;38:17-18;39:1-2,27-28.

erroneous conclusion regarding the proper division.[23] Consider, for
example, 37:5:

MT ירעם אל בקולו נפלאות   עשׂה גדלות ולא נדע׃
"God thunders wondrously with his voice,
   the one who does great things which (lit. and) we do not know."

P   ܢܪܥܡ ܐܠܗܐ ܒܩܠܗ.
ܕܥܒܕ ܬܕܡܪܬܐ ܘܪܘܪܒܬܐ ܘܠܐ ܡܬܝܕܥܢ.
"And God will thunder with his voice,
   He does wonders and great things and it is unknown."

P connected נפלאות with the second stich, hence functioning now
as a second accusative of the verb עשׂה rather than as an adverb
modifying ירעם in stich one. Semantics and in particular parallel verse
influence may have prompted the translator to make such a redivision.
For if we look elsewhere in Job (5:9;9:10;42:3) we find נפלאות as an
accusative in a similar proposition. Consider these passages:

5:9   עשׂה גדלות ואין חקר   נפלאות עד־אין מספר׃
9:10   עשׂה גדלות עד־אין חקר ונפלאות עד־אין מספר׃
42:3b   לכן הגדתי ולא אבין נפלאות ממני ולא אדע׃

In each we find נפלאות as the object of the implied עשׂה or the
stated אבין. Note also in 42:3 the similar לא אדע closes the verse,
quite close to לא נדע of 37:5. Thus, the translator may have
unconsciously or consciously adjusted the division of this verse on the
basis of the syntactic function of נפלאות in parallel passages.[24] The
effect on meaning is clearly innovative, albeit lacking in any major
ideological repercussions.

---

[23] See, for example, 20:17(Vg/Tg);24:22,23-24;27:21;28:4-5;30:7-8,17-18;31:26-
27;32:15-16;34:25-26,32-33;37:5;38:17-18;39:1-2,27-28.

[24] See also Pss 72:18;86:10;98:1 and especially 136:4 where נפלאות likewise appears in
a similar passage.

In the next example, 31:26-27, redivision prompted by inter-verse influence and resulting in an innovative meaning is illustrated. However, here redivision is between verses rather than within a verse.

MT   אם־אראה אור כי יהל   וירח יקר הלך:
      ויפת בסתר לבי   ותשק ידי לפי:

> "If I have seen the light when it shines,
> or the moon moving in splendor;
> and my heart has been secretly (lit. in secret) enticed,
> and my hand has kissed my mouth;"

P   ܐܢ ܚܙܝܬ ܢܘܗܪܐ ܟܕ ܕܢܚ ܣܗܪܐ ܟܕ ܢܗܪ.
     ܐܢ ܐܙܠ ܐܬܦܬܝ ܠܒܝ ܒܟܣܝܐ. ܘܢܫܩܬ ܐܝܕܝ ܠܦܘܡܝ...

> "If I have seen the light when it shines
> or the moon when it burns fiercely;
> If my heart went and was enticed in secret,
> and my hand kissed my mouth;"

P clearly divided the Heb. verse after יקר, understanding יקר as a verb rather than adverb and connecting הלך with the following verse as a second verb for the noun לבי.   On closer examination it becomes evident that it is not merely semantics that caused this redivision of verse but intra-verse influence with the syntax of 26a that produced the syntactical adjustment in 26b, thus resulting in redivision between verses 26 and 27. Consider the following syntactical analysis of these two verses:

(v. 26) MT Conj + V/S + DO1 + SubConj + V/S // Conj + DO2 + Adv + V >>
        P   Conj + V/S + DO + SubConj + V/S // Conj + DO + SubConj + V/S
(v.27) MT Conj + V + PPh(= Adv) + S // Conj + V + S + DO[25] >>
        P   Conj + V + Conj + V + PPh(= Adv) + S // Conj + V + S + DO

The significant syntactic catalyst here is contained in 26a. The MT contains a dependent clause (SubConj + V/S = כי יהל) modifying the

---

[25] The Lamedh functions as an indicator of the direct object in both the MT and P.

direct object (אור) of the verb אראה. P imposed this syntactic order on 26b, hence rightly interpreting ירה as an additional direct object of אראה in 26a, but then analyzing יקר as a verb contained in a dependent clause necessitating the addition of a subordinate conjunction בד. Thus both stichs recorded a DO + SubConj + V/S. With this adjustment the translator of P had but one recourse in dealing with the final הלך in the MT's 26b and that was to connect it with the following verse, hence also altering the word order of verse 27.

As far as effect on meaning is concerned, P's adjustments have resulted in innovative propositions, but not at a significant level, for we still have the same semantic elements only they have been presented in an alternate manner.

II. Clausal Relationships

Within the Hebrew text of Job and for that matter characteristic of the Hebrew language is the ever present, prolific and often superfluous waw conjunctive. The function the waw conjunctive serves , however, is not always co-ordinative in nature. Ronald J. Williams demonstrates this fact by providing an additional twelve functions of the waw conjunctive.[26] Thus, by examining P's translation of the waw conjunctive we can gain a greater insight into how the translator and the Syriac of the Peshitta present clausal relationships, as well as the type of clausal relationship the translator perceived in the MT.

In the MT to Job the waw conjunctive occurs 1203 times. The text of P retains a total of 1029, omitting 141 and providing a substitution in 33 cases. In addition, P also adds a waw conjunctive in 399 cases. It is according to these three adjustments - omission, addition, substitution - that this study is structured.

1. Omission. Omission of the waw conjunctive occurs in approximately 140 places in the text of P.[27] When we consider that there are well over

---

[26] See R. Williams, *Hebrew Syntax: An Outline* (University of Toronto Press, rpt. 1984): 70-72. See also Waltke and O'Connor, *Biblical Hebrew Syntax*, p. 648ff.

[27] See 1:5,7,16,17,18,20,22;2:2,10;3:2,25;5:15;6:14,21,24(2),29;8:3,4,9,16; 9:5,11(2), 16,25,27;10:10,14,16;11:2,3,10(2),15,19;12:3,14(2),15(2); 13:13; 14:7,12,15,18,19, 20,21(2);15:9(2),17,22,30;16:12(2),21;17:7,9,10,15;18:7;19:7(2),23(2),27(2);20:1,9,1 5,18,19;21:4,6,25;22:3,8,29;23:3,8,11,13;24:21;25:5(2);28:20,21;29:6,11(2),17,23;30:

a thousand instances in which a waw conjunctive appears, omission occurs
in about one out of ten occurrences. Omission is not at random; rather
there are specific causes that prompted this omission, namely redundancy
and error.

a. Redundancy. Most prevalent by far is omission of the waw
conjunctive due to redundancy, but it is redundancy dictated by the
following reasons:

(1) the waw conjunctive is unnecessary in conjoining the apodosis to the
protasis in a conditional proposition;

(2) the waw conjunctive is unnecessary in joining two simple verbal
clauses;

(3) the waw conjunctive is unnecessary in the translation of a Hebrew
imperfect consecutive;

(4) where both stichs of a verse are introduced by a waw in the MT, but
the first is semantically superfluous, the P omits it;

(5) the waw conjunctive is totally superfluous - it is not being used to
conjoin clauses or lexical items, it does not introduce a new section.

Consider the following representative examples:

9:11 MT הן יעבר עלי ולא אראה   ויחלף   ולא־אבין לו:
                    "If he passes by me, (lit. and) I do not see (him),
                    and (if) he sweeps by, (lit. and) I do not perceive him."

P   ܗܐ ܐܢ ܕܠ ܒܝ ܠܐ ܚܙܐ ܐܢܐ ܠܗ.
          ܘܐܢ ܕܚܕܪ ܥܠܝ ܠܐ ܪܓܫ ܐܢܐ ܠܗ
                    "Behold, if he passes by me, I do not see him,
                    And if he circles round about me, I do not perceive him."

The MT presents a conditional statement in each stich. The two
stichs themselves are conjoined by a waw conjunctive. Within each stich
the Hebrew introduces the apodosis also with a waw conjunctive. This
conjunction, however, is superfluous and best left untranslated in English
or at most rendered by the word "then". In Syriac, by contrast, the

---

3(2),4,26,31;31:1,14,17,27,34;32:14;33:20;34:8,25,29(3);35:5;36:5,7,19,26;37:2;38:3(
2),15, 23,27,32; 39:4,25,28;40:5,7,9,11,25;41:3,4,12,16,18,21;42:4,7,8,17.

apodosis is juxtaposed directly after the protasis without an intervening particle, hence the Heb. conjunction is omitted.[28]

In the next example, 38:3, the MT contains two verbal clauses conjoined by the waw conjunctive in the second stich, and both stichs are likewise conjoined by another waw conjunctive. The translator omitted both conjunctions.

38:3 MT   אזר־נא כגבר חלציך   ואשאלך והודיעני:
"Gird your loins like a man,
and I will question you and (you will) make known to me."

P   ܐܣܘܪ ܠܘ ܐܝܟ ܓܒܪܐ ܚܨܝܟ. ܐܫܐܠܟ ܐܘܕܥܝܢܝ.
"Gird up your loins like a mighty man!
I will ask you, tell me!"

The waw joining the verbal forms in stich two was deemed unnecessary by virtue of the translator's stylistic preferences. For elsewhere in the text of Job wherever there exists a similar clausal relationship of two verbs conjoined, the P omits the waw and directly juxtaposes them.[29] The omission of the waw between stichs is unusual for P rarely omits a conjunction joining two stichs.[30] The omission here then may be the translator's technique of indicating poetic heightening, for the P now presents a verse that contains three intense statements in rapid succession. Note also that in 40:7 this exact verse is repeated and in 42:4 a similar one occurs. In both places the waw joining both stichs is omitted as well as the waw conjoining the verbal clauses, hence uniformity does prevail.

In the next example, 17:7, the translator omitted the waw of the imperfect consecutive, a technique not uncommon when adjusting the tense system between Hebrew and Syriac.[31]

---

[28]For further examples see 8:4;10:14;11:10(2);12:14;14:15,21;19:7;21:6;23:8; 34:29;36:5. The subject of the conditional statement as an element of style is also dealt with in Chapter VI: Sentence Type: Conditionals.

[29] See 1:16,17,18,20;8:9;14:12;15:17;20:19;29:11;40:7,11;42:4.

[30] See below, pp. 116f.

[31] See also 1:7;2:2,10;3:2;5:15;29:17;42:7.

17:7 MT   וְיִצְרַי כַּצֵּל כֻּלָּם: וַתֵּכַהּ מִכַּעַשׂ עֵינִי
"My eye has grown dim from pain,
and my members - all of them - are like a shadow."

P   ܟܐܒܬ݁ ܗܝ ܡܢ ܟܐܦܐ ܥܝܢܝ. ܘܗܝ ܚܘܫܒܝ ܟܠܗܘܢ ܐܝܟ ܛܠܠܝܬܐ.
"My eye suffered from anger,
and all my thoughts are like shadows."

Note, however, that the P does not omit every waw that is joined to
the imperfect consecutive form, for if the conjunction truly serves the
purpose of continuing a series of clauses it will be preserved. In the
present example the waw is superfluous, serving the purpose only of
preserving the imperfect consecutive form. This verse is not directly
conjoined or dependent on the previous verse, but is an independent
statement.

So, likewise, does P omit the initial waw conjunctive in the
following example.

28:20   MT   :וְאֵי זֶה מְקוֹם בִּינָה   וְהַחָכְמָה מֵאַיִן תָּבוֹא
"And from where does wisdom come?
and where is the place of understanding?"

P   ܚܟܡܬܐ ܐܝܡܟܐ ܐܬܝܐ. ܘܐܝܢܘ ܗܘ ܐܬܪܐ ܕܣܘܟܠܗ.
"From where does wisdom come?
and what is the place of her understanding?

The waw conjunctive does not initiate a new stanza or topic in this
verse. It does not serve the purpose of conjoining this verse to the
previous verse. It is superfluous, hence the translator omitted it.
Compare however the nearly identical verse, 28:12 וְהַחָכְמָה מֵאַיִן
תִּמָּצֵא וְאֵי זֶה מְקוֹם בִּינָה . In this case the translator preserved the
initial conjunction, for here it does serve not as a "true" conjunction, but
rather as an indicator that a new section is beginning in this poem on
wisdom. Often in the P's text of Job where both stichs of a verse begin
with the waw conjunctive the second will almost universally be preserved
- indicating that the translator viewed it as an immediate continuation of
the previous stich - but the first waw will only be preserved if that verse

begins a new topical unit or if the entire verse is a direct continuation of the previous one.[32]

At times, too, it seems that P merely found the waw conjunctive superfluous, not due to any particular type of clause it was contained in; it just may have been semantically inappropriate. Such is the case in the next example:

6:29 MT שבו־נא אל־תהי עולה ושבו עוד צדקי בה:

"Return, please, let there be no injustice!
And return once more, my justice is in it!"

P .ܪܠܘܢ ܐܝܟ ܦܘܬܗܘܢ ܘܠܐ .ܪܫܥ ܬܘ ܬܘܒܘ.
ܬܘܒܘ ܬܘܒ ܡܟܠ ܕܘܗ.

"Return now and you will not be like the wrong-doer!
Return then and be justified!"

Each stich of the verse contains a strong imperative followed by an exclamatory statement. The conjunction introducing the second stich is inconsequential and in fact it tends to interrupt the intensity of the flow of these two statements. This may have led to its omission in the text of P.[33] Note in this particular verse intra-verse influence may also be present, for both stichs begin similarly with שבו. The first, however, lacked the conjunction, thus P may have omitted the conjunction in the second in order to harmonize it with the first stich.

b. Error. In many verses where P omits the waw conjunctive one other cause must also be considered, namely error. Owing to the shape of the conjunction itself it is not hard to believe that haplography with a neighboring Waw, Yodh or Nun may be responsible for its omission.[34] Consider the following example:

---

[32] See, for example, 9:25;14:18;17:9,10,15;21:25;22:8,20,21;29:23;32:14 where the P omits the initial waw of the verse. Compare, for example, 4:12;10:18;12:7; 28:12; 30:9, 16;33:19;34:16;36:17 where P preserves the initial waw thereby indicating that a new unit has begun.

[33] See also, for example, 1:1;8:8;11:3;12:3,15b;14:19;15:22;37:2;40:5;41:21 where simple superfluity may have resulted in the omission of the waw conjunctive.

[34] See, for example, 1:1;8:8;11:3;14:18;17:9;20:18;29:23;37:2.

9:25 MT וימי קלו מני־רץ   ברחו לא־ראו טובה:

"And my days are swifter than a runner,
they flee, they do not see goodness."

P ܢܘܡܬܐ ܡܢ ܗܠܝܢ ܩܛܝܢܝܢ܂ ܗܘܘ ܘܠܐ ܚܙܘ ܛܒܬܐ܂

"My days are swifter than a runner,
they flee and they do not see goodness."

P does not translate the initial waw conjunctive. The cause may be
that P deemed it superfluous on the grounds that this verse should not be
conjoined to the previous verse as a continuation of that proposition ("the
earth is given in the hands of the wicked; he covers the faces of its judges;
if [it is] not [he], then who is it"). However, this verse does begin a new
unit describing the days of Job and his commiserations, so following his
tendencies the translator of P should have translated the waw. If we note,
however, that the verse begins with a waw/yodh sequence, error suggests
itself, i.e. haplography of the initial waw.[35]
2. Addition. Given P's tendency to omit redundant waw conjunctives, it
would seem peculiar for the translator to add a waw conjunctive in nearly
four hundred instances. However, where the conjunctive is added the
cause is quite apparent. At times the insertion of a larger addition
necessitated the inclusion of a waw conjunctive,[36] in a few instances P
explicitly expresses an implied conjunction,[37] while at other times
parallel verse or intra-verse influence resulted in the addition of a waw
conjunctive.[38]

For the most part, however, P's additions fall under the causal
heading of language difference, specifically in the area of style given the
following circumstances:

---

[35] Two other verses begin with a similar semantic sequence, 7:6 ימי קלו מני־ארג and
17:11 ימי עברו. In neither is a waw conjunctive present. Parallel verse influence may be
suggested, however it is hard to believe their lack of an element as minute as a waw
caused the translator to omit it in 9:25.
[36] See, for example, 1:10;2:11;8:18;12:25;14:2;15:34;17:9,10,15;19:16;21:5; 22:17;
24:11, 15,16,24;26:10;28:17;29:18;31:24;32:11;33:9,14;34:8;38:29; 39:13.
[37] See, for example, 6:29;7:16;8:10;11:18;38:15,31.
[38] 1:17,18;2:10;3:13;6:29;8:5;9:21;15:23;29:8,24.

(a) where the MT verse contains two independent propositions (one per stich) without a linking waw conjunctive >>>> P will add the linking conjunctive;

(b) where the MT lacks a waw conjunctive at the beginning of a verse when that verse begins a new semantic unit or that verse directly continues the semantic thought of the previous verse >>>> P will add the waw conjunctive.

A. In well over two hundred cases P adds a waw conjunctive to the second or third stich of a verse.[39] The type of clausal pattern this addition creates is not new, but in fact reproduces a clausal pattern common in the poetic sections of the MT to Job. The pattern is: verse = proposition 1 + waw + proposition 2 (+ waw + proposition 3).[40] Moreover, this addition in P is not random but highly predictable given the presence of certain qualifications.

First, the second or third stichs must be independent propositions, i.e. not just the continuation of stich one. Consider the following example, 38:2:

MT מִי זֶה מַחְשִׁיךְ עֵצָה בְמִלִּין בְּלִי־דָעַת׃

"Who is this who darkens counsel
with words without knowledge?"

---

[39] See 3:4,6,7,11,13,15,16,18;4:5,6,15,16(2),21;6:4(2),15,16,17,18,19,29; 7:8,11, 13,15,18;9:12-15,23,24,32;10:1,3,19,20;11:16;12:3,4,5,14;13:1,2,4, 12,27,28;14:1,5, 13(2),14, 15,16;15:10,26,30;16:2,4,7,9,10(2),13,14;17:1,12,13,14;18:3,13;19:3,15, 17,23,24;20:12,14,15,16,17,19,20,21,22,23,28;21:7,10,16,19,30;22:4,23;23:6,9,10;2 4:1,3,4,11,13,14,15,20;26;2,7,9,13;26:6,10, 19,20;28:4,8,9,16,17,18,19,24;29:2,3,7, 25;30:1,7,12,13(2),14, 15,16,18,21,22(2),24,25;31:30,32,33,36,37; 32:10,11(2),12, 15,16,17,18,19,22;33:2,5,6,9,10,11,24,25;34:4,16,36,37;35:3,9,16;36:4,11,13,16, 21, 24,25,26,27,28(2),29,31,33;37:12,13(2),16,17,19,20,22,24;38:8,23,24,26,41; 39:1,4,7,16,19, 21,23,25,26,29;40:2,8,13, 17,18,22,23,24,30,32;41:5,7,9,11,15,19, 20,21,26.

[40] Statistically speaking there are 937 bicolons and 72 tricolons where this verse pattern is possible in the MT for a total of 1081. The tricolon number was doubled because there are two stichs that have the possibility of the waw conjunctive (i.e. 937 + 72 + 72 = 1081). The narrative sections were excluded owing to their prosaic structure, i.e. the Prologue and the Epilogue, the narrative introduction to Eliphaz's speech (32:1-5) and the introductory verses identifying the speaker of each speech (27 verses). Of the 1081 possibilities the MT preserves this pattern in 580 verses, while the P's addition of the waw conjunctive, creating the same pattern, occurs in an additional 231 verses. Thus, P preserves this pattern in a total of 811 instances.

P   ܡܢܘ ܗܢܐ ܕܡܬܝܥܛ ܒܘܠܝܬܐ ܘܒܡܠܐ ܕܠܐ ܐܝܕܥܬܐ.

"Who is this who takes counsel
with words without knowledge?"

In this example both stichs add up to one independent proposition,
hence stich two is merely a continuation or the completion of the first
stich. Thus, the insertion of a waw conjunctive would be inappropriate.

Furthermore, the second (or subsequent stichs) must not be joined
to the first by means of an existing conjunction in the MT. So for
example in 6:5:

MT   :הינהק־פרא עלי־דשא   אם־יגעה־שור על־בלילו

"Does the wild ass bray over grass,
or does the ox low over its fodder?"

P   ܕܠܡܐ ܡܣܡܣܡ ܥܪܕܐ ܥܠ ܥܣܒܐ.
        ܐܘ ܢܥܓܐ ܬܘܪܐ ܥܠ ܣܝܒܪܬܗ.

"Lest a wild ass snuffs at the grass,
or a bull bellows over dry fodder."

This holds true, too, if the translator perceived that a conjunction
or preposition were implied in the MT as, for example, in 37:7:

MT   :ביד־כל־אדם יחתום   לדעת כל־אנשי מעשהו

"He seals up the hand of every man
(that) all men may know his work."

P   ܒܝܕ ܟܠ ܐܢܫ ܚܬܡ. ܘܢܘܕܥ ܠܟܠ ܐܢܫ ܐܘܪܚܬܗ.

"He sealed up the hand of every man
that he will make known to every man his ways."

In each of the above two cases the presence or implied presence of
a conjunction makes the addition of the waw conjunctive unnecessary.

The waw conjunctive is thus added wherever both stichs form
independent assertions and the second or subsequent stichs lack the waw
conjunctive or an existing or implied conjunction. Now consider the
following representative passage, 4:15-16.

In 4:12-21 Eliphaz tells of a night "visitor" delivering a message in the still of the night, "when deep sleep falls upon men" (v. 13). Dread and trembling befalls him so much so that all his bones took to shaking (v. 14). What follows in the next two verses (15-16) - our representative passage - is his description of the "spirit-visitor" who would deliver the message (vv. 17-21).

וְרוּחַ עַל־פָּנַי יַחֲלֹף   תְּסַמֵּר שַׂעֲרַת בְּשָׂרִי:

יַעֲמֹד   וְלֹא־אַכִּיר   מַרְאֵהוּ

תְּמוּנָה לְנֶגֶד עֵינַי   דְּמָמָה וָקוֹל אֶשְׁמָע:

"a spirit passed by my face, the hair of my flesh stood up,

it stood still, but I could not recognize its appearance

- an image before my eyes -

then I heard a whisper and a voice:"

The Hebrew achieves this breath-taking effect by the minimal use of the waw conjunctive in this unit (vv. 15-16), thereby enabling the text to flow quickly and freely through a rapid succession of somewhat cloudy, eerie imagery and subdued sensations. The reader himself is captured by the vision so much so that he and Eliphaz are one and the same, reliving this experience. One can almost envision Eliphaz upon his bed in the dead still of the night, at that moment when sleep just about befalls a man and the mind wanders between consciousness and dreamland, suspended between breaths, as the vision enfolds before him.

Following P's tendency to conjoin independent propositions within a verse and between verses that conjoin a semantic unit, the translator has added four waw conjunctives to these two verses:

ܘܪܘܚܐ ܥܠ ܐܦܝ ܥܒܪܬ. ܘܐܣܬܡܪܬ ܣܥܪܐ ܕܒܣܪܝ.

ܘܩܡܬ ܘܠܐ ܐܣܬܟܠܬ. ܘܠܐ ܗܘܐ ܕܡܘܬܐ ܠܩܕܡ ܥܝܢܝ.

ܘܢܫܡܬܐ ܘܩܠܐ ܪܟܝܟܐ ܫܡܥܬ ܕܐܡܪ.

"And a spirit passed over my face

<u>and</u> the hair of my flesh stood up,

<u>and</u> I stood up but I did not understand,

<u>and</u> there was no form before my eyes,

<u>and</u> a soft whisper and a voice I heard which was saying:"

The message is still preserved in P, but the "heightening effect" produced by the rapid juxtaposition of clauses in the MT is lost.[41] Instead of providing but the tiniest, tastiest morsels of imagery, the translator has added an overabundance of "waw" seasoning that has destroyed the literary piquancy of this eerie recipe.

Not all waw additions within a verse have such a dramatic effect on the style of the text as in this example.[42] Most for that matter carry little stylistic variation. To cite just one example, consider 34:4:

MT   מה־טוב: בינינו נדעה נבחרה־לנו משפט
"Let us choose for ourselves what is right,
Let us know amongst ourselves what is proper."

P   ܥܩܒ ܗܘܐ. ܒܝܢܬܢ ܡܛܠ ܘܢܕܥ ܠܢ ܓܒܐ.
"Let us choose for ourselves a what is just,
and let us know amongst ourselves what is proper."

P has added the waw conjunctive to the second stich of this verse, thereby continuing the see-saw effect of verse structure begun in verse 2 and now carried through verse 5 without interruption. The majority of waw additions follow this pattern of "Proposition A + waw + Proposition B," so frequent in the text of Job.

B. Just as P has the tendency to add a waw conjunctive to the second or third stich of a verse under specific circumstances, so too does the translator of P add a waw conjunctive at the beginning of a verse, albeit less frequently, with only 127 instances attested.[43] The reasons for this addition are twofold:

---

[41] See Robert Alter, *The Art of Biblical Poetry* (New York: Basic Books, Inc., Publishers, 1985) where he frequently uses the term "heightening" in his analyses of Hebrew poetry.

[42] Another example of the insertion of waw conjunctives in P, reducing the dramatic effect of the MT, occurs in the unit which contains 3:4,6-7.

[43] See 1:10,16,17,18,22;2:5,10;3:1,18;4:16;5:26;6:11,21;7:10,19;8:5,9,10,14,17;9:21, 28, 30,34;10:2,7,10,12,17,19,22;12:4,8,12;13:16;14:2,8;15:26,30,31,32;16:10,13; 17:5;18:5, 9,12,15;19:5,7,12,18,24;20:8,15,23,26;21:18,20, 24;22:17;23:2,4,5,11,15; 24:2,3,6,11, 20,21,23;25:3;27:6,7,15,21;28:2,6,8;29:5,21,22;30:5,13,21,22;31:9, 29, 34,38;33:27,33; 34:26,33,37;35:7,14; 36:6,11,14,20,24,29,30,32;37:1,5,10,18,20; 38:21,41;39:3,14,28, 29;40:11, 13;41:4,10,11,24,25.

(1) the verse initiates a new semantic unit; or

(2) the verse directly continues the semantic unit initiated in the previous verse.

Consider the following group of verses 1:16-19:

MT   16 . עוד זה מדבר וזה בא ויאמר אש אלהים נפלה

מן־השמים ותבער בצאן ובנערים   ותאכלם

ואמלטה רק־אני לבדי להגיד לך:

17 . עוד זה מדבר וזה בא ויאמר כשדים שמו

שלשה ראשים ויפשטו על־הגמלים ויקחום

ואת־הנערים הכו לפי־חרב

ואמלטה רק־אני לבדי להגיד לך:

18 . עוד[44] זה מדבר וזה בא ויאמר

בניך ובנותיך אכלים ושתים יין   בבית אחיהם הבכור:

19. והנה רוח גדולה באה מעבר המדבר

ויגע בארבע פנות הבית ויפל על־הנערים וימותו

ואמלטה רק־אני לבדי להגיד לך:

"While this one was speaking another one came along and said:
 'Fire of God fell from the heavens and burnt the sheep
and the young men and consumed them;
and I alone escaped to tell you.'
While this one was speaking another one came along and said:
'The Chaldeans were gathered into three units
and made a dash for the camels and took them.
And they smote the young men by the edge of the sword;
and I alone escaped to tell you.'
While this one was speaking another one came along and said:
'Your sons and daughters were eating and drinking wine
in the house of their eldest brother.
And behold a great wind came along from across the desert
and it struck the four corners of the house
so that it fell upon the young people and they died;
and I alone escaped to tell you.'"

---

44 Reading עוד for MT עד following many MSS and vv. 16 and 17.

In the previous verse we hear about the rustling of Job's cattle and she-asses by the Sabeans and the subsequent killing of the herders (v. 15). In verses 16-19 the narrative of loss continues with the destruction of Job's sheep, shepherds (v. 16), camels, camel-drivers (v.17) and ultimately the death of his sons and daughters (vv. 18-19). Verse 16 is somewhat unique in that it introduces the phrase מדבר וזה בא ויאמר עוד זה found again in vv. 17 and 18.[45] The translator of P prefixes each of these phrases with the waw conjunctive: ܗܕܐ ܗܘ ܡܬܒܠܠ ܟܕ ܐܬܐ ܐܚܪܝܢܐ ܘܐܡܪ ܠܗ.

In vv. 17-18 the waw directly links the verse with the preceding one, thus providing a direct continuation of the destruction scene. In v. 16 the same is also true, but more importantly this verse initiates a new stylistic unit with the introduction of the phrase עוד זה מדבר וזה בא ויאמר. Hence, the waw conjunctive serves as an introductory particle to this unit. Furthermore, we might also say that the waw was then added to vv. 17-18 under parallel verse influence with v. 16, where presumably it was first added, and then inserted in vv. 17 and 18 to preserve the uniformity of a phrase all three had in common.

3. Substitution. Substitution of a Heb. waw conjunctive occurs in 33 places in P-Job. Nine Syriac conjunctions are used as substitutions for the Heb. waw. These are ܕܝܢ,[46] ܐܘ,[47] ܐܦܠܐ,[48] ܕ,[49] ܠܝܬ,[50] ܡܛܠ,[51] ܗܟܢ,[52] ܐܦ[53] and ܒ.[54] It would be convenient and significant to discover that P's substitution of conjunctions was guided by the Versions, in particular by the LXX or Targum, so that, for example, wherever P substituted or inserted ܕܝܢ the LXX read with δε or where P had ܠܝܬ LXX read γαρ. This, however, is not necessarily the case. P may add a

---

[45] This unit is further bounded by the concluding phrase ואמלטה רק אני לבדי להגיד לך found at the end of vv. 15,16,17 and 19.

[46] See 1:11;3:11;11:5;13:4;16:21;21:32;33:1.

[47] See 2:5;6:22,23;14:18;15:7,14;21:15;25:4;34:29.

[48] See 5:6.

[49] See 5:12;14:5;19:8;21:6,22;27:22;31:1;35:15;42:3,11.

[50] See 19:28.

[51] See 23:16.

[52] See 31:8.

[53] See 34:12;35:13.

[54] See 31:26.

waw conjunctive where LXX reads δε[55] or where LXX reads και,[56] or
P may add the conjunction where LXX preserves none.[57] The Targum
by contrast tends to parallel the MT. Even where a conjunction may be
implicit in the MT the Targum, contrary to LXX, does not add one. The
choice of substitution is, rather dependent on the type of clause the
translator perceived in the MT.

Language difference is no doubt a significant factor in P's need to
substitute for a waw, as well as the resulting choice of conjunction.
Consider, for example, Syriac's expression of the alternative conjunction
"or". Although Hebrew possesses the conjunction אֹ "or", it regularly
uses the waw conjunctive in the same capacity.[58] Syriac, by contrast,
substitutes the conjunction ܐܘ wherever an alternative is intended or
perceived to be implied. So, for example in 14:18:

MT   :וְאוּלָם הַר־נוֹפֵל יִבּוֹל וְצוּר יֶעְתַּק מִמְּקֹמוֹ
     "But a mountain falls (and) crumbles away
     and a rock is removed from its place;"

P   ܫܘܪܝܬܐ ܪܒܬܐ ܢܦܠ .ܘܨ ܪܒܐ ܢܫܬܢܐ
     ܐܘ ܫܡܥ ܟܐܦܐ ܕܗܕܐܠ ܡܢ ܕܘܟܬܗ
     "Truly a great mountain falls,
     or a great rock is moved from its place."

Most commentators and English translations are in agreement in
their translation of the waw conjunctive as simply "and", thus continuing
a list of natural items (mountain, rock [v. 18]; stones, soil [v. 19]) that are
worn away, used in an analogy for the disintegration of "the hope of
man". P, by contrast, felt that alternative elements were intended in v. 18
and for that matter in v. 19 where, however, the MT preserves no
conjunction. Hence, P translated Heb. waw by the Syr. ܐܘ, plus added
the conjunction ܐܘ to the following verse.

---

[55] See, for example, 3:4,11,13;4:15.
[56] See, for example, 3:7;4:5,6,16.
[57] See, for example, 3:15,16,18;4:21.
[58] See Williams, #433, p. 71.

In the next example, explicit exegesis and inter-verse influence are the motivations for the substitution of a Heb. waw conjunctive.

1:11   MT   ואולם שלח־נא ידך וגע בכל־אשר־לו
                          אם־לא על־פניך יברכך:

> "(lit. And) however, stretch out your hand
> and strike everything which he has,
> (and see) if he will not curse you to your face."

P . ܠܗ ܐܝܬ ܕܟܠ ܠܒܠ ܬܩܘܦ ܐܝܟ ܐܦܩܐ ܝܢ ܬܘܒ
                          ܐܠܐ ܒܐܦܝܟ ܢܨܥܪܟ.

> "But, however, extend your hand
> and strike everything which he has
> (and see) if he will not revile you to your face."

P clearly understood the clausal relationship between vv. 10-11, with v. 11 serving as a statement contrary to v. 10, hence Heb. waw = "but". P translated explicitly with ܝܢ. We see in these example that the effect on meaning is still synonymous. The P has maintained the meaning of the MT, albeit in a somewhat structurally different proposition.

In each of the above examples ambiguity is likewise a consideration. For given the variety of functions the waw conjunctive serves, a certain uncertainty does at times exist. The intended meaning is in most cases elucidated by context. However, where context serves as an inadequate guide to meaning, P's substitution provides a more precise conjunction that clarifies the ambiguity. Consider, for example, 19:8:

19:8   MT   ארחי גדר ולא אעבור ועל נתיבותי חשך ישים:
> "He has walled up my way so that (lit. and) I cannot pass,
> and he has set darkness upon my paths."

P   ܐܘܪܚܬܝ ܣܓ ܗܕ ܘܠܐ ܐܥܒܪ ܘܗܘܣܬ ܚܫܘܟܐ ܥܠ ܫܒܝܠܝ.
> "He has fenced in my ways so that I may not pass,
> and he has placed darkness upon my paths."

In stich one the MT contains a waw conjunctive. It does not serve to join two independent clauses, i.e. "He has walled up my way and I cannot pass", but rather the conjunction has a subordinating effect "that, so that", thereby making the proposition "I cannot pass" subordinate or dependent on the first stich, i.e. "he has walled up my way so that I cannot pass".[59] The translator of P clearly understood this relationship hence his translation of the Heb. waw by the Syriac - ܠ This translation has thus clarified an inherent ambiguity in the MT conjunctive waw.

Thus, we see that whereas substitution for the waw conjunctive in P is governed by a variety of causes - language difference, explicit exegesis, inter-verse influence, ambiguity - the effect this substitution has on the meaning of the MT is at once both clarity of the MT, for the translator, but synonymy for the evaluator.

*   *   *

After evaluating P's translational tendencies in the area of syntax, particularly in regard to word order and clausal relationships involving the waw conjunctive, we have seen:
(1)   word order is predominantly influenced by transposition and redivision, secondarily influenced by the universal adjustments precipitated by language difference, ambiguity, error and intra-/inter-verse influence and resulting, with the exception of verse redivision, in synonymy in meaning.   Where redivision did occur innovative propositions ensued.   Where ambiguity was cited as a cause for an adjustment to the text of P, clarity from the translator's perspective was also noted;
(2)   in clausal relationships involving the waw conjunctive, the universal adjustments of omission, addition and substitution were seen to govern the translator's treatment of the text.   We saw that omission was caused mainly by redundancy and error, addition by language difference, and substitution by language difference, ambiguity, explicit exegesis, and inter-verse influence.   In terms of effect on meaning, synonymy with only variation in structure or style prevails.

---

[59] See BDB, p. 254a, s.v. w #3; Waltke and O'Connor, #34.6 and 39.2.2.

V

Semantics

A comparative study of the semantics in the MT and the P presents an utopian playground for the semanticist, for in the transfer from source language to target language the P has yielded a plethora of examples exhibiting both universal and semantically based adjustments. Consider the data supply:

Addition: nearly 400 examples

Omission: over 130 examples

Substitution: nearly 1500 lexemes were examined

However, because of this wealth of examples an almost insurmountable problem arises: discussing each and every example would result in a tome more weighty and loquacious than the dialogues of Job and his friends. Hence, just the choicest examples (from my perspective) have been used to discuss each type of adjustment. Additional examples are found in the footnotes and appendices.

I. Addition. Nearly four hundred cases of addition were discovered in the text of P. This addition can be as small as a bound morpheme or as lengthy as an independent clause. The choice of what was added is dictated *mainly* by ambiguity, error, explicit exegesis, parallel verse influence and ideology.[1] At times more than one cause is responsible, while in a few passages an addition defies any explicable cause.

Two special types of translation techniques involving addition have also been uncovered: paraphrase and the doublet. These are discussed in separate excursuses below.

1. Ambiguity/Error.   Forty-three cases of addition prompted by an ambiguity (at least from the translator's perspective) and/or error in the text of the MT were uncovered. Eighteen cases resulted in synonymous propositions, twenty-four in innovative propositions and one in an antithetic statement. Most error comes into play when the translator had two or more options at his disposal when resolving an ambiguity, but subsequently selected the wrong one, hence an error from the evaluator's perspective.   Occasionally error in translation occurs without any inherent ambiguity in the text, such is the case, for example in 29:10.

MT   קוֹל־נְגִידִים נֶחְבָּאוּ   וּלְשׁוֹנָם לְחִכָּם דָּבֵקָה:
        "The voice(s) of the nobles are hushed,
        and their tongue clings to their palate."

P   ܘܩܠܐ ܕܓܘܕܝܐ ܕܐܬܛܫܝܘ. ܘܠܫܢܗܘܢ ܕܒܩ ܠܚܟܐ ܕܦܘܡܗܘܢ
        "The voice of the nobles (which) were hidden,
        and their tongue cleaved to the roof of their palate,"[2]

In stich two P has added ܚܟܐ "roof of", i.e. to the roof of their palate. The palate is the roof of the mouth, thus the addition of ܚܟܐ is unnecessary and redundant. Clearly P's reading is an erroneous attempt at paraphrasing Heb. חֵךְ, where "roof of their mouth" (ܦܘܡܗܘܢ ܚܟܐ) would be a more correct attempt. Hebrew חֵךְ occurs an additional six times in Job: thrice it is rendered by the exact equivalent

---

[1] Language difference is not included here because additions in semantics due to language difference more properly belong to the area of Grammar. So, for example. in the topic of tense P's tendency to translate the imperfect by a participle when present tense is indicated naturally requires the addition of a personal pronoun (e.g. 7:19). So too P's frequent use of the enclitic pronoun (e.g. 36:24) is technically an extra element in the text, but this too is better relegated to a discussion of Grammar than of Semantics. See Chapter III: Grammar: Tense and Pronoun.

[2] P concludes in the next verse (11), "because the ear which heard praised me, and the eye which saw bore witness to me."

שׁע (12:11;20:13;34:3) and thrice by the general term פּ חך
(6:30;31:30;33:2); thus error here is even more certain, for P's tendency
is either to simply provide the exact equivalent or simplify the term.

a. Synonymy. In those cases where synonymy occurs it seems at times
the translator was overly cautious, adding a proper name (1:5,13 ܐܝܘܒ)
or pronominal suffix (9:23;17:6[3]) where its implied presence in the MT
is *fairly* certain. In other cases the translator may have wished to clarify
a *possible* ambiguity of a word. Such is the case in 7:6 where P reads
ܢܘܠܐ ܡܢ "thrum of the loom" for Heb. ארג "loom", i.e. "my days are
swifter than the thrum of the loom". Thrum refers to the loose warp
threads that remain on the loom after the cloth is cut off. Compare the
Targum here which similarly reads מחי גרדית "thread of a weaver". It
is not the loom itself or the thrum that provides the imagery of swiftness
of motion in this comparison, but the shuttle, around which the thread is
wound and which is slid back and forth through the alternate warp
threads, that more clearly provides a picture of speed. Thus neither P's
addition nor the Targum's clarify this comparison.

In 28:9 the Heb. reads בחלמיש שלח ידו "He puts his hand on
the flint". P adds (ܛܠܝܢܝ) ܟܐ ܦ "rock (of flint), thereby more precisely
indicating the form in which flint occurs in nature. P's addition may also
be the result of parallel verse influence with Dt. 8:15 and 32:13 where
Heb. צור החלמיש and חלמיש צור, respectively, are rendered ܟ ܦ ܐ ܟ
ܕ ܛܠܝܢܝ in the P. Note חלמיש also occurs in Ps. 113:8b and Is. 50:7
where, however, P translates with the general term ܟܐ ܦ ܐ "rock".

In 31:9 P reads ܐܢܬܬܐ ܢܘܟܪܝܬܐ "a strange woman" for MT
אשה "woman, wife", thus clarifying that Job should not be enticed by a
strange woman, while simultaneously distinguishing this "woman" from
his wife referred to in the following verse.

In 39:27 clarification of a possible ambiguity also occurs. Here P
adds ܡܠܬܐ "word, command" (ܒܦܘܡܟ ܡܠܬܐ ܥܠ) where the MT reads
על־פּיך "(Is it) by your (lit.) mouth that the eagle rises on high . . .".
Now it is commonly known that Heb. פה is used as a metonymy for
"word, command, speech, that which issues forth from the mouth", hence

---

[3] LXX and Vg also add the pronominal suffix here.

the meaning is not really uncertain.[4]   Given P's tendency for over-
precision it has specifically stated this, here and similarly in the OT,
wherever פה denotes "a command".[5] Contrast P's translation with that
of the Tg (על מימירך), QTg (על מאמרך) and LXX (ἐπὶ σω
προστάγματι) which rather replace Heb. פיך with their equivalent
of "your command".

One further example of P's clarification of a Heb. term that does
contain an inherent ambiguity is P's translation of Heb. אוכל in 31:23b.

MT   ומשאתו לא אוכל
"And I could not endure because of His majesty"

P   ܡܢ ܘܗܢܐ ܠܐ ܐܨܛܒܝܬ ܠܡܣܝܒܪ
"And I was not able to endure because of the trembling."

Heb. √יכל has two basic meanings "to be able" and "to prevail,
endure", dictated by how this verb is used.[6] Standing alone it is best
translated "to prevail, endure". When followed by an infinitive (at times
also an imperfect or imperative) describing the primary verbal action, it
then serves as an auxiliary verb with the meaning "to be able".   In
Targumic Aramaic this ambiguity is solved simply by using √יכל +
infinitive when Heb. √יכל = "to be able" is indicated (Job 4:2;33:5) and
the √סבב "to endure, prevail" when Heb. √יכל = "to prevail, endure"
(Job 31:23;42:2).   P, by contrast, handles this situation differently,
choosing to add in order to achieve clarity rather than provide a lexical
substitute. Thus, in our present example 31:23b, P not only provides the
equivalent for Heb √יכל = √ܨܒܐ , but then adds the infinitive ܠܡܣܝܒܪ
"to endure" in order to clarify that Heb. √יכל is here used with the
meaning "to endure, prevail". This correspondence is unique to P-Job.
Although there is no one standard equivalency used in the P to the OT for
Heb. √יכל = "to prevail" there are five options that are attested: √ܡܨܐ

[4] See BDB, p. 805a, s.v. פה 2c.
[5] See, for example, Gen 41:40;45:21; Exod 17:1;38:21; Num 3:16,39;14:41;22:18;
24:13; 1 Sam 15:24; 2 Kgs 23:35.
[6] See BDB, pp. 407-408, s.v. יכל.

"to be able, have the power, be allowed; it may, it can" + ܣܟܠ for emphasis;[7] √ܡܨ alone;[8] √ܚܣܢ Ethp. "to be strong, take courage";[9] √ܙܟܐ Ethp. "to overcome, overpower";[10] and √ܫܟܚ Ethp. "to be able".[11]

Heb. √יכל occurs thrice elsewhere in Job (4:2;33:5;42:2), all, however, carry the meaning of "to be able" followed by an infinitive (4:2), an imperative (33:5) or an implied infinitive (42:2). P accordingly translates √יכל by √ܫܟܚ with the respective verbal forms in two cases (4:2;33:5). This is a standard translation technique for Heb. √יכל = "to be able" in the P.[12] In 42:2 P uses √ܡܨ "to be able, have the power, be allowed" as an equivalent for Heb. √יכל[13] and then explicitly expresses the implied infinitive in the MT "I know that you are able (to do) all", hence P's addition of ܠܡܥܒܕ.[14]

In each of these cases of ambiguity, the addition in P has resulted in a clarity to the text of the MT from the translator's perspective. When compared to the MT, however, the meaning inherent in the text is still preserved, hence synonymy prevails.[15]

b. Innovative. Twenty cases of ambiguity necessitating addition and resulting in an innovative meaning in the text of P were discovered. Most, however, do not provide a significantly distinct proposition that radically alters the entire sense of the passage, but rather provide a bit of additional information that incorporates the existing elements of the MT. Consider, for example, 19:24a:

---

[7] See Num 13:30; Judg 16:5; Obad 7; Hos 12:5; Ps 129:2; Esth 6:13.

[8] See Gen 32:26,29.

[9] See Jer 3:9.

[10] See 1 Sam 17:9;26:25; 2 Chr 38:22; Jer 1:19;15:20;20:7; Ps 13:5.

[11] See Gen 30:8; 1 Kgs 22:22; Isa 16:12; Jer 20:9,11;

[12] See, for example, Gen 13:16;15:5;19:19,22;31:35;43:32;44;22,26;45:1,3; 48:10; Exod 7:21,24;10:5;12:39;15:23;19:23; Num 11:4; Josh 24:19.

[13] See Payne-Smith, p. 293b, s.v. ܡܨ.

[14] For an interesting example involving linguistic interference of Heb. √מצא "to find" with Syr. √ܡܨ "to be able", see below p. 131.

[15] Further examples of ambiguity resolved by an addition to the text and resulting in synonymity occur in 3:19 (-ܢ [LXX]); 6:21 (ܗܟܢ); 7:21 (ܗܠܢ ܗܡܢ); 22:21(ܠܟ); 24:1(ܡܢܗ); 28:24 (-ܢ ܠܐ); 31:24 (ܐܢ ܗܘܐ); 32:2 (ܠܐ).

MT ‎בעט־ברזל ועפרת   לעד בצור יחצבון:
"With a pen of iron and lead may they be forever engraven
on a rock."

P   ‎ܚܡܣܐ ܘܦܪܙܠܐ. ܘܒܩܢܝܐ ܕܐܒܪܐ ܠܥܠܡ.
‎ܢܬܓܠܦܘܢ ܥܠ ܛܪܢܐ.
"And with a iron pen and with a lead pen
may they forever be engraven upon a rock."

P understood Heb. ‎בעט־ברזל ועפרת "with a pen of iron and
lead" as describing not one, but two writing instruments, hence its
translation ‎ܚܡܣܐ ܘܦܪܙܠܐ ܘܒܩܢܝܐ ܕܐܒܪܐ "and with an iron pen and
with a lead pen", adding ‎ܒܩܢܝܐ in order to clarify this ambiguity.

So too, in 39:1, P adds the preposition ‎ܒ, thereby understanding
Heb. ‎יעלי־סלע "(Do you know the time when) the mountain-goats of
the crag (give birth)" into ‎ܒܛܘܪܐ ܕܝܥܠܐ "(Do you know the time
when) the mountain-goats (give birth) in the crags." Thus, uncertain as
to whether the MT phrase represented a construct chain serving as the
subject or whether the nomen rectum implied the dative of place, P added
the preposition, thereby clarifying this ambiguity.

In 27:9a we find an example of ambiguity that is resolved by a
unique type of interpretive addition.

MT ‎הצעקתו ישמע אל
"Will El hear his cry (when distress comes upon him)?"

P   ‎ܡܛܠ ܕܠܐ ܫܡܥ ܐܠܗܐ ܩܠܐ ܕܨܠܘܬܗ.
"Because God does not hear the sound of his prayer
(when misfortune comes upon him)."

Consider here the meaning of Heb. ‎צעקתו as discerned by the
translator of P. Heb. ‎צעקה denotes "a cry", especially a cry of distress
directed toward the Lord.[16] P does not simply provide an equivalent,

---

16 See BDB, p. 858, s.v. ‎צעקה.

e.g. √ܝܠܠ "to wail, shout, cry"[17], √ܓܥܐ "to low, bellow (like a bull), hence to call out"[18] or √ܩܥܐ "to call, shout (with the voice or with a trumpet)"[19]. It first interprets what a "cry of distress directed toward the Lord" would be, hence ܨܠܘܬܐ "a prayer" - a reasonable assumption[20] - and then sought to indicate that this prayer was audible to the ear and not silent, hence the addition of ܒܩܠ "(lit.) in the sound of".

Thus, by addition and interpretation P has clarified the ambiguity it saw in Heb. צעקה. This is not just a case of restatement in other words, i.e. paraphrase,[21] but a phrase that provides additional information: Job's cry was in the form of a prayer spoken aloud.

It is not P's treatment of Heb. צעקה that is responsible for the major theological departure in this verse, but rather P's choice of sentence type. P has obviously transformed MT's question in which one would hope Job sees a positive response, i.e. that God does hear his cry, into a declaration carrying just the opposite sense, i.e. God does not hear his prayer at a time of distress. One might suggest that P's translation is born as a result of what is happening in the story: Job is afflicted, crying out to God. From Job's perspective the unceasing continuity of his persecution may indicate God is not listening to him. Thus, the translator clearly betrays his own interpretation of the machinations of Job's mind.[22]

In 11:7 is an example of ambiguity and linguistic interference involving the Heb. √מצא. Consider this verse in the MT and P's treatment of Heb. √מצא:

---

[17] See Payne-Smith, p. 192b. s.v. ܠܠ and ܓܥܠܠ. For specific cases of Heb. צעקה = Syr. ܓܥܠܠ see Gen 27:34; Exod 11:6;12:30; 1 Sam 4:14; Is. 5:7; Jer 48:3;49:21; Zeph 1:10; and Neh 5:1.

[18] See Payne-Smith, p. 75b, s.v. ܓܥܐ. For specific cases of Heb. צעקה = Syr. ܓܥܐ see Gen 18:21;19:13; Exod 3:7,9; 1 Sam 9:16; Jer 48:5; and Ps 9:13.

[19] See Payne-Smith, p. 119a, s.v. ܩܥܐ. See Jer 25:36 where Heb. צעקה = Syr. ܩܥܬܐ.

[20] See also Job 34:28a and Exod 22:22 for this same equivalency.

[21] The issue of paraphrase is discussed below, pp. 153f.

[22] For P's treatment of Interrogative sentences see Chapter VI: Style, Sentence Type: Interrogative.

MT החקר אלוה תמצא   אם עד־תכלית שדי תמצא:

"Can you find out the deep things of Eloah,
or can you find out the limit of Shaddai?"

P   ܒܥܩܒܗ ܕܐܠܗܐ ܡܫܟܚ ܐܢܬ ܠܡܕܥ.
        ܐܘ ܥܕ ܠܠ ܣܘܦܗ ܕܥܫܝܢܐ ܡܫܟܚ ܐܢܬ ܠܡܩܡܬ.

"Are you able to know of the searching of God,
or are you able to understand[23] the end of the Mighty One?"

Heb. מצא "to find" occurs in both stichs of this verse, both with a
somewhat extended meaning "to find out, explore, discover."[24] In only
three other verses in the Hebrew Bible does √מצא carry this extended
meaning (Job 37:23; Ec. 3:11;8:17[3]). P omits translating one (Job
37:23) and the other two simply provides the standard equivalent for Heb.
√מצא > √שכח "to find". In our verse from Job (11:7), P translates each
occurrence by √שכח + an infinitive. Syriac √שכח carries the meaning
"to find, find out, discover". However, when it is followed by an
infinitive (or future or same tense), as in the present verse, it rather
serves as an auxiliary verb meaning "to be able, to find it possible; one
can, one may".[25] One wonders if linguistic interference might have
influenced the translator of P in his choice of lexemes here, in that he
may have connected Heb. √מצא with its Syriac cognate √ܡܨܐ. In Syriac
this root ܡܨܐ means "to be able, have the power, be allowed", a root that
we have also seen used as an equivalent for Heb. יכל (Job 42:2).[26]
Viewed from this perspective, it became essential for the translator to
provide an infinitive (or other verbal form) to complete the verbal
clauses. And so the translator did, adding ܠܡܕܥ to stich one and
ܠܡܩܡܬ to stich two. Note, too, that the translator selected different
qualifying infinitives in each case. Thus, not only further clarifying the

---

[23] Literally √ܩܡ "to stand" + ܥܠ "to stand upon = to understand". See Payne-Smith,
p. 494b, s.v. ܩܘܡ.

[24] See BDB. p. 592f. s.v. מצא, 2a. See also the comments in Dhorme, p. 160; Habel,
p. 208; Pope, p. 83; ICC, p. 107, p. 69.

[25] See Payne-Smith, p. 576, s.v. ܫܟܚ. See above, pp. 128f, where √שכח = √יכל.

[26] See above, p. 128.

ambiguity and apparently incomplete verbal clauses containing Heb.
√מצא, but lending a little variety to each stich while providing greater
semantic agreement with the following objects.[27]

More significant, ideologically speaking, is P's resolution of
ambiguity in 10:21. Here P's addition of the seemingly insignificant
adverbial particle ܬܘܒ *seems* to lend a whole new nuance to the Heb text.

MT   בטרם אלך ולא אשוב אל ארץ חשך וצלמות:
       "Before I go from where (lit. and) I will not return
       to a land of darkness and shadowy-death."

P   ܒܛܪܘ ܐܙܠ ܐܢܐ ܘܠܐ ܬܘܒ ܐܗܦܘܟ.
       ܠܐܪܥܐ ܚܫܘܟܬܐ ܘܡܢ ܛ̈ܠܠܝ ܡܘܬܐ.
       "Before I go from where (lit. and) I will not again return
       to a dark land and one of the shadows of death."

P adds the adverb ܬܘܒ to its equivalent of Heb. ולא אשוב "I will
not return", thus reading ܗܦܘܟ ܠܐ ܬܘܒ "I will not again
return". The implications of the adverb ܬܘܒ in P's "Before I go from
where I will not again return" suggests that Job has at least once before
tread a path to a certain destination from which he had returned. If this
phrase appeared, for example, in a context of a merchant engaging on a
perilous journey or a warrior setting off for battle, the idea of having
returned once - safely - but possibly not again would seem less peculiar,
if odd at all. What makes this suggestion peculiar in the present case is
the destination stated in stich two "(P) a dark land and one of the shadows
of death".

---

[27] For further examples of ambiguity and/or error resolved by addition but resulting in
less significant innovations in semantics see 4:11;6:28;7:2;10:22;13:17(LXX);16:10c
(Tg.,Vg);18:10b;19:24;24:15;27:20;38:34b;42:3. For other examples of ambiguity/ error
and linguistic interference resulting in an addition to the text of P, see 24:24 (Heb. √קפף
with √קצף); 27:19 (Heb. √אסף confused with √יסף); 29:17 (Heb. עם confused with עם);
29:19 (Heb. של confused with צל). In 25:5 P clearly had trouble with Heb. √אהל which
has been connected with √הלל "to shine", resolving the uncertainty of this term by
appealing to context, thereby translating ܠܐ ܡܫܟܚ ܠܡܕܟܐ "is not able to be pure" a
translation used in 25:4 and 25:5b for Heb. √זכה "to be pure".

This may be an oversensitive reading on my part. However, if we consider Job's statement in Chapter 29 wherein he wishes for his former days when Eloah protected him (29:2) and Eloah's lamp shone upon Job's head (29:3a) and especially לאורו אלך חשׁך "by His light I walked through darkness" (29:3b), P's suggestion is not that peculiar. Job has walked a *dark* path before, and with God's help has survived. The counsel of God (29:4) which once rested upon Job's tent is no longer there according to P. Now he is once again going to a dark land from which this time he will not return.

Thus, by the addition of a mere adverbial particle, P may have alluded to and tied in Job's past tribulations to his present plight and suggested that Job's situation is now quite different. God is not just testing him as in the past - from which he survived by God's help - but he has been abandoned.

Another example of semantic ambiguity resolved by addition and resulting in a significantly innovative meaning occurs in 23:6:

MT   :הברב־כח יריב עמדי   לא אך־הוא יָשִׂם בִּי
"Would he contend with me by means of great strength?
No! He would (only have) to pay attention to me."

P   ܟܡܐܘ ܐܪܝܢ ܐܪܘܫܐ ܘܐܝܢ ܓܒܝ.
           ܘܐܠܐ ܗܘܐ ܘܐܠܘܬܐ ܡܩܬܪ ܓܠ.
"Does he judge (lit. with) me by a multitude of strength?
And if He would not, He places fear upon me."

From the variety of translations suggested by commentators on this verse it is obvious that the meaning of certain elements within this verse (רב־כח and -ב in stich one; אך in stich two) and the semantic relationship of stich one to two is not unanimously agreed upon. Agreement, however, is found regarding the verbal clause יָשִׂם בִּי,[28] seen here as the idiom meaning "to direct the heart (mind) toward, pay

---

[28] See Dhorme "Is it by bringing to bear great might that He would dispute with me? No! He would only have to listen to me!"(p. 345); Habel "Would he use great force to contend with me? No! Surely he must heed me."(p. 344); Pope "Through an attorney would he sue me" Nay, he himself should give heed to me." (p. 170); ICC "Would he contend with me in the greatness of his power? Nay: but he would give heed unto me." (p. 201).

attention to"[29] with the object לב/לבב unexpressed, but implied, and not
the transitive verb √שׂים "to put, place", which would require a direct
object. This idiom does find a cognate equivalence in Syriac,[30] but
without the direct object in this case P clearly missed it, viewing ישׂם in
its non-idiomatic capacity and thus in need of an object. Accordingly, P
resolved this ambiguity by adding a direct object ܕܚܠܬܐ "fear". The
choice of object is directly dependent on either the tone of this particular
passage -for later we do read (23:15) that Job is terrified of God (√בהל
and √פחד) - or by a theological presupposition on the part of the
translator that God does place "fear" upon men in order to achieve his
means. Clearly, then, ideology is also a motivation in P's choice for the
direct object in this verse.[31]

The effect this addition has on the meaning of the text of the P as
compared to the MT is clearly distinct. Given the variety of English
renditions of the Hebrew the basic sense can still be understood as:
(1) Job asks, "Will God deal with him using all his great strengths?"
(2) No!Such means are unnecessary. God only has to pay attention to Job.
By contrast, P relates:
(1) Either God will judge him with great strength,
(2) or failing this He will place fear upon him.[32]
c. Antithesis. Only one example was found in which ambiguity resolved
by addition resulted in a *possible* antithetic proposition in P. Consider
30:23:

MT   כי ידעתי מות תשיבני   ובית מועד לכל־חי:
"For I know you will bring me (to) death
and (to) the meeting place for all the living."

---

[29] See BDB, p. 963b, s.v. שׂים /שׂום, 2b.

[30] See for example Deut 32:46; 1 Sam 9:20; 2 Sam 18:3; Ezek 40:4;44:5b; Job 2:3.

[31] Elsewhere in the MT when this idiom is used without the direct object לבב/לב P
rectifies the ambiguity of the situation in a variety of ways none of which include the
addition of the direct object ܕܚܠܬܐ "fear". See Ezek 44:5a and Isa 41:22 where ܠܒ is
added; Hag 2:15,18 where no object is expressed; Judg 19:30 where √ܩܒܠ Ethp. "to be
accepted; think, suppose" replaces √שׂים; Job 4:20 where √ܣܡ is rendered in the Ethp.;
and Isa 41:20 where √ܒܝܢ Ethp. "to notice, regard, consider" replaces √שׂים.

[32] Further examples of ambiguity resolved by addition and resulting in a significant
semantic departure from the MT occur in 9:24c;14:20;22:16b and 23:13.

P   ܡܛܠ ܝܕܥ ܐܢܐ ܕܡܢ ܡܘܬܐ ܬܗܦܟܢܝ.
    ܠܒܝܬ ܘܢܝܫܐ ܕܟܠܗܘܢ ܚܝܐ.

"Therefore I know that you will return me from death
to the house and meeting place of all the living."

Most modern commentators and English Bibles are in agreement in
supplying the preposition "to" in the MT translation. It is in the first
stich that the addition of the preposition "to" is most significant: "For I
know that you will bring me (to) death". Likewise the preposition "to" is
added in the second stich, "(to) the meeting place for all the living", i.e.
eventual death, thereby continuing the thought of the first. Job has just
described how God has tormented him (vv. 19-22), following this it
seems quite natural and logical to understand this verse in a negative
light. By contrast, P relates just the opposite. By adding the preposition
ܡܢ "from", God is rescuing him from death and bringing him back to the
place of the living, i.e. life. P's assertion here seems rather contextually
inappropriate given what has just occurred in the previous verses: He was
cast into the mire becoming like dust and ashes (v. 19); he cried to God
but was not answered; he stood up but was paid no heed (v. 20); God
made him His enemy, persecuted him by the might of His hand (v. 21);
made him ride upon the wind and tossed by the sea (v. 22). These are
hardly the actions of a friendly deliverer. Nonetheless, P chose to
contradict the context by supplying the preposition ܡܢ in the ambiguous
phrase תשיבני מות.

This addition might be an error - the translator was not paying
attention to the greater contextual arena - but if we note that P has
connected the following verse (v. 24) with this one, translating it also in a
positive way, error seems unlikely. In the MT, verse 24 begins a new
semantic unit reading אך לא־בעי ישלח־יד אם בפידו להן שוע
"But does not one in a heap of ruins stretch out (his) hand or in his
disaster (cry) for help?". By contrast, P reads "But he will not stretch
out his hand against me and when I cried out to him he will deliver me"
(ܒܪܡ ܠܐ ܠܘܬ ܢܘܫܛ ܐܝܕܗ ܥܠܝ ܘܟܕ ܓܥܝܬ ܠܘܬܗ ܢܦܨܝܢܝ). True,
the MT is a bit obscure, but P clearly considered this a continuation of v.
23, thereby continuing its optimistic point of view. Thus, ambiguity is

not the only force moving P in its choice of clarification in 30:23. The
translator's theological perspective also breaks through.

2. Implicit to Explicit Exegesis. Of the four hundred additions in the
text of MT nearly twenty-five percent - 83 examples to be precise -
occurred because of explicit exegesis. The majority are orthographic
representations of an implied preposition in the text of the MT. Thus we
find explicitly expressed the prepositions   -ܒ [33], -ܠ [34], ܡܢ [35], ܐܝܟ
[36], ܥܠ [37], ܠܟ [38], ܐܟܘܬ [39], ܟ [40] and ܒܝܕ [41] ; the preposition with a
suffixed pronominal element;[42] ; verbal suffixes;[43] and the relative
pronoun.[44]

As indicated in the footnotes, the Versions quite often also express
these minute implied semantic elements and it is here that the distinction
between versional parallels and versional influence becomes most clear.
An implied element in the Hebrew text that is so clearly understood that it
need not even be written should not be considered influential to P just
because the Versions, especially LXX, also recognized its implicitness.
Thus in the case of implicit to explicit exegesis, versional *parallel* is a
more proper term for the similarity in texts than versional *influence* .

P also adds a few words and phrases that are also implied in the
MT. Thus we find P providing a more semantically substantial verb
where the MT records no verb, but implies the present tense of "to be" or
the like. So, for example, in 2:4 P adds ܕܢܬܦܨܐ n "that he might be
saved" to the Heb. "Skin for skin and all which a man has he will give for
his soul", thus explicitly providing the obvious reason why a man would

---

[33] See 5:11,14(2); 10:11; 12:12(LXX),25; 15:2,5,10c; 24:19; 27:20; 29:3; 30:17; 31:34;
32:11,21;33:11,15;34:20;36:17;37:16;38:26;39:24;40:12(Tg,LXX);41:4b.

[34] See 17:13;22:7(LXX,Tg,Vg);23:9(Vg);27:20b;29:7,23a;30:23,26;37:7.

[35] See 9:28;28:2;33:17(LXX,Tg,Vg);34:25b;42:14.

[36] See 24:5(LXX,Tg,Vg);29:23b.

[37] See 17:9;20:22(LXX,Vg),24;22:14.

[38] See 24:12.

[39] See 3:16.

[40] See 9:11b(LXX);12:15b(LXX);31:24(2).

[41] See 29:17 (LXX).

[42] See ܘܒܗ in 4:2(LXX); ܡܢܗ in 13:24;14:5;15:9(LXX); ܡܢܗܘܢ in 16:5(Vg); ܒܗܘܢ in
32:6; ܠܗ in 11:3(LXX),19(LXX); 33:32; ܠܗܝܢ in 17:10; ܠܗܝܢ ܡܢ in 19:14; ܠܗܘܢ in
35:12; ܠܗܘܢ in 39:14; ܥܠ in 19:12a.

[43] See 16:9;19:16;32:15,16;38:4(LXX,Vg),18(LXX,Vg);42:4.

[44] See 15:28;31:35 (actually -ܕ ܡܢ);38:26; מחיר in 21:31 and -ܕ מחיר in 37:15.

sacrifice everything he has; in 8:18 P (and Vg) adds the implied ܘܐܡܪ ܠܗ ܕ- "and it will say to him that" to the MT וכחש בו לא ראיתיך "(and [if] he is swallowed from his place) then it will deceive him [saying] 'I have never seen you'"; in 17:1 P (LXX,Tg, and Vg) explicitly states the verb ܛܝܒܘ "is ready" where MT reads קברים לי "the grave (is ready) for me"; in 18:10 P provides the verb ܬܬܟܪܟ "is coiled" for the MT ומלכדתו עלי נתיב "and his snare is upon the path"; in 22:25 P even provides the imperfect of √ܗܘܐ "to be" implied in the MT וכסף תועפות "(And Shaddai will be your precious ore) and [he will be] your precious silver". So, too, does P explicitly state implied infinitival complements in 20:9 (ܠܡܚܙܝܗ), 40:5 (ܠܡܡܠܠܘ) and 42:2 (ܠܡܥܒܕ).

In 13:22 (and 33:5) P supplies the implied direct object ܦܬܓܡܐ "word" to the phrase והשיבני "(or I will speak) and he will return (word to) me", i.e. answer me;[45] in 17:5 it is the implied subject ܪܚܡܐ "friend" that P explicitly indicates for the Heb. לחלק יגיד רעים "one who denounces friends for a share"; in 22:24 P reads ܕܗܒܐ ܕܐܘܦܝܪ "the gold of Ophir" where the MT only states the place name. The association of Ophir with gold is, to borrow a cliché, as old as the hills; nonetheless P explicitly expresses it.[46] In 29:19b P gave in to the common biblical simile "as numerous as the sand of the seas" when it added ܕܝܡܡܐ "of the seas" to the MT וכחול ארבה ימים "and like the sand I will increase [my] days." If this comparison were not so common one might cite parallel verse influence, too, for the phrase "like the sand of the seas" does appear in Job (6:3), as well as the more commonly quoted occurrences in Genesis (e.g. 32:13;41:49). In 42:2 P adds the implied demonstrative ܗܠܝܢ in the phrase ידעת כי־כל תוכל "I know that you are able [to do] all [these things]." Whereas we have

45 For a discussion of this idiom, see Chapter VI: Style: Idiom.

46 If we compare the MT and P in this verse it is clear that P also took some poetic liberties in translating the rest of this verse, no doubt due to the textual difficulty of the verbal element in stich one. The MT reads: ושית על־עפר בצר ובצור נחלים אופיר "and [if you] place precious ore upon the dust and [the gold of] Ophir in the rocks of the wadies;". P reads ܘܬܟܢܫ ܟܣܦܐ ܐܝܟ ܥܦܪܐ. ܘܐܝܟ ܚܠܐ ܕܢܚܠܐ ܕܗܒܐ ܕܐܘܦܝܪ "And you will gather silver like dust, and the gold of Ophir like the sand of a wadi."

seen a variety of semantic elements explicitly expressed in P-Job, they all
have one thing in common: they all result in synonymous propositions.
3. Parallel Verse Influence. The term parallel verse influence as defined
in the Model is a term used to describe a motivation in which the
semantics, be it a single element or an entire verse, has influenced the
translator to make an adjustment in another place in the text. The parallel
verse need not be limited to the immediate vicinity, but can occur
anywhere in a given text or for that matter, as we shall see, within the
Hebrew bible itself. Although we speak of parallel *verse* influence,
influence within a verse can and does occur, that is influence between
stichs. Parallel verse influence is thus distinct from intra-/inter-verse
influence in that it is a semantic element(s) that is influential as against a
grammatical element. In P-Job eleven examples of parallel verse
influence were uncovered, five within a verse and six from verses outside
the verse.

So, for example, in 3:6b P adds ܡܢܝܢܐ "number" no doubt
influenced by its presence in the MT in 3:6c (מספר); in 6:10b P adds
ܘܬܒ found in 6:10a (עוד) in the MT; in 13:25a P adds ܝܒܫܐ
"withered" drawn from 13:25b (יבש) in the MT; in 34:10c P adds ܠ-
ܚܣ "far be it for" paralleling Hebrew חלילה ל- in 34:10b; and in
34:21a P adds ܟܠܗܘܢ paralleling the use of כל in 34:21b. In each of
these examples a single semantical element has been added to one stich on
the basis of its presence in another stich within the same verse. The
essence of the meaning of the verse, however, remains the same albeit an
extra semantic element now exists in the P.

Looking beyond the individual verse, six examples of very obvious
parallel verse influence were discovered. This influence need not be
from a verse that necessarily precedes the influenced verse, but may just
as easily be influenced by what follows or is even contained elsewhere in
the Hebrew Bible. This points to a very important point: the translator of
P had a thorough knowledge of the text he was working with, i.e. he
obviously read the text more than once, thereby providing him with key
phrases that he early on could make use of and in a sense foreshadow
what is to come. Consider, for example, 1:6. The MT reads:

ויהי היום ויבאו בני האלהים להתיצב על־יהוה
ויבוא גם־השׂטן בתוכם:

"And so it was one day the sons of God came to present themselves before the Lord and the adversary also came among them."

P translates similarly, but at the conclusion adds ܠܡܩܡ ܩܕܡ ܡܪܝܐ "to stand before the Lord". Now ܠܡܩܡ ܩܕܡ ܡܪܝܐ is used as the equivalent of Heb. להתיצב על יהוה earlier in this verse, so we might say parallel stich influence prompted the translator to add this same phrase at the end of this verse to explain why the adversary appeared before the Lord. However, if we examine the Hebrew at 2:1 we find the identical verse preserved with this concluding phrase extant:

ויהי היום ויבאו בני האלהים להתיצב על־יהוה
ויבוא גם־השׂטן בתכם להתיצב על־יהוה:

Hence, P added this phrase on the basis of its appearance in 2:1, thereby harmonizing both verses.[47]

In 2:10 we find another example of parallel verse influence, but with a slightly different twist. This time the passage that is added in 2:10 is not just drawn from another verse, in this case from 1:22, but is P's interpretive rendering of a difficult clause that appeared in the MT. Consider these two verses:

2:10 MT   ויאמר אליה כדבר אחת הנבלות תדברי גם את־הטוב
נקבל מאת האלהים ואת־הרע לא נקבל
בכל־זאת לא־חטא איוב בשׂפתיו:

---

[47] For similar additions due to very obvious parallel verse influence, see 21:21b where P adds ܠܒܢܘܗܝ "for his sons" drawn from 21:19a; 33:9 where P prefixes ܕܐܡܪܬ - ܗ "for you say that" drawn from 33:8a (אך אמרה); 34:6 where P omits translating stich one, but then prefixes ܡܟܒ "what/who is" to stich two (אנוש חצי בלי־פשׁע) misunderstanding Heb. אָנוּשׁ "incurable" as if Heb. אֱנוֹשׁ "man", influenced no doubt from 34:7a (מי־גבר כאיוב); and 41:7a (גאוה אפיק מגנים "his back is rows of shields") P omits translating אפיק מגנים , misinterprets גאוה as "valley", hence ܢܚܠܐ which is connected with 41:6b. P then adds ܦܘܡܗ "his mouth" as the subject of 41:7b drawn from 41:6a (דלתי פניו מי פתח).

"And he said to her, 'You speak as one of the foolish women speaks. Shall we indeed accept what is good from the Lord and not accept what is bad.' In all this Job did not sin with his lips."

P ܐܡܪ ܠܗ̇. ܐܝܟ ܕܡܡܠܠܐ ܚܕܐ ܡܢ ܣܟܠܬܐ ܡܡܠܠܬܝ܂
ܛܒܬܗ ܕܐܠܗܐ ܩܒܠܢ ܘܒܝܫܬܗ ܠܐ ܢܩܒܠ. ܘܒܗܠܝܢ ܟܠܗܝܢ
ܠܐ ܚܛܐ ܐܝܘܒ. <u>ܐܦ ܠܐ ܓܕܦ ܥܠ ܐܠܗܐ</u> ܒܣܦܘܬܗ.

"He said to her, 'You speak as one of the foolish women speaks. We have received the good things from God and shall we not receive his misfortunes.' And in all these (things) Job did not sin, <u>indeed he did not blaspheme God</u> with his lips."

1:22 MT: בכל־זאת לא־חטא איוב ו<u>לא־נתן תפלה לאלהים</u>:
"In all this Job did not sin and <u>he did not ascribe wrong-doing to God</u>."

P ܘܒܗܠܝܢ ܟܠܗܝܢ ܠܐ ܚܛܐ ܐܝܘܒ. <u>ܐܦܠܐ ܓܕܦ ܥܠ ܐܠܗܐ</u>.
"And in all these (things) Job did not sin. <u>Indeed he did not blaspheme against</u> <u>God</u>."

The catalyst or catch phrase in this situation is the Heb. בכל־זאת לא־חטא איוב "in all this Job did not sin" which appears in both 1:22 and 2:10. In 1:22 it is followed by the Heb. ולא־נתן תפלה לאלהים "and he did not ascribe wrong-doing to God" for which P provides the translation ܐܦܠܐ ܓܕܦ ܥܠ ܐܠܗܐ "Indeed he did not blaspheme against God", clearly an interpretive rendering of the difficult Heb. נתן תפלה "lit. to give unsavoriness, unseemliness".[48] It is precisely this same Syriac translation that is added in 2:10 after the common catch phrase בכל־זאת לא־חטא איוב, thus pointing to a very

48 See BDB, p. 1074a, s.v. √תפל. Heb. תפלה also occurs in Job 24:12 where however, the translator understood it as derived from the √פלל "to pray", hence a prayer, and in Jer. 23:13 where P translates ܕܢܟܠܘܬܐ "falsehood, treachery, unfaithfulness", clearly not derived from √פלל but from √תפל as in 1:22.

obvious case of harmonizing parallel verses. It would have been very
interesting if the translator of P had also added his translation of Heb.
בשפתיו = ܒܣܦ̈ܬܗ in 2:10 to 1:22.

4. Ideology. In three verses, the presence of an addition in the text of P
clearly and primarily points to ideological concerns as the motivational
factor behind the addition. All are reflective of Job's character and his
relationship with God. Let us consider each of these in turn.

16:5 MT   אאמצכם במו־פי   וניד שפתי יחשׂך:
               "I could strengthen you with my mouth
               and the solace of my lips could restrain."

P   ܟ̈ܝܘܬܟܘܢ ܓܝܪ ܒܡ̈ܠܝܟܘܢ.
               ܘܡܡܠܠܐ ܕܣ̈ܦܘܬܝ ܠܐ ܚܣܟ ܡܢܟܘܢ ܣܚܣܟܡܢ.
               "For I have searched you out by your words,
               and the speech of my lips has not spared you."

In this first example, it is P's view of Job's character that is
betrayed by his translation. In the MT Job has just labelled the friends
"miserable comforters" (16:1), full of "windy words" that might,
hopefully, soon end (16:2). Job states he could speak and chastise (16:4).
Then in 16:5 he states that he could "strengthen" them and "assuage their
pain", possibly alluding to his former days, when he served in this
capacity. Hence, Job could agree with the friends in order to spare their
feelings and comfort them. As the chapter continues, however, we see
that Job realizes this would not assuage his own pain (16:6) for God and
man are both against him. P, by contrast, gives no allusion to the Job of
old, Job the comforter. This is achieved mainly by the addition of the
negative particle in stich two, thereby continuing the thought of Job the
chastiser begun in v. 4. P may have had trouble translating Heb. √אמץ in
stich one and ניד in stich two and thus chose to follow the context
established in v. 4 "I also could speak as you do, if you were in my place;
I could join words together against you and shake my head at you". Or P
may have felt the transition in vv. 4-5 unacceptable - from Job the
chastiser to Job the comforter - and inappropriate given his
circumstances. Thus he modified his translation in order to maintain the

continuity of the justifiable role of chastisement and complaint Job is now
assuming.

In the next two examples, 27:10 and 32:2, Job's and God's
character come under scrutiny:

27:10   MT   אם־על־שדי   יתענג   יקרא   אלוה   בכל־עת:

"Will he take delight in Shaddai?
Will he call (upon) Eloah at all times?"

P   ܐܢ ܓܝ ܥܠ ܚܣܝܢܐ ܢܬܬܟܠ ܘܠܐܠܗܐ ܢܩܪܐ ܒܟܠܙܒܢ.
             ܐܠܗܐ ܢܥܢܝܗܝ ܘܢܫܡܥܝܘܗܝ.

"For if he should trust in (lit. upon) the Mighty One,
and he will call to God in every time.
God will answer him and will hear him."

In this verse P clearly understood the Hebrew as the protasis of a
conditional statement. What then of the apodosis? P supplies it by its
addition of a third stich and in doing so sheds light on the translator's
view of Job and God, namely that whoever trusts in and calls upon God
will be answered, provided he is not one of the ungodly referred to in
verse eight. This apodosis seems to be more of a response to the MT's
question in v. 9 "Will God hear his cry, when trouble comes upon him?".
However, P understood v. 8 as the question ("Does God listen to the cry
of the ungodly when evil befalls them?") and vv. 9 and 10 as the answer
in the form of conditional statement ("No, God does not answer [v. 9]
unless he places his trust in God [v. 10]). True, P's translation has also
arisen from this erroneous assumption, but nonetheless it does present an
attitude contrary to what Job believes in the MT, i.e. that God will
respond. Hence Job the optimist of the Prologue still abides in the
dialogues according to P, as well as the view of the righteous, caring
God.

32:2 MT   ויחר   אף   אליהוא   בן־ברכאל   הבוזי   ממשפחת   רם
               באיוב   חרה   אפו   על־צדקו   נפשו   מאלהים:

> "Then Elihu the son of Barakh'el the Buzite, of the family of Ram, became angry. He was angry at Job because he justified himself rather than God."

P.ܘܐܬܚܡܬ ܐܠܝܗܘ ܒܪ ܒܪܟܐܝܠ ܒܘܙܝܐ ܡܢ ܫܪܒܬܐ ܕܪܡܘ
ܐܬܚܡܬ ܪܘܓܙܗ ܥܠ ܐܝܘܒ. ܥܠ ܕܙܕܩ ܢܦܫܗ ܝܬܝܪ ܡܢ ܐܠܗܐ.

> "And Elihu son of Berakiel the Buzite, from the family of Ramu was angry. His anger was kindled against Job because he justified himself more than God."

The meaning of the preposition מן at the end of this verse is our concern. Its meaning is not so readily apparent as can be seen from the number of possible translations forwarded by commentators: more than, rather than, before. P resolved this ambiguity by adding ܝܬܝܪ, i.e. ܡܢ ܝܬܝܪ "more than", and in doing so the translator betrayed his own (or his religious background's) perspective. It is not that Elihu is angry with Job because he justified himself, i.e. he maintained his innocence, rather than believing God had a purpose in Job's misfortune. P, by contrast, intimates that Elihu was angry because Job went beyond this. He justified himself "more than" God, i.e. he put his value above that of God's intentions.

5. Uncertainty. In a number of places the text of P finds an addition - usually just a word or two - that defies an explanation for its being added. None produce any significantly different propositions. So, for example, in 2:9;13:13;19:22 P adds the particle ܐܦ "indeed, also" - just for emphasis?; in 19:22, 27:11 and 33:6 P adds an extra pronoun - also for emphasis?; in 9:26 P adds ܣܓܝܐܬܐ in ܐܠܦܐ ܣܓܝܐܬܐ ܕܒܥܠܕܒܒܐ "many ships of the enemies" for Heb. אניות אבה "skiffs of reed" - clearly Heb. אבה was confused with איבה "enmity", but was it also misread as ארבה √רבה "to be many", hence the addition of ܣܓܝܐܬܐ ?. In cases such as these no clear cut explanation can easily be put forward.[49]

---

[49] See also the following verse where similar additions occur: נפה in 11:4; Syr. ܐܢܫ ܟܠ for Heb. באנוש in 13:9 (note LXX here read τα ταντα); ܒܠܚܘܕ in 13:15; ܠܫܢܝܐ in 14:18a; ܦܘܡܟ in 15:6; ܗܢܝܢ in 32:5; and ܒܢܝܐ in 36:28.

Excursus I: The Doublet

In his article "Double Readings in the Massoretic Text", S. Talmon distinguished between synonymous readings and double readings.[50] "Synonymous readings cannot be explained as variants with a clearly defined ideological purpose. They are characterized by the absence of any difference between them in content or meaning."[51] These synonymous readings are found in the same subject matter in different books of the O.T. This is the key which differentiates a synonymous reading and a double reading or doublet. A double reading, as Talmon states, "is a kind of modification of synonymous readings, which made it possible for alternative wordings of the same text to be incorporated in a single verse".[52] Talmon's study dealt mainly with synonymous and double readings in the MT and LXX, but as he himself says "conflation is not confined to the Greek versions, but is also found in the Aramaic translations".[53] The P is no exception.

The presence of doublets in P-Job has long been recognized. Early on Mandl briefly discussed the doublet, defining it as a "variant interpretation" which "later came into the original text".[54] The cause of such doublets, he stated, may have stemmed from the translator's freedom of interpretation, but also possibly from error, i.e. dittography, or the variant word(s) may have been present in the text of P's *Vorlage*. These latter two reasons, however, he viewed as less probable. Mandl himself uncovered 22 doublets.[55] This total was not quite accurate, as Baumann was later to show. He raised the total to 60, some of which Mandl had rather classified as additions.[56] A number of Baumann's doublets can also be explained as additions prompted by intra-verse influence,[57]

---

[50] *Textus* 1 (1960): 144-184.

[51] Talmon, *Textus* 1 (1960): 146.

[52] Talmon, *Textus* 1 (1960): 150.

[53] Talmon, *Textus* 1 (1960): 153.

[54] Mandl (1892): 19.

[55] Mandl (1892): 20. See 10:20; 11:3; 12:16,25; 14:5; 15:34; 17:15a; 20:4b,25; 24:11,24; 28:17-19;29:3a,18a;31:24b;33:9b,20b;34:5;36:13,20;41:4,11.

[56] Baumann(1899): 15ff. See 1:1;2:11;4:21;6:28b,29a*,27b;10:8b,20b;11:2b, 3b;12:16,25a;13:25a;14:2a;15:26a;17:9a*,10a,15a;18:11a;19:16b*, 27b; 20:4b,12a/b,25; 22:8,16;23:7a*;24:6a,11a,23a,24a/b;27:10b*;28:19,24a; 29:3a, 18a;30:7b,13a;31:5b,8b, 23a,24b,34*;32:11a;33:9b,14b,20a,26a;34:5a;36:13b,20b,28a;38:9a;39:30b;41:11b (* indicates Mandl considered these additions).

[57] See 2:11;13:25a;19:27b;28:24a;31:8b.

language difference,[58] explicit exegesis[59] or additions necessitated by redivision of the MT verse.[60] However, at least two-thirds of those additions termed doublets by Baumann are unquestionably just that. Thus, the re-discovery or isolation of doublets is not the intent of this discussion, but rather the recognition of different types of doublets is our concern, along with the reason which might originally account for the existence of an alternate reading.

An examination of the doublets in P has revealed three categories:

(1) a second translation of a single term
(2) a second translation of an entire stich
(3) two translations of a single stich where each is developed from a key word contained in the MT and the remainder of each stich is filled out in accordance with P's interpretation of this key word.

1. Double translation of a single term. Over half the cases of doublets involve an alternate translation of a single term. This term can be an exclamatory particle, a conjunction, a noun or a verb. So, for example, the Heb. particle הֵן , carries the inherent ambiguity in its two-fold meaning (1) "behold" (derived from הנה) or (2) and Aramaism "if" akin to Syr. ܐܢ or Aramaic הן. Thrice it is rendered by the doublet ܐܢ ܗܐ "behold, if" in the P (9:11,12;12:14). Noteworthy is the fact that the Tg. reads הא "behold" in each case, whereas the LXX reads ἐαν "if". Thus in P we see a conflation of both readings.

In 9:17 we find an example where error and ambiguity are responsible for P's double reading of MT בשערה. Lacking the distinguishing dot for the letter shin/sin, Heb. שערה can be a homograph for (2) בִּשְׂעָרָה "in a storm" (this is the pointing preserved in the MT) and (2) בִּשְׂעָרָה "with hair". P provides a reading covering both options: (1) ܘܢܒܪ ܟܠܗܘܢ ܕܒܟܠ "that which is in every part of my head" - a paraphrase of בְּשַׂעֲרָה "with hair";[61] and (2) ܒܬܘܩܦܐ "with force", a free rendering of בִּשְׂעָרָה.[62]

---

[58] See 1:1.
[59] See 31:5b;32:11.
[60] See 19:27b;36:28a.
[61] See below, pp. 153-155, for a discussion of paraphrase and this example.
[62] See Mandl, p. 20.

In 13:17 P provides a double translation of Heb. ואחותי. First, it
understood this form as a noun ואחותי "my declaration", hence
ܐܘܚܝܬܝ "my declaration" - this translation is in keeping with the
pointing of the MT - and second, it translated this form as a verb אהבר "I
will say", as if the Heb. was a verbal form derived from √חוה "to tell,
declare". Note the LXX here translates verbally with αναγελλω; thus
versional influence is possible for this second reading, but equally
possibly both the LXX and P verbal variant may be derived from a
different Hebrew *Vorlage*.

In 17:9 it is a verbal form ויאחז "and (the righteous one) holds on
(to his way)" that is rendered twice: ܘܢܫܘܬܩܡ ܐܘܚܝܢ ܟܐܢܐ ܘܢܐܚܘܕ
"and the righteous will hold on (to) his way and he will persevere". The
second reading ܘܢܫܘܬܩܡ "and he will persevere" seems to be an
exegetical statement explaining the meaning of the preceding "the
righteous will hold on to his way".[63] Note too the alternate reading is
preserved after the entire Hebrew clause, rather than directly after the
verb.[64]

In each of these examples and in the other cases of double
translations of a single term or phrase, not discussed above, a certain
ambiguity may have led the translator to include a second possible
translation or an explanatory one. These doublets may very well have
originated as marginal glosses preserved from a variant text and found
their way into the bulk of the text by a later copyist. The same can be
said of the next type of doublet, that is a second translation of an entire
stich, only here the semantic unit is larger in size.
2. Double translation of an entire stich. Double translations of an entire
stich result in alternate readings that do not provide additional
information, but rather an alternate reading of one or more terms in the
MT. Like doublets involving a single term, doublets of an entire stich
may also have begun as glosses that were inscribed in the margin and
eventually found their way into the text at the hands of a later copyist.
These glosses/doublets may also indicate that more than one text-type of
the P was made and was in circulation at a given time. True, we have
Jacobite, Nestorian and Estrangela MSS, but these doublets may indicate

[63] See Mandl, p. 20; Baumann, p. 17 and p. 22.
[64] See Talmon, p. 160, where he discusses such positioning of double readings.

that more than one text type existed within each of these traditions. Hence, these doublets may actually be remnants of another text much like the תרגום אחר (ת"א) found in Rabbinic Bibles which were included in the text because at this point they differed from each other. By including this alternate reading immediately after the primary text, this alternate text reading could be preserved for posterity. Consider two of these examples, 12:25a and 20:4b:

12:25a   MT   יְמַשְׁשׁוּ־חֹשֶׁךְ   וְלֹא   אוֹר:

"They grope around in darkness and there is no light."

P   ܢܓܫܘܢ ܒܚܫܘܟܐ ܘܠܐ ܒܢܘܗܪܐ.

ܢܓܫܫܘܢ ܒܚܫܘܟܐ ܘܠܐ ܢܘܗܪܐ.

"They grope around in the darkness and not with light;
They grope [in] darkness and there is no light."

20:4b   MT   מִנִּי שִׂים אָדָם עֲלֵי־אָרֶץ:

"since man was placed upon the earth."

P   ܡܢ ܕܐܬܒܪܝ ܐܕܡ ܥܠ ܐܪܥܐ.

ܡܢ ܕܥܒܕ ܠܐܢܫܐ ܥܠ ܐܪܥܐ.

"since Adam was created upon the earth;
since he made man upon the earth."

In each of these examples the second translation provides the same semantic information as the first. We note the major variation is in the choice of the verbal root, thus Heb. √משש in 12:25 is rendered by √גשב and then √גשל, √גשב is clearly the cognate for Heb. √משש.[65] In the first reading P also explicitly expresses the preposition ב implicit in the MT, the second reading does not. Note also the variation ܢܘܗܪܐ and ܢܘܗܪܐ.

---

[65] In 5:14b Heb. √משש is also translated by the cognate √גשב and √פגש "to meet" used as a parallel verb in stich a is rendered in P by √גשל.

In 20:4b variation once again occurs in the verbs with Heb. שׂם rendered first by √ברא "to create" and then √עבד "to make, do"; this second equivalent occurs elsewhere in P-Job, whereas √שׂים > √ברא does not.[66] Most interesting is P's translation of Heb. אדם "man", first rather peculiarly by the Hebraism אדם, then by the more common Aramaic equivalent אנשׁא. In P-Job גברא, בר, בני, בנינשׁא, אנשׁ, בר and אנשׁא are found as equivalents for Heb. אדם, אישׁ, אנושׁ and גבר, but never is אדם used but here. Furthermore, when אדם is used in Syriac it bears the connotation of the proper name Adam and not the general "mankind".[67] Thus, P's use of אדם and √ברא makes clear that reference is to the creation of man in Genesis.

Whereas these doublets - representative of the others in this group - do provide delectable tidbits of orthographic variation, verbal variation and even at times a slip betraying the translator's age or inclinations (as in the case of אדם > אדם), they do not provide additional semantic baggage than that contained in the MT. It is thus easy to view these alternate readings as glosses, just like the second translations of single words, that were remnants of another text inscribed in the margins of latter copies and by the time of our manuscript (6th-7th C.E.)[68] had made their way into the body of the text.

3. In this final type of doublet the translator has created two stichs out of one Hebrew stich, not by reproducing the same information with alternate equivalents, but by extracting key words from the Hebrew stich and expanding on them, thereby providing two distinct stichs whose only semantic similarity with the MT is the key words. Four such cases have

---

[66] Of the 37 occurrences of √שׂים in Job, P renders 23 by the cognate √סמ (1:8; 2:3;4:18,20;5:8,11;13:14,27;17:3,12;18:2;19:8;21:5;22:22;23:6;28:3;29:10;33:11; 34:23; 37:15;38:33;40:4,29); five by √בד; (20:4; 31:24; 34:13; 38:10; 39:6) and seven by interpretive or contextual equivalents (פלג in 1:17; סמ in 7:12; ברא in 20:4; שׁוה in 24:25; פק in 34:14; סמ in 36:13; and ימ in 38:5).

[67] See Payne-Smith, p. 3, s.v. אדם.

[68] See Ernst Würthwein, *The Text of the Old Testament: An Introduction to the Biblia Hebraica* (Grand Rapids, Michigan: William B. Eerdmans Publishing Co., 1979): 82; and F.E. Deist, *Towards the Text of the Old Testament* (Pretoria: N.G. Kerkboekhandel Transvaal, 1981):147-148. Note Deist states that the date appearing on the manuscript (1006/7 C.E.) was "probably not the date of the copy itself, but rather the date at which the copy was presented to some monastery".

been found in P-Job (29:3,18;31:23;33:14). Let us look at each of these in turn.

In 29:3a P preserves a second reading. Compare the Heb. and Syr.:

MT בהלו **נרו** עלי ראשי
"when He shined His lamp upon my head,"

P ܟܕ ܦܪܣ **ܫܪܓܗ** ܥܠܝ ܕܚܠܬܗ ܣܡ ܠܥܠ ܡܢ ܪܝܫܝ
"He placed his awe upon my head
when He spread His lamp upon me."

P translates this Heb. stich twice, although each does not contain the same elements. The first Syr. stich incorporates the Heb. עלי ראשי (underscored words) in its translation; alters the tense from a Heb. infinitive construct > Syr. perfect; and interprets (quite freely) Heb. נרו "his lamp" as ܕܚܠܬܗ "his awe". The second translation incorporates Heb. נרו (bold face words), i.e. ܫܪܓܗ; retains the infinitive; and translates Heb. עלי ראשי simply as ܥܠܝ "upon me".

In 29:18 we once again have two Syriac stichs created from key words in one Hebrew stich; here, however, error must also be considered, for the Heb. terms that were expanded were misunderstood.

MT ואמר עם־**קני** אגוע
"And I said, 'I will expire in (lit. with) my nest"

P ܘܐܡܪܬ ܠܥܡܐ ܡܣܟܢܐ ܐܦܪܘܩ ܘܐܝܟ **ܩܢܝܐ** ܐܡܘܬ.
"And I said, 'I will deliver a poor people
and like a reed I will die."

P's expansions are clearly based on the erroneous reading of Heb. עִם "with" as עַם "people", hence ܠܥܡܐ ܡܣܟܢܐ ܐܦܪܘܩ and קִנִּי "my nest" √קנן as ܩܢܝܐ "reed" √קנה II. These misreadings obviously resulted in innovative propositions in P.[69]

[69] See Mandl, p. 20; Baumann, p. 20.

In 31:23[70] error once again resulted in two innovative readings in
P:

MT   כי פחד אלי איד אל:

"For the calamity of El is a fear to me."

P   ܬܚܠ ܕܘ ܐܬܠܟܐ ܐܠܗܐ ܐܘܠܬܐܝ.
        ܗܘܬܒ ܐܟܐ ܥܠ.

"Because the fear of God startled me
and (his) destruction came upon me."

P's first translation incorporates Heb. כִּי פַחַד אֵלָי; however,
אֵלַי "unto me" was misread as אֵל "El". The verb was added to fill out
the verse. In the second proposition, P incorporates Heb. אֵיד אֵל, only
here אֵל was misread as אֵלַי "unto me", just the opposite of the previous
case. Here too a verb was added to fill out the stich. Dhorme suggests
that the second reading was prompted by reading אֵיד אֵל as יאתא לי,
noting that LXX συνεσχεν με "it constrained me" seems to suggests
this.[71] Note, however, the semantic equivalence of איד in Job is always
ܬܒܘܐ,[72] as in this case, which clearly indicates a reading of איד with
the verb added to complete the thought. The other alternative is that the
reading in P is a conflation of both the Heb. nominal and LXX verbal
readings.

Our final example occurs in 33:14b:

MT   ובשתים לא ישורנה: "but twice He does not repeat it."

P   ܗܒܘܪܘܬܐ ܠ ܢܗܒܘ ܥܡܡܣ "and he does not do a second (time)
        ܗܒܢܦܗܐ ܠ ܐܬܦܦܗ and by lips he does not perceive."

P's first reading is developed from the key term בשתים, the
second reading is based on the key term ישורנה. There is some
disagreement as to whether this is a doublet. Baumann maintains it is.

---

[70] See Mandl, p. 35; Baumann, p. 21.

[71] Dhorme, *Job*, p. 460.

[72] See 18:2;21:17,30;31:23. In 30:12 P lacks a translation for Heb. איד.

Dhorme and Mandl suggest that P may have read בשתים as בשפתים, hence P's ܒܣܦ̈ܬܗ. This is not altogether impossible. However, Dhorme's suggestion that Syr. √ܢܣܒ "to do again" is an equivalent for Heb. √שׁור "behold, regard" seems a little strained. He proposes a homonym √שׁור meaning "to repeat" citing the Vulgate *idipsum non repetit* and the sense of the √שׁור he finds in 33:3 and 33:27 with the meaning "to repeat". The √שׁור occurs eleven times in the book of Job. Four times it is translated by a root meaning "to see, behold, regard",.[73] Elsewhere context dictates its translation.[74] Hence the tendency does seem to indicate contextual interpretation in this verse rather than P understanding the existence of a homonym of Heb. √שׁור.

Thus, we see in each of these examples that the translator has provided us with more of a midrashic commentary on a given word than a synonymous reading as in the first two types of doublets.

In this type of doublet it is hard to view the second translation as an alternate or variant reading preserved from another text-type - such as those discussed in (#1) or (#2) - for here both readings complement one another and both are necessary in that each contains a component or key word from the Hebrew stich. Thus, this doublet is one created by a single translator in a single text-type, unlike the first two types of doublets where each reading was (presumably) the work of a different translator and both were joined by a later copyist.

---

[73] See 20:9;35:5 where ܚܘܪ "to look, behold, gaze" is used and 7:8;24:15 where ܚܙܐ "to see" is used.

[74] In 17:15;35:13,14;36:24 ܫܟܚ "to find; be able" is used; in 34:29 ܛܥܐ "to forget" is used; in 33:27 ܬܪܝܨܘܬܐ "uprightness" (clearly an error misreading Heb. שׁוֹר as יָשָׁר); and in the present verse 33:14 ܣܟܠ "to perceive" is used.

Excursus II: Paraphrase

Another special type of translation technique involving a lengthening or addition of a text is paraphrase. Paraphrase by definition is a restatement of a word(s) in other words that results in the same general semantic information. Paraphrase differs from a simple addition to the text in that it replaces a given word with another equivalent expression that does not use the original term. Thus, in a sense it is also a type of substitution that results in a longer but synonymously parallel expression. The reason for paraphrase in most cases is the desire to clarify an ambiguity in a word, but as we shall see language difference and stylistic preferences also seem to play a part.

In P-Job nineteen examples of paraphrase were discovered (see Appendix A). What prompts a translator to paraphrase? In some cases the desire to clarify an ambiguous or uncommon term is obvious. So, for example, with Heb. מליץ (Hiphil participle √ליץ "to scorn"), a term which occurs only here (33:23) and twice elsewhere (Isa 43:27; 2 Chr 32:31) with the meaning "interpreter". P simply rendered it ܕܨܐܬ ܠܗ "one who listens to him"; by contrast in Gen 42:23 the specific ܡܬܪܓܡܢܐ "interpreter" is used.[75] In 38:10 the rare Heb. √שדד "to harrow" occurs, found only here, Isa 28:24 and Hos 10:11. P paraphrases only the Job passage with ܕܒܪ ܦܕܢܐ "to drive the plough", a paraphrastic expression likewise used for Heb. √חרש "to plough" in 1:14 and elsewhere in the OT.[76]

Language difference might also be responsible for a paraphrase. Consider, for example, P's translation of Heb. מלחה "a salt plain" (39:6). Lacking an equivalent noun P chose to paraphrase with two nouns in apposition: ܒܐܪܥܐ ܡܠܚܬܐ "in a land, salt" i.e. in a salty land. The addition of ܐܪܥܐ "land" may also be due to parallel verse influence, for in the two other occurrences of Heb. מלחה in the Hebrew Bible both contain the term ארץ in apposition to מלחה (Jer 17:6) or in close

---

[75] P does not preserve a reading for מליץ in 2 Chr 32:31.

[76] See Deut 22:10; 1 Kgs 19:11. √דבר is used alone in 2 Sam 8:12; Isa 28:24; Amos 6:12.

proximity (Ps 107:34); hence in this particular case P-Job may be harmonizing passages rather than paraphrasing.

However, what would possess a translator to render such a basic term as שֵׂעָרֹה (erroneously understood as) "hair" שֵׂעָרֹה (9:17) by ܗܘ ܟܠ ܕܟܘܠ ܠܒܟܕܗ "that which is in every part of my head"? Syriac possesses and uses the cognate ܣܥܪܐ elsewhere in rendering Heb. שֵׂעָרֹה,[77] even in the book of Job (4:15). Or why render a verb as simple as √ענה "to answer" by the expression ܢܬܠ ܒܡ ܦܘܠܬܐ "to give a word" (32:12)?[78] After all, Syriac does possess the cognate ܥܢܐ "to answer", a very common verb used throughout Job. An evaluator can only appeal to style to explain such paraphrases, for it is through such means that a translator can exert his own independence without presenting radical departures from the base text.

II. Omission. Over 130 cases of omission have been found in P-Job. This omission can be as small as a preposition or a large a unit as a stich or an entire verse.[79] Of the larger missing portions eleven are entire stichs and six entire verses. In only two cases is scribal error by homoioarkton blatantly apparent (8:16b and 40:12a). In two cases the subject matter might be construed as an objectionable statement about God (22:3a החפץ לשדי כי תצדק and 22:26a כי־אז על־שדי תתענג). Their subject matter, however, is no harsher than other statements about God in the text of Job. It is noteworthy that most of these larger omissions occur late in the book of Job (Chapters 22,29-30,38-40) and in two cases are grouped together (30:3-4 and 41:21a,22-24a), suggestive of an earlier damaged text whose lacunae went unnoted by a later copyist. As for the remaining missing portions, it can only be left to supposition to decide whether the translator never translated them or whether the fault lay with a copyist faced with a damaged manuscript or a copyist who simply missed transcribing these passages. Perplexing

---

[77] See 1 Sam 14:45; 2 Sam 14:11; I Kgs 1:52; Pss 40:13;69:5.

[78] For a discussion of this Syriac expression in P-Job, see Chapter VI Style: Idiom.

[79] Remember that omission of specific grammatical elements, e.g. pronominal suffixes, was dealt with in the chapter on Grammar and omission of conjunctions, interjectory particles and the like were covered in the chapters on Syntax and Style.

too is the fact that Lamsa's translation of P-Job does contain these verses without any comment on where he derived them from.[80]

The majority of other omissions are due to three main causes: redundancy, intra-verse influence and error. There a small number of cases where a different *Vorlage*, versional influence, textual difficulty, ambiguity, and ideology might also be suggested.

1. Redundancy. Over 30 examples were discovered in which omission due to redundancy suggests itself as the motivation for omission.[81] Most of these omissions involve particles such as רק in the overly emphatic statement רק אני לבדי להגיד לך (1:15,16,17,19). Notice, too, the uniformity of this omission in each of the four occurrences of this clause.[82] Then, too, P has the tendency to omit one of two compound prepositions, e.g. על when conjoined to מן.[83] Likewise P will omit a word, e.g. דבר (33:32b), or a phrase e.g. מי יתן (19:23b), when its presence is implied by parallelism with the first stich; thus intra-verse influence should also be considered in these cases. This category of omissions clearly produces no drastic semantic effects.

2. Intra-Verse Influence. Approximately 30 cases were found in which intra-verse influence was responsible for the omission of a variety of semantic elements, some as minute as a preposition, e.g. ב in 33:30, or a suffixed preposition, e.g. לי in 33:31, that do little to disrupt the semantic information contained in the MT. Even more substantial information at times is omitted without radically altering the meaning of the MT. Such is the case, for example, in 15:28:

---

[80] See George M. Lamsa, *The Holy Bible From Ancient Eastern Manuscripts* (Philadelphia, 1957); and Edwin M. Yamauchi, "Greek, Hebrew, Aramaic, or Syriac?: A Critique of the Claims of G.M. Lamsa for the Syriac Peshitta," *Bibliotheca Sacra* 131 (1974): 320-331 whose comments are mostly directed toward the Lamsa translation of the New Testament which he states "in some cases, Lamsa has slavishly copied the King James Version, even where the Syriac could be rendered differently" (p. 329). An in depth study of Lamsa's translation of Job might reveal a similar situation.

[81] See, for examples, the omission of רק in 1:15,16,17,19; תמונה in 4:16; על in 9:34;13:21; 19:9,13;30:16,17,30; כי in 12:2;15:14; לו in 12:11(LXX); לה in 13:1; יאכל in 18:13; אפו in 19:23; מי יתן in 19:23b (LXX); -מ in 20:1; עד in 25:5; תחת in 26:5; אני in 29:15; ממעל in 31:28; לי in 31:35; דבר in 33:32; עם in 34:20; וראה in 35:5; אנוש in 36:25b; קול ישאג in 37:4; and מברות תשם in 37:6.

[82] See Chapter II Model of Translation Technique where this example was dealt with in detail.

[83] See 9:34;13:21;19:9,13;30:16,17,30.

MT   וישכון ערים נכחדות בתים לא ישבו למו
אשר התעתדו לגלים:

> "And he lived in desolate cities,
> (in) houses which should not be inhabited,
> which were destined to become ruins."

P   ܘܐܬܬܩܢ ܒܩܘܪܝܐ ܚܪܝܒܬܐ ܕܠܐ ܥܡܝ̈ܢ ܘܐܬܛܝܒ ܠܩܪܒܐ.

> "And he lived (in) desolate villages which are uninhabited,
> and he was prepared for battle."

P omitted translating Heb. בתים and למו, as well as read a
participle for Heb. imperfect ישבו, and supplied an implied relative
pronoun. All these alterations reduce a Hebrew tricolon, whose second
stich was incompletely parallel to and in apposition to stich one, into a
bicolon whose first stich now contains a relative clause. This joining is
innovative but the ultimate meaning still remains the same in the P as in
the MT: He will live in uninhabited cities. P's version is just condensed.

Similarly in 40:18 P joins two synonymously parallel stichs into
one stich by omitting some but not all of the parallel members in stich
two.

MT   עצמיו אפיקי נחושה גרמיו כמטיל ברזל:

> "His bones are channels of bronze,
> his bones are like a rod of iron."

P   ܓܪ̈ܡܘܗܝ ܥܫܝܢܝܢ ܐܝܟ ܢܚܫܐ ܘܐܝܟ ܦܪܙܠܐ.

> "His bones are strong as bronze and as iron."

Thus, once again P has condensed a verse. It still provides the
basic information even though P misunderstood the meaning of Heb.
אפיקי "channels of", clearly understanding it as a participle from the
√אפק "to hold, be strong". Compare the Tg. תקיפין "strong". P
likewise added the particle of comparison in stich one (so also the Tg.)
and then omitted the redundant גרמיו כמטיל "his bones are like a rod
of" already contained in the first stich. Thus, intra-verse influence and
redundancy have worked together in creating one longer stich in the P.

Many omissions due to intra-verse influence, however, do result in innovative propositions. This is only natural since significant semantic elements may be left out. Consider just two of these examples, 11:15a and 19:7.

11:15a MT : כי־אז תשא פניך ממום והיית מצק ולא תירא

"for then you will lift up your face without blemish,
   and you will be firmly established and not be afraid."

P ܡܛܠ ܗܝܕܝܢ ܬܬܪܝܡ ܐܝܕܝܟ . ܘܡܢ ܥܩܬܐ ܠܐ ܬܕܚܠ

"And then you will raise your hands.
   and you will not be afraid from adversity."

P lacks a translation for Heb. ממום in stich one and היית in stich two. The omission of היית in stich two is not responsible for the innovative proposition in stich two, but rather P's understanding of Heb. מצק. As pointed in the MT מֻצָק is a Hophal participle √יצק "to be firmly established". P's translation מן עקתא "from adversity" clearly confused Heb. √יצק with √צוק, i.e. מוּצָק "constraint, distress".[84]

By contrast, P's omission of ממום in stich one resulted from its treatment of the MT idiom נשא פנים.[85] This idiom is here understood as a sign of good conscience, but it can also be used as a sign of boldness as in Job 10:15, there, however, with the object ראש. P may have replaced the object פניך with אידיך in order to avoid a connection with the imagery of 10:15 and rather presented an idiom הרים איד that means "to swear; to present a blessing; to pray".[86] The Heb. ממום + נשא פנים denotes "innocence, lack of guilt". In this context ממום "without blemish" is inappropriate. P's omission and interpretation of the Heb. idiom has resulted in an innovative statement:

---

[84] Tg. ותהוי סנין מחבולא "and you will be cleansed from moral defect" and LXX εκδυση δε ρυπον "and you will put off uncleanliness" also had problems with this Hebrew word, deriving their translations from the Heb. √צוק II/√צק I "to pour out".

[85] See BDB, p. 670a, s.v. נשא 1.b(2). See also Chapter VI: Style: Idiom, pp. 231ff, for a full discussion of this idiom in P-Job.

[86] See Payne-Smith, p. 535a, s.v. רום.

Heb. You will be clear of guilt, firmly established and unafraid. >
Syr. You will pray and therefore not be afraid from adversity.

Both ultimately result in a feeling of security, but the way in which
this security is achieved differs.

19:7   MT :משפט ואין אשוע   אענה ולא חמס אצדק הן
        "Behold/if I cry out 'Violence', I will not be answered,
        (if) I shout out, there is no justice."

P   ܗܢ ܐܢ ܐܙܥܩ ܠܐ ܥܢܐ ܠܝ ܐܢܫ.
    ܘܐܢ ܐܩܪܐ ܠܝܬ ܕܬܒܥ ܠܝ.
    "And if I cry out, no man answers me,
    and if I call out, there is no one who avenges me."

P omits translating Heb. חמס "violence" (so also Vulgate), the
direct quote or exclamation that Job shouts in the first stich. The impetus
for this omission may simply be that the second stich likewise contains a
parallel verb of speaking that could be followed by a direct quote but is
not. Thus P has harmonized both stichs. P's omission would seem to
have little effect on the overall meaning of this passage, for the basic idea
of Job calling out but no one responds still remains. However, by
omitting what he did say, P lacks that inner view into Job's mind of how
he perceived himself being treated, i.e. violently.[87]
3. Error. The third most prevalent reason for omission is error. Scribal
error can be initiated by a similar orthographic environment, such as, for
example, in 8:16 where the entire second stich is omitted ועל־גנתו
ינקתו חצא perhaps through homoioarkton with 8:17a על גל שרשיו
יסבכו. Note both begin with the sequence על-נ. So, too, in 40:12a
ראה כל־גאה הכניעהו omitted by homoioarkton with 40:11b

---

87 Further examples of omission due to intra-verse influence are found in 3:15 (relative
Heh);11:15 (ממום),20(מפה);14:19 (תשטף); 15:14 (כי); 16:16 (על); 18:11 (בעתהו); 19:7
(חמס),23 (מי יתן); 20:25 (מן);21:7 (גם); 24:2 (וירעו); 24:5 (פרכה / יצאו פעלם); 24:15
(ישים); 24:18 (לא יפנה); 27:17 (נקי); 28:19 (לא יערכנה); 29:5 (עוד / עמדי), 15 (אני),
25a (ראש); 30:7 (ינהקו); 32:5 (בפי); 33:3 (דעה), 30 (-נ), 31 (לי); 36:33 (עליו); 39:2
(תמלאנה), 18 (כעת); 40:18 (גרמיו כמטיל).

והשפילהו כל־גאה וראה . Here both begin with the sequence
ראה כל־גאה.

Omission of individual words may too be simply a matter of
unintentional scribal error, for we can never completely discount the
possibility that a scribe's eye skipped over a word, he was momentarily
distracted or so involved with the thought at hand that he didn't recognize
a new semantic border. So, for example, in 10:6 where the MT reads
תדרוש ולחטאתי לעוני תבקש כי "for you seek my sin and y o u
search for my sin", two synonymously parallel stichs A B // B' A'. P
omits translating the final verb תדרש and construes לחטאתי as a
second direct object of the verb תבקש. One can almost imagine the
scribe translating the Hebrew כי (Conj.) + תבקש (V/S) + לעוני (DO1)
+ ולחטאתי (DO2) and then getting to תדרש, deeming it unconnected
with what precedes and follows and hence omitting it.[88]
4. Other Motivations. Textual difficulty and ambiguity, different
Vorlage and/or versional influence might also be feasible for omission
rather than error. Consider, for example the textually difficult נופל
יבול in 14:18:

> MT ממקמו יעתק וצור יבול הר־נופל ואולם
> "But a falling mountain crumbles
> and a rock is moved from its place."

Two verbs in stich one disrupt the parallelism of this Hebrew
verse. Which verb should be preserved? The imperfect יעתק in stich
two suggests יבול, but what then of the preceding נופל, a m.s. active
participle in form? Should it rather be read as an infinitive absolute
נבול, hence both forms derived from the √נבל "to languish, crumble"
or should יבול be read as יפול, hence both would be derived from the
√נפל "to fall"?[89] Commentators are divided on this issue.[90] Note, too,

---

[88] Further examples of omission due to error are found in 13:15 (אוכיח); 14:19 (תשטף);
19:7 (חמס); 21:7 (גם); 22:3a, 26a; 24:2 (ירעו); 24:15 (ישים); 27:3 (עוד נשמתי); 29: 25
(ראש); 30:7 (ינהקו); 31:7 (כפי), 28 (ממעל); 33:31 (לי); 34:6 (אכזב); 35:5 (וראה); 36:33
(עליו); 37:4 (ישאג קול)'; 39:10 (אחריך)'; 40:18b; 41:21 (רעש).
[89] See BDB, p. 615, s.v. נבל.

the LXX and Tg. follow the MT. Textual difficulty is not enough of a
reason for omission, for although נופל may be easier to understand it
might also be a gloss on the difficult יבול. Thus ambiguity in meaning
is also a concern here.[91] P solved this problem by omitting a translation
for יבול, hence:

ܫܪܝܐܝܬ ܛܘܪܐ ܪܒܐ ܢܦܠ. ܐܘ ܣܩܡܐ ܥܫܝܢܐ ܡܬܬܙܝܥ ܡܢ ܕܘܟܬܗ.
"Truly a great mountain falls or a steep rock is moved from its place."

Then too before appealing to error, different *Vorlage* cannot
always be discounted, especially if a versional parallel exists. Consider
one such example, the omission of אליו in 2:13:

MT   וישבו אתו . . . ואין־דבר אליו דבר . . .
          "And they sat with him . . . and no one spoke a word to him"

P   ܘܝܬܒܘ ܥܡܗ . . . ܘܠܝܬ ܕܐܡܪ ܠܗ ܡܠܬܐ . . .
          "And they sat with him . . . and no one said a word . . .".

P omits translating אליו. A simple error? Redundant because of
the earlier אתו, thus making the direct object of דבר implicit? Different
Vorlage might be possible for the LXX also does not translate this word.
However, an exact call is hard to make with such a small semantic unit.
5. Uncertainty. A degree of uncertainty will always exist when making a
judgment call regarding the omission of a semantic element. Sometimes
the margin of uncertainty can be greatly reduced when other causes, e.g.
error by homoioarkton, are fairly evident. But in some cases there just
seems to be no apparent reason why a translator or copyist omitted a
word. So, for example אחריך "after you" in 39:10b:

MT   אם־ישדד   עמקים   אחריך
     "Or will he harrow the vales after you"

---

[90] See Dhorme, p. 204 who favors a derivation from נפל√ for both forms, in contrast to
the ICC, p. 130 and p. 93, Habel, p. 234, and Pope, p. 105 who do not amend the text.
[91] In a number of verses ambiguity in a word may be the cause for its omission. See,
for example, מפח (11:20); כ- (21:12); פרחה (30:12); פי (30:18) and אגמן (41:12).

P   מרבו פג̈ר בארארא כמרא.
"And he may drive a plough in a rugged place."

Do we suggest a different *Vorlage*, a sloppy or sleepy-eyed
copyist? In cases such as this no answer at present may be the best
answer.[92]

III. Substitution. An examination of nearly 1500 lexical correspondences
in the MT and P-Job has revealed a data supply that is rich in examples of
lexical substitutions. An astonishing number of these substitutions stem
from error.[93] For example in 7:5 and 8:17:

7:5   MT   לבש בשרי רמה וגיש עפר   עורי רגע וימאס:
          "My flesh is clothed (with) worms and clod(s) of dust;
          my skin is hardened then breaks out again."

      P   לבד כמני זהבא בארא ש̈בארהא מרהא בכבא. בארהאור מהבכתהמ.
          "My flesh is clothed (with) worms and my body (with) dust;
          my skin has contracted and has rotted away."

In this first example Heb. גיש (K), גוש (Q), a *hapax legomenon*
with the suggested meaning "clod, lump",[94] is translated in P by בארהא
"my body". Since this term is a *hapax* P may have based its translation
on the context: "flesh" in 7:5a and "my skin" in 7:5b. P's translation may
also be an error arrived at through partial phonological resemblance
בארהא/גוש , hence linguistic interference. This is Mandl's
suggestion.[95] Note that the versions had no difficulty with this term.
Tg's גרגשתא "clod, lump" and LXX βωλαξ "clod" follow the meaning
suggested for Heb. גוש/גיש.

---

[92] For further examples of omission where the motivation is unclear see 6:15 (אפיק);
6:28 (בי);13:4 (כל);27:3 (נשמתי);31:7 (כפי);36:18 (בספק);38:20 (כי תביך).
[93] See Appendix B: Errors in the P-Job.
[94] See BDB, p. 159a, s.v. גוש.
[95] See Mandl, p. 15.

8:17 MT עַל־גַּל שָׁרָשָׁיו יְסֻבָּכוּ בֵּית אֲבָנִים יֶחֱזֶה:
"His roots are entwined about the heap;
He shall see the house of stones."

P ܘܥܠ ܓܠܠܐ ܢܬܬܟܝܢ ܥܩܪܘܗܝ. ܘܒܝܬܐ ܕܟܐܦܐ ܢܚܙܐ.
"And its roots lean over the billows.
and he shall see the house of stones."

Error is once again responsible for P's translation of Heb. יסבכו
"they are interwoven, entwined" √סבך by ܢܬܬܟܝܢ "they lean, rest
over" √ܣܡܟ. Here P's departure may be due to a confusion of the
bilabials Bet and Mem.[96] P's alteration may also be due to a
misunderstanding of the object גל "heap", which P, however, understood
by one of its extended meanings "wave, billow". LXX's reading likewise
stem from error by metathesis, and a confusion of sibilants reading Heb.
√סבך as √שכב "to lie down", hence κοιμαται > κοιμαω "to lull,
put to sleep".[97]

"Confusion" of homographic roots is also quite frequent. For
example in 13:12 P renders Heb. מִשְׁלֵי "proverbs (of ash)" by
ܫܘܠܛܢܟܘܢ "your authority". Heb. משלי derived from √משל I/II "to
resemble" and the nominal "a proverb", was confused with √משל III "to
rule, have dominion over". This "confusion" is from the perspective of
an evaluator, for the translator may never have realized he departed from
the meaning that tradition ascribes to the source text. True, the translator
may have intentionally chosen a different interpretation, but this would
assume that he was aware of the original meaning and given P-Job's
propensity for orthographic errors and misrecognition of Hebrew
vocalization a different interpretation in cases of homography seems
unlikely.[98]

Misrecognition of Hebrew vocalization is also responsible for
errors in translation. In 34:18 Heb. הַאֲמֹר is rendered ܕܐܡܪ

---

[96] See Mandl, p. 23.
[97] See Dhorme, p. 122a.
[98] See Chapter III Grammar, p. 62, where the subject of Hebrew vocalization and
homography was earlier discussed.

suggesting P read הָאֹמֵר. Note LXX and Vulgate make the same error.
In 37:23 P understood Heb. רֹב "multitude" as רַב "prince, lord, chief".
Likewise in 40:29 P translated Heb. לנערותיך "for your little girls" by
ܠܝܘܡܬܐ ܕܛܠܝܘܬܟܝ "for the days of your youth", clearly reading Heb.
לנעורתך or לנעורתיך. Examples of semantic substitution such as
these clearly result in innovative propositions.[99]
      Most semantic substitutions, however, involve specific types of
semantically based techniques that are occasioned by a variety of
motivations. Five of these techniques have been isolated in P-Job:
generalization and specification in which the level of semantic
components is decreased or increased, while still preserving a semantic
connection with the original source language; contextual translation, a
substitution that most often has no semantic connection with the original
source language; interpretation, where the semantic connection to the
source language is stretched to the limit; and lexical levelling which, as
we will see, is a secondary technique that results from generalization,
specification, contextual translation and interpretation.[100] Just as
important as recognizing the presence of these types of semantically based
substitutions is the reason behind their usage and the effect these processes
have on the meaning of the target text. It should be noted that these
processes are classified under substitution because they do not affect the
length of the text, in contrast to addition and omission, but rather replace
one lexeme with another, thereby maintaining the same length in the text.
1. Generalization. Over 150 examples of semantic generalization were
found in P-Job. Generalization, to review a term, is the reduction in
semantic components of a word, e.g. king > man. "Man" lacks the
semantic component /+ first-in-power/.[101] The reason for this reduction
falls under two *main* categories: language difference and ambiguity. We
will see, however, a number of examples where other causes resulted in
the generalization of a term.
a. Language difference. Most cases of semantic generalization occur
because the extant vocabulary of our target language, Syriac, lacks the

---

[99] For further examples of substitutions due to error see Appendix B: Substitution in P-Job due to Error.

[100] See Chapter II Model of Translation Technique for a more in depth discussion of these terms.

[101] See Chapter II Model where this example was discussed more fully.

lexical variety of our source language, Hebrew. Thus, failing this variety, the translator of P had but one recourse, to use a term that most closely contained the same semantic units.[102] Consider, for example, the Hebrew nouns כעש "vexation, anger" and תושיה "sound wisdom". Lacking a single lexeme that precisely denotes (1) an element of frustration + anger = vexation כעש or (2) wisdom + level-headedness = sound wisdom תושיה the translator of P rendered these terms by the most essential components present in a lexeme in his language, thus:

(1) כעש - the element of anger, therefore ܪܘܓܙܐ "anger"[103] and

(2) תושיה - the element of wisdom, therefore ܚܟܡܬܐ "wisdom".[104]

Similarly, verbal roots are also generalized when Syriac lacks the more precise lexeme. Consider for example Heb. יצב√ "to set/station oneself; take one's stand" with לפני + person = "to present oneself before". In Job 1:6 and 2:1(2) it carries the implication of the sons of God (and the adversary) being ready for service.[105] Lacking a verb that carries this extra component of standing at attention before a higher authority, P translates with the common √ܩܡ "to stand".[106] Note Targum translates similarly with למקום.

---

[102] It might also be suggested that the oral language may have contained a greater pool of lexical elements than those preserved in extant Syriac literature. But because the translator was preparing an audience-oriented translation he sought a semantically simpler text.

[103] In Job see 5:2;6:2;10:7;17:7. See also Deut 32:19,27; 1 Sam 1:6,16; 1 Kgs 15:30; 21:22; 2 Kgs 23:26; Prov 12:16;17:25;21:19;27:3; Pss 6:8;10:14;31:10; 85:5; Eccl 1:18;2:23;7:3,9; 11:10.

[104] In Job see 5:12;11:6;12:16. In 6:13 ܦܘܪܩܢܐ "redemption, salvation" is used and in 30:22 the textual difficulty of the Heb. text results in an interpretive reading. See also Prov 2:7;3:21;8:14;18:1; Micah 6:9. Note Targum likewise translates חכמה and Vulgate *sapientia.*

[105] See BDB, p. 426, s.v. יצב (c).

[106] In Job see also 33:5;38:14;41:2. In the OT see Exod 2:4;8:16;9:13;19:17;34:5; Num 22:22;23:3,15; Deut 7:24;9:2;11:25;31:14; Josh 1:5;24:1; Judg 20:2; 1 Sam. 3:10;10:19,23; 12:7;17:16; 2 Sam 18:13,30;23:12; 1 Chr 11:14; 2 Chr 11:13; 20:6,17; Zech. 11:14; Jer 46:4; Hab 2:1; Prov 22:29; Pss 2:2;5:6;94:16. In Exod 14:13 ܩܘܐ "to wait, tarry" is used; in Num 11:16; 1 Sam 12:16; Jer 46:14 ܥܬܕ "to be ready" is used; in Ps 36:5 ܗܠܟ "to go" is used - these variants dictated by context; and in 2 Sam 21:5 יצב√ is paraphrased.

b. Ambiguity. There are a good number of cases where generalization occurs, not because Syriac lacks a more complex lexeme, but more so that the lexeme used in Hebrew is a *hapax legomenon* or a rarer or more archaic term. Consider for example the Hebrew words שֶׁמֶץ "whisper", תרדמה "deep sleep" and √שׁזף "to catch sight of, look on". P's translations, as we will see, are not interpretations or contextual guesses, because the basic semantic component was clearly understood.

Heb. שֶׁמֶץ "whisper" is found only in Job 4:12 and 26:14.[107] In 26:14 P provided an interpretive reading (Heb. "and what whisper of a word do we hear against him?" > Syr. "And what evil word was heard against him?"). By contrast in 4:12 P seems to have grasped the concept that "a whisper" is a small or soft sound, hence its translation ܐܪܟ ܘܟܠܗܝܢ "And unto me a word was stolen, and my ear received [something] like a small [portion] of it." P's choice of the semantic components contained in the Heb. שֶׁמֶץ is interesting. Instead of choosing the very general component "sound", it rather selected the notion of "smallness". Note Targum translates similarly קצת דאתמצי "a part of what had reached".

Heb. תרדמה "deep sleep" occurs twice in the book of Job (4:13 and 33:15) and only five times elsewhere in the OT.[108] In 4:13 it is paraphrased by the common noun with qualifying adjective ܫܢܬܐ ܥܡܝܩܬܐ "deep sleep". By contrast in 33:15 P uses the general term ܫܢܬܐ "sleep", omitting the semantic component of "deep". Note that the Targum translates just the opposite in these two verses, i.e. שׁנתא "sleep in 4:13 and paraphrasing with עמקתא שׁינתא in 33:15. The question here is why did P generalize this rare Hebrew term in one verse but paraphrase it in another. The answer seems to lie in the surrounding semantic environment. In 33:15b P generalizes, because the component of "deep" is already contained in a single lexeme: 33:15c Heb. תנומות "slumber" > Syr. ܢܘܡܬܐ "deep sleep". By contrast, in 4:13b the

---

[107] The feminine noun שִׁמְצָה "whisper, derision" also occurs in Exod 32:25 which P translates ܫܡܐ ܒܝܫܐ.

[108] See Gen 2:21;15:12 where ܫܠܝܐ "quiet, stillness; deep sleep, stupor" is used by P; 1 Sam 26:12 and Prov 19:15 where ܫܢܬܐ "sleep" is used; and Isa 29:10 where the adjective ܥܡܝܩܬܐ "deep" is used.

component of deep is found only in the Heb. תרדמה, hence paraphrase may have been deemed essential in order to preserve the meaning of the MT. Note in 4:13a ܫܠܝܐ, which is used in Genesis as an equivalent for תרדמה, is used to translate Heb. שעפים "disquieting thoughts", but ܫܠܝܐ seems to be used with its primary meaning of "quiet, stillness".

Our last example √שׁוף "to catch sight of, look on" occurs but thrice in the OT, twice in Job (20:9;28:7) and once in Song of Songs (1:6) where it is interpretively rendered. In both verses in Job, it is rendered by the common verb ܚܙܐ "to see", given that Syriac lacks a lexeme denoting more than just seeing something, but rather catching a sudden visual image that steals ones full attention.

From this selection of examples of generalization, prompted by the presence of a rare Hebrew lexeme, a number of observations can be made. P clearly understood the basic component of the term as evidenced by its choice of equivalents. P does not necessarily translate a rare term in the same way for each occurrence, as evidenced by its translation of Heb. תרדמה "deep sleep". By contrast, in those cases of generalization prompted by language difference P was fairly uniform in its choice of equivalents; e.g. √יצב almost always - barring interpretive readings - is translated with √ ܩܘܡ.

c. Generalization and the Semantic Environment. In the cases we have seen of substitution due to language difference or ambiguity, P's reason for generalizing a term appears quite justified: Syriac lacked such a precise lexeme or needed to clarify a rare Hebrew term. However, there are also numerous cases where P substitutes a componentially lower lexeme for a higher Hebrew one even when the Syriac language contains this very same word or an equally complex term. Consider three such Hebrew terms, two nouns חך "palate" and כף "palm" and one verb פער "to open wide".

Heb. חך "palate" occurs eighteen times in the OT, seven of which are found in the book of Job.[109] In twelve of these passages P translates with the cognate ܚܟܐ "palate", hence Syriac does possess this lexeme.[110]

---

[109] See 6:30;12:11;20:13;29:10;31:30;33:2;34:3.
[110] See Job 12:11;20:13;29:10;34:3; Prov 24:13; Pss 119:103;137:6; Cant 2:3; 5:16;7:10; Eccl 4:4; Ezek 3:26.

In one verse (Prov 5:3) P is interpretive. In the remaining five passages
P uses the general term פתם "mouth", thrice in Job (6:30;31:30; 33:2)
and twice elsewhere in the OT (Prov 8:7 and Hos 8:1). Why would P
generalize a term when the Syriac language possesses the same cognate
lexeme and there clearly is nothing ambiguous about its meaning? The
answer lies in the semantic environment in which חך appears. When the
environment refers to taste, ܚܟܐ is maintained, as, for example, in Job
12:11:

MT   הלא־אזן מלין תבחן   וחך   אכל יטעם־לו:

"Does not the ear test words and the palate taste food?"

P   ܐܝܟ ܕܐܕܢܐ ܕܫ̇ܡܥܐ ܡ̈ܠܐ. ܘܚܟܐ ܛܥܡ ܡ̇ܐܟܘܠܬܐ.

"The ear hears words and the palate tastes food."

By contrast when the environment refers to speech, generalization
to פתם occurs as, for example, in Job 6:30:

MT   היש־בלשוני עולה   אם־חכי   לא־יבין הוות:

"Is iniquity on my tongue
or does not my palate discern calamity?"

P ≠ ܘܠܐ ܐܝܬ ܥܠ ܠܫܢܝ ܥܘܠܐ. ܐܘ ܦܘܡܝ ܠܐ ܡܡܠܠ ܩܘܫܬܐ.

"Lest there is iniquity on my tongue
or my mouth does not speak the truth."

In our second example, P's treatment of Heb. כף "palm",
generalization is much more uniform. Syriac possesses the cognate
lexeme ܟܦܐ "palm". Excluding those passages where כף refers to the sole
of the foot, hence P's ܦܣܬܐ;[111] the hollow socket of the thigh-joint;[112]
or where it specifically refers to the palm as distinct from the hand;[113] P

---

[111] See also, for example, Job 2:7; Deut 2:5;11:24;28:56; Josh 1:3.
[112] See, for example, Gen 32:26,33.
[113] See, for example, Lev 14:15,18,26,29.

consistently records the generic ܐ݂ܝܕ..[114] In the Heb. text in each case
"palm" is used as a synecdoche for the hand, i.e. a part representing the
whole; hence we might say that P's generalization here is more properly a
stylistic tendency of P's whereby the translator dissolves a
synecdoche.[115] Consider but one of these occurrences, 13:21:

MT   כפך מעלי הרחק   ואמתך אל־תבעתני:
      "Remove your palm from upon me
      and let not your fear frighten me."

P   ܐܝܕܟ ܠܐ ܬܦܘܩ ܡܢܝ. ܘܕܚܠܬܟ ܠܐ ܬܘܠܗܢܝ.
      "Do not remove your hand from me
      and let not your dread terrify me."

Our verbal example of generalization involves √פער "to open
wide", a root that is found but four times in the Hebrew Bible: Job 16:10;
29:23; Isa 5:14; Ps 119:131. This root does have a cognate ܦܥܐ in
Syriac with the same meaning "to open wide". In two of the four
occurrences P uses this cognate to translate the Heb. √פער (Job 29:23; Isa
5:14), but in two verses generalization occurs, with P rendering √פער by
the more common √פתח "to open", a verb that lacks the component of
[+width]. The reason for this non-uniformity in translation again lies in
the semantic environment in which this verb occurs. Where פער < פ̇עܐ
the component of [+width] is essential to the passage, thus:

Job 29:23   ויחלו כמטר לי   ופיהם פערו למלקוש
             "They wait for me as (for) the rain,
             they open *wide* their mouths for the spring rain."

---

[114] In P-Job see 9:30;10:3;11:13;13:14,21;16:17;22:30;27:23;29:9;31:7;36:32;40:32.
Note in 15:32 P even erroneously renders Heb. כפתו "his frond" by ܐܝܕ.

[115] A detailed study of this figure of speech in P-Job would be necessary in order to
determine whether P inherently removes a synecdoche or whether P just preferred to
more generally translate this particular term. This inquiry is unfortunately beyond the
scope of the present study for the figures of speech that were examined are the most
common ones, namely simile, metaphor and idiom. See Chapter VI: Style: Figures of
Speech.

The element of [+width] is essential, for here we have a beautiful image of a man's face tilted skyward, mouth open wide to take in the refreshing drops of spring rain.

In Isa 5:14b the intimation of width is especially prominent and necessitated by parallelism with 5:14a:

לכן הרחיבה שאול נפשה   ופערה פיה לבלי־חק

"Therefore Sheol has enlarged its appetite,
it has opened *wide* its mouth without measure."

By contrast, in the two passages where P does generalize the element of width is not essential, and, in fact, in the Psalm passage quite inappropriate.

Job 16:10   פערו עלי בפיהם בחרפה הכו לחיי

יחד   עלי   יתמלאון:

"They open their mouth against me,
with reproach they smote my cheek,
they mass themselves together against me."

Ps 119:131   פי־פערתי ואשאפה כי למצותיך יאבתי

"I open my mouth and I pant
because I long for your commandments."

An examination of these three vocabulary items (פער and כף, חך) has indicated that where language difference or ambiguity does not explain generalization of a lexeme appeal can be made to the semantic environment as a motivation for the reduction in semantic components. We might say the motivation is intra-verse influence from the semantic environment. The suggestions forwarded here may be a bit subjective on my part, but who is to say that the translator might not have had these same perceptions?[116]

2. Specification. The opposite of generalization is the semantic process of specification in which a componentially more complex lexeme is

---

[116] For further examples of substitutions involving generalization see Appendix C: Generalization in P-Job.

substituted for a componentially less complex one. Once again it is
motivated by ambiguity, language difference and the demands of a word's
semantic environment, i.e. intra-verse influence.

a. Ambiguity and Language difference. In contrast to generalization due
to ambiguity, the process of specification occurs not when uncertainty
exists because of the rarity of a lexeme, but because the lexeme is
polysemous in nature, thus raising an uncertainty as to what the intended
meaning is. Even where context dictates the intended meaning with
crystal-clear clarity it seems to be an inherent tendency in P to specify.
Consider the following examples: the preposition -ל, the nouns אף, יום,
and צבא.

The inseparable preposition -ל, although traditionally translated
"to, for, in regard to", is much more varied in its application than these
basic equivalences.[117] Given this wide margin of translational
possibilities, the P has the tendency to specify the meaning. So, for
example, in 13:7-8 P renders Heb. ל twice by ܠ and once by לגת:

MT   הַלְאֵל תדברו עולה וְלוֹ תדברו רמיה:
        הפניו תשאון   אם־לַאל תריבון:

> "Will you speak falsely <u>for</u> El and speak deceitfully <u>for</u> him?
> Will you show partiality toward him?
> Or will you plead the case <u>for</u> El?"

What exactly does "for" mean in this context? Is it speaking to God
in such negative ways or "on behalf of him, in place of him"?
Uncertainty does exist, which P resolves by substituting the preposition
ܠ "against" and לגת "with", hence:

P   ܠܐ ܡܗܘ ܠܠܠܠܗܬܪ ܐܘܬܦܢ ܐܘܗܐ ܠܠ
                      ܘܡܗܠܠ ܠܠܠܠܗܬܪ ܐܘܬܦܢ ܠܗܠܐ.
         ܟܐܦܗܣܝ ܣܒܬ ܐܘܬܦܢ. ܐܢ ܐܘܬ ܠܐܠܐܪ ܠܓܬ ܐܢ. ܘܢܬ ܣܝܪܢ ܐܘܬܦܢ.

---

117 See BDB, p. 510-518, s.v. ל; Waltke and O'Connor, *Hebrew Syntax*, #10.4 and
11.2.10; and Williams, *Hebrew Syntax: An Outline*, #265-284.

"Will you speak wickedly <u>against</u> God
and will you speak deceitfully <u>against</u> Him?
Do you show him partiality or do you plead <u>with</u> God?"

In 5:22b P chose to substitute ܥܠ for Heb. ܠ twice in the phrase
לשד ולכפן תשחק "you laugh at destruction and famine", guided more
by language difference than ambiguity, for Syriac tends to use the
preposition ܥܠ with the verb ܓܚܟ, in contrast to Hebrew which uses ܠ,
על as well as אל.118

In 2:13 the Hebrew noun יום "day" occurs in the clause וישבו
אתו לארץ שבעת ימים ושבעת לילות "and they sat with him on the
ground seven days and seven nights". It is clearly not an ambiguous
word, but given its usage here the translator of P apparently wanted to
differentiate between day-light hours and night-time hours, hence P's
translation of ימים by ܐܝܡܡܐ "day-light hours". This specification is
not unique to P-Job, but standard in Syriac. In a recent article "West
Aramaic Elements in the Old Syriac and Peshitta Gospels", Jan Jooston
specifically refers to this example, stating that "the use of ܝܘܡ in the
expression 'x days and x nights' is not regular for Syriac. Wherever that
expression occurs in the OT Peshitta the word used for "day" is ܐܝܡܡܐ.
It is, in fact, normal practice in Syriac literature to use ܐܝܡܡܐ
whenever "day" is juxtaposed with 'night'."119

By contrast, the noun אף is ambiguous, because polysemy exists
due to its extended uses. It has the basic meaning of "nose", but at times
is used for part of the nose, i.e. "the nostrils" (Gen 2:7; Job 27:3); or by
synecdoche [part for the whole] it denotes "the face". It is also
figuratively used to designate "anger", with the nose understood as the
organ from which anger radiates. Given this variety the translator of P
was very specific in his treatment of Heb. אף throughout the Peshitta, no
doubt aided by the word's semantic environment. So, for example, in Job
4:9b אף denotes the emotion of "anger", hence P records ܪܘܓܙܐ "anger":

---

118 See BDB, p. 965b, s.v. שׂחק.
119 *JBL* 110/2 (1991): 276.

MT   ומרוח אפו יכלו   "and at the blast of his אף

they are consumed"

P   .ܢܣܬܝܦܘܢ ܕܪܘܓܙܗ ܐܘܪܚܐ ܘܡܢ

"and from the blast of his anger they will be consumed"

Note P parallels the LXX reading αργη "temper" whereas
נחיריה "his nostrils" is found in the Targum. In 27:3 the semantic
environment suggests אף = "nostrils" in the MT: כי כל־עוד נשמתי
בי ורוח אלוה באפי "For as long as my breath is in me and the spirit
of Eloah is in my nostrils (lit. face)". Thus P translates ܒܝ ܡܬܠܗ.
ܒܢܚܝܪܝ ܕܐܠܗܐ ܘܪܘܚܗ "For all of it is in me and the spirit of God is
in my nostrils".[120]

Our last example of specification of a polysemous lexeme involves
the word צבא which carries the basic meaning "host, war, service".[121]
In certain environments this term carries further connotations as follows:

צבא = host (army; heavenly constellations; celestial beings)

= war

= service (military; priestly; hard life)

+ the plural צבאות with יהוה is an epithet

In P-Job צבא occurs thrice (7:1; 10:17; 14:14). In 10:17 P
translates with the usual correspondence and equally general term ܚܝܠܐ
"army, host". Here the basic sense is appropriate.

10:17   MT   תחדש עדיך נגדי ותרב כעשך עמדי

חליפות וצבא עמי:

"You renew your witnesses against me;

and you increase your vexation toward me;

changes and a host are with me."

---

[120] For other examples of אף > ܪܘܓܙܐ see 9:5,13;14:13;16:9;18:4;19:11;20:23,28;
21:17; 32:3;35:15;36:13;40:11;42:7.

[121] BDB, pp. 838-839, s.v. צבא.

P ܘܡܚܕܪܐ ܐܢܬ ܙܝܢܟ ܠܘܩܒܠܝ. ܘܡܣܓܐ ܐܢܬ ܪܘܓܙܟ ܠܘܬܝ.
ܘܚܝ̈ܠܘܢ ܡܫܚܠܦ ܐܢܬ ܥܠܝ.

"And you have set your armour against me,
and you increase your anger towards me,
and you change hosts against me."

P uses a more precise term to indicate the semantic connotation צבא has in the other two verses:

7:1 MT הלא־צבא לאנוש על־ארץ וכימי שכיר ימיו:
"Does not man have a hard service upon the earth,
and are not his days like the days of a wage-earner?"

P ܗܐ ܙܒܢܐ ܗܘ ܠܐܢܫܐ ܥܠ ܐܪܥܐ.
ܘܐܝܟ ܝܘ̈ܡܝ ܐܓܝܪܐ ܐܢܘܢ ܝܘ̈ܡܘܗܝ.
"Behold, there is a time for man upon the earth,
like the days of a wage-earner are his days."

P renders צבא by ܙܒܢܐ "time", thus clearly providing the most basic equivalent for this most infrequent connotation of צבא as "hard service".

14:14 MT אם־ימות גבר היחיה כל־ימי צבאי איחל
עד־בוא חליפתי:
"If a man dies, will he live (again)?
All the days of my service(?) I would wait
till my renewal would come."

P ܐܢ ܢܡܘܬ ܓܒܪܐ ܕܠܡܢܐ ܚܝܐ.
ܘܟܠܗܘܢ ܝܘ̈ܡܬܐ ܕܛܠܝܘܬܗ ܡܣܟܐ
ܠܡܐ ܕܐܬܐ ܣܝܒܘܬܗ.
"If man dies, why does he live?
and all the days of his youth he waits until his old age comes."

Heb. צבאי is rendered ܛܠܝܘܬܗ "his youth", clearly a contextual reading providing the antonym in accordance with P's interpretation of Heb. חליפה "renewal" as ܣܝܒܘܬܐ "old age".

b. Specification and the Semantic Environment. Just as the semantic environment (i.e. intra-verse influence) prompted the translator of P to generalize a term, so too does the opposite occur. The lexeme in the MT was so basic that in certain contexts the translator chose to specify the term (i.e. add semantic components). Consider for example the noun צור and the verb נשׂא.

The noun צור is a commonly occurring noun in Hebrew carrying the basic meaning of "rock". It can denote the substance "rock" in general; a cliff or precipice, i.e. something made of rock; a small rock, i.e. a stone; or a very large rock, i.e. a mountain, depending on the semantic environment. In the book of Job it occurs seven times and in all but one occurrence[122] P translates with a more specific term in accordance with the current semantic environment, hence the following equivalents:

	MT		P
14:18	אולם הר־נופל יבול וצור יעתק ממקמו	>	ܨܦܝܚܐ
	"But a falling mountain crumbles and a צור is removed from its place."		"steep rock, precipice"
18:4b/c	הלמענך תעזב ארץ ויעתק צור ממקמו	>	ܛܘܪܐ
	"Shall the earth be forsaken for you or a צור be removed from its place."		"mountain"
19:24	בעט־ברזל ועפרת לעד בצור יחצבון	>	ܟܐܦܐ
	"With a pen of iron and lead they were engraven upon a צור forever."		"stone"
22:24	ושית־על־עפר בצר וכצור נחלים אופיר	>	ܚܠܐ "sand"
	"If you place gold in the dust and (the gold) of Ophir in the צור of the wadis."		

---

122 In 29:6 the verse is lacking in P.

כ אֶ ‍כפ <   מזרם הרים ירטבו   ומבלי מחסה חבקו־צוּר 24:8

    "They are wet with the rain of the mountains   "stones"

    and cling to the צור for lack of shelter."

עמﬦ﬩גﬦ <   בְּצוּרוֹת יארים בקע   וכל־יקר ראתה עינו 28:10

    "He cuts out channels in the צורות   "his might" (clearly an

    and his eye sees every precious thing."   interpretive reading)[123]

Elsewhere in the Peshitta, specification of this term also occurs, but not to the extent seen in P-Job. The usual lexical choices are more limited, with ܠܛܘܪܐ denoting "a mountain";[124] ܟܐܦܐ "a rock" in general;[125] ܛܪܢܐ "hard rock, flint";[126] ܫܘܥܐ "rock, rocky hill"[127] and ܬܘܩܦܐ "strength",[128] ܬܩܘܦܐ "strong one"[129] or ܐܠܗܐ "God"[130] when צור is used as a epithet of God or heathen gods.

Our second example, the verb שׂגא, is an Aramaism found only in the book of Job (8:11b;12:23;36:24,26;37:23). It carries the basic meaning "to grow, grow great". Although this is an Aramaic root, the translator of P does not necessarily use this same root (סגי/סגא > שׂגא > ܣܓܝ) unless the semantic environment demands a connotation "be, grow great". Where the semantic environment suggests otherwise, the translator provided a more semantically complex and contextually appropriate verb. Consider each of these occurrences:

MT	P

8:11   בלי־מים   ישׂגה־אחו   בצה   בלא   היגאה־גמא <   ܠ "to

    "Can papyrus grow where there is no marsh?   "to sprout up"

    Can reeds ישׂגה without water?"

---

[123] P reads ܟܣܘܡܬܗ ܢܚܪܘܬ ܦܠܓ ܠܢܗܪܐ ܚܒܠ ܘܟܠ ܫܦܝܪ ܚܙܬ .ܥܝܢܗ "He divided rivers by his might and his eye saw everything precious."

[124] See, for example, Num 23:9; 1 Sam 24:3; Isa 10:26;51:1; Jer 18:14; Nah 1:6.

[125] See, for example, Deut 8:15;32:13; Judg 6:21;13:19; Pss 61:3;81:17; Isa 2:19.

[126] See, for example, Exod 17:6;33:21,22; Isa 2:10,21;8:14;48:21; Pss 78:15,20; 105:41;114:8.

[127] See, for example, 2 Sam 21:10; Prov 30:19; Ps 27:5.

[128] See, for example, Deut 32:37; Isa 17:10.

[129] See, for example, Deut 32:31; Ps 62:8.

[130] See, for example, Pss 31:3; 62:7.

12:23 משׁגיא לגוים ויאבדם   שׁטח לגוים וינחם   >   ܛܥܐ

"He makes nations שׂגא and he destroys them;   "to go astray"
He enlarges nations and leads them away."

36:24 שׁררו אנשׁים   אשׁר פעלו תשׂגיא כי זכר   >   ܣܥܪ "to make
"Remember to שׂגא his work of which men have sung."   great"

36:26 הן־אל שׂגיא ולא נדע   מספר שׁניו ולא־חקר   >   ܥܫܢ
"Behold God is שׂגיא , but we know (him/it) not;   "strong"
the number of his years is unsearchable."

37:23 שׁגיא־כח שׁדי לא־מצאנהו   >   ܣܓܝ "great"

ומשׁפט ורב־צדקה לא יענה
"Shaddai, we cannot find him, שׂגיא in power and justice,
and abundant righteousness he does not oppress."[131]

3. Contextual Translation. In the process termed contextual translation
there is no semantic connection between the lexeme in the source
language and the lexeme in the target language. The presumed semantic
environment dictates the choice of correspondence. The translator's
decision to contextualize a word is not a whimsical notion, but rather is
prompted by two types of ambiguity:
(a) the presence of a *hapax legomenon* or rare word;
(b) the presence of a common Hebrew word that was either used with a
slightly different nuance or for some reason was inappropriate to the
semantic environment.

Over eighty examples of contextual translation were discovered in
P-Job. Let us consider six such examples; three are hapax or rare words
and three are common words deemed inappropriate.

A. Contextualization of *Hapax Legomena* and Rare Lexemes.

a. √חלשׁ. Heb. חלשׁ "weak, prostration" is a rare root occurring but
three times verbally in the OT (Exod 17:13; Isa 14:12; Job 14:10), once
nominally (Exod 32:18), and once as an adjective (Joel 4:10). The Syriac
cognate √ܚܠܫ "to be frail, feeble, weak" does occur and is used in Joel

---

131 For further examples of substitution involving specification see Appendix D.

4:10 and Exod 32:18; however, in Job 14:10 P translates with the √ ܒܠܐ "to fade away", a translation based on the semantic environment:[132]

MT   וְגֶבֶר יָמוּת וַיֶּחֱלָשׁ   וַיִּגְוַע אָדָם וְאַיּוֹ:
      "But man dies and is weak/prostrate;
      man expires and where is he?"

English translations of this verse and even the BDB have attempted to correct this disparagement by rendering √חלשׁ by "prostrate", hence man dies and is laid out prone. P obviously did not follow this train of thought. If a man dies how can he be weak?, hence:

P   ܘܓܒܪܐ ܡܐܬ ܘܡܬܚܒܠ. ܘܡܝܬ ܒܪܢܫܐ ܘܠܝܬܘܗܝ.
      "And man dies and fades away;
      and the son of man perishes and he is no more."

b. עטין. Heb. עֲטִינָיו "his pails" is a *hapax legomenon* found in Job 21:24.[133] The P and the Versions translate it as a body part based on context.

MT   עֲטִינָיו מָלְאוּ חָלָב   וּמֹחַ עַצְמוֹתָיו יְשֻׁקֶּה:
      "His pails are full of milk,
      and the marrow of his bones is moist."

P   ܘܓܒܝ̈ܗ ܡܠܝܢ ܚܠܒܐ. ܘܓܪ̈ܡܘܗܝ ܡܠܝܢ ܡܘܚܐ.
      "And his sides are full of fat,
      and his bones are full of marrow."

c. גמא. The Heb. verb √גמא "to swallow" is found only in Job 39:24 and Gen 24:17.[134] P once again lets context guide his translation.

---

[132] P likewise translates contextually in Exod 17:13 (ܬܒܪ "to break") and in Isa 14:12 (ܡܒܗܬܢܐ "an insolent, infamous or outrageous person").

[133] See BDB, p. 742a, s.v. √עטן where reference is made to this root in Modern Hebrew and in Arabic.

[134] In Gen 24:17 P translates with the Aphel of the √ ܓܡܥ "to cause to swallow" which in that context is appropriate.

MT   בְּרַעַשׁ וְרֹגֶז יְגַמֶּא־אָרֶץ   וְלֹא־יַאֲמִין כִּי־קוֹל שׁוֹפָר:
     "With quaking and rage <u>he swallows</u> the ground;
     he cannot stand still at the sound of the trumpet."

P   ܒܙܘܥܐ ܘܒܪܘܓܙܐ ܗܘ ܪܗܛ ܥܠ ܐܪܥܐ.
       ܘܠܐ ܕܚܠ ܡܢ ܩܠܐ ܕܩܪܢܐ.
     "With quaking and with rage <u>he runs</u> upon the earth;
     and he is not afraid of the sound of the horn."

B. Contextualization of Common Hebrew Lexemes.

a. תּוּשִׁיָּה. Heb. תּוּשִׁיָּה "abiding success" occurs nine times in the OT, four of which appear in the book of Job. As we saw above, the translator of the P had the tendency to generalize this term, reading ܚܟܡܬܐ "wisdom" in all but one case, Job 6:13. In this verse P reads ܦܘܪܩܢܗ "his salvation", no doubt translated contextually on the basis of its parallelism with עזרה "help" in stich one and the fact that the translation "wisdom" would be inappropriate in this verse.

MT   הַאִם אֵין עֶזְרָתִי בִי   וְתֻשִׁיָּה נִדְּחָה מִמֶּנִּי:
     "Behold, there is no help in me
     and <u>abiding success</u> is driven from me."

P   ܗܐ ܠܝܬ ܠܗ ܠܥܘܕܪܢܝ ܒܝ. ܘܦܘܪܩܢܗ ܐܬܪܚܩ ܡܢܝ.
     "Behold, his help is not in me
     and <u>his salvation</u> is far from me."

Targum does maintain the usual translation חוכמתא "wisdom", but LXX reads with βοηθεια "help, aid" likewise presenting a term parallel to Heb. עזרה. Note, however, it is possible that P (and LXX) may have read תשועה "salvation" for which ܦܘܪܩܢܐ is the usual equivalent,[135] thus suggesting an orthographic error of two very similar words.

---

[135] See for example Ps 144:10.

b. ‎√ידע‎. Heb. ‎√ידע‎ both verbally and nominally is a very common root, equally common is its cognate in Aramaic and Syriac (‎ידע‎/‎ܝܕܥ‎). Thus there is no question of non-recognition or misunderstanding of its meaning. However, in 24:16 P renders this verb by ‎√ܚܙܐ‎ "to see". Contextualization is the motivation behind this semantic divergence.

MT ‎חתר בחשך בתים   יומם חתמו־למו   לא־ידעו אור:‎
   "In the darkness they dig through houses;
    during the daytime they shut (lit. seal) themselves up;
    they do not <u>know</u> the light."

P ‎ܦܠܬ ܒܚܫܘܟܐ ܒܬܐ. ܘܒܐܝܡܡܐ ܚܬܡ ܐܢܘܢ ܠܗܘܢ‎
  ‎ܘܠܐ ܢܚܙܘܢ ܢܘܗܪܐ.‎
   "In the darkness he breaks (into) houses;
    and in the daytime he seals/marks them,
    so that they do not <u>see</u> the light."

P's translation of the MT departs in more than one item. The implied burglars in the MT become the implied singular burglar in P; Heb. ‎למו‎ understood as the reflexive is rendered by ‎ܠܗܘܢ‎ , now the direct object, with ‎ܒܬܐ‎ "houses" the referent. Thus the meaning has changed from:

MT   The burglars shut themselves up during the daytime >>>>
P   the burglars scout out potential houses for burglary during the
     daytime and mark them with a sign/seal.

P likewise adds the dependent conjunction -‎ܘ‎ "so that", thus making stich two dependent on stich one. Finally, P renders Heb. ‎√ידע‎ "to know" by ‎√ܚܙܐ‎ "to see" which better accords contextually with the direct object ‎אור‎/‎ܢܘܗܪܐ‎ "light". The enigma here remains: since P speaks of but one burglar, who is the subject of the verb ‎ܢܚܙܘܢ‎ "they do (not) see (the light)?" The houses? If so what does this mean: houses that do not see the light?

c. √עשק. Heb. √עשק "to oppress, wrong, extort" is fairly common in both verbal and nominal forms.[136] It presents few translational problems. In the book of Job it occurs twice (10:3 and 40:23). In 10:3 it is rendered by a semantic equivalent √גחך "to oppress", but in 40:23 it is translated by √יגאה "to swell up". This departure is clearly due to context.

MT   הן יעשק נהר לא יחפוז

                      יבטח כי־יגיח ירדן אל־פיהו:

       "If the river <u>oppresses</u> he is not alarmed;

       he is confident when the Jordan bursts forth unto his mouth."

P   ܐܢ ܢܬܬܙܝܥ ܢܗܪܐ. ܠܐ ܢܕܚܠ.

                      ܘܡܬܬܟܠ ܥܠ ܝܘܪܕܢܢ ܕܢܦܘܩ ܠܦܘܡܗ.

       "If the river <u>swells</u>, he is not agitated;

       and he is confident when the Jordan pours into his mouth."

P clearly rendered √עשק "to oppress" by a verb √יגאה "to swell" more semantically appropriate for the noun ܢܗܪܐ "river".[137]

4. Interpretation. As defined in the Model of Translation Technique a semantic alteration will be termed interpretation when the translation can be shown to explain the meaning of a word, phrase or clause. This is a very general statement, for this could encompass almost any departure from the source text such as the addition or omission of an element or the contextual translation of a *hapax legomenon.* All could be considered different means of explaining the text. Therefore interpretation as a type of semantic substitution will be used in a more restrictive sense to reflect a substitution of a word when this substitution can be shown to be reflective of the translator's perspective regarding an underlying ideological comment. This subtle manner of projecting one's views may concern theological issues such as the nature of God, man's relationship with God; or moral issues such as good versus evil, the fate of the wicked. In some instances, too, it seems as if the translator came across a word and simply asked: What does that mean in this context? Then he

---

[136] See BDB, pp. 798-799, s.v. √עשׁק.

[137] For further examples of substitution involving contextualization see Appendix E: Contextualization in P-Job.

drew on his socio-religio-cultural background to find an answer. With this in mind we will examine examples dealing with three topics: the fate of the wicked, the role and nature of God, and especially the character of Job.

A. The Fate of the Wicked.

When the translator of P came across צלעו "his rib" in 18:12 or לצפוניו "for his treasures" in 20:26, he was not faced with a semantic enigma. Both are common lexemes with straightforward meanings. Yet in their semantic environment the translator saw a deeper meaning. Consider each of these examples, statements made by Bildad (18:12) and Zophar (20:26) about the fate of the wicked:

18:12   MT   יהי־רעב אנו ואיד נכון לצלעו:
"His strength is famished and calamity is ready for his rib."

P   ܘܢܗܘܐ ܟܦܢܐ ܚܫܗ. ܘܐܒܕܢܐ ܡܛܝܒ ܠܒܬܪܝܬܗ.
"And famine will be his pain,
and ruin is ready for his posterity."

Although there is a bit of disagreement regarding the derivation of Heb. צלע - either from צלע I from which the noun "rib" is derived[138] or from צלע II "to limp", hence the noun "limping, stumbling"[139] - P clearly understood the former derivation צלע I "rib". P, however, found a deeper association for rib, i.e. not in reference to a wicked man's rib or side, hence a synecdoche for the part referring to the whole, i.e. the wicked, but rather saw in this a reference to his progeny, i.e. a part of him that survives into the future. Calamity is passed from the father to the children. Note rather interestingly Targum here translates צלע by אנתתיה "his wife", clearly interpreting צלע in terms of Genesis where the woman was formed from the rib of man (Gen 2:22).

20:26   M T   כל־חשך טמון לצפוניו תאכלהו אש לא־נפח
ירע שריד באהלו:

---

[138] See Dhorme, p. 263; Habel, pp. 280-281; and Pope, p. 132, 135.
[139] See BDB, p. 854, s.v. צלע II; and ICC, p. 160.

> "All darkness is reserved <u>for his treasures</u>;
> a fire not blown upon will devour him;
> the remnant in his tent will be consumed."

P

.ܘܬܠܬܘܗܝ ܓܠܝܙ ܚܫܘܟܐ ܟܠܗ
.ܚܝܒ ܠܐ ܕܝܢ ܢܘܪܐ ܡܢܠܐܟܬܗ
.ܡܫܟܢܗ ܒܗ ܥܒܕ ܟܐܒ ܘܗܪ

> "And all darkness is reserved <u>for his generation</u>,
> a fire which is not blown out will consume him,
> and the remnant will do evil in his tent."

Our concern here is with the first stich "All darkness is hidden for his treasures", a straightforward clause with no textual difficulties using basic vocabulary items. One question persists, however: What does this mean? The translator of P provides his answer by interpreting Heb. לצפוניו "for his treasures" not as material possessions, but rather as ܠܬܠܬܘܗܝ "for his generations". This statement, as in the previous example, alludes to the fact that the wicked man's descendants will be held accountable for his behavior and fall prey to his fate.

B. God.

The book of Job is replete with references to the nature of God, his role in creation and his relationship with man. In translating these statements the translator of P occasionally provides a little more insight into his (or his religion's) view of God. Consider but two of these interpretive slips.

In Chapter Nine Job bemoans his lack of control when contending with one so majestic and powerful as God. In verse fifteen he states:

MT   אֲשֶׁר אִם־צָדַקְתִּי לֹא אֶעֱנֶה לִמְשֹׁפְטִי אֶתְחַנָּן:
> "Though I am innocent, I cannot answer (him);
> I must implore the favour of <u>my opponent</u>."

P provides the following translation:

P   ܐܠܐ ܐܝܪܪܚܡ ܐܠ ܐܬܠܐ ܟܝ .ܗܠܝܢ ܐܬܚܒܐ.

"Although I am justified, I will not be answered
and I will make supplication to <u>my judge</u>."

Our focus here is on P's interpretation of Heb. מְשֹׁפְטִי , a rare use
of the Pual participle, but generally understood as meaning "my
opponent".[140] P by contrast may have found this concept of opponents
in court objectionable, for in the legal system the defendant and plaintiff
are considered equals before the court. Staying within the realm of the
√שׁפט, P interprets this word as ܕܝܢܝ "my judge", hence placing God on a
higher level and no longer intimating that a battle of equals is underway.
Note the Vulgate translates similarly *sed meum iudicem* "to my judge"
and Targum preserves a similar concept, although periphrastically
expressed, למן דדין יתי "to whomever judges me". The reading of
the LXX (του κριματος μου) implies a reading of מִשְׁפָּט
"judgment".

In the next example, 13:11, the translator of P provides his
understanding of what Heb. שְׂאֵתוֹ "his (God's) majesty,loftiness" means:

13:11 MT עליכם: יפל ופחדו   אתכם תבעת שְׂאֵתוֹ הלא
"Will not <u>his majesty</u> terrify you and his dread fall upon you?"

P   ܕܕܚܠܬܗ ܬܒܗܬܟܘܢ. ܘܙܘܥܬܗ ܬܦܠ ܥܠܝܟܘܢ.
"<u>His fear</u> terrifies you and his terror falls upon you."

Mandl suggests that P's interpretation of שְׂאֵתוֹ "majesty/loftiness"
by ܕܚܠܬܗ "his fear" was prompted by a desire to soften an offensive
expression.[141] This hardly seems the case for there is nothing offensive
about the grandeur of a higher authority intimidating or even frightening
someone, rather it seems that the translator may have just chosen to
define God's majesty in the sense of a fear of reverence.   Targum's

---

[140] See BDB, p. 1048a, s.v. שׁפט. See also Habel, p. 179,182; ICC, p. 90,57; Pope,
p. 69,72.
[141] See Mandl, p. 15.

translation implies this same notion of fear of reverence in its translation
רתיתיה "his trembling".[142]

c. Job.

Chapters 29-31 contain the last soliloquy of Job before the upstart
Elihu professes his opinions and before the Lord's speeches from the
whirlwind awe Job into recanting and being silent. Within Job's last
speech he pines for "the good old days when all was right", when God
was with him; when he held the respect of young and old alike. In the
middle of Chapter 30 his tone changes to one of persecution recounting
the horrors that have befallen him. In Chapter 31 for the last time he
denies any wrong-doing on his part and repeatedly challenges that if he
has done any wrong (unknowingly we presume) then let the chips fall
where they may.

In nine places within this speech, P provides us with a little extra
information regarding Job by lending its interpretation to a number of
common, but somewhat ambiguous words. In 29:4 Job wishes for "his
autumn days" בימי חרפי. What are autumnal days? Some might view
these as a man's final days before death. P, by contrast, translates ܒܝܘܡܬܐ
ܕܒܣܝܡܘܬܝ "in the days of my favour", clearly referring to the time of his
life when he was in God's favour. In 29:7-8 the MT relates that when Job
went out into the city gate the young men saw him and were hushed and
the old men rose and עמדו "they stood".[143] P interprets this verb as ܟܕ
ܗܘܘ ܡܬܕܡܪܝܢ ܒܝ "and they marvelled at me", clearly a more flattering verb.
Furthermore, in 29:21 the text states that men listened to Job and waited;
they וידמו "they were dumb/silent" for my counsel. P interprets this as
ܨܬܘ "they listened" to my counsel. And in reference to his words
29:22 states "my word תטף upon them". P interprets תטף √נטף "to
drop (usually of rain or myrrh)" quite delectably as √ ܒܣܡܬ "to be sweet,
pleasing", i.e. my words were pleasing to them, clearly indicating his
words were palatable to them. In the final verse of Chapter 29, verse 25,
the MT reads אבחר דרכם "I chose their (his peoples) way", a clear yet
ambiguous clause. What precisely does "way" refer to? P doesn't answer

---

[142] In 41:17 Heb. מִשְּׁתוֹ is similarly interpreted ܡܢ ܕܚܠܬܐ "from fear".

[143] In 37:14 P interprets עמד in this same manner.

this question, but does interpret √בחר "to choose" as √בקא "to search out". It is a subtle nuance that the translator might be trying to suggest here. Job does not just select a man's path through life or provide a definitive answer to a legal problem which Job earlier states he was often called upon to solve. Rather he searches for the right way and presents this option.

In Chapter 30 the tone of Job's soliloquy changes; he now bemoans his adversity. Men who once respected him are now viewed as beneath his dignity. In 30:8 he calls them "sons of foolishness", בני בלי־שם "sons without a name". P quite harshly interprets this phrase as בנֵי רֵוּלא "iniquitous sons", clearly viewing them more harshly than Job and in a sense showing his sympathy with Job. In 30:9 Job states "I have become their song (נגינתם) and I am a word (מלה) to them". P clearly viewed these nouns as euphemisms, interpreting them as רֵנֵמהוֹם "their subject of thought" and רֵהמרא "amazement". And finally in 30:16 when Job says "my soul pours itself out (תשתפך) against me", the translator of P wanted to make certain that Job's feelings were adequately depicted by interpreting this phrase to mean "my soul was agitated (אֵתֵתֵזיעֵהֵ)".

The examples of interpretive substitution examined here concerning Job are not necessarily exhaustive, but only representative of this technique and the fact that the translator of Job was clearly in sympathy with Job and wanted to make certain his character was properly portrayed.[144]

Furthermore, these interpretive readings as well as those regarding the wicked and God, unless otherwise noted, are unique to P-Job. They are not the usual translational equivalences found elsewhere in the Peshitta to the OT, thus lending credence to the belief that the translator was truly trying to inject his or his religious circle's ideological perspectives on these subjects rather than just offering a literal translation of the MT.

5. Lexical Levelling. As defined in the Model of Translation Technique, lexical levelling is a type of semantic alteration in which one word is used to translate a variety of terms.

---

[144] For further examples of substitutions involving interpretation see Appendix F.

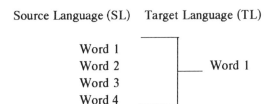

Source Language (SL)   Target Language (TL)

Word 1
Word 2 ——— Word 1
Word 3
Word 4

Lexical levelling might be considered a secondary process because it tends to result from generalization, specification, contextual translation or even interpretation. So, for example, we saw that Heb. אַף "nose, nostril, anger", a polysemous noun, was rendered by the specific Syriac ܪܘܓܙܐ "anger" when the semantic environment so dictated it. Now it is also noteworthy that Heb. רגז "anger" is rendered by the Syriac cognate ܪܘܓܙܐ.[145] Further the specific Heb. terms כעס/כעש "vexation" (anger + annoyance)[146] and עברות (anger + arrogance)[147] are rendered by the general term ܪܘܓܙܐ, given the fact that Syriac lacks the additional lexemes to provide the same variety as the Hebrew. Thus diagrammed:

MT(SL = Hebrew)   P (TL = Syriac)

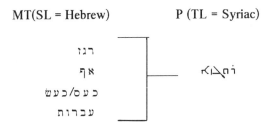

רגז
אף
כ ע ס/כ ע ש   ܪܘܓܙܐ
ע ב ר ו ת

---

145 See 3:17,26;37:2;39:24 and verbally in 12:6. Note in 14:1 P translates ܙܘܥܐ "shakings" for רגז and in 9:6 the verbal √רגז is also translated by the √ܙܘܥ "to shake". In 9:6 the connotation accords well with the semantic environment "He who shakes the earth from its place and its pillars tremble", but in 14:1 P's lexical choice for רגז "anger" as ܙܘܥܐ "shakings" is enigmatic: (MT)"Man born of woman (is) short of days and full of rage" > (P) "Thus is man, born of woman, and he is short of days and one who endures shakings".

146 See 5:2;6:2;10:17;17:7.

147 See 21:30. In 40:11, however, עברות is translated by ܚܡܬܐ "heat, rage, fury" because ܪܘܓܙܐ is reserved as an equivalence for Heb. אַף, which also appears in this verse.

Similarly, we saw Heb. כף "palm" was generalized in P's choice of correspondence אָיד "hand" and when we note that the natural cognate correspondence for Heb. יד is also אָיד, lexical levelling has once again occurred.

MT (SL = Hebrew)   P (TL = Syriac)

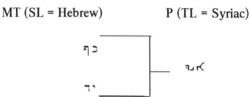

Lexical levelling is not restricted to nominal forms. Examples of verbal levelling are also attested. Consider the following example:

MT (SL = Hebrew)   P (TL = Syriac)

קטל "to kill"	
טרף "to tear"	
רצח "to murder"	מְקַטֶל "to kill"
הרג "to kill, slay"	
מות (Hiphil "to kill, put to death")	
חול (Polal "to be made to writhe")	

In this example we first find the cognate lexical equivalence (קטל > מְקַטֶל)[148]; two examples of generalization (טרף[149] and הרצ[150] > מְקַטֶל); and two examples of language difference. Although Syriac does possess the √ מבהדת "to die" with a causative sense in the Ethpe./Aphel, the translator apparently chose not to use this root in 5:2 and 9:23. In the case of הרג,[151] whereas Syriac does possess this root it carries a totally unconnected meaning "to muse upon, dwell upon in thought".[152] This is

[148] See 13:15;24:14.
[149] See 18:4.
[150] See 24:14.
[151] See 5:2;20:16.
[152] See Payne-Smith , p. 106b, s.v. מְהֵי.

also true of the √שרף. In Syriac it means "to smite, buffet, dash against".153 As for the correspondence חול√ > ﻢ, יחוללו ,154 error may be the culprit. P may have confused חול√ Polal "to be made to writhe" with חלל√ I "to pierce, wound".

An excellent example of contextual translation leading to lexical levelling occurs in 30:12-13:

MT   על־ימין פרחח יקומו רגלי <u>שלחו</u>
                 <u>ויסלו</u> עלי ארחות אדים:
                 <u>נתסו</u> נתיבתי להותי־יעילו לא עזר למו:

"On the right the rabble rise, they <u>push</u> my feet aside,
they <u>cast</u> against me their ways of destruction.
They <u>break down</u> my path, they promote my calamity;
No one helps them."

P

"Upon my right they rose and <u>entangle</u> my feet,
and they <u>entangled</u> me in the paths of their ways,
and they <u>entangled</u> my paths in vain;
and they rejoiced over what has befallen me;
and there will be no help for them."

The translator used the √ܓܕܠ (Parel of √ܓܕܠ) "to entangle" to translate three Hebrew verbs: Piel of שלח "to send, cast away"; סלל√ "to lift up, cast up" and √ נתס "to tear, break down". Heb. √שלח is a very common verb; P seems to have found it inappropriate to the semantic environment ("to send/cast away my feet"), hence choosing to provide a contextual substitute. Heb. √סלל occurs but ten times verbally

---

153 See Payne-Smith, p. 182b. s.v. ܓܦܦ.
154 See 39:1.

in the OT. In six places it is rendered by a semantic equivalent[155] and in
four places, including here, a contextual substitute is provided.[156] P's
choice to contextualize here, as against in Job 19:12 where √חיל "to
prepare a path" is used, may be due to the translator's wish to harmonize
√סלל with the preceding שלח > ܐܘܒܠ and the following נתס > ܐܘܒܠ,
for both here and in 19:12 the direct objects ארחות "paths" (30:12) and
דרכם "their road/way" (19:12) are conducive to the verbal idea of
√סלל "to cast up (a path, road)". The last verb נתס is a *hapax*. Given
the semantic environment already determined by P, it is no surprise to see
this verb likewise rendered √ܐܘܒܠ.[157] This example also demonstrates
that words that are levelled often occur in close proximity.

Interpretation too can result in lexical levelling. Consider P's use
of √ܕܢ:

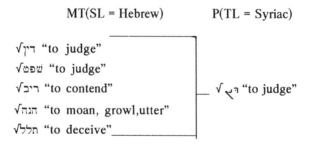

	MT(SL = Hebrew)	P(TL = Syriac)
√דין	"to judge"	
√שפט	"to judge"	
√ריב	"to contend"	√ܕܢ "to judge"
√הגה	"to moan, growl, utter"	
√תלל	"to deceive"	

Syriac ܕܢ is the cognate correspondence for Heb. √דין. Similarly
√ܕܢ for √שפט is due to language difference; Syriac lacks another basic
lexeme meaning "to judge". Heb. ריב > Syr. ܕܢ, by contrast, is a case
of specification. This root means "to strive, contend", both physically and
in the juridical sense, i.e. contention that leads to the intervention of

---

[155] See Jer 18:15 ; Isa 62:10; and Job 19:12 √חיל "to prepare a path; tread, find out";
Prov 15:19 and Isa 57:14(2) √ܦܨܚ "to be/become clear (of a round from rocks)".

[156] See Exod 9:17 √ܫܘܡܣܢ "to grasp firmly, hold fast"; Jer 50:26 √ܒܥܐ "to search out,
investigate"; Prov 4:8 √ܚܒܒ "to love vehemently, embrace"; Job 30:12 √ܐܘܒܠ "to
entangle".

[157] Note also P simply omits an equivalent for the *hapax* פורחח and provides a double
reading for לחותי. See Excursus I: Paraphrase.

justice and an eventual judgment. P specifies that this last aspect is
alluded to, hence √ܕ‌ܝ.

As for the correspondence √הגה > √ܕ‌ܝ, interpretation has
prompted this substitution, for note the cognate √ܗܓܐ does exist in
Syriac with the same meaning. √הגה occurs twice in the book of Job
(27:4; 37:2).

אם תדברנה שֹפתי עולה ולשוני אם־יהגה רמיה   27:4
"If my lips speak iniquity and my tongue, if it utter deceit;"

P generalizes its substitution, reading with the common √ܡܠܠ "to speak:

ܐܢ ܢܡܠܠܢ ܣܦܬܝ̈ ܐܘܠܐ. ܘܠܫܢܝ ܐܢ ܢܡܠܠ ܢܟܠܐ

"If my lips speak iniquity and my tongue, if it speaks deceit"

By contrast, in 37:2 שמעו שמוע ברגז קלו והגה מפיו יצא
"Listen to the thunder of his voice and the rumbling that comes forth
from his mouth" the noun הגה "rumbling" is interpreted as referring to
not just the utterance from God's mouth but his judgment, hence P's ܕܝܢܐ
"judgment".

Heb. √תלל "to deceive" (13:9) is a *hapax legomenon*, hence P's
choice of correspondence is due to contextualization:

MT   הטוב כי־יחקר אתכם   אם־כהתל באנוש תחתלו בו:
       "Is it good when He searches you out,
        or can you deceive Him as one deceives a man?"

P   ܫܦܝܪ ܠܟܘܢ ܕܢܒܨܐ ܠܟܘܢ.
       ܐܘ ܐܝܟ ܕܡܬܚܪܐ ܓܒܪ ܥܡ ܚܒܪܗ ܗܟܢܐ ܡܬܚܪܝܢ ܐܢܬܘܢ ܥܡܗ.
       "Is it good for you that He investigates you,
        or do you contend with Him as one who contends with
        everyone?"[158]

---

[158] For further examples of substitutions resulting in lexical levelling see Appendix G.

*   *   *

What effect do these substitutions have on the meaning of the source text (MT) as transferred into the target text (P)? Substitution stemming from errors - be they errors of linguistic interference, confusion of letters, metathesis of root radicals, confusion of homographs, or misrecognition of Hebrew vocalization - results in innovative propositions. Substitutions involving generalization and specification, since they involve either the addition or omission of a semantic component, while still preserving the basic component(s), yield synonymous propositions that differ at the stylistic level. Lexical levelling in most cases effects the stylistics and fine nuances of the vocabulary by narrowing the semantic variety found in the Hebrew language. In contextual translation and interpretation *can* lie the greatest semantic departures from the MT. For contextual translation not only depends on how well the semantic environment can predict the meaning of an unclear term, but also at times it is uncontrollably subject to the translator's ability to correctly guess; correctly, that is, from the perspective of an evaluator who has both the source and target text at his disposal. As for interpretation, a semantic link still remains between the source text (MT) and target text (P), but extra information is given reflecting the translator's ideology.

VI

Style

The term style, as earlier stated, refers to those elements of choice which an author can impart to a literary work to best express himself. "Expressiveness", as S. Ullmann states "covers a wide variety of linguistic features which have one thing in common: they do not directly affect the meaning of the utterance, the actual information it conveys."[1] Ian Finley, by contrast, wrote, "a poem represents a delicate balance of highly sensitive elements, the changing of any one of which will inevitably upset that balance."[2] Thus, one writer believes meaning is unaffected by stylistic changes, whereas the other sees meaning and style closely linked, with a change in style producing a change in meaning. This topic, style, is addressed in the following pages for just that purpose, that is to discern how the translator of P dealt with the stylistic peculiarities in the MT to Job and how his treatment(s) effect the meaning of the text. Three areas of style are explored: sentence type, figurative language and idiom.

Sentence Type

Sentences are classified in a variety of ways. They can be classified by purpose - declarative, interrogative, imperative, exclamatory - or by their structure - simple, complex, compound, compound-complex.[3] Here, discussion of sentences follows the former manner of classification: purpose. A declarative sentence states a proposition; an interrogative asks

---

[1] *Language and Style*, p. 101.

[2] *Translating.* Teach Yourself Books (Warwick Lane, London: St. Paul's House, 1971), p. 73.

[3] Wooley, Scott & Bracher, *College Handbook of Composition*, pp. 116-118;134.

a question; an imperative expresses a command; and an exclamatory sentence indicates surprise or emphasis. Note, however, the imperative sentence, being specifically concerned with P's treatment of the imperative verbal form, was included in the study of tenses found in Chapter III Grammar: Tense and will not be repeated here. Furthermore, only those sentence types which deviate from the MT will be examined for adjustment, motivation and effect on meaning, not those which are maintained in P-Job. Thus, a MT declarative that is translated as a declarative will not be covered, but rather a declarative that, for example, is transformed into a question will be examined. Sentence type is discussed according to the following outline:

I. Interrogative Sentences

    1. Simple Interrogative Sentence
        a. Heb. הֲ > Syr. Ø
        b. Heb. הֲ > Syr. ܕܠܡܐ
        c. Heb. הֲ > Syr. ܗܐ

    2. Simple Interrogative + Particle
        a. Heb. הלא
        b. Heb. היש
        c. Heb. האף

    3. Disjunctive Questions

    4. Other Interrogatives
        a. Particles אי־זה, אי, מה
        b. Creation of an interrogative sentence

II. Declarative Sentences

    1. Conditional Sentences

III. Exclamatory Sentences
    1. הנה and הן

2. נא

3. גם and אף

I. Interrogative Sentences

In Hebrew both the direct[4] and indirect[5] simple question are introduced by the interrogative Heh. Disjunctive questions[6] likewise use this interrogative particle, most commonly in the combination הַ . . . אִם, but the combinations הַ . . . וְ ; הַ . . . אוֹ and הַ . . . Ø also occur.

Syriac, by contrast, has no special means of indicating the *direct* simple question. As Nöldeke states "such interrogative sentences can only be distinguished from sentences of affirmation by the emphasis."[7] The indirect interrogative, however, can be indicated by the introductory particle ܕܠܡܐ "perhaps, perchance". "Can be indicated" is the key phrase here, for this particle, too, is somewhat flexible in meaning and usage. According to J. Payne Smith it can be translated "that . . . not, lest, not; unless, except (after verbs of fearing); it may be, perhaps, perchance; why?, whether? is it not? not?" and additionally it can be used when "asking a question when the answer is expected to be negative".[8] Furthermore, Nöldeke states that whereas it is used to introduce the indirect interrogative "it is not always easy to distinguish it from the direct".[9] The particle ܕ, indicating dependence, may have an assumed or implicit governing word[10] or ܕ itself can be used as an introductory particle to direct speech.[11] Thus, determining a question much less the type of question is not a simple task in Syriac. As Nöldeke states "the type of question is very often determined by the connection, the enfolding of the clauses, and particularly the change of person necessary in many cases of *oratio obliqua*."[12] Nöldeke's words were in reference to a Syriac text. Here, however, we are working with the text of P-Job, a

---

4 See Williams, #541-542.
5 See Williams, #543; and GKC 150i.
6 See Williams #544; and Andersen 8.6.
7 See Nöldeke, #331.
8 See J. Payne Smith, p. 93a, s.v. ܕܠܡܐ.
9 See Nöldeke, #373.
10 See Nöldeke, #373.
11 See Nöldeke, #367.
12 See Nöldeke, #372.

translation of the Hebrew text of Job, that is a translation from a source
language that in marking questions should lend guidance to determining
the existence of a question in the Syriac text.

Thus, guidance from the Hebrew source text, along with context
and the knowledge that Syriac does not represent the interrogative Heh,
with the exception of the specialized, albeit somewhat fluid, use of
ܕܠܡܐ, would suggest the Syriac treatment of these type of questions by:

1. non-representation of the interrogative particle Heh with
context and emphasis determining the existence of a question;
2. use of the particle ܕܠܡܐ when an indirect question or a
question expecting a negative answer is indicated.

As will shortly be seen, this, however, is not the case.

1. Simple Interrogative Sentence
a. Heb. הֲ > Syr. Ø

The most common way of handling the Heh interrogative is
through omission, or Ø morpheme. The motivation is language
difference, with the effect on meaning synonymy with only a structural
change in representation. So, for example, in 39:19 we have a simple
direct interrogative question:

MT   התתן לסוס גבורה   התלביש צוארו רעמה:
"Do you give the horse might?
Do you garb his neck (with) a mane?

P   ܢܬܠ ܐܢܬ ܠܣܘܣܝܐ ܓܢܒܪܘܬܐ. ܘܡܠܒܫ ܐܢܬ ܨܘܪܗ ܙܝܢܐ.
"(Do) you give the horse might?
Do you clothe his neck (with) armour?

Thus, Heb. ה ... ה > Syr. Ø ... Ø, and this equivalency accords with
the language difference described in the preceding paragraphs. However,
of the 21 simple interrogative questions only ten follow this pattern, that
is omission motivated by language difference resulting in synonymy with

only a structural change.[13] Hence, approximately 50% diverge from the expected norm, and it is here that inquiry is further directed.

In Job 34:31,33 omission of the interrogative also occurs. However, the motivation and effect on meaning differ from the norm. Consider these verses:

34:31 MT כִּי־אֶל־אֵל הֶאָמַר נָשָׂאתִי לֹא אֶחְבֹּל׃

"For has anyone said to God,
'I am mistaken, I will offend no more'."

P ܡܛܠ ܕܐܠܗܐ ܐܡܪ. ܕܫܒܩܬ
ܕܫܒܩܬ ܠܐ ܡܚܒܠ ܐܢܐ ܕܠܐ ܚ̈ܛܗܘܢ

"For God said that I have forgiven,
I am not destroying those who do not sin."

34:33 MT הֲמֵעִמְּךָ יְשַׁלְּמֶנָּה כִּי־מָאַסְתָּ כִּי־אַתָּה תִבְחַר וְלֹא־אָנִי
וּמַה־יָּדַעְתָּ דַבֵּר׃

"Is it on your terms (that) He will requite you since you object?
For you must choose and not I; what you know - Speak!"

ܬܘܒ ܠܐ ܐܘܣܦ ܠܡܡܠܠ ܠܟ ܦܬܓܡܐ ܥܠ ܕܚܛܝܬ.
ܐܢܬ ܓܝܪ ܐܬܒܚܢܬ ܘܠܐ ܐܢܐ. ܘܡܕܡ ܕܝܕܥ ܐܢܬ ܡܠܠ.

"I will not again continue to answer you because you sinned,
for you have been tried and not I; and what you know - Speak!"

In both cases P did not recognize or misunderstood the interrogative. In 34:31, the omission of one אל and, in 34:33, the misdivision of verses - לא אסיף is added from 34:32 - may have necessitated the change from interrogative to declarative. Likewise in 34:31 a question may have been theologically objectionable, i.e. "For has God said . . ." implies God would destroy men without sin.

Another exception in which P does not represent the Heh interrogative is in 27:9.

---

[13] See vv. 1:9;4:2;10:3;20:4;22:15;23:6;35:2;37:20;39:19(2).

MT הצעקתו ישמע אל "Will God hear his cry
כי־תבוא עליו צרה: when distress comes upon him?"

P ܡܛܠ ܕܠܐ ܫܡܥ ܐܠܗܐ ܩܠ ܨܠܘܬܗ.
ܟܕ ܐܬܝܐ ܠܘܬܗ ܒܝܫܬܐ.
"Because God does not hear the sound of his prayer
when evil comes upon him."

Here the formula ܡܛܠ ܕܠܐ is used. The addition of ܡܛܠ ܕ- serves the purpose of connecting this verse to 27:8, rather than as a substitution for the Heh interrogative. Noteworthy, however, is the addition of the negative particle ܠܐ, whereby P translates with the response it believes to be implicit in the Heb. question: Will God hear the cry of the wicked? > God will not hear the cry of the wicked.

b. Heb. הֲ > Syr. ܕܠܡܐ

A second way in which the P represents the interrogative Heh is, as stated, by the particle ܕܠܡܐ. Three times this equivalence occurs in Job. Once in an indirect question (22:13) and twice with questions expecting negative reply (14:14;22:13). This would seem to agree with the usage of this particle, i.e. indicating an indirect question or one expecting a negative response. However, if the other simple interrogatives are examined we note that in 39:19 two questions expecting a negative reply occur and ܕܠܡܐ is not used. Thus, as stated, the use of ܕܠܡܐ is not so clear cut. In the present verse then a further motivation - ideological in nature - seems to be indicated, for all three touch on theological issues:

22:2 MT הֲלאל יסכן־גבר כי־יסכן עלימו משכיל:
"Can man be of service to God;
Surely he who is wise is profitable to himself."

P ܕܠܡܐ ܠܡ ܐܠܗܐ ܐܡܪ ܐܢܬ ܠܓܒܪܐ.
ܕܐܢܬ ܐܫܬܘܝܬ ܠܘܬܗ ܒܚܟܡܬܐ.
"Perhaps, O man, you can say to God
that you are equal with Him in wisdom?"

22:13 MT ואמרת מה־ידע אל הבעד ערפל ישפוט׃

"Therefore you say, 'What does God know?
Can He judge through the deep darkness?' "

P ܘܐܡܪܬ ܐܢܬ ܡܢܐ ܝܕܥ ܐܠܗܐ. ܕܠܡܐ ܠܓܘ ܡܢ ܥܪܦܠܐ ܕܐܢ ܗܘ.

"And you say, 'What does God know?
Perhaps He can judge from the midst of the deep darkness?' "

14:14 MT אם־ימות גבר היחיה כל־ימי צבאי איחל
עד־בוא חליפתי׃

"If man dies, will he live again?
All the days of my servitude I would wait
until my renewal comes."

P ܐܢ ܢܡܘܬ ܓܒܪܐ ܕܠܡܐ ܚܝܐ. ܘܟܠܗܘܢ ܝܘܡܬܐ
ܕܛܠܝܘܬܗ ܡܣܟܐ ܥܕܡܐ ܕܐܬܝܐ ܣܝܒܘܬܗ.

"If man dies, why does he live?
And all the days of his youth (he) waits until his old age comes."

In the first two passages ܕܠܡܐ seems to soften the directness of the question, hence the effect on meaning is synonymy with a variation in intensity. In the last example this substitution plus other internal deviations have resulted in an entirely new meaning that does not reproduce the meaning of the MT, i.e. an innovative effect on meaning.

c. Heb. הֲ > Syr. ܗܐ.

A third way in which the P adjusts for the interrogative Heh is by substitution with the exclamatory particle ܗܐ "behold". This occurs four times (1:8;2:3;6:13,26). Three follow the same pattern of analysis (1:8; 2:3; 6:26):

1:8; 2:3 (Lord to the Satan):

MT השמת לבך על־עבדי איוב

"Have you considered my servant Job?"

P.   ܗܐ ܟܘܡܬܗ ܠܥܒܕܝ ܠܠ ܠܒܕܝ ܐܘܒ

"Behold you have considered my servant Job!"

6:26 (Job to Eliphaz and/or Friends):

MT   נאש אמרי ולרוח   תחשבו מלים הלהוכח

"Do you plan to reprove words,
when the words of the despairing one are like the wind?"

P   ܗܐ ܠܡܟܣܢܘ ܡܠܐ̈ ܬܬܚܫܒܘܢ.
ܘܥܠ ܪܘܚܝ ܬܗܠܟܘܢ ܬܬܚܫܒܘܢ.

"Behold you plan to rebuke [with] words,
and against my spirit you regard my word!"

The Heb. is here using a technique or figure of speech term
Erotesis, the asking of a question without waiting for an answer, that is
asking a question not to obtain information, but rather for stylistic
variation.[14] Thus, P removes this figure of speech by translating with
the implied affirmative response:

                    MT   P

1:8;2:3 (Lord to the satan)
        "Have you considered my servant Job?" > "Yes, of course the satan
                                                has considered Job."

6:26 (Job to Eliphaz and Friends)
        "Do you plan to reprove [with] words?">"Yes, of course the friends
                                        intend to rebuke with words."

However, P does not use just a simple declarative, but rather an
exclamatory statement. The motivation then for the correspondence Heb.
הֲ > Syr. ܗܐ is neither language difference nor stylistic preference, but
rather an intentional ideological reason - these questions are rather highly

---

[14] See Bullinger, p. 944ff. See also A. Gelston, pp. 137, where he also notes P of the
Twelve Prophets similarly avoids questions, especially those rhetorical in nature.

charged - or an unintentional aural error prompted by linguistic
interference. P heard הַ /ha/ and construed it as the cognate ܗܐ /ha'/.
The meaning, however, is still synonymous, varying only in literary
presentation and intensity.

Akin to Heb. הַ > Syr. ܗܐ is the one occurrence of האם > ܗܐ in
6:13. Heb. האם is found only here and in Num 17:28[15] suggesting
ambiguity or a textual difficulty, whereby Heb. האם was understood as
the exclamatory particle הא (+ an enclitic Mem?), hence, P's translation
ܗܐ. The effect on meaning is clarity, for P's translation has clarified the
difficulty of this particle.[16]

2. Simple Interrogative + Particle

a. Heb. הלא

The same equivalences found for the simple interrogative also
occur when the interrogative is combined with a particle. Thus we find
הֲיֵשׁ > ܐܝܬ Ø (e.g. 38:28); הֲיֵשׁ > ܐܝܬ ܗܢܐ (e.g. 6:30); and הֲלֹא >
ܗܐ (e.g. 4:6). More interesting is the treatment of the particle found
with the interrogative. Thus, with the form הלא, the P in all but two
cases (21:29;31:3) omits the negative לא.[17] The common denominator
in all these verses is that the MT contains a negative question that evokes a
positive response. Thus, the P is translating with the response, as, for
example, in 1:10:

MT בעדו שכת הלא־את   P ܐܢܬ ܐܝܟܐ ܐܝܟ ܣܡܬܗ
"Have you not placed => You have placed >"You have rested your
a hedge about him?"   a hedge about him   hand upon him."

---

[15]Likewise translated ܗܐ in the Peshitta to Numbers. See also BDB, p. 50b, s.v. אם
2c.

[16] The meaning of this entire colon is different from the MT owing to the confusion of
pronominal suffixes and not to the translation of Heb. האם > Syr. ܗܐ . See Chapter III:
Grammar: Suffix where this confusion is discussed.

[17] See vv. 1:10;4:6,21;7:1;8:10;10:10,20;12:11;13:11;22:5,12;31:4,15.

The effect on meaning in all cases is synonymy, with a slight change in literary form or in intensity in those that translate הֲ > ܐܘ.

Two verses deviate from this pattern (21:29; 31:3). In 21:29 inter-verse influence with the interrogatives in v. 28 suggests that P is still preserving a question in this verse; that is as Nöldeke said "the enfolding of the clauses" would require this to be an interrogative. "(Have) you not asked travellers?", hence the negative particle is still translated. The other exception in the treatment of Heb. הלא is in 31:3, where P reads with the adversative ܐܠܐ "however, but",[18] apparently for contrast with what precedes and follows.

b. Heb. הֲיֵשׁ

For Heb. הֲיֵשׁ the expected ܐܝܬ Ø (38:28) and the less frequent ܕܐܝܬ ܐܝܬ occur. Of greater interest are the two unexpected equivalences ܐܝܬ ܐܪ, (5:1) and ܠܝܬ (25:3). In 5:1 Heb. "Call now, is there anyone who will answer you?", P seems to have understood the interrogative Heh as if it were a conditional which is contextually possible:

P   ܡܢ ܠܟ ܐܢ ܐܝܬ ܕܢܥܢܝܟ ܠܟ.
           "Call now, if there is anyone who can answer you!"

In 25:3 P has once again supplied the response implicit in the Heb. question:

MT	P
לגדודיו מספר היש	ܗܐܝܬ ܡܢܝܢܐ ܠܚܝܠܘܬܗ
"Is there a number => No, there is no number >	"And there is no
to His troops?" to His troops!	number to His troops!"

c. Heb. הַאַף

P's treatment of הַאַף in 40:8 clearly follows a different line. This time the emphatic אַף is represented in the substitution ܗܘ ܕ- "it is

---

18 See Nöldeke #374D and E.

(you)". The interrogative הֲ is replaced by the conditional אֵך under inter-verse influence with v. 9 which serves as its apodosis.

3. Disjunctive Questions

A disjunctive question is found 50+ times in the book of Job, with the alternative question introduced by אם, ו, אֹו, or Ø.[19] In Syriac, language difference usually dictates that the particle be translated אֹו and so it is in 20 cases, but variation likewise occurs. As in Heb. the conjunctive waw or Ø are also used. Occasionally, variants like אֵ9 (11:2) or the combination אֹו דאֵן (39:9) or אֵ9 (16:3) occur, prompted by ideological concerns, the desire for emphasis, or error.

The equivalences for the Heb. interrogative Heh follow the pattern seen in the simple and simple + particle interrogatives, that is: הֲ = Ø,[20] דאֵן,[21] or אֹו.[22] Where this pattern deviates the motivation is often other than language difference. So, for example, in 11:2 Heb. הֲ ... אם > Syr. Ø(ב) ... אֵ9:

MT   הרב דברים לא יענה   ואם־איש שפתים יצדק

"Should a multitude of words go unanswered?
Or an eloquent man be vindicated?"

P   כמסאֵתא דדברֹיא לא גֵ לֹי.
     אֵ9 גברא דסֹפתֵא לא מתהכֵכבמֹהֹי תכֹדדם.

"In a multitude of words he does not answer.
Indeed an eloquent man can not be vindicated by his words!"

P has once again translated with the response to a Hebrew question which necessitated the addition of the negative particle לא in the second stich.[23]

---

[19] See vv.4:17;6:5,6,22,30;7:12a;8:3,11;10:4,5;11:2,7;13:7,8,9;14:14;15:2,7,8; 16:3; 18:4; 21:4,22;22:3,4;37:15,16;38:12,16,17,22,28,31,32,33,34,35,39;39:1,9,10,11,12, 20,26; 40:2,26,27,28,29,31.

[20] 4:17;7:12a;11:2,7;13:7,8,9;15:2,8;16:3;21:4,22;22:3,4;37:16;38:12,16,17, 22,28,31, 34,35,36;39:1,11,12,20,26;40:2,26,28,29,31.

[21] See vv. 6:5,30;8:3,11;10:4;15:7;39:9,10.

[22] See vv. 18:4;37:15;38:32.

[23] See similarly at 21:4. The change in voice from passive to active is discussed in Chapter III: Grammar: Voice.

Under motivation, inter-verse influence is an important factor resulting in a deviation from the usual equivalences. So, for example, in the MT of 6:6 and 10:5 Heb. אם ... ה is rendered אכ ... אכ . The first אכ hardly seems a likely equivalence for the Heb. interrogative Heh. However, if we examine the preceding verse in each case (6:5 and 10:4) it is here that the first disjunctive question appeared and here that P renders Heb. אם ... ה by a more expected אכ... דלמא. Hence, unlike the Heb., the P does not repeat the interrogative in subsequent disjunctive questions, but rather continues the sequence with just the alternative particle.

Inter-verse influence is also responsible for Heb. ה...ו > Syr. מנו...ה in 38:39. The MT at 38:36,37 and again at v. 41 contains a series of interrogative questions introduced by מי. P by contrast alters the intervening verses (38-40) similarly into questions with the interrogative pronoun מנו. In light of this the P's treatment of the interrogative Heh is understandable here.

The peculiar use of אלו for Heb. ה in 6:22 likewise owes its existence to inter-verse influence. In this case it is not so much a following of a pre-established pattern in the Heb. text that has prompted P to translate with the conditional אלו, a particle used to express a condition that is impossible,[24] but rather P's interpretation of this verse as part of the protasis with the apodosis found in v. 24.

The effect on meaning resulting from P's treatment of the particles involved in disjunctive questions is synonymy with variation in formality in those verses where Heb. הֲ > Syr. Ø; variation in intensity where Heb. הֲ > Syr. אם ; and variation in literary style where Heb. הֲ > Syr. דלמא or wherever the Interrogative Heh is harmonized with the surrounding verses (e.g. by מנו in 38:39). Occasionally an innovative meaning occurs (e.g. 15:11;16:3;'22:3;40:27); however, it is as a result of an alteration in another element of the verse.

---

24 Nöldeke #375.

2. Other Interrogatives

Interrogative sentences, excluding the simple, simple + particle and disjunctive, in which P deviates from the MT involve the particles מה, אי־זה, אי, and the creation of an interrogative sentence where the MT reads with a declarative. The adjustments that are employed are addition, omission and substitution. The effect on meaning in most cases is one of synonymy, with motivations quite varied.[25] Of particular interest is P's treatment that results in an other than synonymous meaning. In 11:8, P treats each interrogative מה differently:

MT   גבהי שמים מה־תפעל   עמקה משאול מה־תדע:

"(It is) higher than heaven - What can you do?
Deeper than Sheol - What do you know?"

P   ܘܪܘܡܐ ܕܫܡܝܐ ܢܕܥ ܐܢܬ.
   ܐܘ ܥܘܡܩܐ ܕܫܝܘܠ ܡܢ ܐܝܟܐ ܗܝ ܝܕܥ ܐܢܬ.

"(Do) you know the height of the heavens?
or (do) you know from whence is the depth of Sheol?"

The function of the interrogatives is ambiguous here, ambiguous in that each stich begins with a comparative statement immediately followed by an interrogative question. Thus, no hint is given for the unique juxtaposition of two independent statements and as such P understood each stich as one independent statement. Thus, the first מה is omitted whereas the second is replaced by ܡܢ ܐܝܟܐ. Inter-verse influence with 11:7 may also be partially responsible for P's treatment here, for in 11:7 we find a disjunctive question:

---

[25] The motivations that occur are: implicit to explicit exegesis (3:11b;15:9b); ideological (9:2); inter-verse influence (11:8;38:38,40); intra-verse influence (14:10); ambiguity (11:8; 38:19,24); parallel verse influence (38:24); and versional parallels (12:14;14:10;38:19,24).

החקר אלוה תמצא   אם עד־תכלית שדי תמצא׃

"Can you find out the deep things of Eloah?
or can you find out the end of Shaddai?"[26]

Thus, the format of v. 7 and the ambiguity of the Hebraic style in v. 8 may have motivated the P to rephrase the structure of v.8 in favor of the clear and certainly more common style of a disjunctive question. P's adjustments in this case have both clarified the MT for the translator of P and his readers and provided a new meaning for the evaluator of the translation.

In 38:38 and 38:40 the P's adjustment has likewise resulted in an innovative meaning. In each case P has harmonized these verses with the immediate context, for at vv. 36,37 begins a series of interrogative מי questions which in the MT is interrupted at vv. 38-40 but then resumed in v. 40. We already saw that P had harmonized v. 39 to fit this pattern and thus, with the present adjustments, the P read with interrogative הכבה in vv. 35-41.

It is also noteworthy that in vv. 38 and 40, P has created questions where the MT read with dependent declarative statements. One other such transformation occurs in 12:14. Consider the MT and P:

MT   הן יהרוס ולא יבנה   יסגר על־איש ולא יפתח׃
     "If he tears down none can (re)build,
     (if) he shuts a man in none can open."

P   ܗܐ ܐܢ ܣܬܪ ܡܢܘ ܕܒܢܐ ܘܐܢ ܐܚܕ ܒܐܦܝ ܓܒܪܐ ܡܢܘ ܕܦܬܚ.
     "Behold, if he demolishes, who can (re)build?
     And if he shuts [the door] in the face of a man, who can open?"

P provides the question for which the MT is the answer. This reversal seems contra to P's usual tendency of providing the response to MT's questions. Versional influence with the LXX may be responsible here which also reads with interrogatives:

---

26 P's use of √גבר twice in this verse, instead of ידע // פעל‍, may be further proof that the P was influenced by v. 7 where √מצא is likewise used in both colons.

LXX Εαν καταβαλη τις οικοδομησει,
εαν κλειση κατ' ανθρωπων τις ανοιξει.
"If he should cast down, who will build up?
If he should shut up against men, who shall open?"

II. The Declarative Sentence

A declarative sentence states a simple proposition: e.g. "In all this Job did not sin; He did not ascribe wrong-doing to God" (Job 1:22). The majority of declarative sentences are maintained by the translator of P-Job. An internal element may at times be altered for semantic reasons or the word order may be transposed in accordance with Syriac syntax rules. These changes do not affect the type of sentence; the declarative statement still remains. However, cases do occur where a declarative is transformed into an interrogative[27] or an exclamatory particle is added, thus effecting a change in sentence type. These transformations are discussed under the new sentence type. One specific type of declarative sentence that is treated in a variety of ways by the translator of P-Job and still remains as a declarative proposition is the conditional sentence.

1. Conditional Sentences

The MT of the book of Job contains over a hundred examples of a conditional sentence, that is a proposition which contains two clauses: a protasis "the if-clause" and a apodosis "the then-clause". Most are maintained by the translator of P. Instead, it is the creation of a conditional proposition that is the most obvious deviation in P-Job. Creation is most commonly achieved by the addition of the conditional particle motivated by implicit to explicit exegesis and resulting in a synonymous effect on meaning with only a structural change in representation.[28] Inter-(e.g. 14:15 with 14:14) and intra-(19:7b with 19:7a) verse influence can also play a significant role in determining that a conditional is, in fact, implicit. In 19:4,7a and 23:8 P again preserves a conditional particle implicit in the MT; however, it is implicit not in its non-representation, but rather inherent in another particle that is polysemous in nature. Thus, in 19:7a and 23:8 the MT contains the

---

[27] See above, pp.202ff.
[28] See vv. 4:2;9:27b,29a;10:15;14:15a,21(2);16:6b;19:7b;21:23a;22:23b;31:5b,7b/c,9b, 16b,17a,24b,27a,29b,39b;34:29(2);35:6;38:21(2).

particle הן, ambiguous in that it has the potential of meaning either "Behold" or "if". P clarifies this ambiguity by its translation ܐܢ.

In 19:4 a slightly different situation occurs. Consider the MT and P:

MT   ואף־אמנם   שגיתי   אתי   תלין   משוגתי:
"And even truly (if) I have erred,
(then) my error lodges with me."

P   ܘܐܢ ܫܪܝܪܐܝܬ ܛܥܝܬ. ܠܘܬܝ ܗܘܬ ܛܥܝܘܬܝ.
"And if truly I have erred,
(then) my error will be mine (lit. to me)."

The MT contains the highly emphatic if not redundant אף־אמנם with a following implicit conditional. It would appear P has replaced this emphatic compound with a conditional and one emphatic particle, but rather P has omitted one redundant emphatic[29] and explicitly stated the conditional as it is wont to do.

In 31:28 and 35:14 P renders Heb. כי by ܐܢ. The motivation is twofold: first, ambiguity - the particle כי is quite polysemous - and second, ideology, more specifically a theological issue. The particle כי "when" presents an act that is certain to occur or to have occurred versus ܐܢ "if" indicating the possibility of an act occurring.   Consider these verses:

(31:28) MT   גם־הוא עון פלילי _כי־כחשתי_ לאל ממעל:
"This also would be an iniquity of my Judge,
for I should have deceived God above."

P   ܐܦ ܗܘ ܗܘ ܫܐ ܟܠܡܢ ܕܥܒܕܬ. ܐܢ ܕܓܠܬ ܩܕܡ ܐܠܗܐ.
"Indeed, He has seen all my contrivances,
if I was unfaithful before God."

(35:14) MT אף _כי־תאמר_ לא תשורנו   דין לפניו ותחולל לו: ף א
"How much less when you say (that) you do not behold Him,
(that) the case is before Him and you anxiously await Him."

---

[29] See below in this chapter where P's treatment of Heb. emphatic particles is discussed.

P. ܡܠ ܐܟ̈ܐ ܐ̈ܪܝܬܗ ܠ ܐ̈ܒܪܬܗ ... ܘܗ̈ܢܬܡܪܬ ܘܗ. ܐܗ̈ܟܐܬܗ ... ܐ̈ܟܘ

"And even <u>if</u> you said 'You do not praise Him;
Plead before Him and make supplication to Him.'"

Thus, using a conditional clearly softens the moral implications of
"deceiving God" (31:28) or "not beholding Him" (35:14).

III. The Exclamatory Sentence

As a powerfully dynamic literary work, the book of Job abounds
with exclamatory sentences. The exclamation or emphasis is most often
achieved through the use of the particles הנה, הן, נא, אף and גם. Thus,
the treatment of an exclamatory or emphatic sentence is more specifically
concerned with P's treatment of a particle that expresses emphasis, and
more particularly with those instances in which P does not preserve the
Heb. particle or in some way alters it.

Emphasis or intensity can also be achieved through the use of the
verbal forms of command - the imperative, emphatic imperative, jussive,
cohortative - or the infinitive absolute in its emphatic role. It can also be
accomplished through the use of the personal pronoun in conjunction with
a verbal form, e.g. אתה אמרת "you, you said!" or "YOU said!".
Emphasis or exclamation achieved in these ways is generally maintained
by the translator of P as seen earlier in the examination of Grammar:
tense and Grammar: pronoun.[30]

1. The Particle הנה.

The particles of exclamation הנה and the shorter form הן, were
investigated by Baumann.[31] Of the 15 occurrences of הנה, he found ten
literally translated by ܟܐ.[32] Of the 31 occurrences of הן , 17 were
likewise literally translated by ܟܐ.[33] Thus, the majority are preserved
with the equivalence ܟܐ. Of those deviations in P where Heb. הנה ≠

---

[30] See above Chapter III for P's treatment of the verbal forms of command, the infinitive
absolute and the pronoun.

[31] Baumann (1899):53.

[32] Baumann's statistics were a bit off. The number in fact is 9. See vv. 1:12,19; 4:3;
13:18; 16:19; 32:12,19;33:2; 40:15.

[33] Baumann's statistics were a bit off. As will shortly be seen rather 14 were literal.

Syr. ܐܘ the adjustments are either omission or substitution.[34] Inter-verse influence or error seem to be the main motivations.[35] Thus in 3:7, P omits Heb. הנה possibly by analogy with v. 6 which likewise begins with הלילה ההוא but lacks the הנה:

MT   אל־יחד בימי שנה   הלילה ההוא יקחהו אפל
                              במספר ירחים אל־יבא:
       אל־תבא רננה בו: הנה הלילה ההוא יהי גלמוד

"That night, let darkness take it,
let it not be joined with the days of the year
and let it not enter into the number of the months.
Behold, let that night be barren,
let a ringing cry not enter into it."

P   ܠܠܝܐ ܗܘ ܢܣܒܝܘܗܝ ܚܫܘܟܐ. ܗܘ ܝܘܡܐ ܠܐ ܢܬܚܫܒ
         ܒܡܢܝܢܐ ܕܝܘܡܬܐ ܕܫܢܬܐ. ܘܒܡܢܝܢܐ ܕܝܪܚܐ ܠܐ ܢܥܘܠ.
         ܠܠܝܐ ܗܘ ܢܗܘܐ ܥܩܪܐ. ܘܠܐ ܬܥܘܠ ܒܗ ܬܫܒܘܚܬܐ.

"That night, let darkness cover it.
Let that day not be reckoned in the number of days of the
year, and let it not enter into the number of months.
Let that night be barren, and let praise not enter into it."

Inter-verse influence with 33:5-6 may also be responsible for the absence of Heb. הנה in 33:7. 33:5 opens with the conditional אם־תוכל השיבני "if you are able, answer me", a conditional statement that is maintained by P ܐܢ ܡܫܟܚ ܐܢܬ ܐܗܦܟ ܠܝ ܦܬܓܡܐ "if you are able, return word (to) me". Verse 6 follows with an initial ambiguous הן (הן־אני כפיך לאל) which, under influence with verse 5, P understood as an Aramaism הן = "if".[36] This non-recognition of the הן as an emphatic in verse 6 may have led to the substitution of the initial

---

[34] Omission of the particle הנה occurs in 3:7;5:27;40:16; and substitution with another particle occurs in 9:19a;33:7a.

[35] Inter-verse influence is a major motivation in 3:7 and 33:7a; and error in 5:27;9:19a;33:7a; 40:16a.

[36] Baumann (1899:53) claims Heb. הן > ܗܐ. This however is not the case. ܗܐ does occur but in the second stich and thus not an equivalence for Heb. הן in stich one.

exclamatory הנה by the transitional ܗܘܐ ܡܢ in verse 7. Baumann suggested this substitution might be an error for the usual equivalence ܗܐ.[37]

The other three cases where Heb. הנה ≠ Syr. ܗܐ were motivated by error. In 40:16a the entire stich is wanting. In 5:27a the Heb. began with הנה־זאת which, if literally translated, would be ܗܐ ܗܕܐ. With the orthographic similarity of these two forms P's translation of just ܗܕܐ might suggest a haplography.[38] In 9:19a P appears to have substituted a ܗܘ for the Heb. הנה. I say "appears to have substituted" because P may have erroneously understood Heb. הִנֵּה as הִנּוֹ = הִנּוֹ "Behold, he".[39] P would then be omitting the exclamatory particle and explicitly expressing an implicit Heb. suffix. Note, however, the Tg. preserves both readings הא הוא, which might suggest a different *Vorlage*. One further appeal might be made to parallel verse influence with 36:26:

$$
\text{ܐܢ ܟܘܠ ܐܬܚܠܡ ܗܘ P.} \qquad \text{אם לכח אמיץ הנה 9:19 MT}
$$
$$
\text{ܗܐ ܐܠܗܐ ܚܠܝܡ ܗܘ P.} \qquad \text{הן־אל שׂגיא ... 36:26}
$$

Whereas in the MT both are distinct - i.e. one an exclamation with unnamed subject (9:19), the other God is specifically stated (36:26) - P translates both with the copula ܗܘ.

In all of these cases (3:7; 5:27a;9:19a;33:7a;40:16a) the effect on meaning is minimal, that is a slight change in intensity and literary style.

2. The Particle הן

With the inherent ambiguity in the particle הן - it is the shorter form of the exclamatory particle הנה and an Aramaism = the conditional ܐܢ "if" - it is not surprising to find both possibilities realized in the P. Of the 66 occurrences outside of the book of Job, P renders only ten by the conditional ܐܢ and the remainder by the emphatic ܗܐ. In P-Job, according to Baumann, 17 are rendered by ܗܐ, four by ܐܢ,

---

37 Baumann (1899):53.

38 See 33:12 where Heb. הן־זאת > ܗܕܐ.

39 So ICC, p. 58, n. 19.

and one by ܐܝܟ.[40] These statistics are not quite accurate. The more accurate correspondences are: הֵן = ܗܐ (17 times); הֵן = ܐܝܟ ܗܐ (3 times); and הֵן = ܐܝܟ (6 times).[41] Attention is here directed to the non-literal correspondences הֵן = ܐܝܟ or הֵן = ܐܝܟ ܗܐ.

a. Heb. הֵן > Syr. ܐܝܟ

As stated above the form הֵן bears an inherent ambiguity. In the examples discussed below the motivations which prompted the translator to select the conditional ܐܝܟ are for the most part context (intra-/inter-verse influence), but in two cases (12:15a; 13:15a) ideology, a theological toning down with versional parallels, in particular with the LXX . Consider, for example, these motivational factors in one of these occurrences, 12:15a. Note that v. 14 is included for contextual setting.

> MT הן יחרוס ולא יבנה יסגר על־איש ולא יפתח:
> הן יעצר במים ויבשו וישלחם ויהפכו ארץ:
> "Behold/If he tears down, it will not be rebuilt,
> (Behold/If) he shuts (a door) upon a man, it will not be opened;
> Behold/If he restrains the waters, they will dry up,
> and (behold/if) he sends them out,
> they will overwhelm the earth."

> p42 ܗܐ ܐܝܟ ܣܬܪ ܗܘ ܕܒܢܐ. ܘܐܢ ܐܚܕ ܒܐܦܐ ܕܓܒܪܐ ܐܝܟ ܗܘ ܕܦܬܚ ܦܐܬܐ.
> ܐܝܢ ܟܠܐ ܠܡܝܐ ܝܒܫܝܢ. ܘܐܢ ܡܫܕܪ ܠܗܘܢ ܗܦܟܝܢ ܐܪܥܐ.
> "Behold, if he demolishes, who can rebuild?
> and if he shuts [the door] in the face of a man, who can open?
> If he rebukes the waters, they dry up,
> and if he sends them forth, they overwhelm the land."

---

[40] Baumann (1899:53).

[41] See vv. 4:18; 8:19; 9:11,12; 12:14; 13:1; 15:15; 21:16,27; 25:5; 26:14; 27:12; 32:11; 33:10 (ܗܘܐ); 36:5,26; 41:1 where הֵן = ܗܐ ; in 9:11,12; 12:14 both correspondences are found; and הֵן = ܐܝܟ in 12:15a; 13:15a; 19:7a; 23:8a; 40:23a (ܕܐܝܟ) and also in 31:35 although Baumann did not include this verse where הֵן‾ occurs not הֵן.

[42] For the addition of the conditional ܐܝܟ in the second stich, implicit in the MT, see Ch. III Sentence Type: Conditionals where this is discussed.

Verses 14 and 15 are situated amidst a doxology (vv. 7-25) extolling the greatness and compassion of the Lord. Understanding Heb. הֵן as the conditional may have seemed less harsh. For, by translating with the conditional, P has softened this harshness, leaving the hint or implication that the possibility of these actions exists, rather than the harsh reality of the bold, outright exclamation: "Behold, he tears down and none can rebuild . . .". Note that the LXX and Vulgate likewise translated in this same manner. Thus, in one example four motivations can be cited: ambiguity, intra-verse influence, inter-verse influence and ideological basis, i.e. theological toning down.

The effect on meaning is first clarity. P's translation of הֵן > ܐܢ has clarified the ambiguity inherent in this particle in that it has made a definite stance on how the text is to be understood. The second effect is synonymy, more specifically a change in the sub-category of literary style. Both MT and P contain the same information, P only preserves it in a less severe tone.

In 13:15a,19:7,23:8a and 40:23a P also translated Heb. הֵן > Syr. ܐܢ. The motivations were also ambiguity, intra-/inter-verse influence and ideological, with the effect on meaning being clarity and synonymy with variation in literary style. The one other passage where the P renders הֵן by ܐܢ is 31:35 which, however, deviates from the pattern of analysis just described. Consider this verse:

MT   מי יתן־לי שמע לי   הן־תוי שדי יענני
                                וספר כתב איש ריבי:

"O that someone would listen to me,
- Behold, my mark! May Shaddai answer me -
And (O that) the man of my quarrel would write a letter!"

P   ܗܝ ܕ݁ܝ ܫܡܒ ܕܝ ܘܐܫܬܒܠ ܠ ܐܝ ܐܟܘܬܘܢ.
         ܐܠܗܐ ܢܫܒ. ܘܢܟܬܒ ܒܡܦܣܐ ܡܢܘ̈ ܕܓܒܪܐ.
         ܘܢܟܒ ܡܢܘ̈ ܕܓܒܪܐ.

"for O that (some)one would listen to me - if it were.
May God answer me and write the judgments of man in a book."

Heb. הֵן, here with maqqeph and reduced vowel הֶן־, appears in stich two joined by maqqeph to the rare Heb. תָּו "mark". This noun occurs but three times in the OT, here, Ezek 9:4,6; and the denominative verb but twice (Ezek 9:4; 1 Sam 21:14).[43] Misunderstanding of this noun has forced the translator to another recourse, namely what Mandl termed "a daring conjecture with a linguistic basis".[44] More likely than conjecture might be aural error for Heb. הֶן־תָוִי /hen tawi/ is phonetically very similar to Syr. ܐܢ ܐܝܬܘܗܝ /'en 'itawhi/. Heb. תוי may also have been understood as the equivalent of Aram. איתוי.[45]

Thus, intra-verse influence, i.e. an error or more specifically linguistic interference with the noun תו, may have prompted the translator to translate Heb. הן by ܐܢ here. Appeal may also be made to versional influence, for the LXX likewise reads with a conditional εἰ.[46] The effect on meaning in this case is obviously innovative, for P's "if it were" bears no semantic relationship to MT's "Behold, my mark".

b. Heb. הן > Syr. Ø.

Of the 31 occurrences of הן it was noted P omits translating הן in nine places. No one cause is responsible for the omission of the exclamatory particle. In some cases there may be a phonetic basis for the omission of the exclamatory particle, in that if translation results in two identical phonetic elements, the first is omitted. This occurs in 33:12 where Heb. הן־זאת should be translated ܗܐ ܗܕܐ, but only ܗܕܐ is found, thus omitting the initial /ha'/. Other cases of omission of the exclamatory particle or definite article before ܗܐ occurred in 5:27a;20:4;35:2. Thus, there may be some linguistic basis for this phenomenon. However, this phenomenon of omission of a similar phonetic element is by no means the rule. Consider the example of

---

[43] In Ezek P clearly understood the meaning of Heb. תו, hence in 9:4 ܬܪܡܐ ܪܘܫܡܐ "to set a mark" and in 9:6 ܪܘܫܡܐ "a mark". In 1 Sam 21:14 P clearly did not understand the verb or an aural error, i.e. confusion of Waw and Bet, might be suggested in explaining Heb. ויתו > Syr. ܘܝܬܒ .

[44] Mandl, p. 30.

[45] Dhorme, p. 461.

[46] Note however the rest of LXX's reading does not parallel P's: χειρα δε Κυριου ει μη εδεδοικειν "... and if I had not feared the hand of God ... ".

33:29a. Here Heb. הֶן־כָּל־אֵלֶּה would literally be translated ܗܐ ܟܠ
ܗܠܝܢ ܐܠܐ , with the exclamatory particle and demonstrative both
containing the initial /ha'/ syllable. In this verse, however, it is rendered
ܟܠܗܝܢ ܗܠܝܢ , i.e. omitting the ܐܠܐ. In 26:14 a similar הֶן־אֵלֶּה occurs
which is rendered ܗܐ ܗܠܝܢ, i.e. preserving the exclamatory particle.
This similarly occurs in 13:1. Clearly this phenomenon is not uniform
throughout P and further motivations must be sought.

Error may also be cited as a motivation for omission. Here, too,
phonology comes into play. The two passages in which omission by
error occur are 24:5a and 28:28a:

	MT	P
(24:5a)	הֵן פְּרָאִים בַּמִּדְבָּר	ܐܝܟ ܥܪܕܐ ܒܕܒܪܐ
	"Behold, (like) wild asses	"Like wild asses in the
	in the wilderness . . ."	wilderness . . ."

(28:28a)

ودحلته دهلكا هو ... وه وه عجدته دكلها.   הֵן יִרְאַת אֲדֹנָי הִיא חָכְמָה
"Behold, the fear of the Lord,   "The fear of God, that is wisdom."
that is wisdom."

In 24:5a P reads with a particle of comparison ܐܝܟ "like" for the
Heb. הֵן "behold"; so also the LXX, Tg., and Vulgate. Baumann[47]
suggests P confused הֵן with הֵ(י)ךְ. However, what seems more
probable is that P (and the Versions) are translating an implicit "like" in
the MT, i.e. "Behold, (like) wild asses in the wilderness . . ." and omitted
the exclamatory because it seemed out of place. Throughout this chapter
describing the wicked activities of man no other exclamations occur, thus
it is hardly rash to propose that P may have harmonized this verse with
its context.

In 28:28a, P lacks a translation for Heb. הֵן , but contains an extra
enclitic particle ܗܘ; thus confusion of הֵן with היא is possible. Note,

---

[47] See p. 55.

however, הן is wanting in some Heb. Mss; thus the difference may be due
to a different *Vorlage.*

In reference to 24:5a two other motivations were alluded to:
versional influence/ parallels and inter-verse influence. In six of the nine
cases where Heb. הן > Syr. Ø versional parallels do occur[48] and in four
of nine inter-/intra-verse influence should be considered.[49]

But above all it is apparent that not one motivation is responsible
for the omission of the Heb. exclamatory הן. And, in fact, in 36:22a
neither one or more motivations seems plausible.

הן־אל ישׂגיב בכחו   MT

"Behold, God acts exaltedly in his strength,"

P . ܕܚܝܠܐ ܒܚܝܠܐ ܡܥܫܢ ܐܠܗܐ "God strengthens with power,"

This stich is preceded by an imperative "Take heed, do not turn to
iniquity"(36:21a) and followed by a series of interrogative מי clauses;
"Who is a teacher like Him? Who has ordained for Him His way? Or who
has said 'You have done wrong?' " (36:22b-23). In this contextual setting
an exclamatory is not inappropriate. The Versions (LXX, Tg, Vg)
record an exclamatory particle. Parallel verse influence with 36:26
might account for the omission - this verse also begins הן־אל שׂגיא.
However, there P translates with an exclamatory ܗܐ. Thus, omission of
the exclamatory in 36:22a may be just an oversight, hence an error.

In all the above treatments of the exclamatory הן uniformity does
exist in one area: effect on meaning. Synonymy with variation in
intensity is unanimous.

3. Particle נא

The particle נא occurs 23 times in the book of Job. In seven
passages it is literally translated ܟܝ,[50] in four there is a correspondence,

---

[48] See 8:20a;24:5a;33:6a,12a;36:30a;40:4a.

[49] See 8:20a;33:6a,12a,29a.

[50] See 4:7;5:1;6:29;8:8;17:3;38:3;40:7. Baumann (p. 53) points out that in 6:29 P also
inserts a ܡ ܬܘܒ after ܟܝ. This may have nothing to do with the particle נא but rather
with the concluding nature of this verse.

albeit not ܪ;[51] in one (40:16a) the entire stich is wanting owed possibly to a case of homoioarkton with 40:15a, both begin with הנה־נא; and finally in eleven places it is wanting without any substitution.[52]

The four verses where P substitutes with another particle (13:6,18;22:21; 42:4) are uniform as regards their effect on meaning, that is all are synonymous to the MT with a variation only in literary style, structural representation or intensity.   Variation, however, is the key word in regard to motivation.   Intra-/inter-verse influence are again present, as is versional influence/parallels.

We see these motivations in 13:6 and 22:21 where each verse is situated at a transitional point in the narrative. Thus, P translates with a transitional particle, rather than with an emphatic. In chapter 12:7-25 Job recites a doxology, with 13:1-5 he claims his knowledge of all he has described plus chastises the friends. In 13:6 the transition occurs, thus P uses ܡܟܝܠ. Job now turns to what he calls "my reasoning" and the "pleadings of my lips". In the 22:21 passage Eliphaz has just described the lot of the wicked (vv. 2-20), with v. 21 he asks Job to agree with his statements; thus a transition has occurred and ܓܝܪ is used by P. Eliphaz now (vv. 22-30) pleads with Job to return to God and admit his error. Thus in each passage P is translating נא by a transitional particle that is clearly more appropriate. Vulgate, too, picks up on this pattern.

In 13:18 P's choice of ܐܦ for נא seems to lack any particular motivation. Here the emphatic is joined to the exclamatory particle הנה־נא > ܐܦ ܗܐ. Note הנה־נא also occurs in 33:2; 40:15 and 40:16. In 40:16a the stich is wanting in P. In the other two examples, contrary to 13:18, P translated simply by ܗܐ, with no formal representation of נא.

In the last passage, 42:4, aural error and intra-verse influence are one explanation for Heb. נא > Syr. ܠܝ -:

MT   :שמע־נא ואנכי אדבר   אשאלך   והודיעני
      "Hear and I will speak;
      I will question you and (you) declare (it to) me!"

<hr>

51 See vv. 13:6 (נא > ܡܟܝܠ);13:18 (נא > ܐܦ); 22:21(נא > ܓܝܪ); and 42:4 (נא > ܠܝ -).
52 See vv. 1:11;2:5;10:9;12:7;17:10;22:22;32:21;33:1,2;40:10,15.

P ܫܡܥܝܢܝ ܘܐܢܐ ܐܡܠܠ. ܐܫܐܠܟ ܘܐܢܬ ܐܘܕܥܝܢܝ.

"Hear me and I will speak;
I will question you, (you) declare (it to) me!"

Aural error - Heb. /na'/ and Syr. /ni/ - and linguistic interference of two very close forms and intra-verse influence with the following 1cs forms, especially the final verbal suffix, also attached to an imperative, are one explanation for Heb. נא > Syr. ‍ני -. Mention must also be made of implicit to explicit exegesis and versional influence. The unstated object of Heb. שמע is obviously the 1pcs pronoun "me" (=Job), for which LXX also added μου.

4. Particles אף and גם

Just as the particles הנה and הן were intertwined, so too are the last two particles, the emphatic אף and גם. They are related not in that one is derived from the other, but rather in that אף is present in both languages, whereas גם is indicative of Hebrew - especially in prose - and not in Syriac. Thus, ܐܦ is found as both a lexical equivalence for Heb. אף and גם in Syriac. This merger of forms (אף and גם > ܐܦ) is the most frequent treatment, with אף > ܐܦ in 11 of its 19 occurrences in Job[53] and גם > ܐܦ in 17 of its 23 occurrences in Job.[54] In only one verse does P omit אף (37:11) and in four places גם (2:10;16:19;21:7;30:2). The motivation in most cases is not discernable unless inter-verse influence be a proper designation for omitting an element which is contextually inappropriate. So, for example, in 37:11, amidst Elihu's speech lauding the wonder of God's hand in nature, comes this verse:

MT :אף־ברי יטריח עב   יפיץ ענן אורו

"He indeed/also loads the cloud(s) with moisture,
the cloud(s) scatters His lightning."

---

[53] See vv. 1:6;2:1;7:11;12:3;13:2,16;15:10(2);16:4;18:5;19:18;23:2;28:27;31:28;33:6;
40:14;41:1.
[54] See vv. 4:19;9:14;14:3;15:4,16;32:10,17(2);35:14;36:33;37:1.

This verse is no more emphatic or transitional than any others in this unit; hence P may have omitted the emphatic אף.

Redundancy might also be cited as a motivation for omission in 16:19. Here the first stich reads:

MT גם־עתה הנה־בשמים עדי

"Indeed now behold my witness is in heaven, . . ."

P ܘܗܫܐ ܗܐ ܒܫܡܝܐ ܣܗ̈ܕܝ.

"And now behold my witnesses[55] are in heaven . . ."

The omission of the particle גם in this case, as well as the other omissions of גם and אף, effect the meaning only in that the level of intensity varies, hence synonymy is still the primary semantic relation.

Of the remaining correspondences for Heb. אף and גם, P employs two different substitutions for the Heb. גם as a result of different motivations. Consider these two verses:

24:19 MT ציה גם־חם יגזלו מימי־שלג שאול חטאו:

"Drought indeed/and heat snatch away the snow-waters,
(so does) Sheol (for) they have sinned."

P ܨܗ̈ܘܐ ܘܫܘܒܐ ܚܛܦܘܢ ܐܝܟ ܡ̈ܝܐ ܕܬܠܓܐ. ܒܫܝܘܠ ܚܛܘ.

"Thirsts and heat, they will seize snow-waters.
They have sinned in Sheol."

30:8 MT בני־נבל גם־בני בלי־שם נכאו מן־הארץ:

"Sons of foolishness,
indeed nameless sons are smitten from the earth."

P ܡܬܗܦܟܝܢ ܒ̈ܢܝܐ ܣ̈ܟܠܐ ܥܡ ܒ̈ܢܝܐ ܥ̈ܘܠܐ.
ܬܡܢ ܢܬܡܟܟܘܢ ܡܢ ܐܪܥܐ.

"The foolish sons will be overthrown with the iniquitous sons.
There they will be brought lower than the earth."

---

55 MT sg. > P pl. See Ch. III for a discussion of Grammar: Number in P-Job.

In the first example, 24:19, it seems clear that the conjunctive waw is intended and implicit in the Hebrew text rather than an emphatic. Moreover, it is two distinct items "drought and heat" that are mentioned, in contrast to verse 30:8 where one 'item' is mentioned, albeit described by two epithets: "sons of foolishness, indeed nameless sons".

As for P's deviations in translating אף, the equivalence אף > ܗܐ in 6:27 has already been dealt with, as has האף > ܘ - ܢ ܕ (34:17) and ܘ - ܗܐ ܐܟ (40:8).[56] In 25:6 אף is rendered ܫܪܝܪܐܝܬ, with little surprise, for this Syriac word is likewise an emphatic. However, here, Heb. אף is followed by כי (= "how much less when") and not simply an emphatic "indeed". Ambiguity or error may have lead to this choice of equivalence. However, it must be noted, Syr. ܫܪܝܪܐܝܬ is the more usual correspondence for Heb. אמנם. So for Heb. אף אמנם in 19:4 and 34:12 P reads ܗܐܟ ܫܪܝܪܐܝܬ (19:4) and Ø ܫܪܝܪܐܝܬ (34:12). Consider these two verses:

19:4 MT ואף אמנם שגיתי אתי תלין משוגתי:
"And even (if) surely I have erred,
(then) my error lodges with me."

P ܗܐܟ ܫܪܝܪܐܝܬ ܛܥܝܬ . ܠܘܬܝ ܗܘܐ ܗܟܝܠ ܛܥܝܘܬܝ.
"and if surely I have erred, (then) my error will be mine."

34:12 MT אף־אמנם אל לא־ירשיע ושדי לא־יעות משפט:
"Indeed truly El will not act wickedly,
and Shaddai will not pervert justice."

P ܫܪܝܪܐܝܬ ܐܠܗܐ ܠܐ ܥܒܕ ܥܘܠܐ.
ܐܦ ܠܐ ܐܠܗܐ ܡܥܘܬ ܐܘܪܚܐ.
"Surely God does not do iniquity,
indeed God does not pervert the path."

---

56 See p. 205.

In both examples, redundancy is the underlying motivation for omission of אף. [57] However, in 19:4 inter-verse influence with v. 5 can by no means be discounted. For this verse (אם אמנם עלי תגדילו ותוכיחו עלי חרפתי) begins with the similar אם־אמנם which m a y have unintentionally (i.e. homoioarkton) or intentionally (desire for contextual harmonization) prompted the translator to translate הא ܐܢ ܨܒ. Thus, vv. 4-5 contain the protasis of the condition and v. 6 the apodosis.

The last deviation, found in 36:29, is Heb. אף אם > Syr. ܡܢܘ:

MT אף אם־יבין מפרשׂי־עב תשׁאות סכתו:

"Indeed can (lit. if) anyone discern the spreadings of the cloud(s), the rumblings of His booth?"

P ܡܢܘ ܢܣܬܟܠ. ܗܦܘܡ ܠܥܢܐ ܡܢ ܣܘܓܐܐ ܘܢܦܪܣ ܠܥܢܢܐ.

"And who can understand
and spread the clouds from the greatness of his booth?"

P's omission of אף may be due to its inappropriateness in this context, or inter-verse influence - in v. 30 P also omits the exclamatory הן - whereas the substitution of ܡܢܘ for אם is motivated by the ambiguity of the multi-functional אם.[58] Here it clearly implies a simple interrogative, i.e. "if someone can understand the spreadings of the cloud(s)" = "can anyone". Since P lacks a simple interrogative particle,[59] rather than merely reproducing the ambiguous Heb. אם by Syr. ܐܢ, it translated with an interrogative pronoun ܡܢܘ "who?". The effect on meaning, however, is still synonymous, varying only in literary style.

---

[57] See discussion of P's treatment of this verse under Sentence Type: Conditional, p.205.

[58] See BDB, pp. 49-50, s.v. אם.

[59] See Chapter V on Interrogatives in P.

Figurative Language

In his lengthy work *Figures of Speech Used in the Bible*,[60] E.W.
Bullinger examined over 200 figures of speech used in the Old and New
Testaments. Examining P-Job in respect to all of these would be an
enormous undertaking, instead two of the most common and prolific
figures of speech were selected: the simile and metaphor.

The late 18th century studies of Mandl and Baumann included this
topic, albeit rather briefly. Mandl's treatment of figurative language is
subsumed under the heading "Die Metaphern".[61] He states that "the
Syriac language is more meagre in figurative expressions", thus often
incapable of reproducing "the pictures and images of a poetical work like
Job. The translator was compelled to render the finest pictures and
images in prose, often completely misunderstood". He then cites roughly
14 examples, some idioms, some personifications, some anti-
personifications, some implied metaphors, as evidence for P's general
tendency to dissolve metaphor.

Baumann[62] likewise fell prey to this generalizing tendency. After
chastising Mandl's treatment of figurative language he cites the chapter,
verse and figurative word or phrase where P diverged from the M T
because of its figurative nature, bringing the number of citations to 55.
He then cites an additional 19 verses where P avoids translating the
figurative language completely.[63] Unlike Mandl, Baumann still credits
the translator with his effort to retain the poetical beauty of the Hebrew,
although at times he fell short of reaching this goal.[64]

It is true that the verses Mandl and Baumann cite do indeed diverge
from the MT. But charging misunderstanding or non-clearness of
expression as the motives hardly seems sufficient. In the following pages
the metaphors and similes in which P diverges from the MT are
discussed. Following these examinations the topic of idiom will be
covered separately. Idiom is a figure of speech. The division here is due
merely to its more extensive depth and length.

---

[60] (Grand Rapids, Michigan: Baker Book House, rpt. 1968 [1898].)
[61] Mandl, pp. 12-13.
[62] Baumann, pp. 55-56.
[63] Baumann, p. 56.
[64] Baumann, p. 56.

Similes and Metaphors.

One rather common and easily recognizable figure of speech is the simile. A simile states quite clearly that some aspect of a person, object, or action bears a resemblance to another. The characteristic which distinguishes a simile from other figures of speech is the use of the preposition -כ "like, as", occurring also in the free form כמו. In Syriac the independent ܐܝܟ is used while the form -ܐܟܘܬ is reserved for suffixed forms.[65]

In the simile comparison is achieved through resemblance. By contrast, in the figure of speech termed the metaphor, comparison is extended one step further, to actual representation. An item now does not merely 'resemble' another, but is actually 'representing' it. The terms "resemblance" and "representation", as E.W. Bullinger states, are the key words in distinguishing the simile from the metaphor.[66]

A distinction must also be made at this point regarding a metaphor and an implied metaphor, more properly termed Hypocatastasis.[67] It differs from a metaphor in that only one of the nouns under comparison is stated, the other being 'implied'. In other words, metaphors are often said to contain three components: the tenor (thing talked about), the vehicle (that to which the tenor is compared) and the ground (the common feature(s) of the image).[68] In a complete metaphor the tenor and vehicle would both be explicitly stated with the ground (hopefully) evident. In the implied metaphor only the vehicle would be explicit, with the context making implicit the tenor. Consider the following two examples from Job:

---

[65] See J. Payne Smith, p. 15b, s.v. ܐܟܘܬ. Unlike the Heb. כמו, Syr. -ܐܟܘܬ does not occur as an independent preposition; thus where the Heb. might read with an unsuffixed כמו, the Syr. would revert back to ܐܝܟ. See for example P-Job in 6:15; 10:22(2); 14:9; 19:22.

[66] *Figures of Speech,* p. 735.

[67] *Figures of Speech,* p. 744-747.

[68] See S. Ullmann, *Language and Style* , pp. 184ff. Similes can also be analyzed according to these components. The only difference is the use of the preposition "like, as", termed "the marker". See also Ernst R. Wendland, *The Cultural Factor in Bible Translation: A Study of Communicating the Word of God in a Central African Cultural Context,* UBS Monograph Series, No. 2 (London: United Bible Societies, 1987), p. 111, who, however ,uses the terms topic, image, ground and marker to describe these figures of speech.

6:12 ‏אם־בשׂרי נחוש:‏   ‏כחי‏   ‏אם־כח אבנים כחי‏

"Is my strength the strength of stones, or my flesh bronze?"

4:8 ‏יקצרהו:‏ ‏עמל‏ ‏וזרעי‏   ‏און‏ ‏כאשׁר ראיתי חרשׁי‏

"As I see those who plough iniquity and sow trouble
will reap it."

In the first example, 6:12, two complete metaphors occur. Here
tenors (my strength/my flesh) and vehicles (strength of stones/bronze) are
explicit, with the ground characteristic understood as the solid, enduring
quality of both stone and bronze to which Job's strength is compared. In
the second example, 4:8 (the implied metaphor), the ground is the only
part explicitly stated, i.e. the comparison understood is that the wicked
are (like) farmers. The wicked (the tenor), however, is not referred to
outright, albeit their actions are: ‏און‏ and ‏עמל‏. The vehicle (farmers) is
likewise not explicit, but the agricultural vocabulary here (‏זרע, חרשׁ,‏
‏קצר‏) serves as the ground which clearly implies the comparison of the
wicked to farmers.

Similes and implied metaphors abound in the book of Job, with
more than a hundred similes found.[69] As for implied metaphors, the text
of Job is replete with the rich imagery of jurisprudence; of God as
warrior (5:18); of night as a barren woman (3:7); of the fool as a tree
(5:3); of darkness as a blanket (23:17), naming here but a few. Complete
metaphors, by contrast, are hardly as prolific, with fewer than 20 found
in the entire text of Job.[70]

Similes.

Of the 110 similes found in the text of Job, roughly 40% are
altered in some way by the translator of the P. More precisely 43 are
altered, ten of which are either totally wanting or lack the preposition of
comparison, and 33 are still a simile but with one or more elements of the

---

[69] See 1:8;2:3,10;3:16(2),24;5:14,25,26;6:7,15(2);7:1,2(2);9:26;10:9,10(2),16,22(2);
11:16,17;12:3,25;13:2,9,28(2);14:2(2),6,9;15:16,24,33(;2);16:2,4; 17:7;19:10,22;20:7,
8(2),18;21:18(2);23:10,14;24:14,24(2);27:7(2),16(2),18(2),20;28:5;29:2,4,14,18,23,
25(2);30:5,14,15(2),18,19;31:18,33,37;32: 19(2);33:6;34:7(2),11;35:8;36:12,22;37:18;
38:3,14,30;39:18,20;40:7,9(2),15,17,18,29;41:10,12,16(2),21,23(2),24;42:7,8,9,15.
[70] See, for example, 6:12,26;7:7;8:2,9,14a;13:4,12;25:6;29:15(2);30:9(2), 29(2).

comparison modified. Furthermore, in 25 places the translator has
created a simile by the addition of the particle ܐܝܟ

1. Similes altered by Removal of the Preposition.

In ten places P no longer preserves a MT simile. In 41:21a,23(2)
the verse themselves are missing. In the other seven places the two major
and most common motivations are: ambiguity of a preposition (20:18;
30:18); and error (20:18;30:18;31:18; 32:19a;36:12;37:18). Language
difference (35:8;36:12), intra-verse influence (35:8) and textual difficulty
(36:12) also occur, albeit with less frequency.

Consider the following representative verses:

30:18   MT :באזרני כתנתי כפי   לבושי יתחפש ברב־כח

"with a multitude of strength he strips off my clothing,
he girds me as (with) the collar of my tunic."

P ܒܣܘܓܐܐ ܕܚܝܠܐ. ܐܠܒܫܬ ܐܠܒܘܫܝ ܘܐܣܘܪܬܗ ܒܟܘܬܝܢܝ

". . . with a multitude of strength.[71]
I put on my clothing and I girded myself with my tunic."

In this first example the fluidity in semantic range often inherent in
the Hebrew prepositions presents an ambiguity. The preposition -כ might
be rendered by the expected "like, as", but equally possible is the
translation "in, with" - as if Heb. -ב. Also possible is the translation "as
with (the edge of my tunic)" - as if the Heb. read כבכתנתי or with the
Heb. preposition -ב implicit. Hence, the translator removed this
ambiguity by translating with a contextually more appropriate
preposition. The effect on meaning is clarity of the ambiguity, as well as
synonymy with only structural variation.

31:18 MT :אנחנה אמי ומבטן כאב גדלני מנעורי כי

"For like a father he reared me from my youth,
and from the womb of my mother he guided me."

---

[71] In P the initial prepositional phrase is joined to the end of v. 17.

ܐܘܫܐܬ ܩܠ̈ܝܠ ܕܡܢ ܠ̈ܠܝ ܝܒܐܬܐ܂ ܘܚܒܢܬ ܩ̈ܢܝ ܐܠ ܩܕܐ. P
ܡܢ ܓܠ ܡ̈ܡܥ ܝܐ ܐܬܡܪܒ

"Because from my youth pains raised me,
and groans from my mother's womb."

In this second example, visual error clearly motivated the
translator to translate Heb. כְּאָב "like a father" by ܐܟܒܐ "pains". This
error clearly resulted in the dissolution of the Heb. simile and in turn
created a new verse.

2. Similes preserved but internal element(s) altered.

As previously stated 33 of the 110 similes in Job were still
preserved as a simile in the P, however, with an element modified.
Twenty-five of these involve a problem in semantics, two in grammar,
five in syntax and one in style.   Some of the most interesting
modifications are found in the area of semantics, so it is from here that
examples will be drawn to elucidate this phenomenon.

As stated 25 cases involve a problem in semantics. Eighteen of
these involve semantics at the word/root level with ambiguity or error as
the principle motivations for modification. Ambiguity can be further
qualified as ambiguity caused by a rare word or *hapax legomenon*, or
ambiguity caused by a semantically polysemous form. Consider the
following representative examples:

15:24   MT   יבעתהו צר ומצוקה
             תתקפהו כמלך עתיד לכידור:
             "Distress and anguish terrify him,
             they prevail over him like a king ready for the onset."

             P . ܢܒܥܬܗܝ ܡܘܡܣ ܐܘܠܨܢܐ ܗܟܢܐ ܘܬܪܒܩܝܘܗܝ
             ܐܝܟ ܡܠܟܐ ܕܥܬܝܕ ܠܩܪܒܐ.
             "Distress will terrify him and calamity will overtake him,
             like a king who is prepared for battle."

In the first example, 15:24, setting aside the redivision of the verse,
the main issue is P's translation of Heb. כידור. This Hebrew term
occurs only here. Hence, we are dealing with ambiguity of the first type,

i.e. of a rare word, in this case specifically a *hapax legomenon*.[72] P translates with the more general term מה֗רבא "battle" that lacks the semantic component of [+beginning phase of an assault] contained in the more specific Heb. כידור "onset".[73] Vulgate translates similarly with *ad praelium* "for the battle". LXX paraphrases with ωσπερ στρατηγος πρωτοστατης πιπτων "he shall fall as a general in the first rank" and Tg.'s גלוגדתא "bier", i.e. a king ready for the bier" provide a different imagery of a fallen king ready for burial, rather than a king on the offensive.

7:2   MT   כעבד ישאף־צל   וכשכיר יקוה פעלו:
           "Like a slave longs for the shadow,
           and like a wage-earner waits for his wages,"

           P   .ܐܝܟ ܥܒܕܐ ܕܗܘܐ ܡܣܟܐ ܠܛܠܠܐ
                  ܘܐܝܟ ܐܓܝܪܐ ܕܡܣܟܐ ܠܡܫܠܡܘ ܥܒܕܗ
           "And like a servant who waits for the shadow,
           and like a wage-earner who waits to complete his work,"

In the second example, 7:2, ambiguity is once again the motivational factor. However, this time it is ambiguity caused by the polysemous word פעל, i.e. "and like a wage-earner waits for his *po'al* ". Heb. פעל carries the basic meanings of "deed, thing done, work".[74] However, here, and in Jer. 22:13 it bears a finer nuance, that of "wages earned from work" or "the completion/end of his toil", that is "like a wage-earner waits for his wages, i.e. the end of his work". P adjusts for this ambiguity by denoting the precise meaning of Heb. פעל in this verse through the addition of the infinitive ܠܡܫܠܡܘ "to complete": "and like a wage-earner who waits to complete his work."

---

[72] See Frederick E. Greenspann, *Hapax Legomena in Biblical Hebrew*, p. 184, where כידור is listed as an absolute *hapax legomenon*. See also Dhorme, p. 219, and ICC, p. 100, who connects this word with the Arabic *kadara* "to swoop, dart down".

[73] See Chapter II Model of Translation: Adjustments for the process of generalization (#d.)

[74] See BDB, p. 821b, s.v. פעל.

30:15   M T   תרדף כרוח נדבתי   ההפך עלי בלהות
                          וכעב עברה ישעתי:

"Terrors are turned against me,
my honor is pursued like the wind
(or: you pursue my honor like the wind),
and my salvation has passed by like a cloud."

P ܫܒܝܠܝ ܠܟ ܘܐܠܨܘ. ܡܕܡ ܐܝܟ ܪܘܦܗ. ܗܦܟܘܗܝ

ܐܝܟ ܥܢܢܐ ܕܥܒܪܐ ܠܟ ܦܘܪܩܢܝ.

"For they turned confusion against me,
and they pursue my paths like the wind,
and my salvation like a cloud which passes by."

The final example of a semantic problem at word level in a simile is found in 30:15, and here, as stated, the motivation is clearly error, more precisely aural error. Heb. נדבתי "my honor" is rendered ܫܒܝܠܝ "my paths", suggesting the translator heard Heb. נתיבה "path", i.e. confusion of dentals. The correspondence Heb. נתיבה > Syr. ܫܒܝܠܐ occurs throughout Job and the OT.[75] Noteworthy is its appearance just two verse earlier in 30:13 which may have subconsciously affected the translator's erroneous choice in the present verse.[76]

What is the effect on meaning of such internal modifications in the Heb. similes? In most cases where ambiguity, implicit to explicit exegesis, or intra-verse influence are the motivations the effect on meaning is clarity (for the translator) and synonymy, with variation at the level of formality, literary style or intensity. Where error is responsible, however, the effect on meaning for the evaluator is clearly innovative. Thus, looking back at P's error in 30:15 (Heb. נדבתי > Syr. ܫܒܝܠܝ) "the pursuit of Job's honor" (MT) versus "the pursuit of Job's paths" (P) are not the same sentiments.

---

[75] See Syr. ܫܒܝܠܐ > Heb. נתיב in Job 18:10;28:7; נתיבה in Job 19:8;24:13;30:13;19:8; 24:13;38:20; Judg 5:6; Isa 42:16;43:16;58:12;59:8; Jer 6:16;18:15; Pss 78:50;119:35,105; Prov 1:15;3:17;7:25;8:2,20; Hos 2:8; Eccl 3:9.

[76] Although the form נדיבה is rather rare in Heb. occurring just here and in Is. 32:8(2) (= √ܢܕܒ in P), the root √נדב is fairly common verbally, nominally and adjectivally, thus excluding ambiguity as a motivation in this case.

3. Similes created.

As stated earlier, in 25 places P creates a simile by the addition of the particle ܐܝܟ. Only three, however, are metaphors transformed into similes.[77] Thus, it is not a matter of P translating a Heb. metaphor as if it were an implied simile, rather other motivations come into the picture. In the text of P-Job, five motivations occur which can explain this transformation: ambiguity, implicit to explicit exegesis, ideology, intra-verse influence, and error.

a. Ambiguity. Of those similes created as a result of ambiguity, ambiguity more specifically occurs in a preposition, less frequently in a word, and once syntactically (27:20b). Consider the following three representative verses:

3:21 (Ambiguity of a preposition)

MT   מִמַּטְמוֹנִים   ויחפרהו   ואיננו   המחכים למות
"who wait for death, but it is not,
and they search for it more than/rather than hidden treasures."

P. ܟܡܘܢ̈ܐ ܐܝܟ ܠܗ ܒܥܝܢ. ܗܘܐ ܠܗܘܢ ܠܡܘܬ ܡܣܟܝܢ
"who wait for death but there is none,
and (who) search for it as if for hidden treasure."

4:12 (Ambiguity of a word)

MT   מנהו: שֵׁמֶץ   אזני   ותקח   יגנב   דבר   ואלי
"A word came stealthily to me,
and my ear caught a whisper of it."

P ܡܢܗ. ܩܠܝܠ ܐܝܟ ܐܕܢܝ ܘܩܒܠܬ. ܐܬܓܢܒ ܦܬܓܡܐ ܥܠܝ
"and a word was stolen by me,
and my ear received (something) like a little of it."

---

[77] See vv. 6:12;7:9;8:9 and p.229, on removal of a metaphor, where this situation is discussed.

27:20b (Ambiguity of syntax)

M T   ‫תשיגהו כמים בלהות לילה גנבתו סופה‬:
"Terrors overtook him like waters,
(at) night the whirlwind carried him away."

P   ܢܘܕܪܟܝܗܝ ܐܝܟ ܐ ܡܝܐ ܐܝܟ ܢܘܙܕܐ.
     ܘܐܝܟ ܥܠܥܠܐ ܕܦܪܚܐ ܐܬܟܪܟܬܗ ܢܘܚܐ ܗܘܐ ܒܠܠܝܐ.

"Confusion will tread upon him like water,
and like a whirlwind which flies the wind will carry him away in
the night."

In each Heb. verse there occurs an ambiguity. In 3:21 it is the
meaning of the preposition ‫מן‬, in 4:12 it is the meaning of the rare Heb.
‫שמץ‬[78] and in 27:20b an ambiguity in syntax occurs in that some doubt
exists as to whether ‫לילה‬ or ‫סופה‬ is the subject of ‫גנבתו‬. In each case
the translator of P resolved the ambiguity by inserting the particle
ܐܝܟ.[79] As regards the effect on meaning, in our first examples - 3:21
ambiguity of a preposition and 4:12 ambiguity of the word ‫שמץ‬ - clarity
from the translator's perspective is obvious. However, the meaning is
still synonymous with variation at the literary level. In the last example,
27:20b ambiguity in syntax, the effect on meaning is clearly innovative
from the evaluator's perspective, for the translator has clearly rearranged
and augmented the Hebrew text. As for the translator and his reader the
meaning may, however, still be synonymous, with his translation being
but an explicit expression of the meaning inherent in the MT.
b./c. Implicit to explicit exegesis and intra-verse influence. Creation of a
simile under these motivations can be demonstrated by appeal to Job
5:14a. In this verse both motivations have prompted the translator to add
the particle ܐܝܟ of comparison:

---

[78] ‫שמץ‬ also occurs in Job 26:14 where P however translates ‫פגעתא דבסר‬.

[79] In 3:21 Syr. ‫ܐܝܟ‬ ‫ܕ‬- has replaced the ambiguous Heb. ‫מן‬. Nonetheless a simile has
still been created.

יומם יפגשו־חשׁך   וכלילה ימששׁו בצהרים: MT

"During the day they grope (as in) the dark,
and they grope around at noon-time as (in) the night."

P . ܟܢ̣ܗ̇ܪܐ ܡ̣ܓ̇ܫ̇ܝ̣ܢ ܐܝܟ ܕܒܚܫܘܟܐ .
ܘܐܝܟ ܒܠܠܝܐ ܡ̣ܓ̇ܫ̇ܝܢ ܒܛܗܪܐ.

"They grope around in the day-time as in the dark,
and they grope at noon as in the night."

As is evident from the English translation of the Heb., the
preposition -כ is implied, i.e. "during the day they grope around (as
in)[80] the dark". P's insertion of the comparative particle may also be
explained by intra-verse influence. In the parallel stich the Heb. text
explicitly states the preposition -כ (כלילה) on the member parallel to
חשׁך.[81] The effect on meaning in this case is once again synonymy with
variation only in structure.

d. Ideology. Creation of a simile for ideological reasons occurs in 10:4;
more specifically it is a case of softening an anthropomorphic allusion to
God.

העיני בשׂר לך   אם־כראות אנושׁ תראה: MT

"Do you have eyes of flesh?
Or do you see as man sees?"

P . ܘܠܡܐ ܐܝܟ ܥܝܢܐ ܕܒܣܪܐ ܐܢ̈ܝܟ .
ܐܘ ܐܝܟ ܕܚܙ̈ܝܢ ܒܢܝ̈ܢܫܐ ܗܘ ܚܙܐ ܐܢܬ.

"Perhaps your eyes are like eyes of flesh,
or is it as man sees you see?"

The comparison here between God and man is clear. Job inquires
as to whether God has eyes like man and hence sees in this fashion. P has
softened the harshness of the first stich ("Do you have eyes of flesh?") by
transforming it into a simile. Not only is the comparative particle ܐܝܟ

---

[80] Note P likewise explicitly records the preposition -ב "in" in this verse.
[81] Heb. parallelism is A B C // C' B' A'.

added, but also the possessive לך is transformed into a vehicle of comparison ("your eyes"). Note, the P also translates with the indirect interrogative particle ܕܠܡܐ in place of the direct Heb. interrogative Heh.[82] This too seems to soften the boldness of this direct Heb. interrogative question. Thus, where the Heb. preserves a direct interrogative possessive statement, the P preserves an indirect interrogative comparison.

Intra-verse influence should also be mentioned here (10:4), for the impetus to translate with a simile may stem from the simile found in the second stich ("Do you see as man sees"). This deviation from the MT still, however, produces synonymy in meaning albeit variation at the literary stylistics level.

e. Error. In four cases error, be it a straightforward error seen below or an error resulting from another motivation such as ambiguity, has resulted in the formation of a simile.

In 27:20b; 29:7; and 34:11 an error has occurred resulting in the formation of a simile. In each case ambiguity is also suspect as a motivation. Ambiguity exists at least from the evaluator's perspective, with P's choice thus appearing as a erroneous resolution of the ambiguity. Thus, in 27:20b, just discussed, the translator may have found no ambiguity in the syntax of Heb. לילה גנבתו סופה and was simply supplying an implicit preposition. However from the evaluator's view of the two grammatical and syntactical possibilities, the P has selected the wrong one.

In 36:5 P's error in word division has resulted in the formation of a simile.

הן־אל כביר ולא ימאס   כביר כח לב: MT
"Behold, God is mighty and does not reject,
(He is) mighty (in) strength of heart."

P ܗܐ ܐܠܗܐ ܚܝܠܬܢ . ܠܐ ܡܣܠܐ ܐܝܟ ܕܕܟܐ ܐܝܟ ܚܠܒܐ.
"Behold, God is powerful,
He does not reject the one who is pure as milk."

See Ch. VI Style: Sentence Type: Interrogative Sentence for P's treatment of Heb. interrogatives.

Heb. כַּבִּיר כֹּחַ לֵב "He is mighty [in] strength of heart" is read as כְּבַר כְּחֵלֶב "as pure as milk". Hence P's ܐܝܟ ܚܠܒܐ . P has likewise redivided the first stich and treated כביר in stich two as if just בּר "pure". The effect on meaning from the evaluator's perspective is clearly innovative.

Metaphor.

Of the sixteen complete metaphors, that is those in which both tenor and vehicle are expressed, only five are rendered literally (25:6;29:15(2);30:29(2)). Of the remaining eleven, three are transformed into a simile (6:12;7:9;8:9)[83] and eight are altered in such a fashion that the metaphor is dissolved (6:26;7:7;8:2,14a;13:4,12;30:9(2)). The motivations necessitating these alterations are as follows. Note in some cases more than one motivation is present.

Ambiguity	6:26;8:12;13:4,12;30:9(2)
Error	7:7;8:2;13:12
Intra-verse influence	6:26;13:12
Versional influence	8:14a

Consider the following representative verse:

13:12 MT זכרניכם משלי־אפר   לגבי־חמר גביכם:
"Your memorials are proverbs of ash,
    your breastworks are breastworks of clay."

P ܐܬܕܟܪܘ ܕܝܢ ܕܫܘܠܛܢܟܘܢ ܡܢ ܥܦܪܐ ܗܘ .
    ܘܡܥܡܪܟܘܢ ܠܘܬ ܛܝܢܐ ܗܘ .
"Remember that your authority is from the dust,
and your habitation is beside clay."

Here two motivations are present: ambiguity of the word (√משל and √נכב) and error resulting from the wrong choice of meaning for

---

[83] See the previous section (Creation of a Simile) where theses verse are included. In these three cases the P seems to have understood an implicit simile rather than a metaphor, hence its explicit expression of the particle ܐܝܟ of comparison.

ambiguous words. Heb. משל and גב are polysemous terms. For משל
three roots occur: משל I "to be like, resemble"; משל II "proverb,
[whence denominative] to use a proverb; and משל III "to rule, have
dominion".[84] גב (> √גבב) on the other hand has but one root in
Hebrew[85] from which is derived the noun גב whose meanings include
"back; mound; boss (of shield); breastworks; brow; rim; elevation".
Although Syr. does not use ܡܬܠ with the meaning of "to rule" - rather
ܫܠܛ - it does have the first two meanings. It likewise possesses the
semantic variety of √גבב, and, in addition, uses √גב ܓܒ/ ܓܢܒ with ܠ,
i.e. ܠ ܠܓܒ prepositionally with the meaning "beside, near"[86]. Thus,
this plethora of meanings for both roots clearly presented an ambiguity.
Error, then, occurred in that the translator of P selected the wrong
meaning for משל and for the first occurrence of √גבב (לגבי)
[Diagrams 1 and 2].

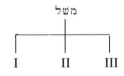

"be like" "proverb" "to rule"

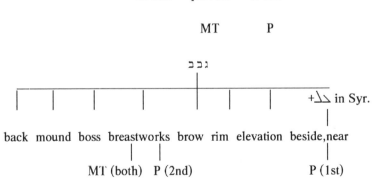

MT (both)   P (2nd)   P (1st)

---

[84] See BDB, pp. 605f, s.v. משל.

[85] See BDB, p. 146, s.v. גבב.

[86] See J. Payne Smith, p. 74, s.v. ܠܓܒ.

Peshitta's translation of the second occurrence of Heb. גנב√
(גביכם "your breastworks") by נכדּוּבכם "your habitation" seems more problematic. נכדּוּבי is translated *contignatio, tabulatum* = "a boardwork, flooring, floor, story" and then extended to mean "a habitation".[87] A breast-work - a temporary, quickly constructed fortification - may have been generalized[88] to "a construction", hence the common נכדּוּבי, or there may be no semantic correlation; P was purely interpretive in its translation.

The effect on meaning is quite obviously innovative. Although ambiguity need not lead to a new meaning,[89] when combined with error as in the present verse (13:12), it has.

Idiom

Idiom, according to the classic definition, is a figure of speech in which the sum of its parts does in no way equal its meaning.[90] According to Mandl, P's treatment of an idiom is to dissolve it.[91] But precisely how P "dissolves" an idiom is not discussed in detail. In two unrelated languages a one to one correspondence in translating an idiom may not be effective; the semantic effect may not necessarily carry over even though the exact words are present. Hebrew and Syriac, however, are closely related so that some literal correspondence might not be too much to expect. Thus, at times, P does translate an idiom, word for word, and achieves the same semantic results as the idiom carried in the MT. Such is the case, for example, in 3:22 where Heb. כי ימצאו־קבר "when they find the grave" i.e. "when they die" is translated כד דנשכחוּן מבּרא "when they find the grave", i.e. "when they die".

A total of 64 idioms were found to deviate from the MT, for a variety of reasons and a variety of ways. Very generally speaking these idioms were:

---

[87] See R. Payne-Smith, p. 857, s.v. נכדּוּבי.

[88] See Chapter II and V for the type of semantically oriented adjustment termed generalization.

[89] See, for example, 13:4 where ambiguity of the word טפלי "plasterers (of falsehood)" has been clarified נכדּוממללי "speakers (of falsehood)", while still preserving the synonymy of the verse, with variation at the literary level.

[90] See Bullinger, p. 819ff.

[91] See Mandl, pp. 12-13.

1. replaced by a Syriac idiom (12)
2. replaced by non-figurative language (42)
3. in ten (10) cases a Syriac idiom was added where the
   MT preserved non-figurative language.

I. Substitution of a Heb. idiom with a Syr. idiom

When a Heb. idiom was replaced by a Syriac idiom three types of semantic relations were found to explain the relationship between these two idioms:

1. Synonymous - a Heb. idiom is replaced by a Syr. idiom with the same meaning:

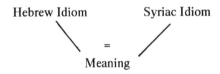

2. Clarity - a polysemous Heb. idiom is replaced by a Syr. one that identifies the intended meaning for the translator:

3. Innovative - a Heb. idiom is replaced by a Syr. one that bears no semantic relationship to the Heb.:

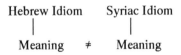

An example of the first type, synonymy, is found in 1:10 (and again in 3:23).[92] Here occurs the Heb. idiom . . . שֹכת בעד "to place a hedge about" which P renders ܥܠ ܐܝܕܟ ܐܬܟܠ ܐܢܬ "to rest one's hand

---

[92] See Mandl, p. 12, who calls P's reading here "loose translations".

upon", both meaning "to protect".[93]   The motivation is clearly one of language difference.   The √שׁוּך does occur in Syriac; however there it means "to finish, bound".[94]   Thus it was necessary for the translator to supply an equivalence in his own language.   Ambiguity or misunderstanding are not appropriate motivations here, for the verb √שׂוּך occurs with its usual meaning "to hedge in" in Hosea 2:8, for which P uses the verb √ܣܚܪ "to fence, hedge",[95] hence clearly understanding its meaning.   The effect on meaning achieved by P's treatment here is synonymy, with a variation in literary style.[96]

An example of the second type, a polysemous Heb. idiom replaced by a contextually more appropriate Syr. one, is found in 42:8 (likewise in 42:9).   Here occurs the Heb. idiom נשׂא פנים "lit. to lift one's face".[97] This Heb. idiom is quite polysemous in nature.   In the book of Job alone it bears four meanings; נשׂא is also used with three other objects for three additional idioms:

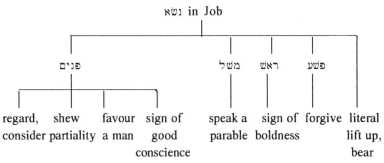

נשׂא in Job

פנים				משׁל	ראשׁ	פשׁע	
regard, consider	shew partiality	favour a man	sign of good conscience	speak a parable	sign of boldness	forgive	literal lift up, bear

---

[93] See BDB, p. 962a, s.v. שׂוּך; and J. Payne Smith, p. 73a, s.v. ܐܓܢ

[94] See J. Payne Smith, p. 363b, s.v. ܣܚܡ; and p. 364a, s.v. ܚܣܡ.

[95] Presuming the translator of Job and Hosea were the same or at least aware of the other's work.

[96] Additional examples are: (9:13) שׁוּב אף "to return nose/anger" > ܚܡܬܐ ܗܦܟ "to change anger" = "to restrain/turn back anger"; (9:14) בחר דברים "to choose words" > ܡܠܬܐ ܕܢ "to arrange words" = "to select the proper way of speaking"; (11:5) שׂפתה פתח "to open lip(s)" > ܣܦܘܬܗ ܢܪܝܡ "to raise lips" = "to speak"; (41:8) אחד באחד "one with one" > ܚܕ ܒܚܕ "one to one" = "to one another"; (41:9) אישׁ באחיהו "a man to his brother" > ܚܕ ܠܚܕ "one to one" + "to one another".

[97] See BDB, p. 670b, s.v. נשׂא.

Thus, to return to our original passage, 42:8, the MT and P read:

MT כי אם־פניו אשא לבלתי עשׂות עמכם נבלה
"Then I will consider him (lit. lift up his face)
by not doing folly with you."

P   ܘܐܦܐ ܕܝܠܗ ܩܒܠܬ ܘܠܐ ܐܒܗܬܟܘܢ ܒܟܘܢ.
"And I will regard him (lit. make his face)
so I will not put you to shame."

The effect on meaning in this case (42:8,9) is one of synonymy
with variation at the level of literary style, for the Syr. idiom (ܐ ܟܒܠ
ܟ ܐܦܗ) still preserves the meaning, although not the same words as the
Heb. idiom (נשׂא פניו). Elsewhere in the P נשׂא is usually rendered by
ܢܣܒ "to take, receive" when followed by the object פנים , when the
intended meaning is "to shew partiality; grant a request; be gracious".[98]
In the next example, one exception to this correspondence occurs.

An example of the third type - a Heb. idiom replaced by a Syr.
idiom that bears no semantic relationship to the Heb. - can likewise be
demonstrated by appealing to this same idiom (נשׂא פנים), but in 11:15.

MT כי־אז תשׂא פניך ממום   והיית מצק ולא תירא:
"Surely then you will lift up your face without blemish
(=sign of good conscience),
and you will be secure and will not be afraid."

P   ܘܗܝܕܝܢ ܬܪܝܡ ܐܝܕܝܟ. ܘܡܢ ܒܝܫܬܐ ܠܐ ܬܕܚܠ.
"And then you will raise your hands,
and you will not be afraid from adversity."

Heb. נשׂא פנים "to lift up one's face" is an expression used as a
sign of good conscience.[99] P usually presents the equivalence ܬܪܡ√ +

---

[98] See Gen 19:21;32:21[20 in P]; Lev 19:15; Deut 10:17; 1 Sam 25:35; Mal 1:8,9;2:9;
Prov 18:5; Ps 82:2.

[99] See BDB, p. 670a, s.v. נשׂא 1b(2).

אפ "to raise one's face" (Num 6:26; 2 Sam 2:22; 2 Kgs 9:32). The P-Job here, however, translates with the Syriac idiom ܪܡ ܐܝܕܐ "to raise one's hands", an idiom carrying three semantic possibilities: to swear; to present a blessing; to pray.[100] All meanings are distinct from the Hebrew, thus producing an innovative meaning. The motivation for this divergence is not only ambiguity inherent in the Heb. idiom, but error resulting from parallel verse influence with 10:15.   There Heb. נשא ראש "to lift up one's head" = 'a sign of boldness' is rendered רמ ܪܝܫ "to raise one's head".

Consider the correspondences for the idiomatic used of נשא in Job:

גבה לבא > נשא פנים	(42:8,9)
רב "lord" > נשוא פנים	(22:8)[101]
נסב לבא > נשא פנים	(13:8,10;32:21;34:19)
רמ רֵיש > נשא ראש*	(10:15)
רמ אַפֵּי > נשא פנים*	(11:15)
תבע מנתא > נשא משל	(27:1;29:1)
שבק חטהא > נשא פשע	(7:21)

Thus for each idiom P provided a different translation which was either a resolution of the idiom (7:21;22:8;27:1;29:1) - discussed in the next section; the idiom preserved formally and dynamically (10:15; 13:8,10;32:21;34:19); replacement of an idiom with a semantically unrelated equivalence (11:15); or a Syr. idiom which preserves the meaning of the Heb. idiom (42:8,9).

II. Heb. idiom replaced by Syr. non-figurative language

The second way in which P adjusts for a Hebrew idiom is again through substitution. However, in these cases an idiom is not replaced by a Syriac one, but rather its figurative language is resolved into non-figurative propositions.   This resolution in P-Job falls into three

---

[100] See J. Payne-Smith, p. 534b-535a, s.v. ܪܡ.

[101] P handles this phrase נשוא פנים "one favoured of face" uniquely in each occurrence. Thus in 2 Kgs 5:1 P translates שביח באפא "glorious in face" and in Isa 3:3;9:14 מיקר אפא "honourable of face".

categories based on motivations: (1) language difference; (2) ambiguity; and (3) error.

1. Language Difference.

Certain Hebrew phrases are simply not used in their idiomatic capacity in Syriac. Thus, the translator of P resolved this Hebraic usage by translating according to the meaning of the Hebrew idiom. So, for example, with the Heb. idioms indicating "in one's presence", i.e. לפני, 102 לעיני, 103 or "within one's hearing" באזני. 104   P, in general, renders all by the simple preposition קדם "before, in the presence of". Similarly, such distributive expressions as לבקרים lit. "to mornings" i.e. "in every morning" (7:18) and לרגעים "to moments" i.e. "at every moment" (7:18) are rendered ܒܨ̇ܦܪܐ "in the morning" and ܒܪܓܫܐ "at the moment"; or שָׁלוֹשׁ פְּעָמִים "twice three" i.e. "three times" > ܙܒܢ̈ܝܢ ܬܠܬ "three times" (33:29). Here, too, are included the Heb. expressions for anger such as חרה אף (19:11) or חרון אפו (20:23). P does not use the term אף "nose" extended to mean "anger", but has a specific term ܪܘܓܙܐ , hence its translations ܪܘܓܙܐ ܚܡܬ (19:11) and ܗܘܐ ܪܘܓܙܗ ܘܚܡܬܗ (20:23).105

The effect on meaning – synonymy with variation at the literary level – indicates that with resolution of this type P clearly understood the Heb. idiom, but did not use or better yet possess a Syriac idiom for these situations, hence its non-figurative translation.

2. Ambiguity.

Ambiguity can exist for a number of reasons in a Heb. idiom. It can be semantically based in an element of the idiom; an element may be polysemous or the entire idiom may be polysemous. With very common idioms, e.g. שׂים לב, the object need not be expressed in the Hebrew,

---

102 See, for example, לפני in vv. 3:24;4:19;8:16;15:4;21:18;34:19; and BDB, p. 816b #4 , s.v. פנים.

103 See, for example, לעיני in vv. 15:15;25:5; and BDB, p. 745a #5, s.v. עין.

104 See, for example, באזני in v. 13:17; and BDB, p. 23b-24a #2a, s.v. אזן.

105 See, for further examples of expressions of anger in Heb. and Syr., vv. 4:9;9:5,13; 14:13;16:9;18:4;19:11;20:28;21:17;32:3;35:15;36:13;40:11;42:7.

thus in some cases going unrecognized as an idiom by a translator. In other cases P clearly missed the idiomatic usage because of the uniqueness or rarity of an idiom.

Returning to the first type of ambiguity, a semantically based ambiguity, we find the idiom קדמוני ברכים in 3:12:

MT   מדוע קדמוני ברכים   ומה־שדים כי אינק:
             "Why did knees receive me?
             And what of breasts that I might suck?"

P   ܠܡܢܐ ܩܒܠܢ ܒܘܪ̈ܟܐ. ܘܡܢ ܐܝܟ ܠܕܝܐ ܝܢܩܬ.
             "Why did knees rear me?
             And why did I nurse from the breasts?"

Heb. √קדם is a denominative verb occurring only in the Piel with the basic connotation "to come or be in front; to meet". Under contextual influence the latter meaning is extended once, here (Job 3:12), to mean "receive". In Syriac the root √קדם is quite common, occurring in the Peal, Pael, and Ethpaal, still, however, with the basic connotation "to go before, be first". P, however, translated with the root √ܪܒܐ "to rear, raise", hence clearly understanding the dynamics of the Heb. idiom, but not understanding or adopting the formal use of the root √קדם. Synonymy is still present in the meaning, with variation at the literary stylistics level.

The second type of ambiguity - a polysemous element or idiom - finds an example in 12:3:

MT   גם־לי לבב כמוכם   לא־נפל אנכי מכם
                           ואת־מי־אין   כמו־אלה:
             "I also have a heart like you,
             I am not inferior to (lit. to fall from) you,
             and who does not [know such things] as these?"

P   ܐܦ ܠܝ ܠܒܐ ܐܝܬ ܠܝ ܐܟܘܬܟܘܢ.
             ܘܠܐ ܡܢܟܘܢ ܒܨܝܪ ܐܢܐ. ܠܡܢ ܗܘ ܡܢ ܐܝܟ ܗܠܝܢ.

"I also have a heart like you, and I was not less than you;
to whom were they like these?"

In the second stich, Heb. נפל occurs in the comparative statement
לא־נפל אנכי מכם. Although the basic connotation of "to fall" seems
clear enough, this root is quite polysemous in its fine nuances and
particularly in its idiomatic capacity.[106] However, only here and Job
13:2 is it used idiomatically with the meaning "to be inferior".[107] In
order to avoid the ambiguity of the possible selections and the rarity of
this expression, P resolved the idiom, translating according to the
intended meaning: ܒ ܪ "be little, less". The overall effect on meaning is
still synonymy with variation at the level of literary style.[108]

As for the third type of ambiguity, the problem of an incompletely
expressed idiom, an excellent example occurs in 23:6:

MT   הברב־כח יריב עמדי   לא אך־הוא ישם בי:
"With a multitude of strength would he contend with me?
No, He would pay attention to me!"

P   ܟܡܘܬ ܐܝܟܐ ܕܐܝܬ ܚܝܠ ܢܕܘܢܢܝ.
                     ܘܐܢ ܠܐ ܗܘܐ ܗܟܢܐ ܕܚܠܬܐ ܣܐܡ ܥܠܝ.
"With a multitude of strength (would) He judge me?
And if He would not, He places fear upon me."

The Hebrew verb שים "to put, place" is used with a variety of
nouns and prepositions to achieve a variety of expressions.[109] One
rather common combination is שים לב "to set the heart/mind (toward)
= "to pay attention to".[110] The familiarity of this idiom is so much so
that at times its complement, while omitted, is still implicit in the text.
Three times in the book of Job the omission of לבב/לב occurs

---

[106] See BDB, pp. 656-658, s.v. נפל.

[107] See BDB, pp. 657b, s.v. נפל 6c.

[108] Vulgate similarly translates Heb. נפל, thus *nec inferior* "not inferior".

[109] See BDB, pp. 962-965, s.v. שים.

[110] See BDB, pp. 963, s.v. שים 2b.

(4:20;23:6; 24:12) and in each case the translator seemed unaware that a complement, i.e. the idiom שׂים לב, was intended. Such is the case in the present example, 23:6. If Heb. √שׂים, a transitive verb, is viewed non-idiomatically an object is wanting. This, in fact, is what P does, supplying the object ܕܚܠܬܐ "fear".

The effect on meaning from the evaluator's perspective is clearly innovative. To the translator and possibly his reader/aural recipient no discernable difference would be found.[111]

The final reason for ambiguity in an idiom - uniqueness or rarity that led to non-recognition - can be seen in 9:27:

MT   אם־אמרי אשכחה שׂיחי   אעזבה פני ואבליגה:
"If I say 'I will forget my complaint,
I will abandon my gloomy countenance
(lit. forsake my face) and be cheerful',"

P   ܐܝܟ ܕܛܥܝ̈ܝ ܠܝ̇ܠܝ ܡ̈ܡܠܠܝ.
         ܐܢ ܐܫܒܩ ܗܘ ܐܝ ܘ ܡ̇ܚܫ̈ܒܬܝ. ܟܐܒ ܐܢܐ.
"Together with mybitternesses I have forgotten my discourses.
If I leave off my thought or my words, I am grieved."

P clearly had difficulties with many elements of this verse. The present issue concerns the translator's treatment of Heb. אעזבה פני. The peculiarity of this expression has produced a plethora of comments and suggested interpretations.[112] The √עזב "to leave, forsake, loose" with the complement פנים is unique to this verse. Most commentators understand this as an idiom meaning "to abandon one's gloomy countenance" which would then accord with the following, also albeit infrequent, √בלג "to be cheerful, smile". To wit, Job is proposing that he change his entire demeanor and, to borrow an old cliche, "put on a happy face". The translator has clearly missed the uniqueness of his

---

[111] For further examples of incomplete idioms in the text of Job and P's treatment see 6:27 (נפל√); 16:4 (חבר√); and 4:20 and 24:12 (שׂים√).

[112] See BDB, p. 737b, s.v. עזב #3 end; Dhorme, p. 141f; ICC, p. 60; Habel, p. 183; Pope, pp. 74-75.

idiom, basing his translation on the usual meaning of עזב√, hence Syr.
ܫܒܩ√ "to leave off". His uncertainty is also apparent in the double
translation of Heb. פני by ܪܢܝ "thoughts" and ܢܒܠ "words". Likewise,
the rarity of Heb. בלג√ was no contextual guide, for that too was
rendered by a possible antonym ܢܬܬܬܠܥ "to be grieved".[113] Thus,
the translator is clearly continuing the bitter sentiments expressed in stich
one, which likewise shows that a secondary motivation of intra-verse
influence has effected P's choice of translation. Versional parallels with
the LXX (στεναξω "I will groan") and Vulgate (*dolore torqueor* "I
am tormented with sorrow) also exist, but context more than direct
influence should be considered. The effect on meaning from an
evaluator's perspective is innovative. As for the translator, from his
perspective the effect on meaning would be clarity of an unclear and
difficult Hebrew passage.

3. Error.

In the previous example (9:27) an error in non-recognition of an
idiom, brought on by ambiguity, caused the translator to translate contra
the MT. This could be considered an error of a secondary nature.
Situations do occur though in which error can be cited as the primary
motivational factor in P's translating a Heb. idiom. In 22:8a this situation
occurs:

> MT   ואיש זרוע לו הארץ
>
>   "the land belongs to the powerful man (lit. a man of arm),"

> P   ܐܬܪ ܠܗ ܙܪܥ ܗܘ ܓܒܪܐ ܐܝܬ
>
>   "there is a man who sows the land for himself,"

P clearly made an error in reading זרוע "arm" > זרע√ I as if
derived from זרע√ II "to sow, plant", i.e. זורע a participle or זרוע an
infinitive absolute. The effect on meaning is innovative. The Heb. text

---

113 בלג√ also is found three other times in the OT; Job 10:20 and Ps 39:14 (ܐܬܬܢܝܚ
"to be at rest") and Amos 5:9 (ܡܫܠܛܒ "to set in authority"). In each case context serves
as the P's guide to translation.

speaks of a powerful man, in a sense intimating that the land goes to the strongest taker. P, by contrast, preserves a more agricultural scene, a man sowing his own land, the underlying connotations of which are: (1) a man is affluent enough that the profit of his land is of his own keeping, or (2) a man must sow his own field, suggesting he was not affluent enough to afford servants to do the work. In light of the second stich - ונשוא פנים ישב בה "and the favoured man lives in it" - the latter case seems true. In other words, the commoner does the work, while the lord lives off it. In Heb. the stichs are synonymously parallel, in the P they are antithetic to one another.[114]

III. Creation of a Syriac Idiom

From the preceding discussion we have seen that to merely state that P dissolves an idiom due to misunderstanding or because P lacks the stylistic capabilities is indeed an overly generalized statement. P's dissolution is due to legitimate motivations of language difference, varieties of ambiguity, and error. Moreover, we saw that substitution by an equivalent Syriac idiom also occurred, prompted by a variety of reasons. It must also be remembered that only a small fraction of the Heb. idioms were in any way altered,[115] thus indicating that neither the translator of P nor his language can be charged with lacking stylistic abilities. Moreover, in ten places, P added an idiom where the MT records non-figurative language.[116]

One such example of the addition of an idiom concerns the translator's treatment of Heb. ענה "to answer". Heb. √ענה occurs 51 times verbally and twice nominally in the book of Job; 42 of which are rendered literally by √ܥܢܐ;[117] and three are interpretively rendered.[118] The remaining six verbal and two nominal occurrences are translated by the idiom ܢܣܒ ܦܬܓܡܐ (32:12;40:2) or ܝܗܒ ܦܬܓܡܐ (9:32;32:3*, 5*,20;33:12; 40:5 - asterisk indicates the equivalence here is for the Heb. nominal מענה). Only in 32:12 is the object אמר "word" expressed in

---

114 For another example see 28:8.

115 The same was seen with the previous section on figurative language. P more often than not preserved figurative elements.

116 See 1:14;2:11;7:16;9:7;11:5;38:35;40:2,5,19.

117 See vv. 5:1;9:14,15;13:22;15:2;16:3;19:16;30:20;32:15,16,17;33:13;35:12.

118 See 32:1 = √ܫܠܝ; 16:8 is paraphrased; and 15:6 = √ܚܣܡ.

the Hebrew text. The idiom ܢܗܒ ܦܬܓܡܐ also occurs once as a translation for the Heb. infinitive construct of √ דבר in Job 11:5: ואולם מי־יתן אלוה דַּבֵּר "But would that Eloah might speak" > P ܦܬܓܡܐ ܒܪܡ ܡܢ ܝܢ ܢܬܠ ܕܢܗܒ ܗܘܐ ܐܠܗܐ "But would that God had given a word, i.e. answered".[119] P appears to have misunderstood the Heb. piel infinitive construct as the noun דָּבָר "word" - as if the Heb. read "But would that Eloah a word" - and then by necessity added the verb ܢܗܒ to complete the thought. P's addition of ܢܗܒ ܗܘܐ is not a translation of the Heb. desiderative מן־יתן, for the standard equivalence ܡܢ ܢܬܠ is present. The effect on meaning in each case is still synonymy with variation only on the literary level.

Outside the book of Job, the cognate ܥܢܐ is the most common equivalence for Heb. ענה, but ܣܗܕ "to witness, testify"[120] and √ܡܟܟ Ethp. "to be brought low, humbled"[121] are well attested when √ענה bears these connotations. There are also well over a dozen other interpretive renderings for individual passages.[122] Of particular interest, however, are five passages (Gen 45:3; 1 Kgs 18:21; 2 Kgs 18:36; Isa 36:21; Ps 119:42) in which P uses the idiom ܢܗܒ ܦܬܓܡܐ or ܢܬܠ ܦܬܓܡܐ. In all but the Genesis passage, P's translation is not just a translation of the verb ענה , but a rendering of Heb. ענה "to answer" + דבר "a word".

Rather interesting, too, is the fact that the Tg. also had recourse to translate the Gen 45:3 passage with the idiom תוב (Aphel) + פתגם "to

[119] The more usual equivalences for √דבר are: verbally ܐܡܪ (2:13;37:20;40:27; 42:7,9) or ܡܠܠ (1:16,17,18;2:10;7:11;9:35;10:1;13:3,7,13,22;16:4,6;18:2; 21:3;32:7, 16,20;33:14,31;34:33,35;42:4); and nominally ܡܠܐ/ܡܠܬܐ (2:13; 4:2;9:14;32:11; 34:35) or ܦܬܓܡܐ (4:12;6:3;26:14;29:22;31:40;33:1,13;42:7).

[120] See Gen 30:32; Exod 20:16; Num 35:30; Deut 5:17;19:16,18; 1 Sam 12:3; 2 Sam 1:16; Isa 3:9; 59:12; Jer 14:7; Ezek 14:4,7; Prov 25:18; Mic 6:3.

[121] See Isa 25:5; Hos 2:17;5:5;7:10;14:9; Pss 22:22;55:20;119:67; Eccl 10:17.

[122] See Exod 24:3 (ܩܠܐ); Deut 25:9 (ܪܘܡ + ܐܦ); Deut 31:21 (ܡܘܪܐ); er. 44:20 (ܐܡܪ); Ruth 1:21; 2 Chr 6:26 (ܗܦܟ Aphel); 1 Sam 9:17 (ܥܢܐ); 1 Kgs 8:35 (ܦܢܐ Ethp.); Ps 81:8 (ܢܣܐ); Ps 119:122 (ܢܟܠ); Ps 147:7 (ܫܒܚ); Prov 15:28 (ܗܝܡܢܘܬܐ); Exod 32:18; Prov 18:23; 26:5 (ܡܠܠ); Prov 29:19 (ܩܒܠ); Ezra 3:11 (ܡܪܢ).

return word" = "to answer",[123] an idiom not unfamiliar to either Hebrew or Syriac.[124] In Hebrew the idiom שׁוּב (Hiphil) "to return" + דבר[125] has two distinct meanings: (1) "to bring back words, i.e. a report or message" and (2) "to return word" = "to answer".[126] In P, we find that the usual equivalence is either ܐܬܒ (Aphel)[127] or ܦܢܝ [128]+ ܦܬܓܡܐ. No distinction is made in regards to the two connotations. Of particular interest here, however, are the departures from this norm, that is in Num 22:8; Deut 1:22 and Isa 41:28 P reads ܝܗܒ ܦܬܓܡܐ and in Prov 18:13 ܬܝܒ ܦܬܓܡܐ, the same idiom we saw above at times used for Heb. √ענה. It is most noteworthy that in two passages (Num 22:8; Deut 1:22) the connotation "to bring back a report/message" is indicated. P's substitution with its own idiom is still contextually appropriate, but here "to give a word" must be understood in a non-idiomatic capacity.[129] Rather peculiar, too, is that in Ezek 9:11 P reverses its translational tendency, rendering the Heb. idiom שׁוּב + דבר non-idiomatically by √ܬܢܐ.

---

[123] In the Targum √תוב (Aphel) is a common equivalence for Heb. √ענה when it denotes "to answer", however, it is usually followed by an object (e.g. פתגמא or מימרא) unless paralleled in the MT or unless the Heb. idiom √שׁוּב + דבר is present. Thus, here the Tg. either understood an object, i.e. דבר + ענה√ or the idiom √שׁוּב + דבר.

[124] See MT at Gen 37:14; Exod 19:8; Num 13:26;22:8; Deut 1:22,25; Josh 14:7;22:32; 1 Sam 17:30; 2 Sam 3:11; 1 Kgs 12:6;20:9; 2 Kgs 22:9,20; 2 Chr 10:6,16;34:16,28; Isa 41:28; Ezek; 9:11; Job 20:2 (w/o דבר); 13:22;33:5;35:4; Prov 18:13;22:21;24:26; Neh 6:4.

[125] In Prov 22:21 the MT reads אמר as the direct object (> P ܗܠܝܢ) and in Job 35:4 מלין (> P ܠܟ).

[126] See BDB, p. 999, s.v. שׁוּב, #3.

[127] See Gen 37:14; Num 13:26; Deut 1:25; Josh 14:7;22:32; 1 Sam 17:30; 2 Sam 3:11 1 Kgs 12:6; 20:9; 2 Kgs 22:9,20; 2 Chr 10:16;34;15; Job 13:22;33:5;35:4; Neh 6:4.

[128] See Exod 19:8; Prov 22:21; 2 Chr 10:6;34:28.

[129] These verse in P read (Num 22:8) "And he (Balaam) said to them, 'Lodge here the night, then I will give you the word as the Lord says to me'. And the leaders of Moab waited for Balaam." (Deut 1:22) "And all of you drew near to me and said 'Let us send out men beforehand that they might explore the land for us and they might give to us a word and show us the way in which we must go and the cities which we may go up to."

Thus, we see the Syriac idiom ܢܬܠ ܦܬܓܡܐ / ܝܗܒ ܦܬܓܡܐ used:

(1) for eight occurrences of Heb. ענה√ "to answer" (Gen 45:3; Job 9:32;32:3,5,20;33:12; 40:2,5);

(2) in five passages in which the MT reads ענה√ "to answer" + דבר "a word" (1 Kgs 18:21; 2 Kgs 18:36; Isa 36:21; Ps 119:42) or אמר (Job 32:12);

(3) and in four passages where the MT preserves the idiom שוב דבר "to return a word" (Num 22:18; Deut 1:22; Isa 41:28; Prov 18:13).

In those passages (#2) where the MT preserves the object דבר or אמר, P may have found the combination Heb. ענה + דבר/אמר "to answer a word" unacceptable, for "to answer" is "to give a word, i.e. a reply", hence the presence of the object is unnecessary and redundant. Thus P replaced ענה with the more generic verb ܝܗܒ or ܢܬܠ "to give" and then retained אמר / דבר with the standard equivalence ܦܬܓܡܐ. Herein may lie the origin of this Syriac idiom. However, what motivated the translator to use this idiom as a translation for Heb. ענה√, especially in P-Job, or to use it, at times, as a substitute for the idiom שוב דבר (#3), extant in Syriac as well as in Hebrew and Targumic Aramaic, can by no means be stated with such ease and certainty. Versional influence is not indicated for, unless noted, the Targum and LXX[130] parallel the MT.

In P-Job there are a few common denominators present:

1. the 1pcs imperfect is often present (9:32;32:20;33:12;40:5);
2. the presence of the idiom פתח שפה (11:5;32:20);
3. the presence of the term מוכיח (32:12;40:2; nearby in 9:33;
4. and it is used for the only two nominal occurrences of ענה√ (32:3,5).

There are, however, verses where ענה√ occurs with one of these features and P still retains the √ ܥܢܐ.[131] Then too, the majority of cases are found in Elihu's speeches (32:3,5,12,20;33:12). The first is spoken

---

[130] LXX most frequently uses the stem αποκριvω (Middle) "to give answer" or "to reply", alone or with an object (λογον, ρηματα, πραγματα) when one is present in the MT.

[131] See 9:14,15;13:22;32:17 where ענה√ is used in the 1pcs imperfect, but P still translates with √ ܥܢܐ .

by Job (9:32) and the second by Zophar (11:5) in his response to Job.
The last two occur in rapid sequence (40:2 and 40:5), first by the Lord
(40:2) and then what might be considered an echo of 40:2 in Job's
response (40:5). Strictly speaking then, no single feature seems to have
motivated the translator to use this idiom, but rather a variety of possible
factors/features. At times, too, the translator may have had a predilection
to translate with figurative language.

VII

Conclusions

In the preceding pages we have seen the application of the TTModel to P-Job in the areas of grammar, syntax, semantics and style. Each area has not been examined exhaustively, but rather a select group of topics have been investigated as sample cases. Although limited, they have yielded quite a large and varied data supply from which we can evaluate the P-Job and the Peshitta as a whole, as well as the translator and the translation process.

Let us evaluate the data that has been collected in the preceding chapters, proceeding from the general to the specific, that is, data related to the Peshitta in general, specific characteristics of the P-Job, the formation and textual transmission of P-Job, and concluding with the effectiveness of this method of gathering data, i.e. the TT Model.

I. Characteristics of the Peshitta in General

The Peshitta in general is a translation that in the transfer from source to target language naturally adjusts certain grammatical, syntactic, semantic and stylistic features in accordance with the Syriac language. This adjustment is to be expected when translating from one language to another no matter how closely related the languages are. Translational elements in all areas provide us with, for the most part, examples of departures that are more correctly language specific, i.e. characteristic of the Syriac language of the Peshitta, than unique to the P-Job. Thus they are the expected, usual correspondences and should not be deemed as evidence of a different *Vorlage* or reflective of subtle ideological insinuations.

259

In the area of grammar, it is characteristic of the Peshitta:

1. to render the Heb. homographs n.m.s./ adj. m.s. טוב and רע by the f.pl. adjective;[1]

2. to render the Heb. singular by the plural when used collectively, the Heb. plural by the singular when used stylistically and the Heb. dual by the plural;[2]

3. to render the Heb. impersonal subject "anyone, one" by an explicit subject;[3]

4. to add the enclitic pronoun primarily in non-verbal clauses and explicitly express the relative pronoun implied in the MT;[4]

5. to render the tenses presented in the MT in accordance with the standard tense system equivalences that exist in the Syriac language;[5]

6. to render the Heb. impersonal active (= passive) by the passive form;[6]

7. to switch word classes as dictated by language difference;[7]

8a. (under certain circumstances) to use an object suffix affixed to a preposition or the Lamedh object marker for a Heb. verbal suffix, especially where the preposition is implicit in the MT;

b. to represent various Heb. prepositions with suffixes by a verbal suffix when the preposition is redundant or inappropriate to the semantic environment;

c. to omit redundant resumptive suffixes;

d. to add a suffix when translating Heb. descriptive clauses with the structure [m.s. adj. in cstr. + dual noun] > Syr. [relative pronoun = m.pl.abs. adj. + n.pl. + suffix].[8]

In the area of syntax, it is characteristic of the Peshitta:

1. to permit a somewhat free arrangement of its principal parts with variation dictated by emphasis or stylistic preferences just like Syriac word order in general. P follows the MT much of the time with an occasional transposition that can only be explained by stylistic preferences

---

[1] See Ch. III Grammar: Gender, p. 63.
[2] See Ch. III Grammar: Number, pp. 64-66.
[3] See Ch. III Grammar: Person, pp. 70-72.
[4] See Ch. III Grammar: Pronoun, p. 75-77.
[5] See Ch. III Grammar: Tense, pp. 80-82.
[6] See Ch. III Grammar: Voice, p. 89.
[7] See Ch. III Grammar: Word Class, pp. 93-94.
[8] See Ch. III Grammar: Suffix, p. 100-101.

of the translator, e.g. the formula "and N1 answered N2 and said" > Syr. "And N1 answered and said to N2".[9]

2. to omit the waw conjunctive when under certain circumstances it is deemed redundant; to add the waw conjunctive when it is implicit in the MT or when certain stylistic conditions are present; to substitute another Syriac conjunction for the Heb. waw conjunctive when the Syriac language provides for the use of a different conjunction in specific types of clauses, e.g. Syriac uses the conjunction ܐܘ "or" for the Heb. waw conjunctive wherever the alternative is intended or perceived to be implied.[10]

In the area of semantics it is characteristic of the Peshitta:

1a. to uniformly add the same clarifying lexeme when translating certain ambiguous (e.g. חלמיש) or polysemous (יכל, פה) lexemes;

  b. to explicitly express prepositions, the relative pronoun and prepositions + suffixes implied in the MT;

  c. to uniformly paraphrase a number of terms (See Appendix A).[11]

2. to omit various redundant lexemes, e.g. emphatic particles, one of two compound prepositions, words clearly implied in one stich by parallelism with another;[12]

3. to generalize a more componentially complex Heb. lexeme when:

    a.) Syriac lacks the lexical variety or componentially complex lexeme, e.g. כעש > ܪ̈ܓܐܬܐ ; חושיה > ܥܒܕܟܐ ; יצבֿ√ > √ܡܢܬ;[13]

    b.) the more complex lexeme is inappropriate to the semantic environment, e.g. פער, כף, חך.[14]

4. to specify a polysemous Heb. lexeme even when the semantics clarifies the ambiguity, e.g. צבא, אף, יום, ל-;[15]

5. to specify a very basic Heb. lexeme when the semantic environment suggests more detailed information, e.g. צור and שׂנא.[16]

---

[9] See Ch. IV Syntax: Word Order: Transposition, pp. 108-111.

[10] See Ch. IV Syntax: Clausal Relationships: The Waw Conjunctive, pp. 118, 122-131.

[11] See Ch. V Semantics: Addition, p. 134-137, 145-149, 161-162.

[12] See Ch. V Semantics: Omission, p. 163.

[13] See Ch. V Semantics: Generalization, p. 171-172.

[14] See Ch. V Semantics: Generalization, p. 174-177.

[15] See Ch. V Semantics: Specification, p. 178-182.

[16] See Ch. V Semantics: Specification, p. 184-186.

6. to contextually translate Hebrew words that are *hapax legomena* or rare lexemes.[17]

7. As a result of the above semantic substitutions the process of lexical levelling occurs in the P.[18]

In the area of style, it is characteristic of the Peshitta:

1. to represent the simple interrogative question - in Hebrew indicated by the interrogative Heh - by Ø morpheme or under certain circumstances by the particle ܕܠܡܐ. These same equivalences occur when the simple interrogative is combined with a particle.[19]

2. to represent the disjunctive question - indicated in Heb. by הֵ . . . אִם - by ܐܪ . . . Ø.[20]

3. to explicitly indicate an implied conditional statement by adding (ה) . . . ܐܝܟ.[21]

4. to indicate the exclamatory sentence by the standard equivalences for Heb. particles: הִנֵּה > ܐܡ ; הֵן > ܐܡ ; נָא > ܠ or Ø; אַף and גַם > ܐܦ.

Note: P freely omits the exclamatory particle when it is redundant or contextually inappropriate.[22]

5. to preserve a Heb. simile, removing the preposition of comparison only in error or when the preposition is inappropriate and altering an internal element only when it contains a grammatical, syntactical or semantical problem;[23]

6. to preserve the precise wording of a Heb. idiom when the Syriac language possesses that same idiom;[24]

7. to substitute non-figurative language for those very basic Heb. idioms that are so frequently used one is not aware that they are idioms, e.g. לְעֵינֵי, לִפְנֵי;[2 5]

---

17 See Ch. V Semantics: Contextualization, p. 193-198.

18 See Ch. V Semantics: Lexical Levelling, p. 185ff.

19 See Ch. VI Style: Sentence Type: Simple Interrogative and Simple Interrogative + Particle, pp. 202-211.

20 See Ch. VI Style: Sentence Type: Disjunctive Questions, p. 211.

21 See Ch. VI Style: Sentence Type: Conditional Statements, p. 215.

22 See Ch. VI Style: Sentence Type: Exclamatory Sentences, p. 217-229.

23 See Ch. VI Style: Simile, p. 233-236.

24 See Ch. VI Style: Idiom, p. 244-245.

25 See Ch. VI Style: Idiom, p. 248.

8. P is not adverse to formulating its own idioms and substituting them for non-figurative language, e.g. Heb. √עזז > Syr. ܦܝܠܬ ܕܬܠ or ܢܚܣܒ.[26]

The Peshitta (including the P-Job) as we have seen is also a translation characterized by a tendency toward explicit exegesis, relying not upon implied elements, but rather the expressly written word to faithfully and clearly project the message of the source text, the MT.

II. Characteristics of the P-Job

Our investigations have similarly revealed characteristics and features found only in P-Job. This uniqueness does not necessarily reflect the work of a different translator but rather may indicate that in its transfer from source to target text P-Job possesses certain translational techniques that are text specific, i.e. only occurring in a specific type of text.

In the area of grammar, it is characteristic of P-Job:

1. to correct gender-number disagreement in the source text (e.g. 1:4b);[27]

2a. to confuse number in homographs which are only distinguishable by the vocalization developed much later in the MT;

b. to adjust the number to achieve grammatical harmonization with the surrounding environment;

c. to adjust the number to accord with the translator's theological belief (e.g. 32:1);[28]

3a. to adjust the person to accord with the translator's theological belief (e.g. 6:13);

b. to adjust the person to achieve grammatical harmonization with the surrounding environment (e.g. 38:11);[29]

4. to adjust the pronoun to harmonize with the surrounding environment;[30]

5a. to confuse the tense when homographs are present;

---

[26] See Ch. VI Style: Idiom, p. 253-257.

[27] See Ch. III Grammar: Gender, pp. 61-62.

[28] See Ch. III Grammar: Number, pp. 67-70.

[29] See Ch. III Grammar: Person, pp. 72-73.

[30] See Ch. III Grammar: Pronoun, pp.76-78.

b. to adjust the tense to harmonize with the surrounding environment;

c. to adjust the tense to harmonize events and to portray the character of Job and God as perceived by the translator;[31]

6a. to alter the Heb. voice when ambiguity is present as to which voice is intended;

b. to adjust the voice to harmonize with the surrounding environment;

c. to be influenced by the versions or at least parallel the versions in a number of radical departures in voice;

d. to adjust the voice to accord with the translator's ideology of Job and the fate of the wicked (e.g. 9:15; 21:33).[32]

7. to alter word class in order to clarify an ambiguity and harmonize with the surrounding environment;[33]

8a. to omit or add a suffix due to orthographic errors or in order to harmonize with the surrounding environment;

b. to add a suffix in order to project ideology perceived by translator.[34]

In the area of syntax it is characteristic of P-Job:

1. to transpose words/phrases where ambiguity of syntax exists in MT;[35]

2. to redivide stichs and verses where ambiguity of syntax exists in MT;

3. to redivide a stich or verse in order to harmonize with the surrounding environment;[36]

4. to add a waw conjunctive under specific rules of style;

5. to substitute another conjunction for the waw conjunctive when the meaning is implied in the conjunctive or intra-/inter-verse influence suggests another conjunction would be more appropriate.[37]

In the area of semantics, it is characteristic of P-Job:

1. to add an element that clarifies an ambiguous (e.g. ארנ) or a polysemous lexeme (e.g. אשׁה) that is text specific;[38]

2. to add an element to a common term in order to clarify and bring out an ideological point (e.g. 23:6 קעצ);[39]

---

[31] See Ch. III Grammar: Tense, pp. 81-87.

[32] See Ch. III Grammar: Voice, pp. 88-89,90-92.

[33] See Ch. III Grammar: Word Class, p. 94.

[34] See Ch. III Grammar: Suffix, pp. 100,102.

[35] See Ch. IV Syntax: Word Order: Transposition, pp. 111-112.

[36] See Ch. IV Syntax: Word Order: Redivision, pp. 113-117.

[37] See Ch. IV Syntax: Clausal Relationships: Waw Conjunctive, pp.128-131.

[38] See Ch. V Semantics: Addition, p. 135

[39] See Ch. V Semantics: Addition, pp. 138-139.

3. to add a word or phrase motivated by parallel verse influence;[40]

4. to add a word or phrase in order to better express ideological concerns (e.g. 16:5);[41]

5. to preserve double readings of a word or stich, or develop two stichs from key words contained in one MT stich;[42]

6. to uniquely paraphrase certain words;[43]

7. to omit a word or phrase that may not accord with translator's ideology;[44]

8. to omit an element in order to harmonize with the surrounding environment;[45]

9. to omit an element due to errors caused by the surrounding orthographic environment;[46]

10. to substitute a more general term for a rare or ambiguous term uniquely in P-Job versus the P in general;[47]

11. to substitute a more specific term for a common one uniquely in P-Job versus the P in general;[48]

12. to contextualize a common term in such a way that is unique to P-Job;[49]

13. to substitute an interpretive reading that reflects the ideological perspective of the translator.[50]

In the area of style, it is characteristic of P-Job:

1. to transform interrogative sentences into exclamatory statements ($\overline{\Pi}$ > ‌‌ܐܘ) carrying the affirmative response implied in the MT question, often with ideological topics;[51]

2. to deviate from the standard Syriac pattern for indicating disjunctive questions (ܘܐ . . . Ø) under inter-verse influence;[52]

---

[40] See Ch. V Semantics: Addition, pp. 147-150.

[41] See Ch. V Semantics: Addition, pp. 150-152.

[42] See Ch. V Semantics: Addition, pp. 153-160.

[43] See Ch. V Semantics: Addition, pp. 161-162.

[44] See Ch. V Semantics: Omission, p. 162.

[45] See Ch. V Semantics: Omission, pp. 163-166.

[46] See Ch. V Semantics: Omission, pp. 166-167.

[47] See Ch. V Semantics: Substitution: Generalization, pp. 173-174.

[48] See Ch. V Semantics: Substitution: Specification, pp. 178-182.

[49] See Ch. V Semantics: Contextualization, pp. 186-188.

[50] See Ch. V Semantics: Interpretation, pp. 188-193.

[51] See Ch. VI Style: Sentence Type, pp. 207-209.

[52] See Ch. VI Style: Sentence Type, pp. 211-212.

3. to deviate from the standard Syriac equivalences for exclamatory particles due to intra-/inter-verse influence or stylistic preferences;[53]

4. to create a simile when an ambiguity exists in a word or preposition that could be resolved by the presence of this figure of speech;[54]

5. to create a simile in order to soften an anthropomorphic allusion to God (e.g. 10:4);[55]

6. to transform metaphors into similes for explicitness or dissolve them by clarifying the ambiguity that may exist in the polysemous nature of the tenor or vehicle of the metaphor;[56]

7. to substitute a Syriac idiom for a Heb. one with a polysemous element;[57]

8. to resolve a Heb. idiom into non-figurative language when the Heb. idiom contains a polysemous element; when the Heb. idiom is not completely expressed, i.e. certain key word(s) are present with the remainder implied; or the Heb. idiom is quite rare.[58]

III. The Formation and Textual Transmission of P-Job

The features and techniques just listed are objective in nature, borne out by observable adjustments and motivations when the P is compared to the MT. By contrast, how these data are interpreted to reflect the formation and textual transmission of P-Job is more subjective in nature, but nonetheless useful in reconstructing the stages of formation and transmission of the Peshitta including the *Vorlage* used, the role of the Versions, Western Aramaic influences and the translator(s) and his ideology.

a. Formation, Transmission and Influential Elements in P-Job.

The text of P-Job is filled with errors in all areas of linguistics, i.e. orthographic errors, phonological errors, confusion of homographs, linguistic interference, errors stemming from misrecognition of syntax, errors that result from the translator's attempt to clarify an ambiguity in

---

[53] See Ch. VI Style: Sentence Type, p. 217ff.

[54] See Ch. VI Style: Figurative Language: Simile, pp. 237-239.

[55] See Ch. VI Style: Figurative Language: Simile, pp. 239-240.

[56] See Ch. VI Style: Figurative Language: Metaphor, pp. 241-243.

[57] See Ch. VI Style: Figurative Language: Idiom, pp. 245-246.

[58] See Ch. VI Style: Figurative Language: Idiom, pp. 247-252.

the MT.[59] While visual errors far outnumber aural errors, the presence
of aural errors does suggest that at one point the text of P-Job may have
been aurally received by the translator via an oral reader. This could
account for such aural errors as Heb. הַ /ha/ > Syr. ܗܘ /ha'/.[60] One
might also suggest that some aural errors originated from lectionary
readings, for select passages from the book of Job were a part of the
service readings. The translator, having frequently heard these passages,
translated from rote and memory, triggered by a reminiscence of a verse
still echoing in his mind rather than paying attention to the *Vorlage*
beside him. So, for example, the translator confused the velars Kaph and
Qoph.[61]

Scribal errors of haplography, dittography, homoioarkton,
confusion of similar consonants are likewise prevalent in P-Job in all
areas examined, thus clearly suggesting the translator prepared his
translation by referring to a Hebrew text beside him.[62] These types of
orthographic errors could suggest a different *Vorlage* used as a source
text by the translator.

The large number of errors resulting from confusion of
homographs, distinguishable only by their vocalization, likewise indicates
the source text used by the translator was unvocalized, a reasonable
assumption when we consider that the origin of the P lies in the early
Christian centuries while systems of Hebrew vocalization - excluding the
matres lectionis - were not developed till after the fifth century C.E.
This confusion of homographs also speaks against the translator working
with an oral reader and suggests the translator was not that well
acquainted with the oral vocalization tradition of the MT.[63]

Furthermore, the wealth of errors in the area of semantics, i.e.
erroneous choice of a polysemous lexeme, confusing lexemes, etc.,
suggest a translator not totally versed in the Hebrew language, one who
may not necessarily be a linguistically proficient scholar, that is more of a

---

[59] See Ch. III Grammar, pp. 66,71,90,94-95,99-100,101-102; Ch. IV Syntax, pp. 111-
112,113-114,121-122; Ch.V Semantics, pp. 134,166-167; VI Style, pp. 209,211,221-
222,229,236-237,243,255-256.

[60] See Ch. II TT Model, p. 48; Ch. VI Style, p. 209,229.

[61] See Appendix B: Errors in the P to Job, in particular 11:6 כפלים > ܦܗܠ; 13:28

רקב > ܐܗܒܘܐ 24:22 √מֹשֶׁךְ > ܡܣܘ as if √מֹשֶׁק.

[62] See Appendix B: Errors in the P to Job.

[63] See, for example, Ch. III Grammar: Number, p. 66; Tense, p. 82.

scribe in nature whose duty was to copy, not analyze and translate.[64]
This non-competency, however, is contradicted by examples of parallel
verse influence from other books in the OT, as well as from P-Job
pointing to the translator's familiarity beyond that of the book of Job.

The presence of doublets likewise points to the existence of more
than one text type of P, one of which gained prominence while the
other(s) remained only as vestiges in the form of double readings. The
combining of these readings provides us with evidence of a later editor/
copyist who inserted the variant readings into the bulk of the text.[65]

The large number of errors in P-Job also bring into question what
influence the Versions, especially the Septuagint, had on the translation of
the text. Many of the departures in P-Job, in particular, the explicit
representation of implicit elements in the MT, find parallels with the
versions, especially the LXX and Targum.[66] However, passages that are
so unique in phraseology or structure with a parallel in a version (usually
LXX) that might suggest a dependence by P, i.e. direct influence, are
rare. If we say that the translator of P was dependent on or at least used
a version for guidance, then we must also pose the question, Why are
there so many errors in P-Job that are not in the Versions, especially the
LXX, if the translator was so dependent on them for guidance?
Wouldn't he have recognized that his text was so divergent from the
LXX? More than likely the translator of P used the LXX sporadically,
referring to it whenever his skills were insufficient to handle a
translational problem.

As for the relationship between the P and Targum, the parallels are
many but direct dependence even less so than with the LXX. There is,
however, evidence of Western Aramaic influence, not so much in the
form of a dependence on the Targum, but rather traits of the language
itself that are present in the P. We saw this in the use of √ ܟܒܢ in its W.
Aramaic meaning "to choose",[67] the double readings reminiscent of the
תרגם אחר and the formation of two stichs from key words from one
Hebrew stich, i.e. more of midrashic exegesis than a double reading.[68]

---

[64] See Ch. V Semantics, pp. 134,166-167 and Appendix B: Errors in the P to Job.
[65] See Ch. V Semantics: Addition: Doublets, pp.153-160.
[66] See Ch. II TT Model, pp. 47-48; Ch. III Grammar, pp. 90-91,100,103; Ch. V
Semantics, pp. 145-146.
[67] See Ch. II TT Model, pp. 41-42; Ch. III Grammar: Gender, pp. 62-63.
[68] See Ch. V Semantics, pp. 155-157.

Furthermore, the tendency for over-explicitness in exegesis and the extraordinary concern in removing any possible semantic or syntactic ambiguities suggest the translator was preparing a translation that was audience-oriented. One might almost say the translator had a lack of faith in the ability of the reader/aural recipient to grasp even the most basic implied element. This tendency toward explicitness is one P-Job shares with the Targumim; one might say it is a characteristic of the Aramaic language style in general rather than an influence from the Targum on P.

In summation, the evidence presented here indicates that P-Job follows the standard rules and preferences of grammar, syntax, semantics, and style found throughout the Peshitta. Departures from this norm are due to text specific situations. Furthermore, contradictions of aural and visual errors, particular attention to parallel passages within and outside the book of Job, a plethora of versional parallels, but few examples that suggest versional influence, the presence of doublets and a scattering of W. Aramaic elements all point to a variety of influences (Diagram 1) and a multi-stage development that worked together in the formation of P-Job and resulted in its unique and distinct character when compared to the P in general.

1. Aurally received via:
     Reader of MT/Lectionary Recall
2. Written text of MT (unvocalized)
3. More than one text-type (doublets)   P to Job
4. Sporadic reference to Versions
5. W. Aramaic Influences

Diagram 1

With this evidence in mind we might posit the stages of formation and transmission as follows:

(1) initial translation(s) from unvocalized *Vorlage* of MT: with numerous orthographic visual errors, Versional Influence (LXX) possible, W. Aramaic influences;

(2) more than one text-type in circulation: evidence from doublets;

(3) one text-type gained prominence: editor/copyist preserved variant readings, i.e. doublets;

(4) creation of lectionary readings for religious services drawn from text;
(5) text of P (to Job) recopied, thus more aural errors from familiarity
with lectionary readings. The copyist most likely did not again consult
the source text (MT) or Versions, thereby retaining original errors in
translation, or even was unaware that errors existed.

b. The Translator and His Ideology.

Although the majority of translational departures from the MT
have resulted in synonymous propositions varying only in structure or
stylistics or insignificant innovative propositions, there are enough
examples of translational departures to reveal that on certain issues the
ideological persuasion of the translator may have differed from that
presented in the MT. A note of caution must, however, be here inserted
when evaluating ideological slips that result from ambiguity, textual
difficulty or errors. The belief presented is not always carried through
or harmonized with the rest of the text, as if the ideological slip was (1)
an error, i.e. the translator thought he was faithfully following the MT;
or (2) when the translator was uncertain of the meaning he translated in
accordance with his ideology, thus unaware as to whether his beliefs
differed from those presented in the MT.

A few occasional translational slips reflect the fate of the wicked,[69]
the character of Job's friends[70] and the subject of wisdom,[71] but the
majority involve the character of Job and the nature of God.

P's divergent characterization of Job and God stems from
translational departures involving grammar, semantics, and style. The P,
in constrast to the MT, depicts Job as a man who has convinced his
friends of his piety (32:1),[72] but who unfortunately finds no help from
God to prove this (6:13).[73] In the MT, Job's plea is a cry of distress
(27:9). In P this emotional, if not hysterical, cry becomes a more
dignified formalized prayer which unfortunately also goes unheeded by
God.[74] Likewise in 20:26 where the MT speaks of Job unable to answer

---

[69] See Ch. III Grammar: Voice, pp. 91-92; Ch. V Semantics: Interpretation: A. The Fate
of the Wicked, pp. 189-190; and Appendix F: Interpretation in the Peshitta to Job.
[70] See Ch. III Grammar, pp. 69-70; Ch. V Semantics, p. 150-151.
[71] See Ch. III Grammar, p. 102.
[72] See Ch. III Grammar: Number, pp. 69-70.
[73] See Ch. III Grammar: Person, p. 71.
[74] See Ch. III Semantics: Addition, pp. 138-139.

God, his opponent, the P states instead that Job will not be answered and
here God is not his opponent but rather his judge.[75] In the past God has
helped Job through the dark times, but this is not the case now according
to P.[76] Job believes God will deal with him with all his great powers,
keeping him in line by placing great fear upon him (23:6). This is a far
cry from the MT's statement that God would not contend with Job by
means of great strength but only pay heed to him (23:6).[77] God's
majesty in the MT is now interpreted as fear in the P (13:11).[78]

Given such a harsh attitude on the part of Job regarding God's
help, it seems peculiar for P to then contradict the MT which infers that
God will bring Job to death (30:23) by adding the preposition "from",
that is God will rather rescue Job from death and bring him back to the
place of the living and then reaffirm his belief that God will respond to
him (27:10). P likewise softens the harsh statement of God the destroyer
by transforming a bold exclamation into a conditional statement that only
suggests the possibility of such actions (12:14-15).[79] So too does the
translator soften a direct anthropomorphic reference to God (10:4).[80]

The optimistic Job so prevalent in the Prologue reappears in the
Dialogue according to P.[81] At times P views Job in a softer light, not
directly calling him a laughingstock, but rather only alluding to such
name-calling by resorting to an analogy of an impersonal subject in Job's
situation who is thought of as a laughingstock (12:4).[82] At other times
the Job of P is forceful, unyielding. He refuses to pay heed to the verbal
barrage of his friends (16:3,5).[83] In P it is Job himself who must
procure the ransom for his life, not the mediator he so strongly pleads
for to intercede on his behalf.[84] Furthermore, the translator of P at

---

[75] See Ch. III Grammar, pp. 91-92; Ch. V Semantics: Interpretation, pp. 190-191.

[76] See Ch. V Semantics: Addition, pp. 141-142.

[77] See Ch. V Semantics: Addition, pp. 142-143.

[78] See Ch. V Semantics: Interpretation, pp. 191-192.

[79] See Ch. VI Style: Exclamatory Sentences, pp. 223-224.

[80] See Ch. VI Style: The Simile: pp. 242-243.

[81] See Ch. III Grammar, pp. 69-70 and n. 15; Ch. V Semantics: Addition, pp. 143-144,151.

[82] See Ch. III Grammar: Person, pp. 71-72.

[83] See Ch. III Grammar: Person, p. 73.

[84] See Ch. III Grammar: Tense, p. 87.

times adjusted the tense and semantics of Job's actions to harmonize events.[85]

IV. Final Comments on the Effectiveness of the TT Model.

Although we have just touched on a few topics in each area of linguistics, a wealth of information has been uncovered, providing the data by which we have begun to characterize and describe P-Job, its textual relationship to the Peshitta as a whole, its formation and transmission as well as the ideology of its translator.

It has also been demonstrated that within each area of linguistics focusing on different aspects of the TT Model is more effective. Thus when grammatical and stylistic topics are at issue, analysis by motivation seemed most productive, whereas studies in syntax were best approached by special attention to type of adjustment and motivation. Studies in semantics too emphasized adjustment and motivation with special attention paid to semantically oriented substitutions. Whereas the effect on meaning that resulted has most often yielded synonymous propositions or insignificant innovative ones, the manner of expressing these propositions has left us with characteristics, features and techniques that more clearly describe the mechanics of the Syriac language of the Peshitta and the translator(s) involved in its production.

In the future, as more topics within each discipline are examined in not only P-Job, but the other books of the Peshitta as well, this investigation should give us a more detailed description of the character of the Peshitta, as well as more clues to its formation. Furthermore, by applying the TT Model to other topics within each discipline, both in the Peshitta and other translated works, not only can the Model itself be expanded to include more adjustments, motivations and effects on meaning, but of those already presented here finer sub-divisions can be incorporated.

---

[85] See Ch. III Grammar: Tense, pp. 84-85; Ch. V Semantics, pp. 150-151.

Appendix A

Examples of Paraphrase in P to Job

1:10 Heb. מסביב "from around" > Syr. ܒܟܠ ܕܘܟܐ "on every side"

1:14 Heb. חרשות "ploughing" > Syr. ܕܒܪ ܦܕܢܐ "to drive the plough"

4:13 Heb. תרדמה "deep sleep" > Syr. ܫܢܐ ܠܡܕܡܟܐ "deep sleep"

9:17 Heb. בשערה "in a storm"[1] > Syr. ܕܒܟܠ ܡܢܬܐ ܕܪܝܫܝ

"that which is in every part of my head"

21:34 Heb. תשובתיכם "your answers" > Syr. ܬܘܒܬܐ ܕܦܬܓܡܘܗܝ

"the returning of his words"

22:6 Heb. תחבל "you take a pledge" > Syr. ܡܫܟܢܬ ܡܫܟܢܐ "you take a pledge"

24:9 Heb. יחבלו "they take a pledge" > Syr. ܡ̈ܫܟܢܐ ܐܪܝܡܘ "they set up pledges"

24:24 Heb. ימלו √מלל "they will languish, wither" > Syr. ܢܝܒܫܘܢ ܘܢܬܦܪܟܘܢ

"they will dry up and be shaken out"

27:8 Heb. יבצע "he will cut off, gain by violence" > Syr. ܕܩܢܐ ܢܟ̈ܣܐ

"who acquired riches"

33:12 Heb. אענך "I will answer you" > Syr. ܐܬܠ ܠܟ ܦܬܓܡܐ

"I will give to you a word"

---

[1] Heb. בשערה is pointed בִּשְׂעָרָה "in a storm" which P obviously erroneously understood as בְּשַׂעֲרָה "with hair". Cp. the Targum דעד חוטי בינתא "unto the strands of a single hair" which likewise misunderstood the Hebrew pointing.

33:12 Heb. לֹא צָדַקְתָּ "you are not right" > Syr. ܡܫܟܚ ܐܢܬ ܠܡܙܕܩܘ
                                                      "you cannot be found just"

33:23 Heb. מֵלִיץ "interpreter" > Syr. ܕܫܡܥ ܠܗ "one who listens to him"

34:10 Heb. מֵרֶשַׁע "from (doing) wickedness" > Syr. ܢܥܒܕ ܥܘܠܐ "He will do wrong"

34:12 Heb. לֹא־יַרְשִׁיעַ "(God) does not do wickedly" > Syr. ܠܐ ܥܒܕ ܥܘܠܐ
                                                      "God does not do iniquity"

38:4   Heb. בְּיָסְדִי "(lit.) in my founding" > Syr. ܟܕ ܣܡܬ ܦܗܘܡ ܫܬܐܣܝܗ
                                                      "when I set the foundations" (Cp. Vg)

39:5   Heb. חֹפֶשׁ "free"   > Syr. ܒܪ ܚܐܪܝܢ "son of free ones" (Cp. Tg.)

39:6   Heb. מְלֵחָה "salt-plain" > Syr. ܒܐܪܥܐ ܕܡܠܚܐ "in a salty plain"

39:10 Heb. שָׂדַד "to harrow"   > Syr. ܢܕܒܪ ܦܕܢܐ "to drive the plough"

41:19 Heb. עֵץ רִקָּבוֹן "tree of rottenness" > Syr. ܣܘܣܐ ܕܢܦܠ ܒܗ ܒܩܠܝܬܐ
                                                      "a tree in which the boring worm falls"

Appendix B

Errors in the Peshitta to Job

The following is a representational list of substitution errors, i.e. errors that do not affect the length of the text. The sign (*) indicates error due to linguistic interference; the sign (#) indicates confusion of homographs; the sign (@) indicates a confusion of consonants; the sign (&) indicates an error due to a misunderstanding of the Hebrew vocalization; unmarked verses contain an error due to metathesis or rearrangement of radicals.

#3:5	כמרירי "deep gloom"	>	ܡܟܖ̈ܝܖ̈ܐ "bitter ones" as if √מרר + כ
*6:7	√מאן "to refuse"	>	√ܡܐܢ "to be wearied with/bored with"
@6:7	לנגוע "to touch"	>	ܒܟܬܫܐ ܕܝܠܗ "with its strife/trouble"
			(confused with רגע I "to disturb")
#6:7	לחמי "my bread"	>	ܩܖ̣ܒܐ "my battle" as if √לחם "to fight"
#6:7	המה "they"	>	√ ܡܗܡ "to murmur, growl" as if √המה
			(so LXX)
@6:7	דוי "illness"	>	ܖܘܝܐ "drunkard" ר/ד confusion
*6:9	√דכא "to crush"	>	√ܕܟܐ "to cleanse, purify"
#6:10	חילה "anguish" √חיל/חול I	>	ܚܝܠܐ "strength" √חיל II
@6:14	למס "to one who despises"	>	ܟܠܐ "to withhold"
	√מסס II		(confused with מאס "to refuse, reject")
#6:16	√עלם I "to conceal"	>	√ܣܓܐ "be abundant"
			(as if Aramaic √עלם "to be strong")
@6:17	√זרב "to be scorched"	>	√ܕܢܚ "to rise"
			(confused with √זרח "to rise")
@6:19	תמא "Tema"	>	ܬܝܡܢܐ "south" (so LXX)
			(confused with תימן "south")

275

#6:23 צר "adversary √צרר III	>	ܡܥܠܨܢ "afflictions" (so Tg.) (confused with √צרר I "distress, straits")
*6:27 √כרה II "to get by trade"	>	√ܟܪܐ Aphel "to sadden, be displeased with"
&6:29 עולה "injustice"	>	ܥܘܠܐ "unjust ones"
*7:5 יתמאס "and it ran" √מסס	>	ܐܬܡܣܝ "it rotted away" √ܡܣܝ
@7:20 נצר "watcher"	>	ܒܪܘܝܗ "creator" (confused with √יצר "to form, fashion")
@8:17 √סבך "to be intertwined"	>	√ܣܡܟ "to lean, rest over" (confusion of bilabials)
#8:19 משׂוש "joy"	>	ܒܨܐ "to examine" (confused with משׁשׁ "to feel, grope")
@9:6 עמודיה "its pillars"	>	ܥܡܘܪ̈ܝܗ "its inhabitants" (ד/ר confusion)
#9:24 אפוא "then"	>	ܪܘܓܙܗ "anger" (confused with אפו "his anger")
#9:30 בבר "with lye"	>	ܕܟܝܘܬܐ "the purity" (confused with בר "pure, clean")
#10:8 √עצב II "to shape fashion"	>	ܠܐܐ "to be weary" (confused with √עצב I "to hurt, pain")
@10:18 יחד "together"	>	ܘܡܢ ܒܬܪܟܢ "and afterwards" (confused with ואחר "and after")
&10:17 עדיך "your witnesses" √עוד	>	ܙܝܢܟ "your armour" (confused with √עדה II "to deck oneself")
@10:22 עיפתה "deep darkness" √עיף/עוף I "to be dark"	>	ܫܗܝܐ "is lonely, void" (confused with √עיף II "be faint, weary")
@10:22 √יפע Hiph. "to shine forth"	>	ܘܡܫܠܗܝܐ "and it is weary" (confused with √עיף/יעף "be weary")
&11:3 מְתים "men"	>	ܡ̈ܝܬܐ "the dead" (confused with מֵתים "the dead")
@11:6 כפלים "double"	>	ܩ̈ܦܠܐ "inner chambers/treasures" (interchange of velars)
*11:7 מצא "to find"	>	ܡܫܟܚ "to be able" (confused with ܡܨܐ "to be able")
&11:11 מְתֵי "men of"	>	ܐܡܬܝ "when" (as if מָתַי "when")
@11:12 נבוב "be hollowed out"	>	ܕܟܐ "pure" (confused with נבר > √ברר)
@11:12 פרא "wild ass" √פרא II	>	ܓܢܒܪ "mighty man" (confused with פרה/פרא I "be fruitful")
@11:12 עיר "colt"	>	ܥܕܪ "help" (confused with עזר "to help")

@12:6 √שלי "be at ease"	>	√ܫܢܐ "be removed" (confused with √שלל I "to draw out" or √שלל II "spoil, plunder")
12:19 √סלף "to twist, pervert"	>	√ܫܦܠ "to bring low" (metathesis and confusion of sibilants)
@13:26 מררות "bitterness" √מרר	>	ܡܪܕܘܬܐ "chastisement" √ܡܪܕ (ܕ/ܪ confusion)
@14:1 √שׂבע "to be sated, satisfied"	>	√ܣܒܠ "to bear, suffer" (error for ܣܒܥ)
@14:6 √רצה "to be pleased with"	>	√ܪܗܛ "to hasten, run" (confused with רוץ "to run")
@15:20 √חול "to writhe in suffering"	>	ܡܬܪܘܪܒ √ܪܒ "to behave arrogantly" (confused with √הלל "to be boastful")
#15:23 לחם II "food"	>	ܠܘܚܡܐ "threat, rebuke" (confused with √לחם I "to fight")
@15:27 פימה "superabundance"	>	ܟܝܡܐ "Pleides" (confused with כימה "Pleides")
@15:27 כסל "loins"	>	ܥܝܘܬܐ "Orion/Aldebaran") (confused with כסיל "Orion")
@15:29 √עשר "to be/grow rich"	>	√ܟܬܪ "to continue" (error for √ܥܬܪ)
*15:29 מנלם < מנלה "acquisition"	>	ܡ̈ܠܐ "words" (as if מנלם < מלים < מלין) (dissimilation and nasalization of Lamedhs)
15:31 תמורתו "his recompense"	>	ܡܘܠܬܗ "his growth" (confused with תמורתו "his palm-tree")
@15:32 √מלא "to fill"	>	ܝܒܫ "to wither" (confused with √מלל "to wither")
@15:32 כפתו "its frond"	>	ܐܝܕܘܗܝ "his hands" (confused with כף "palm")
@16:7 √שׁמם Hiph. "to ravage, devastate"	>	ܢܛܪ "to guard" (confused with שׁמר "to guard")
@16:7 עדתי "my company" √יעד	>	ܣܗܕܘܬܝ "my testimony" (confused with √עדה)
&16:11 אֵל אֶל עויל "God (will deliver me up) to the ungodly"	>	ܠܡܠܐܟܐ ܥܘܠܐ "to the ungodly messenger" (as if אֶל אֶל + removal/toning down of objectionable reference to God)
#17:6 משל "by-word" √משׁל II	>	ܫܘܠܛܢܐ "authority" (confused with √משׁל III)
@17:6 תפת "act of spitting" √תוף	>	ܬܚܦܝܬܐ "veil" (confused with √חָפָה)
@18:3 √טמה "to be stupid"	>	√ܛܟܐ Ethp. "to be clean" (confused with √טמא "to be clean")

@18:7 √צרד "to be scarce, short"   >   √ܨܕܝ "to be deserted"
(confused with √צדה II "to lay waste")

#18:7 אונו "his strength" √און II   >   ܒܟܐܒܚܘܣ "by his pain"
(confused with √און I "trouble, sorrow")

&18:20 שֵׂעַר "horror"   >   ܣܥܪܗܘܢ "their hair"
(confused with שֵׂעָר "hair")

#19:17 √חנן III "to be loathsome"   >   √ܚܢ Ethp. "to implore"
(confused with √חנן I "to implore")

#19:26 √נקף I "to strike off"   >   √ܟܪܟ Ethp. "to go around"
(confused with √נקף II "to go around")

&20:5 מקרוב "from afar"   >   ܡܢ ܟܪܣܗܘܢ "from their belly"
(as if read מִקֶּרֶב)

#20:7 גללו "his dung"   >   ܓܠܠܐ "whirlwind"
(confused with √גלל "wheel, whirlwind")

@20:19 √רצץ "to crush"   >   √ܪܢܝ "to think, consider"
(confused with רצה "to desire")

@20:23 למלא "to fill"   >   ܠܐܒܕܢܐ "for destruction"
(as if read ܠܐܒܕ)

#20:23 בלחומו "his bowels"   >   ܒܬܟܬܘܫܗ "by his warlike strength"
(confused with √לחם I "to fight")

@20:25 גוה "back"   >   ܓܘܗ "his inner parts"
(confused with ג "inside, midst")

@20:27 √קום Polel "to rise up"   >   √ܢܩܡ Ethp. "to take vengence"
(confused with √נקם "to take vengence")

&21:23 עֶצֶם "bone"   >   ܒܚܝܠܐ "with the strength"
(read as עֹצֶם "strength, might")

#&21:24 חָלָב "milk"   >   ܬܪܒܐ "fat" (read as חֵלֶב "fat")

@21:30 יובלו "they will be led"   >   ܡܬܕܟܪ "he remembers"
(error for ܡܬܕܒܪ "he is led")

#21:33 √מתק "be sweet"   >   √ܒܠܥ "to swallow"
(understood √מתק as √מצק "to suck")

#&21:34 מַעַל "faithlessness, treachery"   >   ܩܘܕܡܝ "before me" (read as מֵעָלַי)

@22:8 זרוע "arm" √זרע II   >   ܙܪܘܥܐ "one who sows"
(confused with √זרע I "to sow")

@23:2 מרי "rebellion" מרה   >   ܟܪܝܬܐ "bitter"
(confused with √מרר "be bitter")

#&23:7 משפטי "from my judge"   >   ܒܕܝܢܐ "by judgment"
(read as מִשְׁפָּט "judgment")

@23:9 בעשתו "when he made"   >   ܒܥܝܬ "I sought"
(confused with √בקש "to seek")

@24:11 שורה "olive-row" √שור III	>	ܫܪܘܬܐ "banquet-house" (confused with √ܫܪܐ)
#&24:12 מְתִים "men"	>	ܡܝ̈ܬܐ "dead ones" (read as מֵתִים "dead ones")
#24:12 תִּפְלָה √תפל "unsavouriness"	>	ܨܠܘܬܗܘܢ "their prayer" (confused with תְּפִלָּה "prayer" √פלל)
24:13 במרדי "among those who rebel"√מרד	>	ܒܡܕܖ̈ܝ "in the habitations of" √ܕܘܪ (metathesis of 2nd and 3rd radicals)
24:21 רעה עקרה "he feeds on a barren woman"	>	ܐܢܬܬܐ ܒܝܫܬܐ "an evil woman" (read as if רעה עקרה)
@24:22 √מָשַׁךְ "to draw, drag out"	>	ܩܢܝܐ "possessions" as if מֶשֶׁק (confusion of velars)
@24:22 בחיין "in life" √חיה	>	ܒܚܙܘܐ "in a vision" (confused with √ܚܙܐ "to see")
&24:25 לְאַל "for nought"	>	ܩܕܡ ܐܠܗܐ "before God" (read as לְאֵל)
@26:5 √חול Polal "to be made to writhe"	>	√ܩܛܠ Ethp. "to be killed" (confused with √חלל "to bore, pierce, slay")
@26:9 כסא = כסה "throne"	>	ܬܟܣܝܬܐ "covering" √ܟܣܐ (confused √כסא with √כסה)
26:12 √רגע I "to disturb"	>	√ܓܥܪ "to rebuke" (transposition)
@26:12 רהב "Rahab"	>	ܣܓܝ̈ܐܐ "many" (confused with √רבב or √רבה)
#28:4 √דלל "to hand, be low"	>	√ܕܠܠ "be diminished, become few"
@29:7 עלי קרת "of (lit. upon) the city"	>	ܘܩܪܝܬ "and I called out" (read as קראתי)
@29:7 אכין "I prepare"	>	ܐܝܟ ܒܝܫܐ "like an unfortunate man" (read as כאביון)
@29:18 קִנִּי "my nest" √קנן	>	ܩܢܝܐ "reed" (confused with קָנֶה "reed" √קנה II)
#29:19 טל "dew"	>	ܛܠܠܐ "shadow" (error for ܛܠܐ "dew")
@29:19 בקצירי "in my branches" √קצר II	>	ܒܚܨܕܐ "in the harvest" √קצר I
@29:22 √שנה II "to repeat"	>	√ܦܢܐ "to turn" (confused with √שנה I "to change")
30:2 כלח "firm strength"	>	ܟܠܗ ܚܝܠܐ "all strength" (read as כל כח)
@30:13 יעילו "they will profit"	>	ܚܕܝܘ "they rejoiced" (read יגילו)
@30:15 נדבתי "my honour"	>	ܫܒܝ̈ܠܝ "my paths" (confused with נתיבתי "my paths")

@30:17 נקר√ Piel "to pierce"   >   ܣܩܠ√ "to weigh" (confused with יקר√)

*30:21 שטם√ "to bear a grudge"   >   ܟܠܐ√ "to restrain"

@30:28 חמה "heat, sun" חמם√   >   ܚܡܬܐ "anger"
                                (confused with יחם√)

31:7 מאום "spot, blemish"   >   ܡܕܡ "something"
                                (read as מאומה)

@31:11 עון "sin"   >   ܥܝܢܐ "eye"
                                (read as עין)

#&31:18 כְּאָב "like a father"   >   ܟܐܒܐ "pains"
                                (read as כְּאֵב)

@31:18 אנחנה "I will guide it"   >   ܐܢܚܬܐ "groans"
                                (read as אנחה "sighing, groaning")

&31:30 בְּאָלָה "with a curse"   >   ܠܚܕܐ ܡܢ ܗܠܝܢ "for one of these things"
                                (confused with בְּאֵלֶּה)

&31:32 לָאֹרַח "to the way"   >   ܠܐܘܪܚܐ "to the wayfare"
                                (confused with לָאֹרֵחַ (so LXX)

@31:33 בחבי "in my bosom" חבב√   >   ܒܛܘܫܝܐ "in secret places"
                                (confused with חבה√)

@31:34 בוז "contempt"   >   ܣܘܓܐܐ "multitude"
                                (confused with בוז√ > בַז "spoil, booty")

&31:34 וָאֶדֹּם "and I was silent"   >   ܓܒܪܐ "man"
                                (confused with אָדָם)

31:37 קרב√ "to approach"   >   ܒܩܪ√ "to examine"

31:40 חוח "thorns"/ באשה   >   ܟܘܒܐ "dung"/ ܟܘܒܐ "thorns"
                 "foul weeds"   (P inverts order of DO of each stich)

@32:9 רבים "many"   >   ܣܡܐܐ ܕܝܘܡܬܐ "the multitude of days"
                                (as if רב ימים)

@ 32:1   עד תבונתיכם   בין√   >   ܥܕܡܐ ܕܫܠܡܬܘܢ "until you finished"
      "unto your understandings"   (confused with כון√)

@32:19 כיין "like wine"   >   ܟܐܒ "is pained" (as if כעני "like affliction)

&32:19 כאבות חדשים   >   ܐܝܟ ܐܒܐ ܒܝܪܚܐ "like fruit in (its) month"
         "like new wineskins"   (confused with אבות "fresh, green fruit"
                                and חֹדֶשׁ "month")

&32:22 עֹשֵׂנִי "my Maker"   >   ܥܘܫܢܝ "my strength"
                                (as if עֹשְׁנָא "strength, force")

33:10 תנואות "opportunities"   >   ܥܠܬܐ "occasions"
                                (confused with תואנות "occasions")

#@33:27 ישר שור√ "to relate,   >   ܬܪܝܨܘܬܐ "uprightness"
                  repeat, tell"   (confused with ישר "uprightness")

&34:6 אָנוּשׁ "incurable"   >   ܐܢܫܐ "man" (confused with אֱנוֹשׁ)

@34:9 רצה√ "to take delight in"   >   ܕܚܠ "to fear" (confused with ירא√)

@34:18 רשע "wicked"	>	ܪ̈ܫܢܐ "leaders" (confused with ראש)
@34:20 ויסירו "they will remove"	>	ܡܫܬܘܕܥܝܢ "they recognize" (confused with יכירו √נכר)
@34:24 אחרים "others"	>	ܐܟܚܕܐ "at once, alike" (confused with אחד)
@&34:26 רשעים "wicked ones"	>	ܥܘܠܐ (read as רֶשַׁע "wickedness")
@34:36 על־תשבת "because (his) answers"	>	ܘܠܐ ܡܬܚܫܒ "and he is not counted" (confused with ואל חשבת)
34:37 וירב "and he will multiply"	>	ܘܢܩܪܒ "and he will draw near" (read √רבה as √קרב)
@35:10 זמרות "songs"	>	ܡܚܫܒܬܐ "considerations, thoughts" (confused with מזמות "purposes, thoughts")
&35:11 מַלְּפֵנוּ "(who) teaches us"	>	ܡܢ ܩܕܡ "from before" (read as מִלִּפְנֵי)
@35:13,14 √שׁור "to behold, regard"	>	√ܫܒܚ "to praise" (confused with שׁיר "to sing")
@35:14 √חול Polal "to wait anxiously"	>	√ܒܥܐ Ethp. "to make supplication" (confused with √חלה "to appease")
36:5 כביר כח לב "might (in) strength of heart"	>	ܠܐܝܢܐ ܕܕܟܐ ܐܝܟ ܚܠܒܐ "the one who is pure in milk" (read as כבר כחלב)
@36:15 אזנם "their ear"	>	ܐܘܪܚܗܘܢ "their way" (confused with ארחם "their path")
36:27 לאדו "into his mist"	>	ܒܠܚܘܕܘܗܝ "by himself" (confused with לבדו)
@36:29 תשאות √שׁוא "rumblings"	>	ܣܘܓܐܐ "the greatness" (confused with שׂאת "exaltation" √נשׂא)
@37:3 √שׁרה "to let loose"	>	√ܫܒܚ "to praise" (confused w/√שׁיר "to sing")
*37:4 √עקב "to say"	>	√ܒܨܐ "to search out"
@37:9 מזרים √זרה "scatterers"	>	ܪ̈ܝܦܬܐ "violent rain" (confused with מטרים)
#@37:10 במוצק "in constraint" √צוק I	>	ܡܚܬ Aphel pt. √ܢܚܬ "to cause to descend" (confused with √יצק/צוק "to pour")
@37:11 ברי "with moisture" √רוה	>	ܪܟܝܟܐܝܬ "softly, gently" (confused with √ברר "to purify, clear")
#37:23 רֹב "multitude"	>	ܪܒ "chief, lord" (confused w/ רַב "lord, chief")
#37:23 √ענה III "to be afflicted"	>	confused with √ענה I "to answer"
@37:24 √ראה "to see"	>	√ܙܘܥ "to tremble" (confused with √ירא "to be afraid")
@38:7 ברן "when sung joyously"	>	√ܒܪܐ "he created" (read as ברא)
@38:14 חותם "sealed (clay)"	>	ܒܓܘܫܡܗܘܢ "their body" (read as גותם)
@&39:8 יתור √תור "to search"	>	ܒܣܘܓܐܐ "with a multitude" (read as יֶתֶר)
@39:8 √דרשׁ + אחר "to search after"	>	√ܕܐܫ + ܥܠ "to tread upon" (confused w/ דושׁ)
@39:18 תמריא √מרא "to flap"	>	ܕܩܠܐ "palm-tree" (confused with תמר)

@39:22 לפחד "at terror"   >   ܠܠ ܓܘܡܨܐ "at the pit" (read as פחת)

@40:21 צאלים "lotus"   >   ܛܠܠܗ "his shade" (so Tg.)
                                                (confused with √צלל)

@40:21 ובצה "and marsh"   >   ܕܒܟ "to lay down" (read as רבצה)

@40:22 סכך "to cover"   >   √ܟܪܟ "to encircle, surround"
                                                (confused with √סבכ)

@40:24 בעיניו "by his eyes"   >   ܒܥܢܢܘܗܝ "by his clouds" (confused עין w/ ענן)

&40:29 לנערותיך "for your little girls" >   ܛܠܝܘܬܟ "(days of) your youth"
                                                (read as לנעורתך or לנעוריך)

@40:31 בשכות "with spears"   >   ܒܣܪܐ "flesh" (read as בשׂרות)

@40:31 בצלצל דגים "with   >   ܒܛܠܠܝ ܢܘܪܐ "with the shadows of fire"
          fishing-spears"   (confused with צלל and ܢܘܪ with נסא)

&41:1 אל "unto"   >   ܐܠܗܐ "God" (read as אֵל)

@41:1 מראיו "his appearance" √ראה >   ܡܪܝܪܘܬܗ "his bitterness" (confused with √מרר)

@41:5 בכפל "into the double"   >   ܢܦܠ "(when the net) falls" (confused w/ כנפל)

@41:20 בן "son"   >   ܡܢ "from" (interchange of labials)

41:24 שיבה "gray-headed"   >   ܝܒܫܐ "dry land" (read as יבשה)

@41:25 אין "there is not"   >   ܚܝܠܗ "his strength" (read as אוֹן)

*42:6 √נחם Piel "to repent"   >   √ܣܥܪ Ethp. "to be revived, raised"

Appendix C

Generalization in the Peshitta to Job

The following is a representative collection of substitutions involving generalization in the P to Job.

1:15	שבא "Sabeans"	>	ܓܝܣܐ "band of robbers" (Cp. LXX)
1:17	√פשׁט "to make a dash"	>	√ܢܦܠ "to fall"
3:5	√גאל "to redeem"	>	√ܛܫܐ "to hide, conceal"
3:6	√לקח "to take"	>	√ܛܫܐ "to hide, conceal"
5:5	√שׁאף "to pant after, be eager for"	>	√ܒܠܥ "to devour"
5:11	√שׂגב "be high, lifted"	>	√ܥܫܢ "be strong"
5:13	√לכד "to capture"	>	√ܐܚܕ "to seize"
5:18	√כאב "to wound"	>	√ܬܒܪ "to break"
6:9	√נתר Hiph. "to let loose, free"	>	√ܦܪܣ "to spread out"
6:9	√בצע "to cut off"	>	√ܫܠܡ "to make an end of"
6:10	√סלד "to spring"	>	√ܠܒ Esth. "to be given over"
6:13	√נדח Niph. "be banished"	>	√ܪܚܩ "be far off"
6:15	אפיק נחלים "channels of wadis"	>	ܪܓܠܬܐ "torrents"
6:23	√פדה "to ransom"	>	√ܦܨܐ "to deliver"
6:24	√חרשׁ "to be silent, dumb"	>	√ܫܬܩ "to cease; be still"
6:30	√בין "to understand, discern"	>	√ܡܠܠ "to speak"
7:2	√שׁאף "to pant after, be eager for"	>	√ܣܒܪ "to wait"
7:3	√נחל Hoph. "made to possess"	>	√ܝܪܬ "to inherit"
7:4	√מדד "to continue, extend"	>	√ܡܫܚ "to measure"
7:11	√שׂיח "to muse, complain"	>	√ܬܢܐ "to repeat, say again"
9:12	√חתף "to seize, plunder"	>	√ܬܒܪ "to break"
9:17	√שׁאף "to bruise"	>	√ܡܚܐ "to smite"
9:23	שׁוט "scourge, whip"	>	ܫܒܛܐ "rod"

283

10:11 √גאה "to rise up"   >   √רמם "to be high"

11:3 √בדד "idle talk"   >   על מליך "on account of your words"

13:4 אלל "worthlessness"   >   כלא מדם "nothing"

13:18 √ערך "to arrange"   >   √איתי Aphel "to bring"

14:8 גזע "stock, stem"   >   יעותא "growth"

14:9 קציר "harvest"   >   טרפא "leaves"

15:4 שיחה "muse, complaint"   >   ממללא "speech" (so 21:7)

15:22 √צפה "to spy out"   >   √חזא "to see"

16:8 כחש "leanness, lying"   >   דגלותי "my lie"

16:16 עפעף "eyelids"   >   עיני "my eyes"

17:3 √תקע "to strike oneself"   >   √שיזב "to deliver"

17:6 √יצג "to set"   >   √סמם "(Aphel) to put, place"

18:5 אש "fire"   >   נוהרה "his light"

18:15 נוה "habitation"   >   אתרה "his place"

23:12 √צפן "to hide, treasure up" >   √נטר "to keep"

24:15 נשף "twilight"   >   חשוכא "darkness"

25:3 גדוד "bands, troops"   >   חילא "army"

26:13 √חלל "to pierce, slay"   >   √קטל "to kill"

27:4 √הגה "to utter, moan"   >   √מלל "to speak"

27:5 √גוע "to perish, expire"   >   √מות "to die"

27:6 √חרף "to reproach"   >   √רדי "to chasten, pain"

27:8 √שלה II "to draw out"   >   √שקל "to take, lift up"

27:12 √הבל "to become vain"   >   √רוז "to behave arrogantly"

27:16 √צבר "to heap up"   >   √כנש "to gather"

27:21 √שער "to sweep"   >   √רדי "to drive away"

28:2 √צוק to melt"/√לקח "to take" >   √נסך "to pour out"

28:3 √חקר "to search out"   >   √ידע "to know"

28:5 לחם "bread"   >   מזונא "sustenance"

28:7 √שזף "to behold"   >   √חזא "to see"

28:10 יארים "channels"   >   נהרין "rivers"

28:15 סגור "fine gold"   >   דהבא "gold"

29:13 √רנן "to cause to ring out" >   √חדי "to gladden"

29:17 טרף "prey"   >   שללא "spoil"

30:8 √נכא Niph. "be smitten"   >   √מכך "be humbled, brought low"

30:18 √חפש "to disguise oneself" >   √לבש "to put on"

31:7 מאום "spot, blemish"   >   מדם "something"

31:17 פתי "morsel"   >   לחמא "bread, food"

31:36 √ענד "to bind"   >   √עבד "to do, make"

33:15 תרדמה "deep sleep"	>	ܫܢܬܐ "sleep"
34:20 √געש "be shaken"	>	√ܣܘܦ "to come to an end"
34:24 √רעע "to shatter"	>	√ܒܐܫ Aphel "to afflict"
34:29 √סתר "to hide"	>	√ܗܦܟ "to remove"
35:16 √פצה "to part, open"	>	√ܦܬܚ "to open"
36:22 √ שׂגב "to act exaltedly"	>	√ܥܫܢ "to be strong"
36:33 מקנה "cattle"	>	ܩܢܝ "possessions"
37:14 √עמד "to stand"	>	√ܫܡܥ "to hear, listen to"
37:15 √יפע Hiph. "to cause to shine"	>	√ܓܠܐ "to reveal"
37:21 שחקים "clouds"	>	ܪܩܝܥܐ "firmament"
38:6 אדניה "its pedestals"	>	ܟܢ̈ܦܝܗ "its limits, ends"
38:6 √טבע Hoph. "to be sunk"	>	√ܢܘܚ "to rest"
38:10 √שׁבר "to break"/√שׂים "to put"	>	√ܥܒܕ "to do, make"
38:24 קדים "east wind"	>	ܪܘܚܐ "wind"
38:26 √מטר "to rain down"	>	√ܢܚܬ "to descend"
38:30 √לכד "to capture"	>	√ܐܚܕ "to seize"
38:39 טרף "prey"	>	ܡܐܟܘܠܬܐ "food"
38:41 √כון "to prepare"	>	√ܝܗܒ "to give"
38:41 ציד "hunt"/ אכל "food"	>	ܡܐܟܘܠܬܐ "food"
39:5 √שלח "to send"	>	√ܫܒܩ "to let go"
39:7 תשאות "shoutings"	>	ܩܠܐ "sound, voice"
39:13 √עלס "to flap joyously"	>	ܡܬܪܘܪܒܐ "to rouse oneself up"
39:20 √רעש Hiph. "to cause to quake, shake"	>	√ܙܘܥ Aphel "to set in motion"
39:23 √רנה "to rattle"	>	√ܡܫܬܟܚ Ethp. "is found"
39:26 √אבר "to soar"	>	√ܗܘܐ "to be"
40:10 √עדה "to deck oneself"	>	√ܠܒܫ "to put on"
40:23 √חפז "to be in a hurry, alarmed"	>	√ܙܘܥ "be agitated, stirred up"
40:23 √גוח/גיח "to burst forth"	>	√ܢܣܟ "to pour"
40:25 √משך "to draw out"	>	√ܐܚܕ "to seize"
40:25 √שקע "to press down"	>	√ܐܚܕ "to seize"

Appendix D

Specification in the Peshitta to Job

The following is a representative sampling of verses in which specification of a Hebrew lexeme occurs when translated into the Syriac of the book of Job.

1:6 עַל "upon"	>	קֳדָם "before" (also in 2:1) [so Tg.]
1:11 נגע + בְּ	>	ܩܪܒ + ܠ (also in 2:5)
1:12 אֶל "unto"	>	ܥܠ "upon"
1:14 בָּקָר "cattle, herd, oxen"	>	ܬܘܪܐ "oxen" [so Tg.]
1:16 זֶה . . . . זֶה "this one . . . this one"	>	ܗܘ . . . ܐܚܪܢܐ "he . . . another one" (also in 1:17,18)
1:16 נְעָרִים "lads"	>	ܪ̈ܥܘܬܐ "shepherds" [so LXX]
1:17 √שׂים "to put, place"	>	√ܦܠܓ Ethp. "to divide oneself"
1:17 רָאשִׁים "heads"	>	ܡܢ̈ܘܬ "parts"
1:19 √נגע "to touch"	>	√ܢܩܫ Ethp. "to dash, strike against"
1:19 נְעָרִים "lads"	>	ܛܠ̈ܝܐ "unmarried youths"(m. & f.)
2:7 קָדְקֹד "head"	>	ܡܘܚܐ "brain"
2:8 בְּתוֹךְ "in the midst of"	>	ܥܠ "upon"
2:13 לְ "to"	>	ܥܠ "upon" (so also 6:26;8:8;9:23; 10:6;13:7[LXX],8;15:29;16:9,13; 17:6;29:9;31:24;34:18;38:34; 39:7,14;41:21)
4:13 שְׂעִפִּים "disquieting thoughts"	>	ܫܠܝܐ "quiet, stillness"
5:9 חֵקֶר "searching"	>	ܣܟܐ "limit" (also in 9:10;34:24)
5:21 בְּ "in, with, by"	>	ܡܢ "from" (also in 8:5)
5:22 שֹׁד "devastation, ruin"	>	ܒܙܬܐ "spoil"
5:24 √פקד "to visit"	>	√ܗܦܟ "return"
5:25 צֶאֱצָא "offspring"	>	ܝܠܕ "children"

287

6:20 עד "until"	>	ܠܘܬ "to"
7:5 √רגע "to be hardened"	>	√ܩܦܣ "to be contracted"
7:12 משמר "guard"	>	ܢܛܘܪ̈ܐ "guards, garrison"
7:14 מן "from"	>	ܒ "in"
7:16 √חדל "to cease"	>	√ܦܘܩ "to depart, withdraw"
7:20 ל "to"	>	ܕ- relative pronoun
8:5 אל "unto"	>	ܡܢ "from"
8:8 ל "to"	>	ܒ "in" (also in 9:19:29:3;30:1; 32:4,6;35:2;39:12) [so LXX]
8:17 גל "heap, wave, billow"	>	ܓܠ̈ܠܐ "waves"
9:2 עם "with"	>	ܠ "to" (17:3;34:8)
9:10 √גדל "be/grow great"	>	√ܐܬܥܫ "be strong"
9:14 עם "with"	>	ܩܕܡ "before"
9:20 √צדק "be righteous"	>	√ܕܟܐ "be pure"
9:32 ב "in, with, by"	>	ܠ "to"
10:16 ב "in, with, by"	>	ܥܠ "upon"
10:17 עמדי "with me"	>	ܠܘܬܝ "to me" (17:2)
10:17 עמי "with me"	>	ܥܠܝ "upon me"
11:7 עד "until"	>	ܥܠ "upon"
12:16 עמו "with him"	>	ܕܝܠܗ "his"
12:16 לו "to him"	>	ܕܝܠܗ "his"
12:20 ל "to"	>	ܡܢ "from"
13:20 עמדי "with me"	>	ܡܢܝ "from me"
13:27 שרש "root"	>	ܐܫܬܐ "base, power"
15:6 √ענה "to answer"	>	√ܣܗܕ "to testify" [Tg., LXX]
15:9 עם "with"	>	ܠܘܬ "to"
15:25,26 אל "unto"	>	ܥܠ "upon" (also in 34:14;39:11)
16:11 על "upon"	>	ܠ "to" (also in 33:22;34:15;40:4)
18:5,6 אור "light"	>	ܫܪܓܐ "lamp"
19:19 מתי סודי "men of my council"	>	ܒܢ̈ܝ ܬܪܥܝܬܝ "counsellors of my council"
19:26 אחר "after"/ מן "from"	>	ܥܠ "upon"
20:24 נשק "weapon"	>	ܫܪܝܢ "breastplate"
22:13 בעד "through"	>	ܡܢ ܓܘ "from the midst of"
22:20 יתרם "their remainder"	>	ܫܪܒܬܗܘܢ "their generation"
22:24 ב "in, with, by"	>	ܐܝܟ "like"
23:2 היום "the day, today"	>	ܝܘܡܢܐ "today, at the present time"
23:6 ב "in, with, by"	>	ܥܠ "upon" (also in 26:14)

23:11	אשר "step, going"	>	ܐܪܚܐ "path"
24:10	עמר "sheaf"	>	ܠܚܡܐ "bread"
25:3	√קום "to rise"	>	√ܕܢܚ "to rise (of sun)"
25:4	עם "with"	>	ܡܢ "from"
26:7	על תהו "upon the formlessness">		ܡܢ ܡܕܒܪܐ "from the desert"
28:15	מחירה "its price"	>	ܒܕܡܝܗ "in (as) its blood-price"
29:19	אלי "unto"	>	ܥܠ "upon"
29:24	אל "unto"	>	ܥܠ "upon"
30:14	שאה "ruin, devastation"	>	ܠܥܠܥܠܐ "whirlwind"
31:12	אש "fire"	>	ܢܘܗܪܐ "light"
31:22	שכמה "its shoulder"	>	ܒܗ "its socket"
33:10	ל "to"	>	ܐܝܟ "like" (also in 41:19,20,24,25)
33:25	מן "from"	>	ܐܝܟ ܕܒ- "as what is in"
33:26	אל "unto"	>	ܩܕܡ "before"
34:29	על "upon"	>	ܩܕܡ "before"
34:37	ל "to"	>	ܠ "to"
38:11	√שית "put, place"	>	√ܟܬܪ "to remain"
38:16	בחקר "in the range"	>	ܒܫܬܐܣܘܗܝ "in the foundations"
38:33	חק "statute"/משׁפט "rule"	>	ܢܡܘܣܐ "law"
38:39	√מלא "to fill"	>	√ܣܒܥ "to satiate"
39:7	המון "sound,murmur,abundance">		ܣܘܓܐܐ "multitude"
40:26	אגמון "cord (lit. bulrush)"	>	ܦܓܘܕܬܐ "bridle"
40:28	√לקח "to take"	>	√ܡܢܐ "to count"
41:6	פניו "his face"	>	ܦܘܡܗ "his mouth"
42:15	בתוך "in the midst of"	>	ܥܡ "with"

Appendix E

Contextual Translation in the Peshitta to Job

The following is a representative collection of substitutions involving contextual translation in the P to Job. The asterisked verses (*) indicate contextualization was due to a hapax legomenon or rare term in contrast to the unmarked verses where contextualization was prompted by a word deemed inappropriate by the translator of P.

*4:18	תחלה "error"	>	ܬܗܪܐ "amazement, astonishment"
*4:19	עש "moth"	>	ܥܪܦܠܐ "thick darkness"
*5:5	√לקח "to take"	>	√ܢܣܟ "to pour out"
*5:11	קדרים "dark ones"	>	ܡܟܝܟܐ "humble ones"
5:14	√פגש "to meet, encounter"	>	√ܓܫܫ "to grope around"
6:13	תושיה "abiding success"	>	ܦܘܪܩܢܗ "his salvation"
6:17	√צמת "to be annihilated"	>	√ܦܫܪ "to melt"
7:13	שיח "muse, complaint"	>	ܠܢܘܦܐ "tossing, agitation"
*7:15	מחנק "strangling"	>	ܡܢ ܐܒܕܢܐ "from destruction"
8:18	√בלע "to swallow"	>	√ܥܩܠ "to uproot"
*9:6	√פלץ "to shudder"	>	√ܪܠܠ "to reel"
9:23	√נסה "to try, tempt"/ √מסס "to despair"	>	ܫܠܛܘܬܐ "foolishness"
12:17	שולל "barefoot"	>	ܒܬܗܪܐ "with amazement"
*13:4	טפל "plasterer"	>	ܡܡܠܠܠ "speaker"
13:12	גב "breastwork"	>	1.) ܕܝܪܐ "habitation" 2.) ܠܘܬ ܓܒ "beside"
*13:27	√חקה Hith "to carve a graving, fix a limit"	>	ܚܙܐ "to see"
14:14	צבא "service"	>	ܠܝܡܘܬܐ "youth"
14:14	חליפה "renewal"	>	ܣܝܒܘܬܐ "old age"
*14:15	√כסף "to long for"	>	√ܚܫܒ Ethp. "to consider"

291

*14:17	√טפל "to smear, plaster over">		√פוק Aphel "to remove"
*14:19	ספיחיה "outpourings"	>	הדכ "a clod"
15:4	√גרע "to diminish, restrain"	>	√סגא "to multiply"
15:33	√חמס "to wrong"	>	√נפץ "to shake off"
15:34	שחד "bribe"	>	חנפא "the ungodly ones"
16:5	√אמץ "to strengthen"	>	√בעי "to search"
16:6	יהלך "what will go"	>	חובנ "what can appease"
16:9	√שטם "to bear a grudge"	>	√פסח "to tear asunder"
*16:11	√רטה "to wring out"	>	√שלט Aphel "to deliver"
16:13	√סבב "to surround"	>	√סגא "to increase"
*17:2	התלים "mockery"	>	שקרא "falsehood"
*17:6	√הפת "act of spitting"	>	תחפיתא "veil"
17:7	√כהה "to grow dim"	>	√כאב "to suffer"
17:15	√שור "to behold, regard"	>	√שכח "to find"
18:2	קנצי "snares, traps"	>	סוכסכא "contradiction"
18:3	√טמה "to be stupid"	>	√דכא "to be clean"
19:6	√נקף "to close about"	>	√פשט "to spread out"
19:29	√גור "be afraid"	>	√פרק "to save oneself"
20:2	שעפי "my thoughts"	>	אורחתי "my ways"
*20:22	√שפק "sufficiency"	>	דכאל "which he measured"
20:28	יבול "produce"	>	שתאסא "foundations"
*21:20	כידו "his misfortune"	>	אבדנה "his destruction"
21:21	חצץ "to cut in two"	>	נטר "to keep"
21:27	√חמס "to do violence"	>	√חשב Ethp. "to devise, plan"
21:33	רגב "clod"	>	נקפא "deep hollows"
22:16	√קמט "to seize"	>	√כלא Ethp. "to be hindered"
*22:20	קימנו "our adversary"	>	קשיותהון "their harshness"
*22:25	תועפות "ingots"	>	חשבנא "reckoning"
*24:11	√צהר "to press out oil"	>	√כפן "to be hungry"
24:13	√ישב "to dwell, sit, stay"	>	√הלכ "to walk"
25:5	√הלל I "to shine"	>	משכח למדכו "be able to be pure"
*26:13	שפרה "fairness, clearness"	>	מדבר "(he) guides"
*27:8	√שלה "to draw out"	>	√שקל "to take, lift up"
29:19	√פתח "to open"	>	√נצב "to be planted"
29:24	√נפל Hiphil "to cast down"	>	√הלכ "to walk"
30:14	√גלל "to roll on"	>	√תבר Ethp. "to be shattered"
30:16	√אחז "to seize"	>	√חדר "to surround"
*30:17	ערקי "my gnawing pains"	>	גשמי "my body"

30:24	פידו "his calamity"	>	√פוב "to deliver"
31:11	זמה "plan, device, wickedness">	ܚܛܝܬܐ "sin"
33:3	לב "heart"	>	פמר "mouth"
*33:20	√זהם "to loath"	>	ܠܐ ܣܒܥ "not be satisfied"
33:21	ושפו (Q) "be bare"	>	ܣܘܓܐܐ "multitude"
	ושפי "barrenness"		
34:37	√ספק "to clap"	>	√פהר "to seek"
36:8	√לבד "be captured"	>	ܢܚܬ "to descend"
36:16	√סות Hiphil "to allure"	>	√ܦܨܝ "to deliver"
36:18	√נשה "to turn aside"	>	√ܣܢܩ "to cause to have need of"
36:27	√זקק "to refine, purify"	>	√ܓܒܠ "to form, describe"
*37:1	√נתר "to spring, start up"	>	√ܙܘܥ "to move, shake to and fro"
37:9	√זרה Piel pt. "scatterers"	>	ܙܪܝܦܐ "violent rain"
*37:11	√טרח "to load"	>	√ܒܕܪ Ethp. "be spread out"
*37:16	מפלשי "balancings"	>	ܡܦܩܐ "the going out"
38:27	שאה ומשאה "devastation & desolation"	>	ܠܟ ܠܝܟ "every thicket"
*38:30	√חבא Hith. "to draw back, hide oneself" >	√ܩܫܐ "to become hard"
38:31	√פתח "to loosen"	>	ܚܙܐ "to see"
38:38	√דבק "to cling together"	>	√ܬܩܢ "to fashion"
38:38	רגב "clod"	>	ܫܩܝܦܐ "crags"
39:5	מוסרות "bonds"	>	ܢܝܪܐ "yoke"
39:16	√קשח Hiph. "to treat harshly" >	√ܣܓܐ "to multiply"
39:17	√נשה "to cause to forget"	>	√ܣܓܐ "to multiply"
*39:23	√רנה "to rattle"	>	√ܫܟܚ Ethp. "to be found"
*39:24	√גמא "to swallow"	>	√ܪܗܛ "to run"
39:24	יאמין כי "he does (not) believe that"	>	ܗܘ ܕܚܠ "he is (not) afraid of"
40:11	√פוץ Hiph. "to scatter"	>	√ܫܦܥ "to pour out"
40:12	√דכך "to crush"	>	√ܪܡܐ "to cast"
*40:17	√חפץ "to bend down"	>	√ܙܩܦ "to lift up"
40:17	√שרגc "to be intertwined"	>	√ܙܩܦ "to lift up"
40:29	√קשר "to bind"	>	√ܢܛܪ "to keep"
40:30	√כרה "to bargain"	>	√ܟܢܫ "to be gathered"
*41:10	עטיש "sneeze"	>	ܥܝܢܘܗܝ "his eyes"
41:10	√הלל "to flash forth"	>	√ܡܠܐ "to be full of"
41:11	√מלט Hith. "to escape"	>	√ܝܩܕ "to burn"
41:26	בני־שחץ "sons of dignity/pride" >	ܪܚܫܐ "reptiles"

Appendix F

Interpretation in the Peshitta to Job

The following is a representative collection of verses in which substitution due to interpretation was found. Those verses asterisked (*) indicate the interpretation relates to God; those verses marked with the sign (#) indicate reference is to Job. The remaining verses contain examples reflecting a wide variety of ideological issues.

*1:5 וברכו אלהים "and they blessed God"	>	ܘܨܚܝܘ ܠܐܠܗܐ "and they reviled God" (Tg. and LXX similar)
1:10 √פרץ "to break through"	>	ܣܓܝ√ "to increase"
2:4 √בעד "through, behind, about"	>	ܚܠܦ "for, instead of"
3:12 קדמוני ברכים "knees received me"	>	ܒܘܪܟܐ ܪܒܝܢܝ "knees reared me"
5:3 אויל "foolish one"	>	ܪܫܝܥܐ "wicked one"
5:12 ערומים "crafty, shrewd"	>	ܚܟܝܡܐ "wise ones" (Tg.) (so also in 5:13)
5:17 √יכח "to reproof"	>	ܟܣܐ "to cover, conceal"
6:17 √זרב "be extinguished = dried up"	>	√ܦܫܪ "to melt"
6:22 כח "power, strength"	>	ܩܢܝܢܐ "goods, wealth" (so Tg.)
6:23 עריצים "terrible ones"	>	ܚܣܝܢܐ "strong ones" (so Tg, LXX) (so also in 15:20)
7:2 √שאף "to pant after, be eager for"	>	√ܣܟܐ "to wait"
8:14 מבטחו "his confidence"	>	ܒܝܬܗ "his house" (LXX)
8:21 תרועה "shout for joy"	>	ܬܫܒܘܚܬܐ "glory, praise"
9:6 ממקומה "its place"	>	ܫܪܫܝܗ "its roots (of earth)" (LXX similar)
*9:12 מי ישיבנו "who will return him"	>	ܡܢܘ ܢܦܩܘܕ ܐܝܕܗ "who will command his hand"
*9:15 משפטי "my opponent"	>	ܕܝܢܝ "my judge"
#9:35 כי לא כן אנכי עמדי	>	ܠܐ ܗܟܢܐ ܗܘܬ ܠܘܬܝ ܐܠܦ

295

*10:3 הטוב לך "is it good for you"	> ܠܐ ܟܕܘ ܠܟ "(is) it not enough for you"
10:11 √סכך "to weave together"	> √ܫܪܪ "to strengthen"
*10:13 עמך "with you"	> ܒܪܥܝܢܟ "in your mind"
#10:15 רשעתי "I am guilty"	> ܚܛܝܬ "I have sinned" (so Tg.)
*13:9 √תלל "to deceive"	> ܕܝܢ "to judge"
*13:16 לישועה "salvation"	> ܦܪܘܩܐ "Savior"
#13:20 לא אסתר "I will not be hidden (from your face)"	> ܠܐ ܐܬܛܥܐ "I will not be led astray"
#*13:24 √סתר "to hide"	> √ܗܦܟ "to turn (your face)"
13:27 √חקה "to fix a limit"	> √ܚܙܐ "to see"
14:5 אתך "with you"	> ܦܣܝܩ "decreed"
15:5 √בחר "to choose"	> ܨܒܐ "to take pleasure"
15:13 √שוב Hiph. "to return" + רוח	> √ܪܝܡ "to exalt"
15:30 √סור "to pass/turn away"	> √ܫܛܐ "to go the wrong way, play the fool"
16:5 ניד "movement"	> ܡܡܠܠܐ "speech"
16:8 √קמט "to seize"	> √ܩܘܡ Aphel "to appoint"
16:16 √חמר IV "to be reddened"	> √ܕܠܚ Ethp. "to be disturbed"
16:17 חמס "violence"	> ܥܘܠܐ "iniquity" (LXX, Vulgate)
17:7 יצרי "my members, forms"	> ܬܪ̈ܥܝܬܝ "my doctrines, thoughts"
17:14 שחת "pit"	> ܚܒܠܐ "corruption"
18:7 √שלך Hiph. "to cast aside"	> √ܒܠܥ "to swallow"
18:19 נין "offspring"	> ܫܡܐ "name"
18:19 נכד "progeny"	> ܕܘܟܪܢ "memorial"
#19:7 ואין משפט "and there is no judgment"	> ܠܝܬ ܕܬܒܥ ܠܝ "there is no one who avenges me"
*19:25 אחרין "afterwards"	> ܒܣܘܦܐ "in the end"
*19:25 יקום "he will rise"	> ܢܬܓܠܐ "he will be revealed"
19:28 שרש דבר "root of the matter"	> ܛܒܐ ܡܠܬܐ "a good thing/matter"
20:10 און "vigour, wealth"	> ܝܠܕ "offspring"
20:11 עלומו "his youth/youthful vigor"	> ܡܚܪܐ "morrow"
20:15 √ירש "to dispossess"	> √ܐܒܕ Aphel "to destroy"
20:21 לאכלו "to/for his eating"	> ܡܢ ܬܘܠܕܬܗ "from his generation"
20:23 בטנו "his belly"	> ܒܛܢܗ "his child/conception"
21:11 עויל "little ones"	> ܒ̈ܢܝܢ "sons"
21:23 בעצם תמו "in the substance/bone of his completeness"	> ܒܚܝܠܐ ܕܫܠܡܘܬܗ "with the strength of his full age"
21:28 נדיב "noble one"	> ܙܕܝܩܐ "righteous one"
21:30 √חשך "to withhold/ spare"	> ܡܬܢܛܪ "is kept, reserved"

*#23:16	√רכך "make weak, faint"	>	√ܙܘܥ Aphel "to terrify, disturb"
*#23:16	ושדי הבהילו "And Shaddai terrified me"	>	ܘܪܫܝ ܐܬܬܙܝܥ "and my head was disturbed"
26:3	תושיה לרב "wisdom for a multitude"	>	ܝܘܠܦܢܐ ܣܓܝܐܐ "much doctrine"
26:14	שמץ דבר "a whisper of a word"	>	ܦܬܓܡ ܒܝܫ "an evil word"
27:11	√ירה "to throw, cast; teach"	>	√ܫܠܡ Aphel "to deliver"
27:15	שׂריד "survivor"	>	ܫܪܒܐ "generation"
*28:27	√כון "to prepare, establish"	>	√ܬܩܠ "to compare, weigh"
30:27	√רתח "to make to boil"	>	√ܕܠܚ Ethp. "to be disturbed"
32:11	√יחל "to wait"	>	√ܫܬܩ "to cease, keep silent"
*32:13	√נדף "to drive out"	>	√ܡܚܐ "to smite"
32:15	√חתת "be dismayed"	>	√ܫܬܩ "to cease"
32:17	חלקי "my part, share"	>	ܡܠܬܝ "my word"
33:4	√עשׂה "to make"	>	√ܒܪ "to stir, rouse up"
33:26	בתרועה "with a shout"	>	ܒܫܘܒܚܐ "with glory"
*#34:9	√רצה "to take delight in"	>	√ܕܚܠ "to fear"
*#34:9	√סכן "to profit"	>	√ܙܟܐ "be justified"
*34:12	משפט "judgment"	>	ܐܘܪܚܐ "way"
*34:24	√רעע "to shatter"	>	√ܒܐܫ Aphel "to afflict"
*34:29	√שקט "show quietness"	>	√ܫܒܩ "to leave, forgive"
*34:29	√סתר "to hide"	>	√ܗܦܟ "to remove"
36:14	קדשים "temple-prostitutes"	>	ܟܦܢܐ "famine"
*36:24	√שרר "to sing"	>	√ܫܒܚ "to praise"
*37:2	הגה "rumbling"	>	ܕܝܢܐ "judgment"
*37:13	שבט "rod, scepter; tribe"	>	ܫ̈ܠܝܛܢܐ "rulers"
37:14	√עמד "to stand"	>	√ܫܡܥ "to listen"
38:7	בני־אלהים "sons of God"	>	ܒ̈ܢܝ ܡܠܐ̈ܟܐ "sons of messengers"
38:41	√תעה "to wander"	>	√ܠܗܦ "to be weary, faint"
39:4	√רבה "to be much, many"	>	√ܚܣܠ "to wean"
39:19	רעמה "thunder, mane"	>	ܙܝܢܐ "weapon, armour"
40:16	במתניו "in his loins"	>	ܒܣܬܪܗ "in his secret"
*40:19	דרכי "ways (of El)"	>	ܒܪ̈ܝܬܗ "his creatures"
40:24	ינקב־אף "Can one pierce (his) nose"	>	ܢܬܬܚܕ "Can he be seized"
41:4	בדיו "his parts, members"	>	ܒܚܣܢܗ "about his strength"
41:17	√חטא Hith. "hide oneself; draw back"	>	√ܡܟܟ "be humbled"
41:17	אלים "gods"	>	ܬܩܝ̈ܦܝܢ "strong ones"

Appendix G

Lexical Levelling in the Peshitta to Job

The following is a select list of some of the most frequent examples of lexical levelling in the P to Job. It is not an exhaustive collection. The verses cited are just one example of where levelling occurred, not necessarily the only appearance of this correspondence.

ܙܕܝܩ "righteous"   >   יָשָׁר "righteous" (1:1)

                                >   תָּם "perfect" (9:22)

                                >   נָדִיב "noble" (21:28)

                                >   חַף "clean" (33:9)

ܨܦܪܐ "early dawn"   >   שַׁחַר "dawn" (3:9)

                                >   נֶשֶׁף "twilight" (3:9)

ܡܪܒܥܐ "womb"   >   בֶּטֶן "belly" (3:10)

                                >   רֶחֶם "womb" (3:11)

ܫܠܝܛܢ̈ܐ "rulers"   >   יֹעֵץ "counselors" (3:14)

                                >   שָׂרִים "princes" (3:15)

                                >   נְגִידִים "nobles" (29:10)

                                >   שֵׁבֶר "rod, staff; tribe" (37:13)

ܫܠܝ "be silent, still"   >   שָׁפַט "be silent" (3:13)

                                >   חָדַל "to cease" (3:17)

                                >   שָׁאַן "be at ease" (3:18)

                                >   שָׁלָה "be still, cease, rest" (3:26)

ܒܥܐ "to seek, search" >   חָפַר "to dig" (3:21)

                                >   חָלָה "to entreat favour of" (11:19)

                                >   פָּגַע "to entreat" (21:15)

ܚܣܢ "be strong/strength"   >   חיל "strength" (21:7)

                             >   אמץ "be strong" (4:4)

                             >   חזק "strong" (4:3)

                             >   כח "power, strength" (23:6)

ܐܬܟܒܢ "be humbled"   >   כתת "be beaten to pieces" (4:20)

                       >   דכא "to crush" (4:19)

                       >   חבא Hith. "to hide oneself; draw back" (41:17)

ܒܛܠ "be ineffectual"   >   מהר "be hasty, precipitate" (5:12)

                         >   פרר "to break, frustrate" (5:13)

ܐܬܟܣܟܢܐ "poor"   >   אביון "poor, needy" (5:15)

                   >   דל "poor" (5:16)

ܟܣܐ "to conceal"   >   כסה "to conceal" (16:18)

                     >   צפן "to hide" (17:4)

                     >   כחד "to hide" (15:18)

                     >   עלם "to hide" (28:21)

                     >   יכח "to reprove" (5:17)

ܣܟܠܐ "iniquity"   >   עולה "iniquity" (11:14)

                    >   און "iniquity, sin" (11:11)

                    >   בליעל "worthlessness" (34:18)

ܣܘܚܐ "sin"   >   פשע "transgression" (13:23)

               >   עון "sin, iniquity" (13:23)

ܣܠܐ "to despise"   >   תעב "to abhor" (19:19)

                     >   מאס "to despise" (19:18)

ܡܠܬܐ "word"   >   מלה "word" (13:17)

                >   דבר "word" (15:3)

                >   אמר "decree" (20:29)

ܢܛܪ "to guard"   >   שמר "to guard" (10:14)

                   >   צפן "to hide" (21:19)

                   >   חצץ "to cut in two" (21:21)

                   >   שמם Hiphil "to ravage, devastate" (16:7)

ܢܒܪ "to lead"   >   גזל "to seize, tear away" (24:2)

                  >   נהג "to lead" (24:3)

ܡܐܟܘܠܬܐ "food"   >   אכל "food" (9:26)

>   טרף "prey" (24:5)

>   ציד "hunt" (38:41)

ܫܒܝܠܐ "path, way"   >   ארחה "path" (30:12)

>   נתיבה "path" (30:13)

>   נדבתי "my honour" (error) (30:15)

ܥܒܕ "to do, make"   >   הפך "to turn" (30:21)

>   שׂים "to put, place" (31:23)

>   ענד "to bind" (31:36)

ܣܓܐ "to be great, increase"   >   פרץ "to break through" (1:10)

>   עלם Hith. "to conceal" (6:16)

>   רב "be great" (31:25)

>   כביר "much, many" (31:25)

>   מכביר "much, many" (36:31)

>   יחור "he dwells" (error) (39:8)

>   נשה Hiphil "to cause to forget" (39:17)

>   יבל "to bring" (40:20)

ܦܨܐ "to deliver"   >   ישׁע "to save, deliver" (22:29)

>   פדה "to deliver, save" (33:28)

>   פדע "to deliver" (38:24)

ܚܟܡܬܐ "wisdom"   >   ערומים "crafty" (5:12)

>   תושׁיה "abiding success" (12:16)

>   חכמה "wisdom" (28:12)

>   בינה "understanding" (39:26)

Bibliography

Peshitta

Avinery, I. "Problems de Variation dans la Traduction Syriaque du Pentateuque." *Sem* 25 (1975):105-09.

-------. "On the Nominal Clause in the Peshitta." *JSS* 20(1977):48-49.

Barnes, W.E. "On the Influence of the Septuagint on the Peshitta." *JThS* II(1901): 186-197.

---------. "A New Edition of the Pentateuch in Syriac." *JThS* XV (1914):41-44.

Baumann, E. "Verwendbarkeit der Pesita zum Buche Ijob für die Textkritik." *ZAW* 1898:305-338; 1899:15-95, 287-309; 1900: 177-307.

Bernstein, Georgius Henricus. *Chrestomathia Syriaca.* Lipsiae, 1832.

Bloch, J. "The Authorship of the Peshitta." *AJSL* 35 (1918/19):215-222.

------. "The Printed Texts of the Peshitta Old Testament." *AJSL* 37 (1920/21): 136-144.

Borger, R. "Das Comma Johanneum in der Peschitta." *NT* 29,3 (1987): 280-284.

Brock, Sebastian. "Toward a History of Syriac Translation Technique," pp. 1-14. In *IIIe Symposium Syriacum 1980.* R. Lavenant, ed. Orientalia Christiana Analecta 221. Rome: Pontificum Institutum Studiorum Orientalium, 1983.

Brockelmann, C. *Syrische Grammatik mit Paradigmen, Literatur, Chrestomathie und Glossar.* Leipzig: Veb Verlag Enzyklopädie, rpt. 1981.

Ceriani, A.M. *Translatio Syra Pescitto Veteris Testamenti: Ex Codice Ambrosiano Sec. Fere VI, Photolithographice Edita,* 1876.

Delekat, L. "Die Peschitta zu Jesaja zwischen Targum und Septuaginta." *Biblica* 38,2 (1957):185-199; 38,3 (1957):321-335.

Duval, R. *Traitè de grammaire syriaque.* Paris, 1881.

Gelston, A. *The Peshitta of the Twelve Prophets.* Oxford: Clarendon Press, 1987.

Goldenberg, G. "On Syriac Sentence Structure," pp. 97-140. In *Arameans, Aramaic and the Aramaic Literary Tradition.* Michael Sokoloff, ed. Bar-Ilan University Press, 1983.

304   Peshitta to Job

Goshen-Gottstein, M.H. "Critique on the Leiden Peshitta." In *Text and Language in Bible and Qumran*. Jerusalem: Orient, 1960.

Guillaumont, A. "La phrase dite "nominal" en syriaque." *Comptes rendus du Groupe Linguistique d'Etudes Chamito-Sèmitique* 5(1949):31-33.

Haefeli, Leo. *Die Peschitta des Alten Testaments: mit Rucksicht auf ihre textkritische Bearbeitung und Herausgabe.* Munster: Verlag der aschendorffschen Verlagsbuchhandlung, 1927.

Holtzman, J. *Die Peschitta zum Buche der Weisheit.* Freiburg, 1903.

Hospers, J.H. "Some Remarks with Regard to Text and Language of the Old Testament Peshitta," in Festschrift für Prof. J. van der Ploeg, *Von Kanaan bis Kerala,* 1982.

---------. "The Present-Day State of Research on the Pesitta (since 1948)." In *Verbum: Essays . . . Dedicated to Dr. H.W. Obbink*, pp. 148-57. Studia Theologica Rheno-Traiectine VI. Utrecht, 1964.

Isenberg, Sh. R. "On the Jewish-Palestinian Origins of the Peshitta to the Pentateuch." *JBL* XC (1971): 69-81.

Joosten, Jan. "West Aramaic Elements in the Old Syriac and Peshitta Gospels." *JBL* 110/2 (1991):271-289.

Mandl, A. *Die Peschitta zum Hiob.* Dissertation. Leipzig, 1892.

Maori, Y. *The Peshitta Version of the Pentateuch in its Relation to the Sources of Jewish Exegesis.* Doctoral Dissertation. Hebrew University, 1975.

Martin, J.P.P. "Tradition Karkaphienne, ou la Massore chez les Syriens." *JA* 14 (1869): 245-379.

Muraoka, T. "On the Nominal Clause in the Syriac Gospels." *JSS* 20(1975):28-37.

--------. "On the Syriac Particle ܐܘܟ܆." *Bibliotheca Orientalis* 34(1977):21-22.

Nöldeke, Theodor. *A Compendious Syriac Grammar.* James A. Crichton, trans. London: Clarendon Press, rpt. 1979.

Payne Smith, J. ed. *A Compendious Syriac Dictionary.* Oxford: At the Clarendon Press, rpt. 1979.

----------. *Supplement to the Thesaurus.* Oxford: Clarendon Presss, 1927.

Payne Smith, Robert. *Thesaurus Syriacus.* Oxford: Clarendon Press, 1879, 1901.

Pinkerton, J. "The Origin and Early History of the Syriac Pentateuch." *JThS* 15 (1914):14-41.

Rahlfs, A. "Beiträge zur Textkritik des Peschita." *ZAW* IX (1889): 160-210.

Rignell, L.G. ed. *The Old Testament in Syriac According to the Peshitta Version: Job.* Leiden: E. J. Brill, 1982.

Rosenthal, Franz. *Die Aramäistische Forschung seit Th. Nöldeke's Veröffentlichungen.* Leiden: E.J. Brill, 1939.

Segal, J.B. *The Diacritical Point and the Accents in Syriac.* Oxford University Press, 1953.

Smith Lewis, Agnes ed. *A Palestinian Lectionary containing Lessons from the Pentateuch, Job, Proverbs, Acts and Epistles.* Londres, 1897.

Stenij, E. *De Syriaca libri Jobi interpretatione quae Peschita,* 1887.

Vööbus, A. *Peschitta und Targumim des Pentateuches: Neues Licht zur Frage der Herkunft der Peschitta aus dem altpalästinischen Targum.* Stockholm, 1958.

----------. "Der Einfluss des altpalästinischen Targums in der Textgeschichte der Peschitta des Alten Testaments." *Le Museon* LXVIII (1955): 215-218.

Wernberg-Møller, P. "Some Observations on the Relationship of the Peshitta Version of the Book of Genesis to the Palestinian Targum Fragments Published by Professor Kahle, and to Targum Onkelos." *STh* XV (1961): 128-180.

----------. "Some Scribal and Linguistic Features of the Genesis Part of the Oldest Peshitta Manuscript (B.M. Add. 14425)." *JSS* XIII (1968): 136-161.

Wright, William. *A Short History of Syriac Literature.* Amsterdam: Philo Press, 1966.

Yamauchi, E.M. "Greek, Hebrew, Aramaic or Syriac: A Criticism of Claims of G.M. Lamsa for the Syriac Pentateuch." *Bibliotheca Sacra,* Dallas Tx. 131 (1974): 320-31.

Zipor, Moshe A. "A Striking Translation Technique of the Peshitta." *JSS* 26 (1981): 11-20.

Other Versions

Aejmelaeus, Anneli. "What Can We Know About the Hebrew Vorlage of the Septuagint?" *ZAW* 99 (1987/2): 58-89.

Barnes, W.E. "On the Influence of the Septuagint on the Peshitta." *JThS* II (1901): 186-197.

Bertram, G. "Der Sprachschatz der Septuaginta und der des hebraeischen A.T." *ZAW* 57 (1939):85-101.

Brown, Francis, S.R. Driver and Charles A. Briggs. *A Hebrew and English Lexicon of the Old Testament.* Oxford: Clarendon Press, 1975.

Deist, F.E. *Towards the Text of the Old Testament.* Pretoria: N.G. Kerkboekhandel Transvaal, 1981.

Gammie, John G. "The Septuagint of Job: Its Poetic Style and Relationship to the Septuagint of Proverbs." *CBQ* 49 (1987): 16-31.

Gard, Donald H. "The Exegetical Method of the Greek Translator of the Book of Job." *JBLMS* 8; Pennsylvania: Society of Biblical Literature, 1952.

Gesenius' Hebrew Grammar. E. Kautzsch & A.E. Cowley, eds. Oxford: Clarendon Press, 1980.

Goshen-Gottstein, M.H. "Theory and Practice of Textual Criticism." In *Text and Language In Bible and Qumran.* Jerusalem: Orient, 1960.

Heater, Homer, Jr. "A Septuagint Translation Technique in the Book of Job." *CBQMS* 11; Washington D.C.: Catholic Biblical Association, 1982.

Lambdin, Thomas O. *Introduction to Biblical Hebrew.* New York: Charles Scribner's Sons, 1971.

Marquis, Galen. "Word Order as a Criterion for the Evaluation of Translation Technique in the LXX and the Evaluation of Word-Order Variants: As Exemplified in LXX-Ezekiel." *Textus* XIII (1986): 59-84.

McCarter, P. Kyle. *Textual Criticism: Recovering the Text of the Hebrew Bible.* Old Testament Series. Philadelphia: Fortress Press, 1986.

Orlinsky, J. "The Character of the Septuagint Translation of the Book of Job." *HUCA* 28 (1957): 53-74; 29 (1958): 229-271; 30 (1959): 153-167.

Rabin, Chaim. "The Translation Process and the Character of the Septuagint." *Textus* 6 (1968): 1-26.

Seow, C.L. *A Grammar for Biblical Hebrew.* Nashville: Abingdon Press,1987.

Sokoloff, M. *The Targum to Job from Qumran Cave XI,* 1974.

Sperber, A., ed. *The Bible in Aramaic, Vol. IVB: The Targum and the Hebrew Bible.* Leiden: E.J. Brill, 1973.

Szpek, Heidi M. *Similes and Metaphors in the Targumim: A Comparative Study of the Translational Techniques used by the Aramaic Targumim to the Pentateuch for Similes and Metaphors of the Hebrew Bible.* Unpublished M.A. Thesis. University of Wisconsin-Milwaukee, 1983.

Talmon, Shemaryahu. "Double Readings in the Massoretic Text." *Textus* 1 (1960): 144-184.

Tov, E. *The Text-Critical Use of the Septuagint in Biblical Research.* Jerusalem Biblical Studies 3. Jerusalem: Simor Ltd., 1981.

Tov, E. and B.G. Wright. "Computer-Assisted Study of the Criteria for Assessing the Literalness of Translation Units in the LXX." *Textus* XII (1985): 149-187.

Van der Ploeg, J.P.M. and A.S. van der Woude. *Le Targum de Job de la Grotte XI de Qumran.* Leiden: E.J. Brill, 1971.

Waltke, Bruce K. and M. O'Connor. *An Introduction to Biblical Hebrew Syntax.* Eisenbrauns, 1990.

Weiss, A. De Libri Jobi: *Paraphras Chaldaica Dissertatio Inauguratis.* Vratislavieae, 1873.

Weiss, R. *The Aramaic Targum of Job.* Tel Aviv, 1979.

Williams, Ronald J. *Hebrew Syntax: An Outline.* University of Toronto Press, 1984.

Würthwein, Ernst. *The Text of the Old Testament: An Introduction to the Biblia Hebraica.* Grand Rapids, Michigan: William B. Eerdmans Publishing Co., 1979.

Job

Andersen, Francis I. *Job: An Introduction & Commentary.* Tyndale Old Testament Commentaries. Leicester, England: Inter-Varsity Press.

Bardtke, H. "Profetische Zuge im Buche Hiob." In *Das Ferne und Nahe Wort:* : Fest schrift Leonard Rost. *BZAW* 105 (1967).

Barr, J. "The Book of Job and Its Modern Interpreters." *BJRL* 54 (1971): 28-46.

Davidson, A.B. *The Book of Job.* Cambridge: University Press, 1951.

Dhorme, E. *A Commentary on the Book of Job.* New York: Thomas Nelson Publishers rpt. 1984 (1926).

Diewert, David A. "Job 7:12: Yam, Tannin and the Surveillance of Job." *JBL* 106/2 (1987): 203-215.

Driver, G.R. "Problems in the Hebrew text of Job." *VT* Suppl III (1960): 72-93.

Driver, S.R. and G.B. Gray. A Critical and Exegetical Commentary on the Book of Job. *ICC,* 1977.

Fohrer, Georg. "The Righteous Man in Job 31," pp. 3-22. *In Essays in Old Testament Ethics.* J.L. Crenshaw & John T. Willis, eds. New York: KTAV, 1974.

Freedman, David Noel. "The Elihu Speeches in the Book of Job." *HTR* 61 (1968): 51-59.

Gabel, John B. and Charles B. Wheeler. *The Bible as Literature: An Introduction.* New York and Oxford: Oxford University Press, 1986.

Gammie, John G. "Behemoth and Leviathan: On the Didactic and Theological Significance of Job 40:15-41:26," pp. 217-31. In *Israelite Wisdom: Theological and Literary Essays in Honor of Samuel Terrien.* John G. Gammie, ed. Missoula: Scholars Press, 1978.

Glatzer, N. "The Book of Job and Its Interpreters," pp. 197-220. In *Biblical Motifs.* A. Altman, ed. Cambridge: Harvard University Press, 1966.

-------. *The Dimensions of Job.* New York: Schocken Press, 1969.

Gray, J. "The Book of Job in the Context of Near Eastern Literature." *ZAW* 82 (1970): 251-69.

Guillaume, A. *Studies in the Book of Job: With a New Translation.* Leiden: E.J. Brill, 1968.

Habel, Norman. *The Book of Job: A Commentary.* Philadelphia: The Westminster Press, 1985.

Humbert, P. "Le modernisme de Job." *VT* Suppl III (1960): 150-161.

Kegler, Jürgen. "Hauptlinien der Hiobforschung seit 1956," pp. 9-25. In *Der Aufbau des Buches Hiob*. Claus Westermann, ed. Stuttgart: Calwer, 1977.

Kramer, Samuel Noah. "Man and His God: A Sumerian Variation on the 'Job' Motif." *VT* Suppl 3 (1960): 170-182.

MacKenzie, R.A.F. "The Purpose of the Yahweh Speeches in the Book of Job." *Bib* 40 (1959): 435-445.

Michel, Walter L. "SLMWT, 'Deep Darkness' or 'Shadow of Death'?" *Papers of the Chicago Society of Biblical Research*. XXIX (1984): 5-20.

Patrick, Dale. "Job's Address of God." *ZAW* 91 (1979): 268-282.

Peake, A.S. *The Problem of Suffering in the Old Testament*, 1904.

Pfeiffer, Robert H. *Introduction to the Old Testament*. New York: Harper & Brothers Publishers, 1948.

Pope, Marvin H. *The Anchor Bible: Job*. New York: Doubleday & Company, Inc., 1983.

von Rad, G. "Hiob xxxviii und die altägyptische Weisheit." *VT* Suppl III (1955): 293-301.

Richter, Heinz. "Die Naturweisheit des Alten Testaments in Buche Hiob." *ZAW* 70 (1958): 107-114.

Roberts, J.J. M. "Job and the Israelite Religious Tradition." *ZAW* 89 (1977): 107-114.

Rowley, H.H. *The Book of Job*. The New Century Bible Commentary. Grand Rapids: Wm. B. Eerdmans Publishing Co., 1970.

Rowold, Henry. "Leviathan and Job in Job 41:2-3." *JBL* 105,1 (1986): 104-109.

Sarna, Nahum M. "Epic Substratum in the Prose of Job." *JBL* (1957): 13-25.

van Selms, A. *Job: A Practical Commentary*. William B. Eerdmans Publishing Company: Grand Rapids, Michigan, 1985.

Snaith, N.H. *The Book of Job: Its Origin and Purpose*. London: SCM, 1968.

Terrien, S. *Job: Poet of Existence*. New York and Indianapolis: The Bobbs-Merrill Inc., 1957.

-------. "Quelques remarques sur les affinite de Job avec le DeuteroEsaie." *VT* Suppl 15 (1966): 295-310.

Vawter, Bruce. *Job & Jonah: Questioning the Hidden God*. New York and Ramsey: Paulist Press, 1983.

Westermann, Claus. *Der Aufbau des Buches Hiob*. Stuttgart: Calwer, 1977.

Williams, James G. "You Have Not Spoken Truth of Me: Mystery and Irony in Job."
    ZAW 83 (1971): 231-255.

Wisdom Literature

Bryce, Glendon E. *A Legacy of Wisdom: The Egyptian Contribution to the
    Wisdom of Israel.* Lewisburg and London: Bucknell University and Associated
    University Presses, 1979.

Crenshaw, James L. "Wisdom." In *Old Testament Form Criticism.* John H. Hayes,
    ed. San Antonio: Trinity University, 1974.

----------. *Studies in Ancient Israelite Wisdom.* New York: KTAV, 1976.

----------. *The Old Testament Wisdom: An Introduction.* Atlanta, GA: John
    Knox Press, 1981.

Fichtner, Johannes. Die altorientalische Weisheit in ihrer israelitisch-judischen
    Auspragung. *BZAW* 62. Giessen: Alfred Topelmann, 1933.

Gammie, John, et al, eds. *Israelite Wisdom: Theological and Literary Essays
    in Honor of Samuel Terrien.* Missoula: Scholars Press, 1978.

Gilbert, Maurice, ed. *La Sagesse de l'Ancien Testament.* Gambloux, Belgique:
    J. Duculot & Leuwen University Press, 1979.

Murphy, R.E. "Form Criticism and Wisdom Literature." *CBQ* 31 (1969): 475-83.

Noth, Martin and D.W. Thomas, eds. "Wisdom in Israel and in the Ancient Near East."
    VT Suppl 3. Leiden: E.J. Brill, 1960.

Paterson, John. *The Wisdom of Israel.* London & Nashville: Lutterworth and
    Abingdon, 1961.

Pfeiffer, Robert H. "Edomite Wisdom." *ZAW* 44 (1926): 13-25.

----------. "Wisdom and Vision in the Old Testament." *ZAW* 52 (1934): 93-101.

von Rad, Gerhard. *Wisdom in Israel.* Nashville & New York: Abingdon, 1972.

Rankin, Orvid S. *Israel's Wisdom Literature.* Edinburgh: T. & T. Clark, 1954.

Rylaarsdam, J. Coert. *Revelation in Jewish Wisdom Literature.* Chicago:
    University of Chicago Press, 1946.

Scott, R.B.Y. "The Study of the Wisdom Literature." *Interpretation* 24 (1970):
    20-45.

--------. *The Way of Wisdom in the Old Testament.* New York: Macmillan,
    1971.

Whybray, Roger N. "The Intellectual Tradition in the Old Testament." *BZAW* 135.
    Berlin & New York: Walter de Gruyter, 1974.

Williams, R.J. "Theodicy in the Ancient Near East." *CJJ* 2 (1956): 14-26.

Wood, James. *Wisdom Literature.* London: Gerald Duckworth & Co. Ltd., 1967.

Zimmerli, W. "Concerning the Structure of Old Testament Wisdom," pp. 175-207. In *Studies in Ancient Israelite Wisdom.* James L. Crenshaw, ed. New York: KTAV, 1976.

Linguistics/Translation/Language

Aarts, Jan M.G. and Joseph P. Calbert. *Metaphor and Non-Metaphor: The Semantics of Adjective-Noun Combinations.* Linguistische Arbeiten. Tübingen: Max Niemeyer Verlag, 1979.

Alter, Robert. *The Art of Biblical Poetry.* New York: Basic Books, Inc., Publishers, 1985.

Amos, Flora Ross. *Early Theories of Translation.* New York: Columbia University Press, 1920.

Barr, James. *Comparative Philology and the Text of the Old Testament.* Eisenbrauns: Winona Lake, Indiana, 1987.

---------. *The Typology of Literalism in Ancient Biblical Translations.* Mitteilungen des Septuaginta-Unternehmens, 15. Gottingen, 1979.

Bugarski, Ranko. "Translation Across Cultures: Some Problems with Terminologies," pp. 159-163. In *Scientific and Humanistic Dimensions of Language: Festschrift for Robert Lado.* Kurt R. Jankowsky, ed. John Benjamin Publishing Company, 1985.

Bullinger, E. W. *Figures of Speech Used in the Bible.* Grand Rapids, Michigan: Baker Book House. 1898; rpt. 1981.

Caird, G.B. *The Language and Imagery of the Bible.* Philadelphia: Westminster Press, 1980.

Cohen, L.J. *The Diversity of Meaning.* 2nd Edition. London: Methuen, 1966.

Crim, Keith R. "Old Testament Translations and Interpretation." *Interpretation* 32 (1978): 145ff.

Cunningham, J.V. *The Problem of Style.* Greenwich, Conn.: Fawcett Publications, Inc., 1966.

Dagut, M.B. "Can 'Metaphor' Be Translated." *Babel* 22,1 (1976): 21-22.

De Beaugrande, Robert. *Factors in a Theory of Poetic Translating.* Approaches to Translation Studies, No. 5. Van Gordum, Assen, The Netherlands, 1978.

Empson, W. *Seven Types of Ambiguity.* 2nd Edition. London, 1949.

Finlay, Ian F. *Translating.* Teach Yourself Books. Warwick Lane, London: St. Paul's House, 1971.

Frawley, Wm., ed. *Translation: Literary, Linguistic and Philosophical Perspectives.* Neward: University of Delaware, 1984.

Gavronsky, Serge. "The Translator: From Piety to Cannibalism." *Sub-stance* 16 (1977): 53-62.

Glassman, Eugene H. *The Translation Debate: What Makes a Bible Translation Good.* Downers Grove, IL, 1981.

Greenstein, Edward L. "Theories of Modern Bible Translation." *Prooftexts* Vol. 3 (1983): 9-39.

Hodges, John, Mary E. Whitton & Suzanne S. Webb, eds. *Harbrace College Handbook.* 10th ed. San Diego: Harcourt Brace Jovanich Publishers, 1986.

Holmes, James S., Josè Lambert & Raymond Van den Broeck, eds. *Literature and Translation: New Perspectives in Literary Studies with a Basic Bibliogrphy of Books on Translation Studies.* Leuven/Belgium: Acco, 1978.

Kelly, L.G. *The True Interpreter: A History of Translation Theory and Practice in the West.* Oxford: Basil Blackwell, 1979.

Lado, Robert. *Linguistics Across Cultures.* Ann Arbor: University of Chicago Press, 1957.

Lakoff, George and Mark Johnson. *Metaphors We Live By.* University of Chicago Press, 1980.

Leighton, Lauren G.,trans. & ed. *The Art of Translation: Kornei Chukovsky's A High Art.* Knoxville: The University of Tennessee Press, 1984.

Lyons, John. *Language, Meaning & Content.* Fontana Paperbacks, 1981.

--------. *Language and Linguistics: An Introduction.* Cambridge: Cambridge University Press, 1981.

--------. *Semantics.* Vol. 1 & 2. Cambridge: Cambridge University Press, 1977.

--------. *Introduction to Theoretical Linguistics.* Cambridge: Cambridge University Press, 1969.

Mathews, Jackson. "Third Thoughts on Translating Poetry," pp. 57-66. In *On Translation.* Reuben A. Brower, ed. Cambridge, Massachusetts: Harvard University Press, 1959.

Neubert, Al. "Translation Across Languages or Across Cultures?," pp. 231-239. In *Scientific and Humanistic Dimensions of Language: Festscrift for Robert Lado.* Kurt R. Jankowsky, ed. Amsterdam, 1985.

Newmark, Peter. *Approaches to Translation.* Oxford: Pergamon Press, 1981.

Nida, Eugene A. *God's Word In Man's Language.* New York: Harper & Brothers, 1952.

----------. *Toward a Science of Translating.* Leiden: E.J. Brill, 1964.

----------. *Componential Analysis of Meaning.* The Hague, Paris: Mouton, 1975.

----------. *Exploring Semantic Structures.* Munich: Fink, 1975.

----------. *Language Structure and Translation: Essays by E.A. Nida.*
Stanford, California, 1975.

Nida, Eugene A. and Charles R. Taber. *The Theory and Practice of Translation.*
Leiden, 1974.

----------. *Essays in Biblical Culture and Bible Translation.* New York,
1974.

Pause, Eberhard. "Context and Translation," pp. 384-399. In *Meaning, Use, and
Interpretation of Language.* Berlin, 1983.

Rabbe, Paul R. "Deliberate Ambiguity in the Psalter." *JBL* 110/2 (1991):213-227.

Schwarz, W. *Principles and Problems of Biblical Translation.* Cambridge:
University Press, 1955.

Sebeok, T.A., ed. *Style in Language.* Cambridge, Mass.: M.I.T. Press, 1960.

Silva, Moises. *Biblical Words & Their Meaning: An Introduction to Lexical Semantics.*
Grand Rapids, Michigan: Zondervan Publishing House, 1983.

Steiner, George. *After Babel: Aspects of Language and Translation.* London,
1975.

Stern, David. "Translating the Ancients." *Commentary* 59:6 (June 1975): 44-51.

Stern, Gustaf. *Meaning and Change of Meaning: With Special Reference to the English
Language.* Bloomington: Indiana University Press, 1964.

Taber, Charles R. "Translation as Interpretation." *Interpretation* 32 (1978):
130-143.

Ullman, Stephen. *Meaning and Style: Collected Papers.* Oxford: Basil Blackwell, 1973.

----------. *Semantics: An Introduction to the Science of Meaning.* Oxford: Basil
Blackwell, 1970.

Vermes, G. *Scripture and Tradition in Judaism.* Leiden: E.J. Brill, 1961.

Wendland, Ernst R. *The Cultural Factor in Bible Translation.* UBS Monograph
Series, No. 2. New York: United Bible Societies, 1987.

Woolley, Edwin C., Franklin W. Scott & Frederick Bracher. *College Handbook of
Composition.* Boston: D.C. Heath and Company, 1958.

Index

32:16	80n,114n,115n,123n,145n, 253n,254n		34:3	780n,93n,135,174n,175n
32:17	108-109,123n,253n,297		34:4	108n,123n,126
31:18	87n,89n,123n		34:5	153n(2)
32:19	80n,123n,217n,232n,233, 280(2)		34:6	93n,148,167n,280
			34:7	76n(2),148,232n
32:20	253-257,254n		34:8	87n,108n,117n,122n,288
32:21	145n,214,235		34:9	70n,80n,280,297(2)
32:22	80n,81n,123n,280		34:10	147,274
			34:11	65n,80n,87n,88n(2),90n,101n, 108n,232n,240
33:1	128n,225n,254n		34:12	80n,128n,228-229,274,297
33:2	80n,108n,123n,135,174n,175n, 217n,225n,226		34:13	108n,157n
			34:14	67n,68n,80n,157n,288
33:3	75n,93n,160,166n,293		34:15	80n,288
33:4	83n,85n,297		34:16	65n,93n,121n,123n
33:5	80n,108n,123n,136,137,146, 171n,255n		34:17	71n,75n,80n,228
			34:18	83,170-171,281,287,300
33:6	108n,152,224n(2),226,232n		34:19	75n,80n,247,248n
33:7	218n(2),219		34:20	80n,87n,88n(2),145n,153n, 163n,281
33:8	83n,85n,102n,103n,148n			
33:9	65n,122n,123n,148n,153n(2), 299		34:21	80n,147
			34:22	65n
33:10	80n,83n,85n,108n,123n,220n, 280,288		34:23	157n
			34:24	83n,281,285,297
33:11	83n,85n,123n,145n,157n		34:25	114n,115n,117n,145n
33:12	80n(2),93n,219n,222, 224n(2),253-257,273(2)		34:26	114n,115n,126n,281
			34:27	88n,293
33:13	83n,85n,253n,254n		34:28	80n,139
33:14	80n,92n,122n,153n,158- 160,254n		34:29	80n,99n,102n,117n,119n,128n, 160n,205,285,289,297(2)
			34:30	83n
33:15	65n,83n,145n,173-174,285		34:31	80n,205
33:16	80n		34:32	114n,115n,205
33:17	65n,80n,101,102n,145n		34:33	81n,83n,85n,114n,115n,126n, 205,254n
33:19	65n,87n,88n,93n,121n			
33:20	93n,117n,153n(2),285,293		34:34	80n
33:21	83n,87n,88n,293		34:35	75n,93n,254n(2)
33:22	288		34:36	83n,85n,123n,281
33:23	83n,87,161,274		34:37	65n,80n,87n,90n,123n,126n, 281,289,293
33:24	83n(3),87,93n,123n			
33:25	123n,289			
33:26	83n,87n,93n,153n,289,297		35:1	110n
33:27	83n,93n,126n,160,160n		35:2	93n,205n,222,288
33:28	83n,108n,301		35:3	80n
33:29	80n,223,224n,248		35:4	255n(2)
			35:5	76n,80n,117n,160n,163n,167n
33:30	83n,88n,163		35:6	80n(2),215n
33:31	163,166n,167n,254n		35:7	80n,126n
33:32	80n,145n,163,163n		35:8	75n,232n,233
33:33	83n,126n		35:9	80n
			35:10	67n,76n,281
34:1	110n,247		35:11	281
34:2	76n,97n